Research on Pandemics

T0300405

The lasting turmoil associated with the unprecedented pandemic, triggered by the novel corona virus COVID-19, has dragged the world into a mud of uncertainty. Fiscal stimulation, interest rate cuts, global supply-chain redeployment, "pandemic bond" and circuit breakers kicked in and the world is responding to this great challenge. But how can finance and economic research help the world under such circumstances?

This book dwells on this new area of research and tries to understand how pandemics impact the economic and financial ecosystem of both emerging and advanced economies. Lessons learnt from the experience of previous pandemics maybe presented and discussed through drawing on policy lessons to date. By gathering research on political economy, geopolitical issues, behavioral finance, international institutional responses and medical and health issues resulting from pandemics, the chapters in this edited volume help in expanding the knowledge of social and economic consequences of the pandemic as well as set the foundation for future research. This book would benefit scholars, policy makers and entrepreneurs worldwide as a valuable archive of research on pandemics.

The chapters in this book were originally published as a special issue of *Emerging Markets Finance and Trade*.

Yezhou Sha is Associate Professor of Finance at Capital University of Economics and Business. His research has been published in the *Economic Modelling*, *Pacific-basin Finance Journal*, and *Emerging Markets Finance and Trade*.

Susan Sunila Sharma is Senior Lecturer in the Centre for Financial Econometrics & Department of Finance in Deakin Business School. In 2019, the Web of Science Group recognized her with a distinguished title of a highly cited researcher. Moreover, in 2016, she received a "highly cited early to mid-career Australian female researcher" award at the inaugural "Women in Research" citations awards, hosted by the Thomson Reuters IP and Science and the Australian National University (ANU). Google Scholar counts the citation of her work at over 3,700, with an h-index of 29. She is a co-editor of the journal *Emerging Markets Finance and Trade*, a subject editor of the *Journal of International Financial Markets*

Institutions & Money, and guest editor of multiple issues of *Economic Modelling*. Her research in finance has employed a wide range of recent developments in financial econometrics. Susan's research interests are in the areas of panel predictability models, time series econometric models, price discovery, commodity markets, forecasting and energy markets.

Research on Pandemics

Lessons from an Economics and
Finance Perspective

Edited by
Yezhou Sha and Susan Sunila Sharma

LONDON AND NEW YORK

First published 2022
by Routledge
2 Park Square, Milton Park, Abingdon, Oxon OX14 4RN

and by Routledge
605 Third Avenue, New York, NY 10158

Routledge is an imprint of the Taylor & Francis Group, an informa business

© 2022 Taylor & Francis

British Library Cataloguing in Publication Data
A catalogue record for this book is available from the British Library

ISBN: 978-1-032-10301-3 (hbk)
ISBN: 978-1-032-10302-0 (pbk)
ISBN: 978-1-003-21468-7 (ebk)

DOI: 10.4324/9781003214687

Typeset in Minion Pro
by Newgen Publishing UK

Publisher's Note
The publisher accepts responsibility for any inconsistencies that may have arisen during the conversion of this book from journal articles to book chapters, namely the inclusion of journal terminology.

Disclaimer
Every effort has been made to contact copyright holders for their permission to reprint material in this book. The publishers would be grateful to hear from any copyright holder who is not here acknowledged and will undertake to rectify any errors or omissions in future editions of this book.

Contents

Citation Information

The chapters in this book were originally published in *Emerging Markets Finance and Trade*, volume 56, issue 10 (2020). When citing this material, please use the original page numbering for each article, as follows:

Introduction

Research on Pandemics Special Issue of the Journal Emerging Markets Finance and Trade
Yezhou Sha and Susan Sunila Sharma
Emerging Markets Finance and Trade, volume 56, issue 10 (2020), pp. 2133–2137

Chapter 1

Country Responses and the Reaction of the Stock Market to COVID-19—a Preliminary Exposition
Dinh Hoang Bach Phan and Paresh Kumar Narayan
Emerging Markets Finance and Trade, volume 56, issue 10 (2020), pp. 2138–2150

Chapter 2

Flatten the Curve and Stock Market Liquidity – An Inquiry into Emerging Economies
Omair Haroon and Syed Aun R. Rizvi
Emerging Markets Finance and Trade, volume 56, issue 10 (2020), pp. 2151–2161

Chapter 3

Does the Indian Financial Market Nosedive because of the COVID-19 Outbreak, in Comparison to after Demonetisation and the GST?
Alok Kumar Mishra, Badri Narayan Rath, and Aruna Kumar Dash
Emerging Markets Finance and Trade, volume 56, issue 10 (2020), pp. 2162–2180

Chapter 10

The Disease Outbreak Channel of Exchange Rate Return Predictability: Evidence from COVID-19
Bernard Njindan Iyke
Emerging Markets Finance and Trade, volume 56, issue 10 (2020), pp. 2277–2297

Chapter 11

Fear Sentiment, Uncertainty, and Bitcoin Price Dynamics: The Case of COVID-19
Conghui Chen, Lanlan Liu, and Ningru Zhao
Emerging Markets Finance and Trade, volume 56, issue 10 (2020), pp. 2298–2309

Chapter 12

Constructing a Global Fear Index for the COVID-19 Pandemic
Afees A. Salisu and Lateef O. Akanni
Emerging Markets Finance and Trade, volume 56, issue 10 (2020), pp. 2310–2331

Chapter 13

Accounting Index of COVID-19 Impact on Chinese Industries: A Case Study Using Big Data Portrait Analysis
Pinglin He, Hanlu Niu, Zhe Sun, and Tao Li
Emerging Markets Finance and Trade, volume 56, issue 10 (2020), pp. 2332–2349

Chapter 14

How Does COVID-19 Affect China's Insurance Market?
Yating Wang, Donghao Zhang, Xiaoquan Wang, and Qiuyao Fu
Emerging Markets Finance and Trade, volume 56, issue 10 (2020), pp. 2350–2362

Chapter 15

Household Financial Decision Making Amidst the COVID-19 Pandemic
Pengpeng Yue, Aslihan Gizem Korkmaz, and Haigang Zhou
Emerging Markets Finance and Trade, volume 56, issue 10 (2020), pp. 2363–2377

For any permission-related enquiries please visit:
www.tandfonline.com/page/help/permissions

Notes on Contributors

Hongshan Ai, School of Economics and Trade, Hunan University, Changsha, China; Key Laboratory of Energy Internet Supply-demand and Operation in Hunan Province, Changsha, China.

Lateef O. Akanni, Centre for Econometric & Allied Research, University of Ibadan, Ibadan, Nigeria; Centre for the Study of the Economies of Africa, Abuja, Nigeria.

Huimin Bi, Hunan University of Finance and Economics, Changsha, China.

Conghui Chen, Faculty of Business and Law, University of Northampton, Northampton, UK.

Yongquan Chen, Department of Accounting, School of Economics and Management, North China Electric Power University, Beijing, China.

Aruna Kumar Dash, Department of Economics, The ICFAI Foundation for Higher Education, India.

Mengyao Fu, Department of Accounting, School of Economics and Management, North China Electric Power University, Beijing, China.

Qiuyao Fu, School of Economics, Southwestern University of Finance and Economics, Chengdu, China.

Xin Gu, School of Economics and Management, Southeast University, Nanjing, China.

Omair Haroon, Suleman Dawood School of Business, Lahore University of Management Sciences (LUMS), Lahore, Pakistan.

Pinglin He, School of Economics and Management, North China Electric Power University, Beijing, China.

Fei Hou, School of Management, Xiamen University, Xiamen, Fujian, China.

Guoliang Huang, Department of Accounting, School of Economics and Management, China University of Mining and Technology, Xuzhou City, China.

Bernard Njindan Iyke, Centre for Financial Econometrics, Deakin Business School, Deakin University, Melbourne, Australia.

Aslihan Gizem Korkmaz, Barowsky School of Business, Dominican University of California, San Rafael, CA, USA.

Tao Li, School of Economics and Management, North China Electric Power University, Beijing, China.

Yuankun Li, Economics and Management School, Wuhan University, Wuhan, China.

Ding Liu, School of Economics, Southwestern University of Finance and Economics, Chengdu, China.

Lanlan Liu, Dongwu Business School, Soochow University, Suzhou, China.

Taixing Liu, School of Finance, Capital University of Economics and Business, Beijing, China.

Wen Ming, Key Laboratory of Energy Internet Supply-demand and Operation in Hunan Province, Changsha, China; State Grid Hunan Electric Power Company Limited Economic and Technical Research Institute, Changsha, China.

Alok Kumar Mishra, School of Economics, University of Hyderabad, Hyderabad, India.

Paresh Kumar Narayan, Monash Business School, Monash University, Melbourne, Australia.

Hanlu Niu, School of Economics and Management, North China Electric Power University, Beijing, China.

Beixiao Pan, School of Finance, Capital University of Economics and Business, Beijing, China.

Hongyu Pan, Department of Accounting, School of Business, Guilin University of Technology, Guilin, China.

Dinh Hoang Bach Phan, Department of Economics, Finance, and Marketing, La Trobe Business School, LaTrobe University, Melbourne, Australia.

K. P. Prabheesh, Associate Professor, Indian Institute of Technology Hyderabad, Hyderabad, India.

Xiuhong Qin, Department of Accounting, School of Economics and Management, China University of Mining and Technology, Xuzhou City, China.

Badri Narayan Rath, Department of Liberal Arts, Indian Institute of Technology Hyderabad, India.

Syed Aun R. Rizvi, Suleman Dawood School of Business, Lahore University of Management Sciences (LUMS), Lahore, Pakistan.

Afees A. Salisu, Centre for Econometric & Allied Research, University of Ibadan, Ibadan, Nigeria.

Yezhou Sha, Capital University of Economics and Business, Beijing, China.

Susan Sunila Sharma, Centre for Financial Econometrics & Department of Finance, Deakin Business School, Deakin University, Melbourne, Australia.

Huayu Shen, Department of Accounting, School of Economics and Management, North China Electric Power University, Beijing, China.

Weihong Sun, The West Center for Economics Research, Southwestern University of Finance and Economics, Chengdu, China.

Yulong Sun, School of Economics and Management, North China Electric Power University, Beijing, China.

Zhe Sun, School of Economics and Management, North China Electric Power University, Beijing, China.

Yewei Tao, State Grid Suzhou Electric Power Company Limited, Suzhou, China.

C. T. Vidya, Assistant Professor, Centre for Economic and Social Studies (CESS), Hyderabad, India.

Xiaoquan Wang, School of Insurance, Southwestern University of Finance and Economics, Chengdu, China.

Yating Wang, School of Finance, Capital University of Economics and Business, Beijing, China.

Zuofeng Wu, School of Business, Linyi University, Linyi, Shandong, China.

Yao Xiao, Economics and Management School, Wuhan University, Wuhan, China.

Hao Xiong, School of Accounting, Guizhou University of Finance and Economics, Guiyang, Guizhou, China.

Zhichao Yin, School of Finance, Capital University of Economics and Business, Beijing, China.

Shan Ying, Macquarie Business School, Macquarie University, Sydney, Australia.

Zhen Yu, Economics and Management School, Wuhan University, Wuhan, China.

Zhongfu Yu, Department of Accounting, School of Economics and Management, North China Electric Power University, Beijing, China.

Pengpeng Yue, Department of Finance, Beijing Technology and Business University, Beijing, China.

Donghao Zhang, School of Insurance, Southwestern University of Finance and Economics, Chengdu, China.

Jun Zhang, School of Business, Beijing Wuzi University, Tongzhou, Beijing, China.

Weiqiang Zhang, School of Economics and Management, Southeast University, Nanjing, China.

Xuan Zhang, Institute of Economics and Finance, Nanjing Audit University, Nanjing, China.

Ying Zhang, School of Economics and Management, North China Electric Power University, Beijing, China.

Ningru Zhao, Institute of Economics and Finance, Nanjing Audit University, Nanjing, China.

Yuan Zhong, School of Economics and Trade, Hunan University, Changsha, China.

Haigang Zhou, Department of Finance, Cleveland State University, Cleveland, OH, USA.

Zhengqing Zhou, School of Economics and Trade, Hunan University, Changsha, China.

Introduction

Research on Pandemics Special Issue of *Emerging Markets Finance and Trade*

The special issue of *Emerging Markets Finance and Trade* (EMFT) represents the very first special issue on COVID-19 from a business and economics point of view. EMFT is, therefore, proud to be the first journal to compile literature on COVID-19. This issue contains 19 papers; seven were selected from the virtual symposium on *Pandemics: Lessons from an Economics and Finance Perspective* (May 2020, China) while 12 papers were chosen from the papers received as part of a general call for papers on the theme. All papers were selected following the journal's usual peer review process. Those 19 papers chosen not only expand our knowledge of social and economic consequences of the pandemic but set the foundation for future research.

The coverage of the special issue is broad as it covers a wide range of topics, such as the effects of COVID-19 on stock markets, foreign exchange markets, insurance markets, and households. The first paper by Dinh Phan and Paresh Kumar Narayan provides an overview of the response and reaction of 25 countries' stock markets to the COVID-19 pandemic. Their study documents possible overreaction during early stages of pandemic and identifies patterns in market correction with time.

The second paper by Omair Haroon and Syed Aun Rizvi examines the impact of COVID-19 pandemic on liquidity of 23 emerging markets. They provide evidence of a significant negative relationship between the number of confirmed COVID-19 cases and liquidity in 23 emerging financial markets.

In the third paper, Alok Kumar Mishra, Badri Narayan Rath, and Aruna Kumar Dash investigate the impact of the pandemic on the Indian financial market. Their main contribution is in the finding that the Indian stock market experienced a negative return growth and an increase in volatility from COVID-19. They compared the impact of COVID-19 with those of other policy shocks in India (such as demonetization and GST) and found that these two policies actually had a positive effect on market returns and contributed to less volatility.

The next four papers have a common feature; they consider firm or sector level data to examine the impact of COVID-19 on the Chinese stock market. Xin Gu, Shan Ying, Weiqiang Zhang, Yewei Tao, for instance, examine the impact of COVID-19 on economic activities in Zuzhou, China. They use daily electricity usage data for 34,040 enterprises as a proxy for economic activity and find that the impact of COVID-19 had a heterogenous effect on firms belonging to different sectors.

In addition, other three papers by Pinglin He, Yulong Sun, Ying Zhang, and Tao Li; Huayu Shen, Mengyao Fu, Hongyu Pan, Zhongfu Yu; and Yongquan Chen and Hao Xiong, Zuofeng Wu, Fei Hou, and Jun Zhang document similar findings that different sectors and firms are affected differently by the impact of the COVID-19 pandemic in the case of China.

The eighth paper by Xiuhong Qin, Guoliang Huang, Huayu Shen, and Mengyao Fu examine the impact of COVID-19 on firm-level cash holding and document that the pandemic had a significant positive effect on cash-holding levels of Chinese listed firms.

Ding Liu, Weihong Sun, and Xuan Zhang make up the ninth paper. They conduct a time-frequency analysis of the macro-financial variables to examine its resilience in fighting the COVID-19 pandemic in China. They note that Chinese businesses and financial cycles were very close to a contraction phase before the onset of COVID-19, which, they argue, places China in a better position compared to other emerging economies in the fight against the pandemic.

The tenth paper by Bernard Iyke focuses on the predictability of exchange rate returns of 25 countries. He used disease outbreak as a predictor variable. This study provides novel evidence that outbreaks, such as COVID-19, contain valuable information that can be used to predict exchange rate returns and volatility.

The work of Conghui Chen, Lanlan Liu, and Ningru Zhao, is about the impact of fear sentiment originating from the COVID-19 pandemic on Bitcoin price dynamics. They construct a proxy for fear sentiment using hourly Google search queries on coronavirus-related words. They provide evidence that negative Bitcoin returns are adversely affected due to the market downturn and its safe-haven properties are worth further investigation. They suggest Bitcoin does not exhibit safe-haven properties during extreme crisis periods.

The next two papers construct unique indexes in response to the COVID-19 pandemic. Afees Salisu and Lateef Akanni construct a global fear index resulting from COVID-19 and use this index to predict OECD and BRICS stock returns. They document that the inclusion of this global fear index in the predictability model during the pandemic period outperforms the benchmark constant-return model.

On the other hand, Pinglin He, Hanlu Niu, She Sun, and Tao Li construct an accounting index for COVID-19 and examine its impact on various Chinese industries. They document that manufacturing, sports and entertainment, hotels, and catering and residential service industries were significantly affected by the pandemic while other industries (such as basic industry) were found to be relatively stable during the pandemic phase.

The fourteenth paper by Yating Wang, Donghao Zhang, Xiaoquan Wang, and Qiuyao Fu investigates how COVID-19 has impacted China's insurance market. They discover strong evidence that the Chinese insurance market is adversely affected by the COVID-19 pandemic.

The next three papers focus mainly on the most vulnerable economic units, such as labor force, households, and global trade networks during the COVID-19 pandemic. Pengpeng Yue, Aslihan Korkmaz, and Haigang Zhou show that households that have a family member, relative, colleague, fellow student, friend, acquaintance in the same community or village infected by COVID-19 lose confidence in the economy. They are more likely to change their risk behavior and become risk averse.

Zhichao Yin, Taixing Liu, and Beixiao Pan document a significant decline in household consumption during the COVID-19 pandemic. They further note that urban household consumption during the pandemic was promoted by mobile payment while rural households remain unaffected.

Interestingly, Zhen Yu, Yao Xiao, and Yuankun Li find evidence that the COVID-19 pandemic alters human behavior and negatively affects the labor force participation rate. They further suggest that this negative impact could be due to the cultural attitude toward uncertainty avoidance.

In the second last paper, Vidya C.T., and K.P. Prabheesh examine trade interconnectedness among 15 global trading countries during COVID-19 outbreak. They document a drastic reduction in trade connectedness, connectivity, and density amongst countries during pandemic.

The last paper is by Wen Ming, Zhengqing Zhou, Hongshan Ai, Huimin Bi, Yuan, Zhong. They examine the impact of the COVID-19 pandemic on air quality in the case of China and document that air quality improved during this pandemic phase, but this effect is temporary.

Very little is known especially with respect to social and economic implications of COVID-19 and we believe this special issue forms a foundation for this new area of research. These 19 papers provide fresh and new insights on economic consequences of COVID-19, however, there are still several aspects of COVID-19 research that remains to be done. Here we outline some of the areas which require further investigation.

First, studies such as Yue et al. and Yin et al. emphasize household consumption during pandemic periods. These studies are based on survey data; however, the conclusions are mainly drawn from Chinese households. Similar work should be done for other Asian economies, such as Indonesia and India to identify if there are specific patterns in household responses to COVID-19 in emerging markets.

Second, Yating et al. provide an excellent insight on the performance of insurance companies during the COVID-19 pandemic. This paper lays the foundation and motivation for future research on the insurance industry. The focus should be on understanding how insurance companies in other emerging economies responded to the COVID-19 crisis. Are there specific patterns in responses? Answers to this question will aid policy formulation. It will be more useful to also understand how different types of insurance products (such as life insurance, health insurance, travel insurance) were impacted by COVID-19.

Third, few studies show that COVID-19 has a heterogenous effect on sectoral returns. Some sectors are more vulnerable (such as manufacturing) during COVID-19 while others show resilience or growth (such as medical). However, it will be worth investigating the impact of COVID-19 on tourism and travel-related firms, such as hotels, airlines, and rental transportation. This is because tourism and travel, particularly the international component, is an industry that has come to a stop.

Finally, there is one paper by Ming et al. which examines air quality during COVID-19 in China. This paper is inspirational and demands an extension of the literature which examines determinants of carbon dioxide emissions (see, for example, Sharma 2011) during the COVID-19 pandemic period. The validity of the Environmental Kuznets Curve (EKC) can be tested during the COVID-19 period.

In closing, we acknowledge some of the studies that have already been published and attempt to make a link with what has been published in this issue. Papers in this issue on global fear index and sentiment relate to papers published in the energy literature showing the response of energy markets to sentiments (see Haroon and Rizvi 2020; Huang and Zheng 2020; Narayan 2019, 2020). Studies on reaction of stock markets (and its volatility) from COVID-19 complement studies that explore similar types of effects but in the energy market (see Devpura and Narayan 2020; Liu et al 2020; Gil-Alana and Monge 2020; Qin, Zhang, and Su 2020;; Fu and Shen 2020; Al-Awadhi, Al-Saifi, Al-Awadhi, & Alhamadi 2020; Ali, Alam, and Rizvi 2020; Zhang, Hu, and Ji 2020). Finally, a range of studies in this special issue show sectoral heterogeneity, a finding first established by Narayan and Sharma (2011) at the sector level when modeling oil price shocks. More robustness tests on this pattern of relation is needed, particularly using emerging market data.

References

Al-Awadhi, A. M., K. Al-Saifi, A. Al-Awadhi, and S. Alhamadi. 2020. Death and contagious infectious diseases: Impact of the COVID-19 virus on stock market returns. *Journal of Behavioral and Experimental Finance* 27:100326. doi:10.1016/j.jbef.2020.100326.

Ali, M., N. Alam, and S. A. R. Rizvi. 2020. Coronavirus (COVID-19) – An epidemic or pandemic for financial markets. *Journal of Behavioral and Experimental Finance* 27:100341. doi:10.1016/j.jbef.2020.100341.

Devpura, N., and P. K. Narayan. 2020. Hourly oil price volatility: The role of COVID-19. *Energy Research Letters* 1 (2). In Press.

Fu, M., and H. Shen. 2020. COVID-19 and corporate performance in the energy industry. *Energy Research Letters* 1 (1):12967. doi:10.46557/001c.12967.

Gil-Alana, L. A., and M. Monge. 2020. Crude oil prices and COVID-19: Persistence of the shock. *Energy Research Letters* 1 (1):13200. doi:10.46557/001c.13200.

Haroon, O., and S. A. R. Rizvi. 2020. COVID-19: Media coverage and financial markets behavior—A sectoral inquiry. *Journal of Behavioral and Experimental Finance* 27:100343. doi:10.1016/j.jbef.2020.100343.

Huang, W., and Y. Zheng. 2020. COVID-19: Structural changes in the relationship between investor sentiment and crude oil futures prices. *Energy Research Letters* 1 (2). In Press.

Liu, L., E. Z. Wang, and C. C. Lee. 2020. Impact of the COVID-19 pandemic on the crude oil and stock markets in the US: A time-varying analysis. *Energy Research Letters* 1 (1):13154. doi:10.46557/001c.13154.

Narayan, P. K. 2019. Can stale oil price news predict stock returns? *Energy Economics* 83:430–44. doi:10.1016/j.eneco.2019.07.022.

Narayan, P. K. 2020. Oil price news and COVID-19—Is there any connection? *Energy Research Letters* 1 (1):13176. doi:10.46557/001c.13176.

Narayan P. K. and S. S. Sharma. 2011. New evidence on oil price and firm returns. *Journal of Banking and Finance* 35:3252–62.

Qin, M., Y. C. Zhang, and C. W. Su. 2020. The essential role of pandemics: A fresh insight into the oil market. *Energy Research Letters* 1 (1):13166. doi:10.46557/001c.13166.

Sharma, S. S. 2011. Determinants of Carbon dioxide emission: Empirical evidence from 69 countries. *Applied Energy* 88:376–82. doi:10.1016/j.apenergy.2010.07.022.

Zhang, D., M. Hu, and Q. Ji. 2020. Financial markets under the global pandemic of COVID-19. *Finance Research Letters* 101528. doi:10.1016/j.frl.2020.101528.

Yezhou Sha

Susan Sunila Sharma

Country Responses and the Reaction of the Stock Market to COVID-19—a Preliminary Exposition

Dinh Hoang Bach Phan and Paresh Kumar Narayan

ABSTRACT

As the coronavirus pandemic (COVID-19) has amplified so has country responses to it. With COVID-19 taking its toll on humans, as reflected in the number of people infected by, and deaths from, COVID-19, countries responded by locking down economic activity and peoples movement, imposing travel bans, and implementing stimulus packages to cushion the unprecedented slowdown in economic activity and loss of jobs. This article provides a commentary on how the most active financial indicator – namely, the stock price – reacted in real-time to different stages in COVID-19's evolution. We argue that, as with any unexpected news, markets over-react and as more information becomes available and people understand the ramifications more broadly the market corrects itself. This is our hypothesis which needs robust empirical verification.

1. Introduction

When it comes to containing pandemics, particularly when a pandemic is as devastating as COVID-19, that brings the world to a standstill, there is no rule-book, there are no policy prescriptions, and there are no models (neither economic nor medical) that governments can draw upon. At these times, the rule for pandemic containment is self-taught, self-learnt, or learnt from the experience of other countries. Much of this learning takes place as the pandemic ages. This is precisely what the early experience of COVID-19 has taught us. So much is the uncertainty surrounding COVID-19 that we are still learning. How will COVID-19 unfold and at which point its devastation will come to a halt are unpredictable. If the crisis has stressed governments and people alike globally, medical science finds itself in a space never before. Medically, COVID-19 is not all about developing a vaccine but also about understanding its origins, evolutions, mutations and, as a result, its life. Answers to these questions will take many months if not years. Global social and economic stability rests on the accuracy of answers to these questions. It is within this spirit of learning not the medical side of COVID-19 but its economics, and not knowing what to expect in days and weeks to come let alone months, that this paper settles on starting with the basics – primarily, providing a snapshot of how different countries responded to the declaration of COVID-19 as a pandemic by the World Health Organization (WHO). In other words, we study the timing of government actions and policy responses. We relate, albeit casually, those policy responses to reactions of arguably the most active financial indicator – namely, the stock price. Obviously, stock price is not the only indicator but it is the leading indicator. We focus on understanding the reaction of stock price because we believe this pandemic can potentially instigate a global financial crisis.

We aim to identify any patterns in these relations that could potentially have implications for how countries should position themselves to react to future pandemics. Our aim is not to cover all aspects of the relation between the pandemic and the financial system for we cannot, both because of lack of data and time. Our ultimate goal is to set the foundation for what will be a large volume of empirical literature on this pandemic and its ramifications for the global economy.[1]

COVID-19, we would like to argue, represents the fear of the unknown and arguably the father of all fears that have engulfed global financial and economic systems. We further argue that it is this fear that leads to reactions, not only from governments but also from businesses. By the time governments have reacted and, as a result, businesses have reacted without much choice, individuals have no space to react – they simply become "reaction takers." By way of theory, then, we are guided in our interpretation of the behavior of stock prices by investor underreaction and overreaction theories (Daniel, Hirshleifer, and Subrahmanyam 1998; Hong and Stein 1999; Hong, Torous, and Valkanov 2007). All stakeholders in our story of COVID-19 are investors. This is not difficult to see. Every stakeholder is expected to make a loss from this crisis. Governments are lead investors. Their objective function is to minimize loss to businesses and households. Given this objective, when an unprecedented crisis takes shape, about which nothing, or at best, very little is known, governments initial reaction will be to overreact because of the fear generated by the crisis. However, as more information about the crisis becomes available – that is, as governments become more comfortable in dealing with the crisis and learn more about the crisis, they will correct their reactions. Markets are a function of government. Markets will, therefore, react consistent with government reactions. When governments overreact, this will transmit to the market. Therefore, we should see a market overreaction and, as governments correct their reactions, the market will do so too. This type of government overreaction and reaction-correction type behavior should be observed from market fundamentals, which in our case is the stock price.[2]

In this paper, we study government responses to COVID-19 for the top-25 countries most affected by the COVID-19 in terms of infected cases and deaths, and utilize daily time-series data on those countries stock returns to infer any patterns in policy responses and reactions of stock returns. We unravel new insights. The data signal possible overreaction and market correction. When we observe how each of the 25 countries' stock market (proxied by price returns) reacted to cases of COVID-19 infections and deaths, we see that during the early stages stock prices in the vast majority of the countries reacted negatively. However, with time, as countries reached 100,000 infections and 100 deaths, for example, the reaction in 50% of the markets was positive, suggesting a possible market correction.

We also show that in the absence of any guiding model or prescriptions on how countries should react to an event as unprecedented as COVID-19, some countries were slow in imposing travel bans and lockdowns – two arms of governments containment policy regarded as central to containing the spread of infections and indeed deaths. We find it difficult to converge to claiming what policy response worked most but we stand to infer that travel ban (because it prevented imports and exports of the virus) was effective, followed by country lockdowns (because they prevented the spread of virus through ensuring social distancing). It appears from the data, and commonsense too, that preventing virus trading through closing borders and stopping it from spreading (through lockdowns which reflect social distancing measures) are effective measures. One does not need to engage in empirical analysis to confirm what is an obvious case.

2. An Assessment of Country Speed of Reaction to COVID-19

In this section, we use multiple types of data to comment on the hypothesis that countries were slow to react to the pandemic. Our approach is we calculate the number of days it took for countries to record the first death, 100th death, 1000th death, 5000th death, 10,000th case and 100,000th case from the day the WHO declared COVID-19 as a pandemic. The list of events is reported in Table 1 and the calculated days appear in Panel A of Table 2. We calculate the number of days recorded to obtain those levels of death and case from the time each of those 25 countries announced country lockdowns. This statistic appears in Panel B of Table 2.[3]

We start with data in Panel A. There are several important messages here. First, even before the WHO declared COVID-19 a pandemic, 12/25 countries had recorded at least one death. Second, the total number of deaths had reached 100 in Italy and China 6 days and 43 days before the pandemic was declared. Third, in five countries (the US, Spain, France, the UK, and South Korea) it took less than 10 days for those countries to reach 100 deaths, and except for South Korea, in the other 4 countries within 10 days of 100 deaths

Table 1. List of events.

	Panel A: Macro events			
	WHO declares pandemic	Lockdown	Stimulus package	Travel ban
United States	11-Mar-20	19-Mar-20	6-Mar-20	31-Jan-20
Spain	11-Mar-20	14-Mar-20	17-Mar-20	10-Mar-20
Italy	11-Mar-20	10-Mar-20	11-Mar-20	10-Mar-20
France	11-Mar-20	16-Mar-20	17-Mar-20	17-Mar-20
Germany	11-Mar-20	20-Mar-20	1-Mar-20	17-Mar-20
United Kingdom	11-Mar-20	16-Mar-20	17-Mar-20	25-Mar-20
China	11-Mar-20	23-Jan-20	1-Feb-20	27-Mar-20
Turkey	11-Mar-20	12-Mar-20	18-Mar-20	13-Mar-20
Belgium	11-Mar-20	17-Mar-20	28-Mar-20	20-Mar-20
Netherlands	11-Mar-20	15-Mar-20	18-Mar-20	17-Mar-20
Brazil	11-Mar-20	21-Mar-20	16-Mar-20	27-Mar-20
Canada	11-Mar-20	16-Mar-20	18-Mar-20	16-Mar-20
Russia	11-Mar-20	30-Mar-20	24-Mar-20	31-Jan-20
Switzerland	11-Mar-20	13-Mar-20	16-Mar-20	17-Mar-20
Portugal	11-Mar-20	18-Mar-20	18-Mar-20	17-Mar-20
Austria	11-Mar-20	10-Mar-20	18-Mar-20	17-Mar-20
India	11-Mar-20	24-Mar-20	19-Mar-20	3-Mar-20
Israel	11-Mar-20	19-Mar-20	30-Mar-20	30-Jan-20
Ireland	11-Mar-20	12-Mar-20	16-Mar-20	–
Sweden	11-Mar-20	11-Mar-20	15-Mar-20	2-Mar-20
Peru	11-Mar-20	30-Mar-20	30-Mar-20	15-Mar-20
South Korea	11-Mar-20	24-Feb-20	4-Mar-20	6-Mar-20
Japan	11-Mar-20	13-Mar-20	5-Mar-20	1-Feb-20
Chile	11-Mar-20	19-Mar-20	19-Mar-20	16-Mar-20
Poland	11-Mar-20	10-Mar-20	19-Mar-20	13-Mar-20

	Panel B: Cumulative infected cases				
	First case	100 cases	1,000 cases	10,000 cases	100,000 cases
United States	21-Jan-20	3-Mar-20	11-Mar-20	20-Mar-20	28-Mar-20
Spain	1-Feb-20	3-Mar-20	10-Mar-20	18-Mar-20	2-Apr-20
Italy	31-Jan-20	24-Feb-20	1-Mar-20	11-Mar-20	31-Mar-20
France	25-Jan-20	1-Mar-20	9-Mar-20	20-Mar-20	15-Apr-20
Germany	28-Jan-20	1-Mar-20	10-Mar-20	20-Mar-20	8-Apr-20
United Kingdom	31-Jan-20	6-Mar-20	15-Mar-20	27-Mar-20	–
China	17-Nov-20	19-Jan-20	25-Jan-20	1-Feb-20	–
Turkey	12-Mar-20	19-Mar-20	23-Mar-20	31-Mar-20	–
Belgium	4-Feb-20	7-Mar-20	17-Mar-20	30-Mar-20	–
Netherlands	28-Feb-20	7-Mar-20	16-Mar-20	30-Mar-20	–
Brazil	26-Feb-20	15-Mar-20	22-Mar-20	5-Apr-20	–
Canada	26-Jan-20	12-Mar-20	22-Mar-20	3-Apr-20	–
Russia	1-Feb-20	18-Mar-20	28-Mar-20	10-Apr-20	–
Switzerland	26-Feb-20	7-Mar-20	14-Mar-20	27-Mar-20	–
Portugal	3-Mar-20	14-Mar-20	21-Mar-20	5-Apr-20	–
Austria	26-Feb-20	9-Mar-20	17-Mar-20	1-Apr-20	–
India	30-Jan-20	17-Mar-20	30-Mar-20	14-Apr-20	–
Israel	22-Feb-20	14-Mar-20	23-Mar-20	11-Apr-20	–
Ireland	1-Mar-20	15-Mar-20	24-Mar-20	14-Apr-20	–
Sweden	1-Feb-20	7-Mar-20	16-Mar-20	12-Apr-20	–
Peru	7-Mar-20	18-Mar-20	1-Apr-20	15-Apr-20	–
South Korea	20-Jan-20	21-Feb-20	26-Feb-20	3-Apr-20	–
Japan	24-Jan-20	22-Feb-20	21-Mar-20	–	–
Chile	4-Mar-20	17-Mar-20	26-Mar-20	–	–
Poland	4-Mar-20	15-Mar-20	26-Mar-20	–	–

	Panel C: Cumulative death			
	First death	100 deaths	1,000 deaths	5,000 deaths
United States	1-Mar-20	18-Mar-20	26-Mar-20	2-Apr-20
Spain	5-Mar-20	14-Mar-20	21-Mar-20	29-Mar-20

(Continued)

Table 1. (Continued).

Italy	23-Feb-20	5-Mar-20	13-Mar-20	23-Mar-20
France	15-Feb-20	16-Mar-20	25-Mar-20	4-Apr-20
Germany	10-Mar-20	24-Mar-20	3-Apr-20	7-Apr-20
United Kingdom	6-Mar-20	19-Mar-20	29-Mar-20	–
China	11-Jan-20	28-Jan-20	11-Feb-20	–
Turkey	19-Mar-20	29-Mar-20	11-Apr-20	–
Belgium	12-Mar-20	25-Mar-20	3-Apr-20	–
Netherlands	7-Mar-20	21-Mar-20	1-Apr-20	–
Brazil	18-Mar-20	29-Mar-20	11-Apr-20	–
Canada	10-Mar-20	2-Apr-20	16-Apr-20	–
Russia	27-Mar-20	12-Apr-20	–	–
Switzerland	6-Mar-20	26-Mar-20	–	–
Portugal	18-Mar-20	29-Mar-20	–	–
Austria	13-Mar-20	31-Mar-20	–	–
India	13-Mar-20	6-Apr-20	–	–
Israel	21-Mar-20	12-Apr-20	–	–
Ireland	12-Mar-20	4-Apr-20	–	–
Sweden	12-Mar-20	29-Mar-20	15-Apr-20	–
Peru	20-Mar-20	8-Apr-20	–	–
South Korea	21-Feb-20	20-Mar-20	–	–
Japan	13-Feb-20	13-Apr-20	–	–
Chile	23-Mar-20	–	–	–
Poland	13-Mar-20	7-Apr-20	–	–

This table reports the list and date for important events taken by WHO and each country (Panel A), cumulative infected cases (Panel B), and cumulative deaths (Panel C).

there was a 10-fold increase in deaths. The speed of deaths was rapid in these four countries. Fourth, China (−43 days), Italy (−6 days), Spain (3 days), and France (5 days) fastest to reach 100 deaths. This was followed by Turkey, Brazil, Portugal, and Sweden who took 18 days. Fifth, Japan (at 33 days) was the slowest to reach 100 deaths (except Chile that didn't reach to 100 deaths at the time of writing this paper), followed by Israel and Russia (32 days). Sixth, reading data on speed to 5,000 deaths suggests Italy was the fastest (13 days) followed by the Spain (18 days). Overall, we see that within 27 days of COVID-19 becoming a pandemic all five advanced countries had recorded 5000 deaths.

To conclude reading this table, we turn to the last two columns which report 10,000 and 100,000 cases from the time COVID-19 was declared a pandemic. Twenty-two countries had reached 10,000 cases at the time of writing this paper. We observe that Italy took 0 days to reach 10,000 cases while Spain took 7 days, and the US, France and Germany took 9 days. Peru took the greatest number of days (35) to reach 10,000 cases, followed by Ireland and India (34 days).

Panel B has corresponding information on the number of days to different levels of death and recorded cases from the day of lockdown. We see that 17/25 countries imposed a country lockdown before any deaths were recorded.

Table 2. Timeline of events.

Panel A: Number of days from WHO pandemic declaration to events					
	First death	100 deaths	1,000 deaths	5,000 deaths	10,000 cases	100,000 cases
United States	−10	7	15	22	9	17
Spain	−6	3	10	18	7	22
Italy	−17	−6	2	12	0	20
France	−25	5	14	24	9	35
Germany	−1	13	23	27	9	28
United Kingdom	−5	8	18	–	16	–
China	−60	−43	−29	–	−39	–
Turkey	8	18	31	–	20	–
Belgium	1	14	23	–	19	–
Netherlands	−4	10	21	–	19	–
Brazil	7	18	31	–	25	–
Canada	−1	22	36	–	23	–
Russia	16	32	–	–	30	–
Switzerland	−5	15	–	–	16	–
Portugal	7	18	–	–	25	–
Austria	2	20	–	–	21	–
India	2	26	–	–	34	–
Israel	10	32	–	–	31	–
Ireland	1	24	–	–	34	–
Sweden	1	18	35	–	32	–
Peru	9	28	–	–	35	–
South Korea	−19	9	–	–	23	–
Japan	−27	33	–	–	–	–
Chile	12	NA	–	–	–	–
Poland	2	27	–	–	–	–

Panel B: Number of days from lockdown to events					
	First death	100 deaths	1,000 deaths	5,000 deaths	10,000 cases	100,000 cases
United States	−18	−1	7	14	1	9
Spain	−9	0	7	15	4	19
Italy	−16	−5	3	13	1	21
France	−30	0	9	19	4	30
Germany	−10	4	14	18	0	19
United Kingdom	−10	3	13	–	11	–
China	−12	5	19	–	9	–
Turkey	7	17	30	–	19	–
Belgium	−5	8	17	–	13	–
Netherlands	−8	6	17	–	15	–
Brazil	−3	8	21	–	15	–
Canada	−6	17	31	–	18	–
Russia	−3	13	–	–	11	–
Switzerland	−7	13	–	–	14	–
Portugal	0	11	–	–	18	–
Austria	3	21	–	–	22	–
India	−11	13	–	–	21	–
Israel	2	24	–	–	23	–
Ireland	0	23	–	–	33	–
Sweden	1	18	35	–	32	–
Peru	−10	9	–	–	16	–
South Korea	−3	25	–	–	39	–
Japan	−29	31	–	–	–	–
Chile	4	–	–	–	–	–
Poland	3	28	–	–	–	–

This table reports the number of days from country lockdown (Panel A) and WHO pandemic declaration (Panel B) to important events.

3. WHO Declaration of Pandemic Vs Travel Ban

Reading the last column of Panel A, Table 1 tells of the dates on which some level of travel ban was imposed by each of those 25 countries. Some important facts are. First, Israel, the US, and Russia were the first countries to impose any sort of travel ban effective from 30 and 31 January 2020. These dates imply that these countries imposed some form of travel ban well before the WHO declared COVID-19 a pandemic. Second, while WHO declared COVID-19 a pandemic on 11 March 2020, Spain, Italy, India, Sweden, South Korea, and Japan also had already imposed some level of travel bans.

We consider the reaction of stock markets to COVID-19 events. The list of stock indexes for 25 countries is reported in Table 3, and their returns on the event dates are reported in Table 4. On 11 March 2020, when the WHO declared COVID-19 a pandemic, 24 out of 25 countries' stock market recorded a negative growth – returns were in the −0.095% (Turkey) to −7.945% (Brazil) range. We see that in 12 of the 25 countries (France, Germany, the UK, China, Turkey, Belgium, the Netherlands, Switzerland, Portugal, India, Sweden, and Poland) the day of travel ban had a positive effect on the market with stock markets recording a positive growth, in the 0.264% to 5.011% range. And, in another six countries (the US, Brazil, Austria, Israel, South Korea, and Japan), the negative effect on the stock market was less when the travel ban was imposed compared to when COVID-19 was declared a pandemic. Only six countries (Spain, Italy, Canada, Russia, Peru, and Chile)

Table 3. List of countries and stock indexes.

Country	Stock index
United States	S&P 500 Composite
Spain	IBEX 35
Italy	FTSE MIB Index
France	France CAC 40
Germany	DAX 30 Performance
United Kingdom	FTSE ALL SHARE
China	Shanghai SE A Share
Turkey	BIST National 100
Belgium	BEL 20
Netherlands	AEX Index
Brazil	Brazil Bovespa
Canada	S&P/TSX Composite Index
Russia	MOEX Russia Index
Switzerland	Swiss Market (SMI)
Portugal	Portugal PSI-20
Austria	ATX – Austrian Traded Index
India	Nifty 500
Israel	Israel TA 125
Ireland	ISEQ All Share Index
Sweden	OMX Stockholm 30 (OMXS30)
Peru	S&P/BVL General (IGBVL)
South Korea	Korea SE Composite (KOSPI)
Japan	NIKKEI 225 Stock Average
Chile	S&P/CLX IGPA CLP Index
Poland	WARSAW General Index

Table 4. Stock index returns (%).

	Panel A: Macro events			
	WHO declares pandemic	Lockdown	Stimulus package	Travel ban
United States	−5.010	0.470	−1.720	−1.786
Spain	−0.337	−8.208	6.210	−3.259
Italy	0.327	−3.333	0.327	−3.333
France	−0.570	−5.924	2.803	2.803
Germany	−0.352	3.632	−0.274	2.227
United Kingdom	−1.387	−4.982	1.587	4.394
China	−0.948	−2.789	−8.034	0.264
Turkey	−0.095	−7.533	−1.394	2.078
Belgium	−0.228	−0.269	−1.260	5.011
Netherlands	−0.111	−3.786	−4.868	1.781
Brazil	−7.945	−5.359	−14.978	−5.666
Canada	−4.709	−10.409	−7.902	−10.409
Russia	−0.243	1.334	6.968	−1.032
Switzerland	−0.473	1.167	−1.693	3.182
Portugal	−0.468	−5.166	−5.166	4.394
Austria	−2.377	−0.781	−8.108	−1.284
India	−0.154	1.942	−2.944	1.573
Israel	−3.438	4.276	2.134	−0.478
Ireland	−2.348	−10.465	−8.257	–
Sweden	−1.433	−1.433	−3.497	0.615
Peru	−3.768	0.137	0.137	−4.700
South Korea	−2.824	−3.952	2.218	−2.184
Japan	−2.297	−6.274	1.080	−1.010
Chile	−2.196	5.788	5.788	−13.837
Poland	−5.702	−1.285	4.302	3.868

	Panel B: Cumulative infected cases				
	First case	100 cases	1,000 cases	10,000 cases	100,000 cases
United States	−0.266	−2.851	−5.010	−4.433	3.297
Spain	0.392	0.799	−3.259	−3.503	−0.081
Italy	−2.314	−5.586	−1.508	0.327	1.053
France	−2.713	0.444	−8.764	4.892	−3.835
Germany	0.897	−0.274	−1.417	3.632	−0.230
United Kingdom	−1.172	−3.561	−4.982	−5.092	–
China	0.332	0.658	−8.034	−8.034	–
Turkey	−7.533	−0.447	−1.823	1.783	–
Belgium	2.777	−7.880	−0.269	−1.260	–
Netherlands	−3.748	−7.956	−3.786	2.349	–
Brazil	−7.262	−14.978	−5.359	6.318	–
Canada	−0.702	−13.176	−5.403	−1.226	–
Russia	−0.189	−5.170	1.334	−0.889	–
Switzerland	0.321	−5.708	−1.693	−2.281	–
Portugal	1.523	−4.459	−1.926	1.149	–
Austria	−0.351	−9.441	−1.284	−2.807	–
India	−0.904	−2.322	−3.696	0.000	–
Israel	−1.680	−4.789	−0.856	−0.960	–
Ireland	−0.154	−8.257	6.710	−2.021	–
Sweden	−0.020	−5.460	−3.497	0.000	–
Peru	−5.409	−5.877	−3.977	−0.054	–
South Korea	0.535	−1.499	−1.284	0.034	–
Japan	0.133	−3.398	2.003	–	–
Chile	1.492	0.644	2.735	–	–
Poland	−1.244	−2.334	2.603	–	–

	Panel C: Cumulative death			
	First death	100 deaths	1,000 deaths	5,000 deaths
United States	4.501	−5.322	6.054	2.257
Spain	−2.581	−8.208	−3.363	−1.756
Italy	−5.586	−1.798	6.874	−1.100
France	0.273	−5.924	4.372	4.508

(Continued)

Table 4. (Continued).

Germany	−1.417	10.414	−0.472	2.756
United Kingdom	−3.561	0.860	0.636	–
China	0.754	−8.034	0.387	–
Turkey	−0.447	−0.074	−0.075	–
Belgium	−15.328	1.799	−1.333	–
Netherlands	−7.956	−1.931	−2.543	–
Brazil	−10.925	1.635	1.474	–
Canada	3.012	1.705	−0.425	–
Russia	−3.634	−1.847	–	–
Switzerland	−4.093	2.362	–	–
Portugal	−5.166	1.019	–	–
Austria	0.478	0.595	–	–
India	3.258	0.000	–	–
Israel	−0.856	−0.960	–	–
Ireland	−10.465	4.743	–	–
Sweden	−11.173	2.085	−3.663	–
Peru	−1.798	0.996	–	–
South Korea	−1.499	7.180	–	–
Japan	−0.140	−2.362	–	–
Chile	−5.348	–	–	–
Poland	3.868	1.361	–	–

This table reports stock index returns (%) on the dates of events. If the event falls on a non-trading day, we consider the stock return on the next trading day. It is worthy to note that although the first COVID-19 infected case in China was on 17 November 2019, it was not fully aware by the general public until China officially reported to WHO on 31 December 2019. Therefore, it is more accurate to report the stock return in China on 31 December 2019 in this table.

were worse off upon imposing travel ban compared to the declaration of pandemic. The reason seems to be that the virus had already taken its toll on these countries, suggesting that the imposition of travel bans was too late. Overall, it is clear from this data that for 75% of the countries most affected by COVID-19, some sort of travel ban had helped financial markets recover. In countries where markets did not recover, we infer that travel bans were a policy too late. In other words, in 18/24 countries travel ban either had a positive return (which was the case in 12 countries) or the negative return was smaller compared to when COVID-19 was declared a pandemic. An event study-based empirical analysis should be undertaken to confirm whether returns did behave in the manner the raw data suggests.

Overall, we believe that a pattern in the response of the stock market is visible in Figure 1. In this figure, we plot the reaction of each countries stock price returns to infections (1st, 100th, 1,000th, and 10,000th) to COVID-19. What we hypothesized earlier – see Section I – that there is an overreaction of the stock market to COVID-19 given that it is an unprecedented event and resulting deaths are a source of fear. We argued that the market is going to correct itself with time as more information about COVID-19 becomes available. Like when the WHO declared COVID-19 a pandemic, 24/25 markets in our sample reacted negatively, with the 1st and 100th infection, we see that 16/25 markets reacted negatively and with time (by the time each of those countries reached 10,000th case) only 12/22 markets reacted negatively. Figure 1 makes this pattern in the data more visible, suggesting a possible overreaction and market correction. We observe a similar pattern from the reaction of stock returns to COVID-19-related deaths (Table 4, Panel C): Upon first death, 18/25 markets reacted negatively but by the time 100th death was recorded only 10/24 (Chile did not reach 100th death by the time of writing this paper) markets reacted negatively. We posit a possible market overreaction and correction. This hypothesis needs empirical testing, such as the one based on an event-study methodology. We leave this for future research.

4. The Role of Lockdowns and Stimulus Package

4.1. Lockdowns

Did lockdowns cushion the effect of COVID-19 on stock markets? In eight countries (the US, Germany, Russia, Switzerland, India, Israel, Peru, and Chile), the effect of lockdown on stock markets was positive. Except for Switzerland, in the remaining seven countries, the announcement of lockdown had the most positive response of their markets compared to pandemic declaration and travel ban. This suggests that the single biggest confidence booster to the stock market was not travel bans but lockdowns.

4.2. Stimulus Package

All the 25 countries we consider announced some measure of stimulus. In 11 countries, the day stimulus package was announced, the stock market reacted positively. Of these 11 countries, nine (Spain, Italy, Russia, Israel, Peru, South Korea, Japan, Chile, and Poland) recorded a stronger positive response of their stock markets compared to the imposition of the travel ban. However, a pattern we observe is that the success of stimulus package in stimulating a positive response of the stock market is achieved for countries which had already imposed travel bans and in most cases lockdown.

5. Discussion

Governments moved at different speeds to embrace and implement policies with respect to the declaration of COVID-19 as a pandemic. It was more a case of learning from the experience of other countries and then devising a response. There were also different magnitudes of travel bans. Some countries like US imposed travel bans to and from a particular country while a country like India took a more stringent approach to close its borders. There is no uniformity, neither in the policy stance taken by governments nor in implementation of policies.

It is difficult to concretely tell what precisely worked for countries. Judging by the reaction of the stock markets it seems a combination of travel bans, lockdowns, and stimulus packages did work in containing stock markets. Data suggest that the declaration of COVID-19 was the single most devastating event for stock markets. The bulk of the respite to markets resulted from travel bans.

The data signal possible overreaction and market correction. When we observe how each of the 25 countries' stock market (proxied by price returns) reacted to cases of COVID-19 infections and deaths, we see that during the early stages stock prices in the vast majority of the countries negatively reacted but with time as countries reached 100,000 infections and 100 deaths, for example, the reaction in 50% of the markets was positive suggesting a possible market correction.

6. Concluding Remarks and Directions for Future Research

The descriptive analysis we provide lays the foundation for more data analysis in search of how COVID-19 has impacted the financial system. The data we present offer a contemporaneous effect on the stock market from specific events associated with COVID-19. Our goal was to provide an understanding of government responses to COVID-19 and seek an understanding of their consequences. Our goal was not to engage in econometric analysis – something we leave for future research. Econometric work is needed to establish the causal relation between COVID-19 and financial markets. In econometric models, both time-series and panel data, the events we identify should be

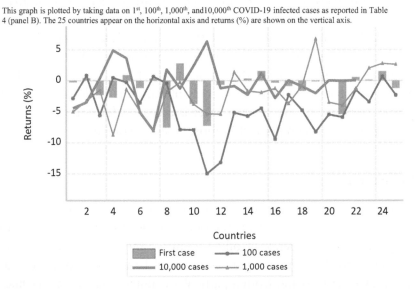

This graph is plotted by taking data on 1st, 100th, 1,000th, and 10,000th COVID-19 infected cases as reported in Table 4 (panel B). The 25 countries appear on the horizontal axis and returns (%) are shown on the vertical axis.

Figure 1. Response of stock prices to COVID-19-infected cases. This graph is plotted by taking data on 1st, 100th, 1,000th, and 10,000th COVID-19 infected cases as reported in Table 4 (panel B). The 25 countries appear on the horizontal axis and returns (%) are shown on the vertical axis.

captured directly (in the form of dummy variables or through constructed indices) because our discussion here shows that they did play a role. Econometric analysis should confirm whether the effects were statistically significant and robust.

In explaining the data, we observe and hence document a possible over-reaction of stock markets and market correction with time. This is a hypothesis that also needs to be empirically tested. This hypothesis can also be tested by using an event study approach.

Notes

1. Some recent papers are Narayan (2020), Gil-Alana and Monge (2020), Liu, Wang, and Lee (2020), Zhang, Hu, and Ji (2020), Haroon and Rizvi (2020), Ali, Alam and Rizvi (2020), Al-Awadhi et al. (2020), Fu and Shen (2020), Qin, Zhang, and Su (2020), and Apergis and Apergis (2020).
2. Typically, in financial economics, modeling stock returns' response to shocks entails controlling for both market risk and macroeconomic risk factors (see Birz and Lott 2011; Fama and French 1993, 2012). Given the discussion, we present on the status obtained by COVID-19, primarily the fact that it is considered an unprecedented event, by default implies that when in effect COVID-19 has no competition in terms of risk. In other words, macroeconomic and/or market risks should not matter. Thus, the loss from not accounting for commonly known risk factors of returns is all but trivial and does not influence the story we tell.
3. This paper has three main datasets. First, the daily number of infected cases and deaths for countries are obtained from Our World in Data (https://ourworldindata.org/), which is collaboratively organized by University of Oxford researchers and Global Change Data Lab. The data from Our World in Data has been widely used in research, teaching and media by Harvard University, Stanford University, University of Cambridge, University of Oxford, The Wall Street Journal, The New York Times and more. Second, the list of country stock indexes and their daily stock prices are collected from the Datastream database. Finally, the dates of events, namely, WHO pandemic declaration, travel ban, lockdown, and the stimulus package, are collected from various internet sources such as the WHO website, the New York Times, the Washington Post, BBC, CNN, CNBC, and the Guardian.

References

Al-Awadhi, A. M., K. Al-Saifi, A. Al-Awadhi, and S. Alhamadi. 2020. Death and contagious infectious diseases: Impact of the COVID-19 virus on stock market returns. *Journal of Behavioral and Experimental Finance* 27:100326. doi:10.1016/j.jbef.2020.100326.

Ali, M., N. Alam, and S. A. R. Rizvi. 2020. Coronavirus (COVID-19) – An epidemic or pandemic for financial markets. *Journal of Behavioral and Experimental Finance* 27:100341. doi:10.1016/j.jbef.2020.100341.

Apergis, E., and N. Apergis. 2020. Can the COVID-19 pandemic and oil prices drive the US partisan conflict index? *Energy Research Letters* 1 (1):13144. doi:10.46557/001c.13144

Birz, G., and J. Lott. 2011. The effect of macroeconomic news on stock returns: New evidence from newspaper coverage. *Journal of Banking & Finance* 35 (11):2791–800. doi:10.1016/j.jbankfin.2011.03.006.

Daniel, K., D. Hirshleifer, and A. Subrahmanyam. 1998. Investor psychology and security market under-and overreactions. *Journal of Finance* 53 (6):1839–86. doi:10.1111/0022-1082.00077.

Fama, E., and K. French. 1993. Common risk factors in the returns on stocks and bonds. *Journal of Finance* 33:3–56.

Fama, E., and K. French. 2012. Size, value, and momentum in international stock returns. *Journal of Financial Economics* 105 (3):457–72. doi:10.1016/j.jfineco.2012.05.011.

Fu, M., and H. Shen. 2020. COVID-19 and corporate performance in the energy industry. *Energy Research Letters* 1 (1):12967. doi:10.46557/001c.12967

Gil-Alana, L. A., and M. Monge. 2020. Crude oil prices and COVID-19: Persistence of the shock. *Energy Research Letters* 1 (1):13200. doi:10.46557/001c.13200

Haroon, O., and S. A. R. Rizvi. 2020. COVID-19: Media coverage and financial markets behavior—A sectoral inquiry. *Journal of Behavioral and Experimental Finance* 27:100343. doi:10.1016/j.jbef.2020.100343.

Hong, H., and J. Stein. 1999. A unified theory of underreaction, momentum trading, and overreaction in asset markets. *Journal of Finance* 54 (6):2143–84. doi:10.1111/0022-1082.00184.

Hong, H., W. Torous, and R. Valkanov. 2007. Do industries lead stock markets? *Journal of Financial Economics* 83 (2):367–96. doi:10.1016/j.jfineco.2005.09.010.

Liu, L., E. Z. Wang, and C. C. Lee. 2020. Impact of the COVID-19 pandemic on the crude oil and stock markets in the US: A time-varying analysis. *Energy Research Letters* 1 (1):13154. doi:10.46557/001c.13154

Narayan, P. K. 2020. Oil price news and COVID-19—Is there any connection? *Energy Research Letters* 1 (1):13176. doi:10.46557/001c.13176

Qin, M., Y. C. Zhang, and C. W. Su. 2020. The essential role of pandemics: A fresh insight into the oil market. *Energy Research Letters* 1 (1):13166. doi:10.46557/001c.13166

Zhang, D., M. Hu, and Q. Ji. 2020. Financial market under the global pandemic of COVID-19. *Financial Research Letter* 101528. doi:10.1016/j.frl.2020.101528.

Flatten the Curve and Stock Market Liquidity – An Inquiry into Emerging Economies

Omair Haroon ⓘD and Syed Aun R. Rizvi ⓘD

ABSTRACT

In this study, we focus on two dimensions of COVID-19 pandemic and their impact on liquidity in emerging equity markets, the real human costs and the government response. Using a sample of 23 emerging markets across three regions, our findings suggest that decreasing (increasing) trend in the number of confirmed coronavirus cases is associated with improving (deteriorating) liquidity in financial markets. We also find that policy interventions in terms of restrictions on movement and businesses are associated with improved liquidity. Results suggest that flattening curve of coronavirus infections helps reduce uncertainty among investors.

1. Introduction

The coronavirus pandemic (COVID-19) has the potential to be the largest macroeconomic shock to not only developed but developing and emerging economies over the past 100 years (Hevia and Neumeyer 2020). The recent coronavirus outbreak has not only had an unprecedented economic and social impact but also shaped media and news conversations. Terms like R_0 (the basic reproduction number), R (the effective reproduction rate), and "flattening the curve" (of epidemic spread) have been debated and discussed in almost all news and media outlets. "Flattening the curve" has also been suggested as a measure of success of policy makers and public health officials in fighting the pandemic (The Economist 2020). The social media even witnessed the hashtag "#FlattentheCurve" going viral and mathematical and statistical explanations of these terms becoming ubiquitous in print and online media (Rhodes, Lancaster, and Rosengarten 2020). In an effort to curb exponential growth in coronavirus infections, governments around the world have instituted restrictions on movement and businesses.

Analysts have highlighted capital outflows, tightening financing conditions and policy constraints as contributors to additional severity of the economic impact of impending global recession on emerging economies

(S&P Global, 2020). These factors also constrain the policymakers in terms of providing support to businesses and improving liquidity in the financial markets. Popular financial press has voiced concerns over the extremely difficult task of policy makers trying to balance curbing the spread of infections and ensuring economic stability. Long horizon portfolio rebalancing while ensuring personal liquidity is a common theme arising out of this situation (e.g. BCG 2020; Lesser 2020; Matinna 2020). Such concerns become even more important for developing countries (Deloitte 2020). COVID-19 not only induced unprecedented uncertainty in the financial markets (Baker et al. 2020; Narayan and Phan 2020) but also caused substantial shifts in real demand patterns and business practices (Barrero, Bloom, and Davis 2020). This situation has raised concerns over draining liquidity in the financial markets (Adrian and Natalucci 2020; Wilkes 2020). In the face of heightened risk and uncertainty, transaction and other costs lead to increase in bid-ask spreads (Glosten and Milgrom 1985; Hasbrouck 1988), signifying deterioration of liquidity in financial markets. In times of financial and economic crises, deteriorating financial and market liquidity reinforce each other's descent (Brunnermeier 2009; Brunnermeier and Pedersen 2009; Geanakoplos 2010). Liquidity has been shown to dry up before crises hit real economy (Næs, Skjeltorp, and Ødegaard 2011). Liquidity in stock markets has also been suggested as informing economic condition of the related economy (Apergis, Artikis, and Kyriazis 2015).

Recent studies on the impact of COVID-19 on financial markets focus on returns, volatility and systematic risk (Al-Awadhi et al. 2020; Albulescu 2020; Apergis and Apergis 2020; Fu and Shen 2020; Gil-Alana and Monge 2020; Haroon and Rizvi 2020; Liu, Wang, and Lee 2020; Narayan 2020; Qin, Zhang, and Su 2020; Zhang, Hu, and Ji 2020). We contribute to this evolving literature by investigating whether "flattening the curve" in terms of cumulative growth of pandemic and government interventions in terms of restricting peoples' mobility improves liquidity in the equity markets of emerging economies. We focus on two dimensions of the pandemic and their impact on liquidity in emerging equity markets. First dimension is the real human costs by investigating rate of spread of infections, specifically efforts to "flatten the curve". Second dimension is the response from various governments in the form of enforcing social distancing through closing educational institutions, businesses, transportation, etc. We find that decreasing (increasing) trend in the number of confirmed coronavirus cases is associated with improving (deteriorating) liquidity in financial markets of emerging economies. We also find that policy interventions in terms of restrictions on movement and businesses are associated with improved liquidity. If the investors place trust on such policy measures, they could feel more confident in trading in financial markets (Chiu 2019).

Countries around the world have either announced or are in the process of announcing stimulus packages to, among other goals, improve liquidity in the financial markets (IMF 2020). The risk of economic uncertainty translating to illiquidity in financial markets is greater for emerging markets because of constraints on fiscal and monetary freedom for policy makers, inability of investors to rapidly rebalance portfolios and higher asymmetry of information (Chowdhury, Uddin, and Anderson 2018). We focus on emerging markets because of their growing importance and significant differences from developed markets in terms of their institutional and regulatory environments (Bekaert, Harvey, and Lundblad 2007). Lee (2011) also suggested that pricing of liquidity risk differs across countries depending on geographic, economic, and political environments.

In this study, we investigate the relationship between the shape of curve depicting coronavirus related medical cases and deaths and consequential interventions by the governments impact investor behavior in emerging markets. We study whether flattening of the curve of COVID-19-related cases and deaths translate into economic impact on financial markets through liquidity. We use daily changes in moving averages of the number of coronavirus related deaths and cases as ascending (positive changes), flat (no change) and descending (negative changes) curve. Our findings suggest that liquidity in the financial markets is directly (inversely) associated with descending (ascending) curve of coronavirus related deaths and cases. Investors typically display aversion to uncertainty (Ellsberg 1961). It is very difficult to predict what would be the eventual economic impact of coronavirus pandemic and therefore we can expect flight-to-safety behavior from investors (Boscaljon and Clark 2013). Our study demonstrates that flattening the curve did help ease uncertainty concerns among the investors. These findings inform us that flattening the curve is not only significant for health systems to efficiently cope with this pandemic but also improves investor confidence and decreases uncertainty in the equity markets.

The following section discusses briefly the data and methodology utilized in this study followed by analysis of our findings and conclusion.

2. Data and Methodology

With COVID-19 being a very recent phenomenon, the span of data available is limited, since first confirmed case was reported in December 2019. Owing to this we have utilized data from January 1, 2020 till April 30, 2020, which has witnessed the rise of COVID-19 cases from 0 to over 3 million worldwide according to World Health Organization (WHO) data.[1] The financial markets globally have shrunk by over a third during this time (Haroon and Rizvi 2020). With focus on emerging markets we have utilized data for 23 countries. Morgan Stanley Capital International (MSCI) classification for emerging

Table 1. List of emerging markets.

America	Europe and Middle East	Asia
Argentina	Czech Republic	China
Brazil	Egypt	India
Chile	Greece	Indonesia
Colombia	Hungary	South Korea
Mexico	Poland	Malaysia
Peru	Qatar	Pakistan
	Russia	Philippines
	South Africa	
	Turkey	
	United Arab Emirates	

The Emerging market used in this research. We have used the Morgan Stanley Capital International (MSCI) classification for emerging markets to identify our sample. The only exclusions from the MSCI classification in our sample are Saudi Arabia and Thailand due to non-availability of uniform data. The emerging markets have been further classified in three distinctive categories owing to geographical location, America, Europe and Middle East, and Asia.

markets has been utilized to identify emerging markets. The complete list of sample countries is provided in Table 1.

For equity market data we have used the MSCI Country Indices for these 23 countries. The reason for using MSCI for all is to ensure standardization in calculation of index price as highlighted by Haroon and Rizvi (2020). Daily returns are calculated using the equation $r_t = ln(P_t) - ln(P_{t-1})$. Here, r_t and P_t denote daily return and price at the business day t respectively. Related daily data of country indices is collected for liquidity measures, which are summarized in Table 2.

For measurement of volatility, we use Exponential GARCH models, which have been extensively used in studying the volatility of stock markets in finance literature. Yu and Hassan (2008), Rizvi, Arshad, and Alam (2018), etc. have all relied on asymmetric GARCH model developed by Nelson (1991) suggesting a better fit of EGARCH model for volatilities. The EGARCH model presides over other models with its ability to allow for a more stable optimization of routines, and no parameter constraints.

Table 2. Variables description.

Liquidity	Liquidity is measured as the spread between high and low of the index as a proportion of opening price. The higher this number, the more illiquid market is considered.
Volatility	Volatility is calculated using EGARCH of daily returns of index. This is similar to the model used by Haroon and Rizvi (2020) and Ali, Alam, and Rizvi (2020) while investigating financial market volatility in times of COVID-19
Stringency Index	Stringency Index is created using 17 measures of government actions in response to COVID-19. 8 indicators record information on containment and closure policies. 4 record economic policies and 5 measure health system policies (See: Hale et al. 2020)
COVID Case Curve	The COVID Case Curve is calculated as the percentage change of 7 day moving average of reported COVID cases. As it reduces and approaches zero, the curve flattens
COVID Death Curve	The COVID Death Curve is calculated as the percentage change of 7 day moving average of reported COVID deaths. As it reduces and approaches zero, the curve flattens

The construct of each variable used in the study.

For understanding the impact of flattening the curve, the case curve and death curve is calculated as daily change in seven day moving average of new cases or number of COVID related deaths respectively, as officially announced by each country. The moving average as a measure for flattening of a curve is commonly used in literature Philips curves and yield curve (see Dolan 1999; Fernald, Keane, and Mosser 1994; Galí and Gambetti 2019; etc.)

For understanding the relationship between how flattening of the curve and liquidity of the markets, we use the panel regressions with robust standard error. Country fixed effects are included in every regression to incorporate the unique characteristics of each country. The inquiry is controlled for market volatility and stringency of lockdown measures in each country. The model used in this article are as follows where, *Liq* represents Liquidity in the market; *Vol* is the GARCH Volatility; *SI* is Stringency Index; *Case* is Flattening the curve measure of COVID-19 cases; and *Death* is Flattening the curve measure of COVID-19 Deaths.

$$Liq_{it} = \alpha + \beta_1 Vol_{it} + \beta_2 SI_{it} + \beta_3 Case_{it} + \varepsilon \qquad (1)$$

$$Liq_{it} = \alpha + \beta_1 Vol_{it} + \beta_2 SI_{it} + \beta_3 Death_{it} + \varepsilon \qquad (2)$$

$$Liq_{it} = \alpha + \beta_1 Vol_{it} + \beta_2 SI_{it} + \beta_3 Case_{it} + \beta_4 Death_{it} + \varepsilon \qquad (3)$$

3. Empirical Analysis

We have used three models to explore the impact of flattening of the curve on the liquidity on the emerging markets. Table 3 presents these results from which interesting insights can be drawn. COVID Case Curve is calculated as percentage change of 7 day moving average of reported COVID cases. As it increases it significantly increases the illiquidity in the emerging markets, which is understandable owing to uncertain macroeconomics conditions and investment climate uncertainty. However, as a corollary, flattening or declining curve is associated with improving liquidity in financial markets. This is in-line with works of Rehse et al. (2019), Easley and O'Hara (2010), Ozsoylev and Werner (2011) and Routledge and Zin (2009), which conclude an increase in spreads thus illiquidity in the face of economics and financial uncertainty. These findings prevail for emerging markets from America, Europe, and Middle Eastern region but not for Asian emerging markets (see Tables 4–6). Interestingly for Europe, the impact of flattening of the curve is much higher than other regions. This maybe owing to the exponential increase in cases in European continents from zero to nearly 1 million during our sample period as per WHO data.

Table 3. Regression results (emerging markets).

	Model 1	Model 2	Model 3
Volatility	0.0153**	1.985***	2.013***
	(2.08)	(5.18)	(5.34)
Stringency Index	0.132	−5.954**	−5.639**
	(0.20)	(−2.49)	(−2.49)
COVID Case Curve	0.510***		0.995**
	(2.91)		(2.52)
COVID Death Curve		0.94	0.00112
		(0.54)	(0.00)
Constant	3.510***	12.01***	11.45***
	(4.05)	(3.46)	(3.48)

The results for Panel Fixed Effects robust estimators for three models with Liquidity of the financial markets as dependent variable. The rationale for using fixed effect robust estimators is the nature of data and results of diagnostics. In the interest of brevity the diagnostics are not provided in the article and are available with the authors at request. t statistics are provided in parentheses. The superscripts *, ** and *** denote significance at the 10%, 5% and 1% levels, respectively.

Table 4. Regression results (American emerging markets).

	Model 1	Model 2	Model 3
Volatility	0.0143*	1.792***	1.850***
	(2.52)	(6.30)	(7.57)
Stringency Index	−0.719	−3.990	−3.947
	(−1.81)	(−1.70)	(−1.87)
COVID Case Curve	1.261**		0.992
	(3.18)		(0.61)
COVID Death Curve		189.1	142.1
		(1.58)	(0.73)
Constant	5.997***	9.807**	9.686**
	(12.69)	(2.76)	(3.07)

The results for Panel Fixed Effects robust estimators for three models with Liquidity of the financial markets as dependent variable. Sample is restricted to Emerging markets from America region. The rationale for using fixed effect robust estimators is the nature of data and results of diagnostics. In the interest of brevity the diagnostics are not provided in the article and are available with the authors at request. t statistics are provided in parentheses. The superscripts *, ** and *** denote significance at the 10%, 5% and 1% levels, respectively.

At the same time, increase in stringency tends to significantly reduce illiquidity situation as per Table 3 for all emerging countries. The stringency index, as explained in Table 2, captures the government response across multiple areas in dealing with this pandemic. As Battalio and Schultz (2011) highlighted that regulatory certainty assists in improving liquidity situation in markets and spreads tend to reduce. This arises out of confidence of investors in regulatory bodies being proactive and taking charge of anomalies and having a clear direction. But again these findings are insignificant in the case of Asian markets similar to the case of flattening the curve measures. These findings tend to conform to work of Carruthers and Stinchcombe (1999), who suggest that in the social structure of society, ramification of legal structures and signals tend to improve investor confidence and increase liquidity both in bearish or bullish markets. Several studies have noted that Asian equity markets are structurally different from emerging markets elsewhere in terms of liquidity transmission

Table 5. Regression results (Europe and Middle Eastern emerging markets).

	Model 1	Model 2	Model 3
Volatility	7.692***	3.708**	3.712**
	(5.40)	(2.48)	(2.42)
Stringency Index	0.549	−19.53***	−19.82***
	(0.60)	(−6.48)	(−5.46)
COVID Case Curve	0.791**		−0.321
	(2.29)		(−0.45)
COVID Death Curve		85.44*	95.71
		(1.84)	(1.68)
Constant	2.410*	31.89***	32.34***
	(1.90)	(7.13)	(5.99)

The table presents the results for Panel Fixed Effects robust estimators for three models with Liquidity of the financial markets as dependent variable. Sample is restricted to Emerging markets from Europe and Middle East region. The rationale for using fixed effect robust estimators is the nature of data and results of diagnostics. In the interest of brevity the diagnostics are not provided in the article and are available with the authors at request. t statistics are provided in parentheses. The superscripts *, ** and *** denote significance at the 10%, 5% and 1% levels, respectively.

Table 6. Regression results (Asian emerging markets).

	Model 1	Model 2	Model 3
Volatility	3.174	2.134	2.140
	(1.45)	(1.15)	(1.16)
Stringency Index	1.718	−2.817	−2.791
	(1.67)	(−0.68)	(−0.68)
COVID Case Curve	0.159		0.258
	(1.38)		(0.67)
COVID Death Curve		0.0233	−0.135
		(0.03)	(−0.21)
Constant	0.338	6.866	6.812
	(0.24)	(1.17)	(1.17)

The results for Panel Fixed Effects robust estimators for three models with Liquidity of the financial markets as dependent variable. Sample is restricted to Emerging markets from Asian region. The rationale for using fixed effect robust estimators is the nature of data and results of diagnostics. In the interest of brevity the diagnostics are not provided in the article and are available with the authors at request. t statistics are provided in parentheses. The superscripts *, ** and *** denote significance at the 10%, 5% and 1% levels, respectively.

(Choi et al. 2017), corporate governance structures, financial liberalization (Arshad, Haroon, and Rizvi 2019), information transparency (Millar et al. 2005) and trading costs (Domowitz, Glen, and Madhavan 2001). While our results point us into this direction, a deeper inquiry into this dimension is warranted especially with this pandemic, as more data becomes available for further robust modeling.

As a robustness check we had used percentage change of 5 day moving average of reported COVID cases and deaths as an alternate measure of flattening of curve. Also we used Turnover by Volume as alternate measures of liquidity. Our earlier findings hold these robustness check. In the interest of brevity, the results are available from the author and not presented in the tables.

4. Conclusion

While the world grapples with the unprecedented economic and social disruption caused by COVID-19, the financial markets around the world have also been severely affected. However, the pandemic has raised awareness among the general public about various measures of gauging the spread of infectious diseases and policy choices for the government in order to curb the spread of coronavirus. Widespread use of the term "flattening the curve" has generally attained an interpretation that interventions by policy makers have slowed down the growth of pandemic in a country. We examine whether such understanding translates into bringing ease to volatile financial markets in emerging economies in these uncertain times. We find that declining (ascending) curve of the number of coronavirus related cases and deaths is generally associated with improving (deteriorating) liquidity in equity markets of emerging economies. We also find that policy interventions by the governments in the form of curbs on gatherings and movement of people have helped improved liquidity in these markets as well. With increasing uncertainty among investors in the middle of a pandemic, our results are consistent with earlier studies (e.g. Baur and Lucey 2010; Connolly, Stivers, and Sun 2005) demonstrating that equity investors turn to safer assets (e.g. gold, bonds, etc.) in uncertain times. However, our study also shows that declining number of coronavirus cases and deaths also signal decreased uncertainty and improved liquidity in the equity markets. Our results are similar for geographically clustered emerging markets, except for Asian emerging markets where we do not find association between flattening the curve or stringency of government's curbs and liquidity in financial markets. As more data streams on pandemic, financial markets and economic numbers, this study can be expanded by including more unique economic data of each emerging country to understand their unique characteristics.

Note

1. https://www.who.int/emergencies/diseases/novel-coronavirus-2019/situation-report.

ORCID

Omair Haroon 🆔 http://orcid.org/0000-0003-3872-7734
Syed Aun R. Rizvi 🆔 http://orcid.org/0000-0002-6976-299X

References

Adrian, T., and F. Natalucci. 2020. COVID-19 crisis poses threat to financial stability. Accessed May 4, 2020. https://blogs.imf.org/2020/04/14/COVID-19-crisis-poses-threat-to-financial-stability/.

Al-Awadhi, A. M., K. Al-Saifi, A. Al-Awadhi, and S. Alhamadi. 2020. Death and contagious infectious diseases: Impact of the COVID-19 virus on stock market returns. *Journal of Behavioral and Experimental Finance* 27:100326. doi:10.1016/j.jbef.2020.100326.

Albulescu, C. 2020. Coronavirus and financial volatility: 40 days of fasting and fear. *arXiv preprint arXiv:2003.04005.*

Ali, M., N. Alam, and S. A. R. Rizvi. 2020. Coronavirus (COVID-19) — An epidemic or pandemic for financial markets. *Journal of Behavioral and Experimental Finance* 27:100341. doi:10.1016/j.jbef.2020.100341.

Apergis, E., and N. Apergis. 2020. Can the COVID-19 pandemic and oil prices drive the US partisan conflict index? *Energy Research Letters* 1 (1):13144. doi:10.46557/001c.13144

Apergis, N., P. G. Artikis, and D. Kyriazis. 2015. Does stock market liquidity explain real economic activity? New evidence from two large European stock markets. *Journal of International Financial Markets, Institutions and Money* 38:42–64. doi:10.1016/j.intfin.2015.05.002.

Arshad, S., S. A. R. Rizvi, and O. Haroon. 2019. Understanding Asian emerging stock markets. *Bulletin of Monetary Economics and Banking* (12th BMEB Call for Papers Special Issue):1–16.

Baker, S. R., N. Bloom, S. J. Davis, and S. J. Terry. 2020. COVID-induced economic uncertainty. No. w26983. USA: National Bureau of Economic Research.

Barrero, J. M., N. Bloom, and S. J. Davis. 2020. COVID-19 is also a reallocation shock No. w27137. USA: National Bureau of Economic Research.

Battalio, R., and P. Schultz. 2011. Regulatory uncertainty and market liquidity: The 2008 short sale ban's impact on equity option markets. *The Journal of Finance* 66 (6):2013–53. doi:10.1111/j.1540-6261.2011.01700.x.

Baur, D. G., and B. M. Lucey. 2010. Is gold a hedge or a safe haven? An analysis of stocks, bonds and gold. *Financial Review* 45 (2):217–29. doi:10.1111/j.1540-6288.2010.00244.x.

BCG. 2020, April 24. COVID-19BCG Perspectives. Accessed May 4, 2020. https://media-publications.bcg.com/BCG-COVID-19-BCG-Perspectives-Version3.pdf.

Bekaert, G., C. R. Harvey, and C. Lundblad. 2007. Liquidity and expected returns: Lessons from emerging markets. *The Review of Financial Studies* 20 (6):1783–831. doi:10.1093/rfs/hhm030.

Boscaljon, B., and J. Clark. 2013. Do large shocks in VIX signal a flight-to-safety in the gold market? *Journal of Applied Finance* 23 (2):120.

Brunnermeier, M. K. 2009. Deciphering the liquidity and credit crunch 2007-2008. *Journal of Economic Perspectives* 23 (1):77–100. doi:10.1257/jep.23.1.77.

Brunnermeier, M. K., and L. H. Pedersen. 2009. Market liquidity and funding liquidity. *Review of Financial Studies* 22 (6):2201–38. doi:10.1093/rfs/hhn098.

Carruthers, B. G., and A. L. Stinchcombe. 1999. The social structure of liquidity: Flexibility, markets, and states. *Theory and Society* 28 (3):353–82. doi:10.1023/A:1006903103304.

Chiu, Y. C. 2019. Macroeconomic uncertainty, information competition, and liquidity. *Finance Research Letters*. doi:10.1016/j.frl.2019.08.010.

Choi, W. G., T. Kang, G. Y. Kim, and B. Lee. 2017. Global liquidity transmission to emerging market economies, and their policy responses. *Journal of International Economics* 109:153–66. doi:10.1016/j.jinteco.2017.08.001.

Chowdhury, A., M. Uddin, and K. Anderson. 2018. Liquidity and macroeconomic management in emerging markets. *Emerging Markets Review* 34:1–24. doi:10.1016/j.ememar.2017.10.001.

Connolly, R., C. Stivers, and L. Sun. 2005. Stock market uncertainty and the stock-bond return relation. *Journal of Financial and Quantitative Analysis* 40 (1):161–94. doi:10.1017/S0022109000001782.

Deloitte. 2020, March. Flattening the curve Impact on the Indian banking and capital market industry. Accessed May 4, 2020. https://www2.deloitte.com/content/dam/Deloitte/in/Documents/financial-services/in-fs-flattening-the-curve-impact-on-the-indian-banking-and-capital-markets-noexp.pdf.

Dolan, C. P. 1999. Forecasting the yield curve shape evidence in global markets. *The Journal of Fixed Income* 9 (1):92–99. doi:10.3905/jfi.1999.319234.

Domowitz, I., J. Glen, and A. Madhavan. 2001. Liquidity, volatility and equity trading costs across countries and over time. *International Finance* 4 (2):221–55. doi:10.1111/1468-2362.00072.

Easley, D., and M. O'Hara. 2010. Liquidity and valuation in an uncertain world. *Journal of Financial Economics* 97 (1):1–11. doi:10.1016/j.jfineco.2010.03.004.

Ellsberg, D. 1961. Risk, ambiguity, and the savage axioms. *Quarterly Journal of Economics* 75 (4):643–69. doi:10.2307/1884324.

Fernald, J., F. Keane, and P. C. Mosser. 1994. *Mortgage security hedging and the yield curve.* Vols. 26, No. 10. USA: Federal Reserve Bank of New York.

Fu, M., and H. Shen. 2020. COVID-19 and corporate performance in the energy industry. *Energy Research Letters* 1 (1):12967. doi:10.46557/001c.12967

Galí, J., and L. Gambetti. 2019. Has the US wage phillips curve flattened? A semi-structural exploration. No. w25476. USA: National Bureau of Economic Research.

Geanakoplos, J. 2010. The leverage cycle. *NBER Macroeconomics Annual* 24 (1):1–66. doi:10.1086/648285.

Gil-Alana, L. A., and M. Monge. 2020. Crude oil prices and COVID-19: Persistence of the shock. *Energy Research Letters* 1 (1):13200. doi:10.46557/001c.13200

Glosten, L. R., and P. Milgrom. 1985. Bid, ask and transaction prices in a specialist market with heterogeneously informed traders. *Journal of Financial Economics* 14 (1):71–100. doi:10.1016/0304-405X(85)90044-3.

Hale, T., A. Petherick, T. Phillips, and S. Webster. 2020. Variation in government responses to COVID-19. Working Paper. UK: Blavatnik School of Government, 31.

Haroon, O., and S. A. R. Rizvi. 2020. COVID-19: Media coverage and financial markets behavior—A sectoral inquiry. *Journal of Behavioral and Experimental Finance* 27 (100343):100343. doi:10.1016/j.jbef.2020.100343.

Hasbrouck, J. 1988. Trades, quotes, inventories, and information. *Journal of Financial Economics* 22 (2):229–52. doi:10.1016/0304-405X(88)90070-0.

Hevia, C., and P. A. Neumeyer. 2020. A perfect storm: COVID-19 in emerging economies. VoxEU CEPR Policy Portal. Accessed May 4, 2020. https://voxeu. org/article/perfect-stormCOVID-19-emerging-economies.

IMF. 2020. Policy responses to COVID-19. Accessed May 4, 2020. https://www.imf.org/en/Topics/imf-and-COVID19/Policy-Responses-to-COVID-19.

Lee, K. H. 2011. The world price of liquidity risk. *Journal of Financial Economics* 99 (1):136–61. doi:10.1016/j.jfineco.2010.08.003.

Lesser, R. 2020, March 19. 6 steps to sustainably flatten the coronavirus curve. *Fortune.* USA. https://fortune.com/2020/03/19/coronavirus-COVID-19-flatten-curve-solution/

Liu, L., E. Z. Wang, and C. C. Lee. 2020. Impact of the COVID-19 pandemic on the crude oil and stock markets in the US: A time-varying analysis. *Energy Research Letters* 1 (1):13154. doi:10.46557/001c.13154

Matinna, T., 2020, March 27. Flattening the curves. Mackenzie Investment Insights. Accessed May 4, 2020. https://www.mackenzieinvestments.com/content/dam/mackenzie/en/insights/mi-todd-mattina-monthly-commentary-march-27-en-web.pdf.

Millar, C. C., T. I. Eldomiaty, C. J. Choi, and B. Hilton. 2005. Corporate governance and institutional transparency in emerging markets. *Journal of Business Ethics* 59 (1–2):163–74. doi:10.1007/s10551-005-3412-1.

Næs, R., J. A. Skjeltorp, and B. A. Ødegaard. 2011. Stock market liquidity and the business cycle. *The Journal of Finance* 66 (1):139–76. doi:10.1111/j.1540-6261.2010.01628.x.

Narayan, P. K. 2020. Oil price news and COVID-19—Is there any connection? *Energy Research Letters* 1 (1):13176. doi:10.46557/001c.13176

Narayan, P. K., and D. H. B. Phan. 2020. Country responses and the reaction of the stock market to COVID-19—A preliminary exposition. *Emerging Markets Finance and Trade.* 56 (10):2138–2150. doi:10.1080/1540496X.2020.1784719

Nelson, D. B. 1991. Conditional heteroskedasticity in asset returns: A new approach. *Econometrica* 59:347–70. doi:10.2307/2938260.

Ozsoylev, H., and J. Werner. 2011. Liquidity and asset prices in rational expectations equilibrium with ambiguous information. *Economic Theory* 48 (2–3):469. doi:10.1007/s00199-011-0648-0.

Qin, M., Y. C. Zhang, and C. W. Su. 2020. The essential role of pandemics: A fresh insight into the oil market. *Energy Research Letters* 1 (1):13166. doi:10.46557/001c.13166

Rehse, D., R. Riordan, N. Rottke, and J. Zietz. 2019. The effects of uncertainty on market liquidity: Evidence from hurricane sandy. *Journal of Financial Economics* 134 (2):318–32. doi:10.1016/j.jfineco.2019.04.006.

Rhodes, T., K. Lancaster, and M. Rosengarten. 2020. A model society: Maths, models and expertise in viral outbreaks. *Critical Public Health* 30 (3):253–56. doi:10.1080/09581596.2020.1748310.

Rizvi, S. A. R., S. Arshad, and N. Alam. 2018. A tripartite inquiry into volatility-efficiency-integration nexus - case of emerging markets. *Emerging Markets Review* 34:143–61. doi:10.1016/j.ememar.2017.11.005.

Routledge, B. R., and S. E. Zin. 2009. Model uncertainty and liquidity. *Review of Economic Dynamics* 12 (4):543–66. doi:10.1016/j.red.2008.10.002.

S&P Global. 2020, May 19. COVID-19 Impact: Key Takeaways From Our Articles. https://www.spglobal.com/ratings/en/research/articles/200204-coronavirus-impact-key-takeaways-from-our-articles-11337257.

The Economist. 2020, February 29. COVID-19 is now in 50 countries, and things will get worse. https://www.economist.com/briefing/2020/02/29/COVID-19-is-now-in-50-countries-and-things-will-get-worse.

Wilkes, T. 2020. The plumbing behind world's financial markets is creaking. Loudly. Accessed March 15. https://www.reuters.com/article/us-health-coronavirus-markets-crisis-ana/the-plumbing-behind-worlds-financial-markets-is-creaking-loudly-idUSKBN2120NJ.

Yu, J., and M. Hassan. 2008. Global and regional integration of the Middle East and North African (MENA) stock markets. *The Quarterly Review of Economics and Finance* 48 (3):482–504. doi:10.1016/j.qref.2006.06.003.

Zhang, D., M. Hu, and Q. Ji. 2020. Financial markets under the global pandemic of COVID-19. *Finance Research Letters* 1015.

Does the Indian Financial Market Nosedive because of the COVID-19 Outbreak, in Comparison to after Demonetisation and the GST?

Alok Kumar Mishra, Badri Narayan Rath, and Aruna Kumar Dash

ABSTRACT

We investigate the impact of COVID-19 on the Indian financial market and compare it with the outcomes of two recent structural changes of the Indian economy: demonetization and implementation of the Goods and Services Tax (GST). Using daily stock return, net foreign institutional investment, and exchange rate data from January 3, 2003 to April 20, 2020, we find negative stock returns for all the indices during the COVID-19 outbreak, unlike during the post-demonetization and GST phases. Markov switching vector autoregression shows the impact of COVID-19 on stock returns is severe in comparison to that of demonetization and the GST.

1. Introduction

As of June 9, 2020, the COVID-19 outbreak had spread to 213 countries, with nearly 7 million confirmed cases and 404,396 deaths worldwide (World Health Organization website, https://covid19.who.int/). This pandemic has impacted the world's economies, and India, the focus of our study, is not immune. One opinion is that India is facing a prolonged period of economic slowdown, although the exact magnitude of the economic loss cannot be predicted (Dev and Sengupta 2020).

This paper aims to examine the impact of the COVID-19 outbreak on the Indian financial market, proxied by stock returns, the exchange rate between the Indian rupee (INR) and the US dollar (USD), and foreign institutional investor (FII) net inflows. The aim is to compare the outcomes of the effects of COVID-19 with those of two other major economic policy events in India, namely, demonetization (November 8, 2016) and implementation of the Goods and Services Tax (GST, July 1, 2017). Both policies had implications for India's equity and foreign exchange markets. As India was adjusting to the aftermath of the demonetization and the GST, the unprecedented outbreak of the COVID-19 pandemic halted all progress and posed a major challenge. The government's response to COVID-19 was a lockdown, restricting people's movement and business activities. An immediate effect of COVID-19 was also noted in the Indian financial markets,[1] which further motivated us to examine the dynamic impact of the COVID-19 pandemic on Indian equity and foreign exchange markets.

A research strand related to our paper examines, for instance, the dynamic relation between stock returns, exchange rates, mutual funds, and oil and gold prices (Dhingra, Gandhi, and Bulsara 2016; Edelen and Warner 2001; Garg and Dua 2014; Jain and Biswal 2016; Katechos 2011; Mishra 2004; Narayan, Narayan, and Prabheesh 2014; Sensoy and Tabak 2015). These studies show that India's stock market is influenced by mutual funds (Edelen and Warner 2001; Narayan, Narayan, and Prabheesh 2014), gold and crude oil prices (Jain and Biswal 2016), currency risk (Garg and Dua 2014), exchange rates and foreign equity flows (Dhingra, Gandhi, and Bulsara 2016; Mishra 2004), and long-range dependence (Sensoy and Tabak 2015).

A second strand of research to which our study relates examines the effect of pandemics on financial markets (Al-Awadhi et al. 2020; Ali, Alam, and Rizvi 2020; Apergis and Apergis 2020; Barro, Ursúa, and Weng 2020; Donadelli, Kizys, and Riedel 2017; Gil-Alana and Monge 2020; Gormsen and Koijen 2020; Granger, Huang, and Yang 2000; Haroon and Rizvi 2020; Ichev and Baker Marinc 2018; Lagoarde-Segot and Leoni 2013; Narayan 2020; Phan and Narayan 2020; Zhang, Hu, and Ji 2020; Fu and Shen 2020; Liu, Wang and Lee 2020; Qin, Zhang and Su 2020). These studies show how financial markets and their volatility and the energy markets have been impacted by COVID-19. Of these, the works closest to ours are those of Ali, Alam, and Rizvi (2020); Al-Awadhi et al. (2020); Katechos (2011); Phan and Narayan (2020); Sensoy and Tabak (2015). These studies show that global financial market risks and uncertainty have increased substantially in response to the pandemic, with significant negative effects on stock returns.

We add to the understanding of COVID-19's effect on India's stock market by proposing a dynamic model that relates stock returns, the INR–USD exchange rate, and FII flows. To examine the impact of COVID-19, we consider the equity indices of the BSE (Bombay Stock Exchange), such as Standard & Poor's (S&P) BSE Sensex, BSE mid-caps and small-caps, and the BSE 100, along with three sectoral indices (BSE-Auto, BSE-Bankex, and BSE-Realty). The foreign exchange market is proxied by the nominal bilateral exchange rate between the INR and the USD. Since FIIs are an important component of the Indian financial market, we consider net foreign investment.

Our empirical approach is motivated by the portfolio balance model (Branson 1983; Frankel 1983). According to this model, an exogenous increase in stock prices will increase the demand for money in anticipation of future expected returns. The short-term interest rate will therefore rise, which will attract more foreign investment in the domestic economy. Our study uses daily data spanning from April 8, 2003 to April 20, 2020. The logical rationale behind the use of this data period is to consider various structural reforms, such as the implementations of demonetization in 2016 and of the GST in 2017, in addition to the COVID-19 pandemic in 2020. Demonetization and implementation of GST are two recent major economic reforms that India has undertaken, where the market has responded differently. In the case of COVID-19 pandemic outbreak, the financial market responded negatively. The impact is also found severe. As most of our data is in time series in nature, the trend break is also found to be significant. This has motivated us to understand whether the outcome of the COVID-19 impact in comparison to two major economic reforms is tremendous. To comparatively assess the impacts of these three shocks (demonetization, GST, and COVID-19), first, we estimate the growth rates, returns, and volatility of these key indicators and compare the results. In the second stage, we employ a Markov switching vector autoregressive (MS-VAR) model to examine the nonlinear dynamics among these variables.

The major findings of the study are as follows. First, the stock returns of all the indices are negative during the COVID-19 outbreak, which was not the case during the post-demonetization and GST phases. Second, the volatility of the benchmark stock price is 2.77, compared to 0.51 and 0.59 in the post-demonetization and GST phases, respectively. Third, the consequences of the IRF (impulse response function) of the MS-VAR model indicate that shocks (innovation) in exchange rate returns have asymmetric impacts on stock returns in the COVID-19 phase. However, shocks in stock returns negatively affect exchange rate returns in both the short and long run. Fourth, the transition matrix shows that the impact of COVID-19 is determined to be severe in the context of India's stock liquidity index (Sensex), in comparison to the impact of demonetization and GST implementation.

The remainder of the paper is organized as follows. Section 2 presents the methodology and data. Section 3 discusses the statistical analysis and empirical results. Finally, Section 4 highlights the main conclusions and policy implications.

2. Methodology and Data

2.1. Markov-switching VAR (MS-VAR) Model

In the empirical literature, the impact of the event on the stock market is generally analyzed by the event study methods. However, in the event analysis, the t-test or other nonparametric tests are used to test the null hypothesis (example, no abnormal returns in case of stock market) at the time of the event. This may lead to misleading results because of the kurtosis and volatility-clustering characterization of the financial time series, especially the data on securities which are continuously traded in the market. To avoid this limitation of the event study approach, we proposed to model the returns in the event of window through a Markov Switching model with two regimes: Regime 1: Normal market conditions; Regime 2: Abnormal market conditions. The general idea behind the class of Markov switching models is that the parameters and the variance of an autoregressive process depend upon an unobservable regime variable which represents the probability of being in a particular state of the world. A major advantage of the MS-VAR model is its flexibility in modeling time series subject to nonlinearity and regime shifts. The model is estimated based on the Gausssian Maximum Likelihood estimation (for detailed discussion see Castellano and Scaccia 2010). The MS-VAR model is presented as follows.

The portfolio balance model (Branson 1983; Frankel 1983), as highlighted in the introduction, is modeled by employing a three-variable MS-VAR model. These variables include the return on the liquidity index Sensex ($RSEN$), net FIIs ($NETFII$), and the return on the exchange rate of the INR versus the USD ($RUSD$).

Let $z_t = [RSEN_t, NETFII_t, RUSD_t]'$ be a 3×1 vector of observations at time t. Specifically, the structural representation of the M-state MS-VAR can be expressed as

$$\beta_{0,s_t} z_t = \mu_{st} + \beta_{1,s_t} z_{t-1} + \ldots + \beta_{p,s_t} z_{t-p} + \varepsilon_t, \varepsilon_t \tilde{N}(0, \omega_{st}) \qquad (1)$$

where ε_t is the structural error term, which follows a Gaussian distribution, with a diagonal covariance matrix ω_{st} at time t. The reduced form of the model can be obtained by premultiplying $\beta^{-1}_{0,st}$ on both sides of Equation (1), yielding

$$z_t = \alpha_{st} + \gamma_{1,s_t} z_{t-1} + \ldots + \gamma_{p,s_t} z_{t-p} + \varphi_t, \varphi_t \tilde{N}(0, \Sigma_{st}) \qquad (2)$$

where $\alpha_{st} = \beta^{-1}_{0,st} \mu_{st}$ represents the 3×1 time-varying intercepts and $\gamma_{i,st} = \beta^{-1}_{0,st} \beta_{i,st}, i = 1, 2, \ldots, p$, denotes the 3×3 VAR coefficient matrices at time t. The covariance matrix for the reduced-form error $\varphi_t = \beta^{-1}_{0,st} \varepsilon_t$ can be decomposed as $\Sigma_{st} = \beta^{-1}_{0,st} \omega_{st} \beta^{-1}_{0,st}$

The regime indicator variable S_t is assumed to follow an M-state Markov process with transition probabilities $Pr(S_t = j|S_{t-1} = i) = P_{ij}, i, j = 1, \ldots, M$. The transition probabilities of the Markov Switching process determine the probability of the volatility switching to another regime, and thus the expected duration of each regime (Chevallier, 2011a). Transition probabilities can be constant or a time-varying function of exogenous variables (Cai 1994; Gray 1996; Hamilton and Susmel 1994). The model is estimated based on a Gaussian maximum likelihood procedure. The calculation of the covariance matrix uses using the second partial derivatives of the log-likelihood function, and the transition matrix P controls the probability of a switch from state 1 to 2:

$$P = \begin{bmatrix} p_{11} & p_{21} \\ p_{12} & p_{22} \end{bmatrix}$$

where the sum of each column in p is equal to one.

In this paper, the Markov switching model is estimated by assuming two states. The choice of the two-state process is motivated by the fact that this model is intuitively appealing for tracking the bull–bear cycle of the Indian equity market for the three phases of post-demonetization, GST implementation, and the COVID-19 outbreak.

Since the MS-VAR model is nonlinear, a generalized impulse response function is defined as the difference between a shock trajectory (i.e. incorporating the initial identified shock) and a baseline trajectory (i.e. without the initial identified shock). All exogenous random variables, except the initial identified shock, are identical between these two trajectories (Karame 2010, 2015; Koop, Pesaran, and Potter 1996).

2.2. Data and Measurement of Variables

The empirical analysis is based on daily data from January 3, 2003 to April 20, 2020. The selection of the time span is based purely on the availability of data. The study uses three key variables: stock returns, exchange rate returns, and FII net investment. We use the daily stock closing prices of the Sensex as the benchmark and other indices (BSE 100, mid-caps and small-caps, and sectoral indices) and estimate the first difference of the natural logarithmic stock prices series to obtain stock returns. However, the growth rate of the stock indices and the exchange rates are computed as the ratio of the difference between the current and previous prices upon previous price. The volatility series is calculated using a five-day rolling standard deviation method. This study uses nominal bilateral exchange rate data between the INR and the USD and calculates the return series. The FII net investment is estimated by taking the difference between FII gross purchases and FII gross sales. A positive sign for this net investment series indicates inflows, and negative figures indicate outflows. Since both the stock and foreign exchange markets do not trade on weekends or holidays, we adjust the COVID-19 series accordingly by mapping the exact dates between these four series. In addition to the three key indicators, we use data on the number of confirmed COVID-19 cases from January 30, 2020 to April 20, 2020.

We use three binary dummy variables to denote the periods after the demonetization and the GST and the period of the COVID-19 outbreak; these are, respectively, equal to one for the post-demonetization or GST period and after the Ministry of Health and Family Welfare of the Government of India reported the first COVID-19 case, and zero otherwise. Specifically, from November 8, 2016 to April 20, 2020 denotes the post-demonetization period, from July 1, 2017 to April 20, 2020 the GST period, and from January 30, 2020 to April 20, 2020 the COVID-19 outbreak period. All the data were collected from the CEIC database, which provides the most accurate and in-depth data available on the Indian economy and more than 200 other countries.

3. Empirical Results

3.1. Preliminary Analysis

This section starts with preliminary evidence on the relation between stock returns, exchange rate returns, FII net investment, and the COVID-19 outbreak by presenting a range of descriptive statistics, returns, growth rates, volatilities, and correlations among the key indicators. Figure 1 shows the plots of the four data series. The FII net flows and the number of new COVID-19 cases are shown in the first row of the figure and return series of the exchange rate and stock price are presented in the second row of Figure 1. We notice that all four series show diverse shape.

We present descriptive statistics in Panel A of Table 1. We note that the average positive daily return of the INR versus the USD is minimal (0.01) in comparison to the average daily return of the Sensex and the broad stock index (BSE 100) during the sample period. The kurtosis coefficient, a measure of the thickness of the tail of the distribution, is quite high for all the variables, which follow a platykurtic distribution, with a fatter shorttail. This result implies that a Gaussian distribution for the respective variables cannot be assumed. This finding is further strengthened by the results of a Jarque–Bera test. The Jarque–Bera test indicates that the returns on both assets are not normally distributed (unconditionally), since the time series appear to be slightly skewed (negatively skewed for both stock indices, such as RSEN and RBSE 100, and positively skewed for the return series of the INR versus the USD exchange rate). Hence, this result rejects the null hypothesis of normality at any conventional confidence levels.

Panel B, of Table 1 reports statistically significant correlation coefficients between stock returns, exchange rate returns, and net FIIs. A significant negative correlation is found between the returns on the exchange rate and stock indices and net foreign investments. However, the correlation coefficient between net FII investment and the exchange rate return is extremely low (−0.05), in comparison to the correlation coefficient between the exchange rate and stock price returns. This result supports the stock-oriented model of a negative relation between stock prices and exchange rates.

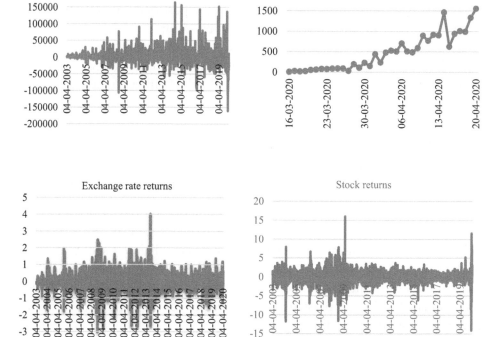

Figure 1. Time series plots of data series.
This graph is plotted by computing the returns of Sensex and exchange rate (INR vs. US$). Both the return series exhibit volatility clustering and their trend is stationary. The tendency of positive COVID-19 is kept on mounting at an alarming rate from April 2020 onwards.

After presenting the descriptive statistics, we analyze the growth rates, returns, and volatilities of the stock prices, the exchange rate, and FII net flows by comparing three events. The post-demonetization phase is considered to be from November 9, 2016 to June 30, 2017 and the GST phase from July 1, 2017 to January 29, 2020. Similarly, January 30, 2020 to April 20, 2020 covers the COVID-19 phase. We arrive at the following insights. First, the Sensex stock prices show negative growth (−22.65%) during the COVID-19 pandemic phase, compared to positive growth rates of 12.07% and 31.9% during the post-demonetization and GST phases, respectively.

Second, other stock indices, such as mid-caps and small-caps, and all sectors, except healthcare, show drastic negative growth rates during the COVID-19 phase, compared to the post-demonetization and GST phases. Third, both the returns and volatility series of the stock indices also reveal a precarious scenario during the COVID-19 phase, in comparison to the other events. All the stock indices, except healthcare, show negative returns and high volatility during this ongoing COVID-19 pandemic. Fourth, among

Table 1. Descriptive statistics.

	RSEN	RBSE100	NETFII	RUSD
Panel A: Summary Statistics				
Mean	0.05	0.05	2808.44	0.01
Median	0.09	0.11	1792.00	0.00
Maximum	15.98	15.49	163775.7	4.01
Minimum	−14.10	−13.88	−161203.9	−3.00
Std. Dev.	1.45	1.46	16203.60	0.45
Skewness	−0.21	−0.40	0.74	0.15
Kurtosis	15.03	14.26	21.78	9.15
Jarque-Bera	24793.59	21796.74	60671.97	6496.65
Probability	0.00	0.00	0.00	0.00
Observations	4101	4101	4101	4101
	RSEN	RBSE100	NETFII	RUSD
Panel B: Correlation Matrix				
RSEN	1			
RBSE100	0.98	1		
	(0.00)			
FIITNET	0.057	0.06	1	
	(0.00)	(0.00)		
RUSD	−0.30	−0.30	−0.05	1
	(0.00)	(0.00)	(0.00)	

Figures in parentheses are probability values.
This table reports the summary statistics of the variables (Panel A) and the pair wise correlation matrix (Panel B).

the three major stock indices, the growth and returns of small-cap companies perform worse than the mid-caps and BSE Sensex, whereas the BSE Sensex stock price is more volatile compared to the mid-cap and small-cap stock indices. Fifth, among the sectors, Realty, Metal, Bankex, and Auto perform the worse in terms of stock returns and stock price growth. The important demand for health-care products and services during the COVID-19 pandemics likely reflected in their positive stock price returns with low volatility. After healthcare, fast-moving consumer goods companies are the second-best performers during the ongoing pandemic, which also show a relatively less affected sector as compared to other sectors. Sixth, by accounting for nominal exchange rate movement between the INR and the USD, our results reveal that the INR depreciated by 7.2% during the COVID-19 phase, as opposed to its 2.95% appreciation during the demonetization phase; however, the INR depreciated by 9.94% during the GST phase, more than during the COVID-19 phase. When we compare the exchange rate volatilities, however we again find that the exchange rate series is more volatile during the COVID-19 phase than in the post-demonetization and GST phases.

Finally, the net FII flow figures show negative growth during all three phases, but this indicator is less volatile in the COVID-19 phase compared to during the other two phases. This result implies that, although the average gross sales of FIIs are higher than their average gross purchase, the growth of FII outflows from the Indian financial market is still lower in the COVID-19 phase compared to the post-demonetization and GST phases. This finding is not surprising, because the uncertainty due to COVID-19 pandemic is higher in developed countries and other emerging countries such as China, Russia, and Brazil. Therefore, though foreign investors are pulling out their funds, particularly from short-term debt funds, during the ongoing COVID-19 outbreak, its growth as well as volatility figures are still much lower in comparison to the post-demonetization and GST phases.

3.2. MS-VAR Results

In this section, after discussing the preliminary analysis, we present the MS-VAR results. Prior to this, however, we need to address the stationarity of the data series. To do so, we employ both augmented Dickey–Fuller (ADF) and Phillips–Perronunit root tests. The unit root test results reveal that all four variables—Sensex returns (*RSEN*), BSE 100 returns (*RBSE 100*), exchange rate returns (*RUSD*), and net FII flows (*NETFII*)—are stationary in levels, that is, $I(0)$.[2]

We further investigate the distributional pattern of the stock returns, exchange rate returns, and net FII flows by applying the BDS test of Broock et al. (1996). This is a well-established technique to check the spatial dependence and nonlinearity of a time series. In particular, this test identifies if a time series is an independent and identically distributed process. Our results reject the null hypothesis of independent and identical distributions for all epsilon (ε) values of close points and m embedding dimensions at the 1% significance level. Epsilon (ε) represents the distance between a selected pair of points for measuring the independent and identical distribution of residuals, whereas the embedding dimensions represent the number of consecutive points used in the set. Thus, the results of the BDS test suggest a likely nonlinear structure in the stock and exchange rate returns and net FII flows.

Table 2 reports the maximum likelihood estimates of the Markov switching model, an intercept switching VAR model with regime-dependent variances but constant autoregressive coefficients. The coefficients are obtained with the expected maximization algorithm. The MSI(2)-VAR(2)-EVENT(3) model refers to the average return of series of the daily stock indices—both liquidity (Sensex) and broad based (BSE 100)—in both stages 1 and 2, respectively, for three different events, such as the most immediate effects of the demonetization, the implementation of the GST, and the impact of the COVID-19 outbreak in the Indian equity market.

In this model, the intercept is assumed to be state dependent. The order of is set to $P = 2$ (and $P = 1$ in some cases) by minimizing the Akaike information criterion (AIC). In the model, the first regime ($S_t = 1$) represents a bear (depression) state, while the second regime ($S_t = 2$) represents a bull (growth) state, since regime 1 coefficients are smaller than regime 2 coefficients. The

Table 2. Markov Switching intercepts VAR based on MLE results.

S&P BSE SENSEX as Dependent Variable	Demonetization Phase	GST Phase	COVID-19 Phase	S&P BSE 100 as a Dependent Variable	Demonetization Phase	GST Phase	COVID-19 Phase
Regime1—Dependent Intercepts							
1	−3.975 (−14.699)	0.146 (6.152)	−1.520 (−7.898)	C_1	−0.142 (−0.372)	−0.175 (−0.570)	−0.893 (−4.024)
Dummy$_1$(−1)	4.291 (11.304)	−0.103 (−1.763)	−6.641 (−10.156)	Dummy$_1$(−1)	0.229 (0.475)	0.444 (0.919)	−6.695 (−10.522)
Regime2—Dependent Intercepts							
C_2	0.180 (6.477)	−5.662 (−18.049)	0.136 (5.662)	C_2	0.064 (2.398)	0.056 (2.246)	0.089 (3.745)
Dummy$_2$(−1)	−0.155 (−3.036)	5.991 (12.533)	0.298 (1.298)	Dummy$_2$(−1)	−0.047 (−0.869)	−0.036 (−0.571)	0.315 (1.412)
Autoregressive Coefficients							
RSEN(−1)	−0.005 (−0.288)	0.017 (1.137)	0.026 (1.660)	RBSE 100(−1)	0.054 (3.329)	0.055 (3.412)	0.056 (3.509)
RSEN(−2)	−0.076 (−4.663)		−0.073 (−4.551)	RBSE 100(−2)	−0.046 (−2.786)		
NETFII(−1)	2.57E-07 (0.166)	−3.68E-06 (−2.831)	−2.28E-06 (−1.489)	NETFII(−1)	1.14E-06 (0.733)	1.30E-06 (0.933)	−2.78E-06 (1.949)
NETFII(−2)	1.06E-07 (0.069)		−1.41E-06 (−0.938)	NETFII(−2)	8.34E-07 (0.546)		
RUSD(−1)	−0.083 (−1.619)	−0.061 (−1.268)	−0.006 (−0.122)	RUSD(−1)	−0.076 (1.436)	−0.049 (−0.952)	−0.037 (−0.721)
RUSD(−2)	−0.110 (−2.172)		−0.059 (−1.130)	RUSD(−2)	−0.114 (2.167)	−0.114 (−0.952)	
Variances							
σ_1^2 RSEN	1.789 (39.222)	1.757 (42.142)	1.933 (42.145)	σ_1^2 RETBSE	2.131 (45.268)	2.136 (45.277)	2.036 (44.638)
σ_1^2 NETFII	978.292 (3.273)	−44.384 (−0.178)	362.993 (1.174)	σ_1^2 NETFII	1076.505 (3.872)	1055.121 (3.642)	137.007 (0.437)
σ_1^2 RUSD	−0.201 (−16.695)	−0.182 (−16.979)	−0.133 (−12.514)	σ_1^2 RUSD	−0.198 (−18.643)	−0.198 (−18.567)	−0.169 (−15.200)
Transition Matrix Coefficients							
P11-C	−1.135 (−3.473)	4.389 (24.482)	−0.060 (−0.282)	P11-C	−2.65 (−3.757)	−3.564 (−3.312)	−0.960 (−2.739)

(*Continued*)

Table 2. (Continued).

	S&P BSE SENSEX as Dependent Variable			S&P BSE 100 as a Dependent Variable		
	Demonetization Phase	GST Phase	COVID-19 Phase	Demonetization Phase	GST Phase	COVID-19 Phase
P21-C	−3.845 (−24.778)	1.483 (4.190)	−3.860 (−23.610)	−4.668 (−25.926)	−4.647 (−26.668)	−4.152 (−20.672)
Diagnostic Statistics						
Resid Covariance	79256500	84705921	80332916	79037700	84247094	84282924
Log Likelihood	−54306.360	−54492.190	−54397.930	−54252.130	−54442.770	−54559.280
AIC/SC	26.515/26.574	26.595/26.640	26.560/26.619	26.489/26.548	26.571/26.616	26.628/26.673
Number of Coefficients	38	29	38	38	29	29

Figures indicated in parenthesis are Z-statistics

This table presents MSI (2)-VAR (2)-EVENT (3) with regime-dependent variances and with constant autoregressive coefficients. The parameters are estimated by using the Expectations-Maximization (EM) algorithm. The estimated coefficients indicate that the nonlinear model fit the data better in COVID-19 period in the context of the return Sensex and the phase of demonetization in the case of return on BSE 100.

COVID-19 dummy is highly statistically significant in regime 1 in the context of both Sensex and BSE 100 returns. Examination of the coefficients of the two intercepts (c_1 and c_2), which are both statistically significant, shows the presence of switches in growth (in terms of returns) between the two regimes. In regime 1 (bear), the average daily return of the Sensex is negative in both the demonetization and COVID-19 phases (−3.97% and −1.52%, respectively) and positive (0.14%) in the GST phase. However, the daily average return of the BSE 100 is negative (−0.14%, −0.17%, −0.89%, respectively) in the demonetization, the GST and COVID-19 phases. However, in regime 2 (bull), the average returns of the Sensex (except in the GST phase) and the BSE 100 are positive across all phases. In regime 1, the demonetization and COVID-19 dummies are statistically significant in the case of Sensex returns with a one-period lag. It is important to note that the COVID-19 dummy negatively affects Sensex returns for a one-day lag, but the demonetization dummy has a positive impact. Similar findings are found in the case of the BSE 100, although the demonetization and GST dummy coefficients are not statistically significant. However, their impact is positive in regime 2 bull, except for the demonetization dummy in the case of Sensex returns and the demonetization and GST dummies in the case of the BSE 100. The autoregressive coefficients are negative, implying negative serial correlation in the return series of stock indices. Interestingly, we find the exchange rate (INR vs. USD) returns and stock returns to have a negative impact in the context of both regimes and stock indices. This empirical finding strengthens our theoretical argument of the negative relation between stocks and the foreign exchange rate, as noted by the portfolio balance (stock-oriented) approach.

The estimated coefficients presented in Table 2 indicate that, overall, the nonlinear models fit the data better in the COVID-19 period in the context of Sensex returns, and in the demonetization phase in the context of BSE 100 returns, in comparison to other phases. Similarly, the nonlinear models with regime-dependent variance fit the data better, as indicated by the higher estimated log-likelihood values. The volatility of Sensex returns is very high in the COVID-19 period, and the volatility of the BSE 100 is very high in the demonetization phase, as indicated by their corresponding variances. The AIC favors the demonetization phase over the GST and COVID-19 phases in the context of both Sensex and BSE 100 returns, although the difference is extremely small among three phases. The intercept regime-dependent MS(2)-VAR(2)-EVENT(3) model passes all the misspecifications tests and demonstrates robustness by negative log-likelihood and positive AIC values.

The transition matrix with constant expected durations is reported in Table 3. In this table, P_{11} is the probability of staying in regime 1 and P_{22} is the probability of being in regime 2, and P_{12} is the probability of transition from regime 1 to regime 2 and P_{21} is the probability of transition from regime 2 to regime 1. In the demonetization period in the context of Sensex returns, during the bear phase,

Table 3. Transition probabilities and expected duration matrix.

Demonitisation: RSEN				Demonitisation: RBSE 100			
	Regime 1	Regime 2	Duration		Regime 1	Regime 2	Duration
Regime 1	0.317 (P11)	0.682 (P12)	1.464	Regime 1	0.981 (P11)	0.018 (P12)	53.864
Regime 2	0.014 (P21)	0.985 (P22)	67.959	Regime 2	0.981 (P21)	0.018 (P22)	1.018
	GST:RSEN				GST:RBSE 100		
Regime 1	0.251 (P11)	0.748 (P12)	1.336	Regime 1	0.299 (P11)	0.700 (P12)	1.426
Regime 2	0.013 (P21)	0.986 (P22)	73.281	Regime 2	0.018 (P21)	0.981 P(22)	53.487
	COVID 19: RSEN				COVID 19: RBSE 100		
Regime 1	0.985 (P11)	0.014 (P12)	70.668	Regime 1	0.018 (P11)	0.981 (P12)	1.018
Regime 2	0.704 (P21)	0.295 (P22)	1.418	Regime 2	0.018 (P21)	0.981 (P22)	55.479

P11 ... P22 are transition probabilities. The average expected duration of being in regime one is computed using formula suggested by Hamilton (1989).

This table presents the transition matrix with constant expected durations in both the regimes. The estimated probabilities associated with both the regimes suggest that the impact of COVID-19 is severe in the context of Sensex in comparison to the impact of demonetization and GST implementation. The average expected duration of return Sensex being in the Regime 1 (bear phase) is nearly 70 days, while that of Regime 2 (Bull phase) is only 2 days.

the estimated probability of being in regime 1 is 31.73%. On the other hand, the probability of the series switching from regime 1 to regime 2 is 68.26%. However, once the economy finds itself in the bull phase (regime 2), the probability that it will be in a bull phase is estimated to be 98.52%. The probability that the series will switch from regime 2 to regime 1 is lower (1.47%).In the GST phase, the estimated probability that the Sensex return will remain in regime 1 is 25.15%; however, the probability that they will continue to remain there during the bull phase (regime 2) is 98.63%. Interestingly, the results show that, in the COVID-19 phase, the estimated probability of the Sensex return continuing to remain in regime 1 (bear phase) is 98.58%. On the other hand, the probability that the Sensex return will switch from regime 1 to regime 2 is 1.41%. The probability that the Sensex return series will switch from regime 2 to regime 1 is higher (70.49%). However, the estimated probability associated with the Sensex return remaining in the bull phase (regime 2) is only 29.50%.

These results suggest that the impact of COVID-19 is severe in the context of the Indian liquidity index, Sensex, in comparison to the impact of demonetization and the implementation of the GST. The average expected duration of the Sensex return in regime 1 (bear) is nearly 70 days, whereas that for regime 2 (bull) is only 2 days. Similarly, in the demonetization period, the average expected duration of the Sensex return in regime 1 is nearly 2 days, whereas that for regime 2 is almost 68 days. In the GST phase, the average expected duration of the Sensex return in regime 1 is nearly 2 days,whereas that for regime 2 is almost 74 days.

However, in the context of the broad-based stock index, the BSE 100, the impact of demonetization is severe in comparison to the impact of the implementation of the GST and the COVID-19 outbreak. The probability of BSE 100 returns remaining in the bear phase (regime 1) is 98.14% in the demonetization phase; however, the probability of them remaining there in regime 2 is lower (1.85%). The transition probability from regime 1 to regime 2 is 1.85%, whereas the probability of switching from regime 2 to regime 1 is 98.14%. The average expected duration for BSE 100 returns in regime 1 is 52 days, whereas that for regime 2 is 1 day. However, during the COVID-19 phase, the average expected duration of return BSE 100 in regime 1 is only 1 day, whereas that in regime 2 is almost 55 days.

3.2.1. MS-VAR Impulse Response Function

The results from the comparative return and volatility analysis for the demonetization, GST, and COVID-19 phases, as well as the findings for the transition probabilities and expected durations in the previous section motivated us to examine the potential dynamic nonlinear response of all the variables in the system to a shock or innovation in each variable in both the short and long run. The regime-dependent impulse response functions are derived from the MSI(2)-VAR(2)-EVENT(3) model (Koop, Pesaran, and Potter 1996). Although we generated the impulse response function results for all the phases, only important results inconsistent with previous findings are presented here. The generalized Markov switching impulse response function of Sensex (liquidity index) returns in the COVID-19, GST, and demonetization phases are presented in Figures 2 and 3, respectively. In Figure 2, during the COVID-19 phase, a one-standard-deviation shock (innovation) to net foreign investment (*NETFII*) has no noticeable impact on the Sensex return in periods 1 and 2. From the second period onwards, the response gradually declines until the third period, when it hits its steady-state value. Beyond this period, the Sensex return remains in the positive region. Similarly, a one-standard-deviation shock to the exchange rate (INR vs. USD) return has a negative impact on the Sensex return, and this negative effect increases sharply up to the second period, when it hits its steady-state value and, after that, decays toward zero.

Thus, it can be concluded that innovation in the exchange rate return has asymmetric impacts on stock returns. However, a one-standard-deviation shock to the Sensex return initially increases *NETFII* up to the second period. This positive response is flattened up to the third period, after which it sharply declines until the sixth period, when it hits its steady-state value. Therefore, it can be concluded that shocks to the Sensex return will have asymmetric impacts on net foreign investment in both the short and long run. Similarly, a one-standard-deviation shock in the Sensex return hurts the exchange rate.

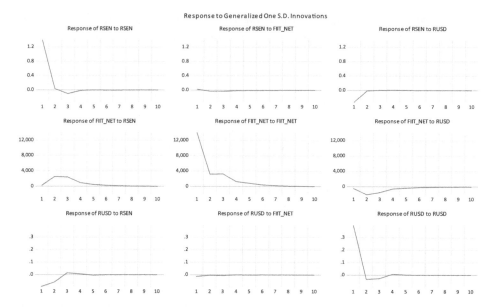

Figure 2. GIRFS return Sensex-COVID-19.
This graph is the dynamic responses of return Sensex, net foreign investment and exchange rate due to the generalized one standard deviation shock to each of the variables in 10 days' time ahead in the COVID-19 phase.

In Figure 3, the generalized impulse response function of the BSE 100 (broad-based index) return generated by Markov switching VAR with two regimes is presented for the demonetization phase. In line with the Sensex return, a one-standard-deviation shock to the net FII initially decreased the BSE 100 return until the second period, after which the effect dissipates. However, a one-standard-deviation shock to the exchange rate (INR vs. USD) return has an initially negative impact on the BSE 100 return. This negative effect increases sharply up to the second period and then flattens, up to the fourth period, after which it hits its steady-state value. Similarly, a one-standard-deviation innovation to the BSE 100 return has initially increases the net FII up to the second period. The response gradually declines from the third period onwards, up to the ninth period; after the 10th period, the effect decays toward zero. Thus, shocks to the BSE 100 return will harm *NETFII* in both the short and long run. Similarly, a shock in the exchange rate return will have asymmetric impacts on *NETFII*. Finally, a one-standard-deviation innovation to the BSE 100 return has a negative impact on the exchange rate return. This result is in line with the portfolio balance approach (Branson and Frankel 1983) to determining exchange rates.

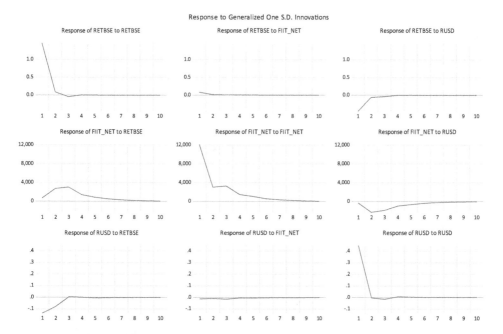

Figure 3. GIRFS return BSE 100-Demonetization.
This graph is the dynamic responses of return BSE 100, net foreign investment and exchange rate due to the generalized one standard deviation shock to each of the variables in 10 days' time ahead in the demonetization phase.

4. Conclusions

This paper examines the impact of the COVID-19 outbreak on Indian financial markets, emphasizing the dynamic interlinkages between stock returns, net FII flows, and exchange rate volatility. The outcomes of the COVID-19 outbreak are being compared with those of two recent major structural changes of the Indian economy, namely, demonetization and implementation of the GST. The MS-VAR nonlinear dynamic model—MSI(2)-VAR(2)-EVENT(3)—is employed to estimate regime-dependent intercepts, autoregressive coefficients, variances, transition probabilities, and expected durations between the regimes by using an expectation maximization algorithm.

The main findings of the study are as follows. First, benchmark BSE Sensex stock prices experience a negative growth of −22.6% during the COVID-19 phase, compared to positive growth during the demonetization and GST phases. Second, the stock returns of all the indices are negative during the COVID-19 phase, unlike during the demonetization and GST phases. Third, the volatility of benchmark stock prices is 2.77 in the COVID-19 phase, compared to 0.51 and 0.59 in the demonetization and GST phases, respectively. Fourth, realty has been the worst-affected sector by the COVID-19 pandemic, with stock price declines of −41.67%, unlike in the other sectors. However, of all the sectors, Bankex's stock returns are the most volatile. Fifth, the INR has depreciated by 7.2% against the USD and is also more volatile during the COVID-19 phase, compared to the other two phases. However, net FII flows are more volatile in the GST phase compared to the COVID-19 phase. Sixth, the impact of COVID-19 is severe in the context of the Indian stock liquidity index, the BSE Sensex, in comparison to the impacts of demonetization and implementation of the GST. The average expected duration of the Sensex return in regime 1 (bear) is nearly 70 days, whereas that for regime 2 (bull) is only 2 days. However, we find that, in the context of a broad stock index, that is, the S&P BSE 100, the impact of demonetization is significant in comparison to the impact of the GST and COVID-19. Seventh, the consequences of the impulse response function of the MSI(2)-VAR(2) model assumes that the shocks (innovation) to the exchange rate return have asymmetric impacts on stock returns in the COVID-19 phase. Even so, the return on the exchange rate is negatively impacted due to the shock in stock returns in both the short and long run. A shock in net FII has a positive impact on the stock return and a negative impact on the exchange rate return in both the short and long run during the post-COVID-19 period.

Our findings have important policy implications for the Reserve Bank of India (RBI) in this crisis period. They suggest that RBI should be extremely cautious in its intervention during the period of INR depreciation. We propose that RBI intervene in forward contract policy, along with determining the trading limits for commercial banks to arrest speculative forces and stop the precipitous fall of the INR against the USD. This approach will stabilize the Indian financial market and especially the equity market by minimizing the outflow of FIIs. The research in this paper could be extended by considering switching between multiple regimes based on the examination of time-varying causality, rather than our prespecified regimes in the MS-VAR model.

Notes

1. India's stock market capitalization declined by 27.4% in March 2020; however, it jumped back up by 14% in April 2020. The FII net investment, which was INR 89.702 billion in February 2020, decreased drastically and was negative in both March and April 2020. In the foreign exchange market, we note that the nominal bilateral exchange rate between the INR and the USD has been depreciating during this ongoing COVID-19 phase, dropping to 76.06 on 23 April 2020, a depreciation of 6.4%.
2. The unit root tests results are not presented here due to space constraints, but they are available upon request.

References

Al-Awadhi, A. M., K. Al-Saifi, A. Al-Awadhi, and S. Alhamadi. 2020. Death and contagious infectious diseases: Impact of the COVID-19 virus on stock market returns. *Journal of*

Behavioural and Experimental Finance 27 (September):100326. doi:10.1016/j.jbef.2020.100326.

Ali, M., N. Alam, and S. A. R. Rizvi. 2020. Coronavirus (COVID-19)–An epidemic or pandemic for financial markets. *Journal of Behavioral and Experimental Finance* 27:100341. doi:10.1016/j.jbef.2020.100341.

Apergis, N., and E. Apergis. 2020. Can the COVID-19 pandemic and oil prices drive the US Partisan Conflict Index?. *Energy Research Letters* 1 (1): 13144. doi:10.46557/001c.13144.

Barro, R. J., J. F. Ursúa, and J. Weng 2020. The coronavirus and the great influenza pandemic: Lessons from the "Spanish flu" for the coronavirus's potential effects on mortality and economic activity. *National Bureau of Economic Research Working Papers* No. 26866. https://www.nber.org/papers/w26866.pdf

Branson, W. H. 1983. Macroeconomic determinants of real exchange risk. In *Managing foreign exchange risk*, ed. R. J. Herring, 33–74. Cambridge: Cambridge University Press.

Broock, W. A., J. A. Scheinkman, W. D. Dechert, and B. LeBaron. 1996. A test for independence based on the correlation dimension. *Econometric Reviews* 15 (3):197–235. doi:10.1080/07474939608800353.

Cai, J. 1994. A Markov model of switching-regime ARCH. *Journal of Business & Economic Statistics* 12 (3):309–16. doi:10.1080/07350015.1994.10524546.

Castellano, R., and L. Scaccia. 2010. Bayesian hidden Markov models for financial data. In *Data analysis and classification: From exploration to confirmation*, ed. F. Palumbo, C. N. Lauro, and M. J. Greenacre, 453–61. Berlin-Heidelberg: Springer.

Chevallier, J. 2011a. Macroeconomics, finance, commodities: Interactions with carbon markets in a data-rich model. *Economic Modelling* 28 (1–2):557–67. doi:10.1016/j.econmod.2010.06.016.

Chevallier, J. 2011b. Detecting instability in the volatility of carbon prices. *Energy Economics* 33 (1):99–110. doi:10.1016/j.eneco.2010.09.006.

Dev, S. M., and R. Sengupta 2020. Covid-19: Impact on the Indian economy. *Indira Gandhi Institute of Development Research Working Paper*No.2020-013. http://www.igidr.ac.in/pdf/publication/WP-2020-013.pdf

Dhingra, V. S., S. Gandhi, and H. P. Bulsara. 2016. Foreign institutional investments in India: An empirical analysis of dynamic interactions with stock market return and volatility. *IIMB Management Review* 28 (4):212–24. doi:10.1016/j.iimb.2016.10.001.

Donadelli, M., R. Kizys, and M. Riedel. 2017. Dangerous infectious diseases: Bad news for main street, good news for wall street? *Journal of Financial Markets* 35 (C):84–103. doi:10.1016/j.finmar.2016.12.003.

Edelen, R. M., and J. B. Warner. 2001. Aggregate price effects of institutional trading: A study of mutual fund flow and market returns. *Journal of Financial Economics* 59 (2):195–220. doi:10.1016/S0304-405X(00)00085-4.

Frankel, J. A. 1983. Monetary and portfolio-balance models of exchange rate determination. In *Economic interdependence and flexible exchange rates*, ed. J. S. Bhandari, B. H. Putnam, and J. H. Levin, 84–115. Cambridge: MIT Press.

Fu, M., and H. Shen. 2020. COVID-19 and corporate performance in the energy industry. *Energy Research Letters* 1 (1): 12967. doi:10.46557/001c.12967.

Garg, R., and P. Dua. 2014. Foreign portfolio investment flows to India: Determinants and analysis. *World Development* 59:16–28. doi:10.1016/j.worlddev.2014.01.030.

Gil-Alana, L. A., and M. Monge. 2020. Crude oil prices and COVID-19: Persistence of the shock. *Energy Research Letters* 1 (1): 13200. doi:10.46557/001c.13200.

Gormsen, N. J., and R. S. J. Koijen 2020. Coronavirus: Impact on stock prices and growth expectations. *University of Chicago, Becker Friedman Institute for Economics Working Paper* No. 2020-22. doi:10.2139/ssrn.3555917.

Granger, C. W. J., B. N. Huang, and C. W. Yang. 2000. A bivariate causality between stock prices and exchange rates: Evidence from recent Asian flu. *The Quarterly Review of Economics and Finance* 40 (3):337–54. doi:10.1016/S1062-9769(00)00042-9.

Gray, S. F. 1996. Modelling the conditional distribution of interest rates as a regime switching process. *Journal of Financial Economics* 42 (1):27–62. doi:10.1016/0304-405X(96)00875-6.

Hamilton, J. D. 1989. A new approach to the economic analysis of nonstationary time series and the business cycle. *Econometrica* 57 (2):357–84. doi:10.2307/1912559.

Hamilton, J. D., and R. Susmel. 1994. Autoregressive conditional heteroskedasticity and changes in regime. *Journal of Econometrics* 64 (1–2):307–33. doi:10.1016/0304-4076(94)90067-1.

Haroon, O., and S. A. R. Rizvi. 2020. COVID-19: Media coverage and financial market behaviour-A sectoral inquir. *Journal of Behavioural and Experimental Finance* 2020. doi:10.1016/j.jbef.2020.100343.

Ichev, R., and M. Baker Marinc. 2018. Stock prices and geographic proximity of information: Evidence from the Ebola outbreak. *International Review of Financial Analysis* 56:153–66. doi:10.1016/j.irfa.2017.12.004.

Jain, A., and P. C. Biswal. 2016. Dynamic linkages among oil price, gold price, exchange rate, and stock market in India. *Resources Policy* 49:179–85. doi:10.1016/j.resourpol.2016.06.001.

Karame, F. 2010. Impulse-response functions in Markov-switching structural vector autoregressions: A step further. *Economics Letters* 106 (3):162–65. doi:10.1016/j.econlet.2009.11.009.

Karame, F. 2015. Asymmetries and Markov-switching structural VAR. *Journal of Economic Dynamics & Control* 53:85–102. doi:10.1016/j.jedc.2015.01.007.

Katechos, G. 2011. On the relationship between exchange rates and equity returns: A new approach. *Journal of International Financial Markets, Institutions and Money* 21 (4):550–59. doi:10.1016/j.intfin.2011.03.001.

Koop, G., M. H. Pesaran, and S. M. Potter. 1996. Impulse response analysis in nonlinear multivariate models. *Journal of Econometrics* 74 (1):119–47. doi:10.1016/0304-4076(95)01753-4.

Lagoarde-Segot, T., and P. L. Leoni. 2013. Pandemics of the poor and banking stability. *Journal of Banking & Finance* 37 (11):4574–83. doi:10.1016/j.jbankfin.2013.04.004.

Liu, L., E. Z. Wang, and C. C. Lee. 2020. Impact of the COVID-19 pandemic on the crude oil and stock markets in the US: A time-varying analysis. *Energy Research Letters* 1 (1): 13154. doi:10.46557/001c.13154

Mishra, A. K. 2004. Stock market and foreign exchange market in India: Are they related? *South Asia Economic Journal* 5 (2):209–32. doi:10.1177/139156140400500202.

Narayan, P. K. 2020. Oil price news and COVID-19—Is there any connection?. *Energy Research Letters* 1 (1): 13176. doi:10.46557/001c.13176

Narayan, P. K., S. Narayan, and K. P. Prabheesh. 2014. Stock returns, mutual fund flows and spillover shocks. *Pacific-Basin Finance Journal* 29:146–62. doi:10.1016/j.pacfin.2014.03.007.

Phan, D. H. B., and P. K. Narayan. 2020. Country responses and the reaction of the stock market to COVID-19 - A preliminary exposition. *Emerging Markets Finance and Trade* 56 (10): 2138–2150. doi:10.1080/1540496X.2020.1784719.

Qin, M., Y. C. Zhang, and C. W. Su. 2020. The Essential Role of Pandemics: A Fresh Insight into the Oil Market. *Energy Research Letters* 1 (1): 13166. doi:10.46557/001c.13166

Sensoy, A., and B. M. Tabak. 2015. Time-varying long term memory in the European Union stock markets. *Physica A: Statistical Mechanics and Its Applications* 436:147–58. doi:10.1016/j.physa.2015.05.034.

Zhang, D., M. Hu, and Q. Ji. 2020. Financial markets under the global pandemic of COVID-19. *Finance Research Letters* 101528. doi:10.1016/j.frl.2020.101528.

How Do Firms Respond to COVID-19? First Evidence from Suzhou, China

Xin Gu [ID], Shan Ying, Weiqiang Zhang, and Yewei Tao

ABSTRACT

In this article, daily electricity usage data for 34,040 enterprises in Suzhou (China) were examined for economic activity associated with the response to COVID-19. Employing a difference-in-differences estimation model, we find that the manufacturing industry incurred the greatest negative effect while industries such as construction, information transfer, computer services and software, and health care and social work were positively impacted by COVID-19. Private firms suffered more than state-owned enterprises and foreign-owned firms, and smaller firms experienced an additional 30% decline compared to large-sized firms.

1. Introduction

Since the World Health Organization declared the Coronavirus Disease 2019 (COVID-19) outbreak a pandemic on March 12, 2020, the disease has caused dire consequences globally for both public health and the real economy. The economic crisis triggered by COVID-19 is different from previous crises (Reinhart 2020) with respect to the urgency, scope, and magnitude of negative demand and supply shock. It has led to a sharp slowdown in growth which is amplified by the almost complete restrictions on economic activities (Ding et al. 2020). Firms have been adversely impacted in both the supply and the demand chain. Our main interest is in how firms across industries reacted to the pandemic shock. The goal is to provide guidance to policymakers and practitioners on appropriate methods for economic recovery.

In the first quarter of 2020 the United States, Japan, the United Kingdom, Germany, and France experienced a decline of 1.22%, 0.85%, 1.98%, 2.22%, and 5.83%, respectively, in their gross domestic product (GDP). The growth rate of the global economy is projected to fall to − 3% over 2020, creating a far worse recession than the 2008 global financial crisis. Likewise, China is facing an economic downturn due to the pandemic. As reported by China's National

Bureau of Statistics, its service industries have suffered the most, falling by more than 16% over the first quarter of the year 2020. Manufacturing industries have had an average loss of 10.7% and currently are trying to recover from the sudden stop in external demand.

This article provides direct evidence of the impact of the pandemic on the firms' activities. Using daily firm-level electricity consumption data, we are able to track the real economic activities associated with the response to COVID-19. Employing a difference-in-differences (DID) estimation method, 34,040 micro-enterprises were selected for evaluation in the period from December 31, 2019, to March 31, 2020. The data for the same period in 2018–2019 are also examined as a control group. The lunar calendar is applied to define the event date considering the seasonal variations in firms' performance related to the Chinese Lunar New Year. In order to remove the noise caused by the week-long holiday in the Spring festival, the seventh day of the first lunar month of 2020 was selected as the cutoff to define the before and after periods.

Our findings are three-fold. First, there was a sudden and massive reduction in firms' electricity consumption in response to the COVID-19 pandemic. Consumption declined by an average of 57% at the aggregate level. Second, the responses to the shock of the pandemic depended on the type of firm. Manufacturing industry enterprises (relative to other industries) were then most adversely impacted – a 37% reduction relative to other industries. Third, short-term dynamic responses of firms to the COVID-19 outbreak were observed with production starting to recover from the second week after the treatment date (January 31, 2020), and by the end of March 2020, some firms were even using more electricity than they were before the pandemic.

Much of the existing literature on public health crises indicates that pandemics or crises have a significant impact on economic activities. Influenza and other epidemics are found to damage economic growth by causing temporary or permanent loss (illness or death) in the labor force (Fan, Jamison, and Summers 2016; Potter 2001). The travel restrictions and limits on commercial activities imposed to prevent the spread of pandemic led to a reduction in the mobility of production factors (Guerrieri et al. 2020; James and Sargent 2002; Verikios et al. 2010). Evaluate the potential economic cost of modern epidemics and find that the degree of GDP loss in a country is generally in the range of 0.5–2%. Moreover, the negative impact of such infectious diseases is distributed unevenly across industries: industries such as transport, catering, and tourism are likely to be constrained by demand shocks, while industries related to manufacturing and mining face large supply shocks (Bloom, de Wit, and Carangal 2005; Eaton et al. 2016; Hepburn et al. 2020; Keogh-Brown and Smith 2008; Lee and Warner 2005).

Articles motivated by the COVID-19 outbreak mainly focus on the dynamics of the pandemic and its macroeconomic consequences (Apergis and Apergis 2020; Ali, Alam, and Rivzi 2020; Fu and Shen 2020; Gil-Alana and Monge 2020; Haroon and Rizvi 2020; Liu, Wang, and Lee 2020; Narayan 2020; Qin, Zhang, and Su 2020; Qiu, Chen, and Shi 2020). They have studied the relationship between pandemic incidence and economic outcomes both at the local level and in the aggregate outcome. However, there are very few quantitative attempts to identify how firms respond to the COVID-19 pandemic. Our article contributes to the literature in several aspects. First, our results complement articles investigating the economic impact of COVID-19 by providing evidence on a situation with respect to electricity consumption in China. Second, high-frequency data provide a unique perspective on how firms have been reacting to the pandemic. Third, we further examine how the impact of the pandemic on firms in Suzhou varies by the ownership structure and other corporate characteristics. With observed effects across industries, our results provide information that can help us consider the broader economic implications of the disease's impact.

This article proceeds as follows. Section 2 describes the data and provides descriptive statistics. The empirical methodology is presented in Section 3. The results are presented in Section 4 and the conclusion is in Section 5.

2. Data Sources and Description

2.1. Data

The analysis is based on daily data from three sources that indicate COVID-19-affected activities in China in a period of 2019–2020. First, we collect original electricity usage data covering 34,040 enterprises in Suzhou from the State Grid Suzhou Electric Power Company Limited, China. The data on electricity consumption enable us to construct a measure of firm-level exposure to a particular shock and thus track the changes of the real-world economic activities. We then winsorize the original data at the 1st and 99th percentile. Second, we use some variables such as industry information, ownership, and firm size (registered capital) obtained from the State Administration for Industry and Commerce of the People's Republic of China. Third, we have taken COVID-19 case counts from the WIND economic database[1] which provides daily updates on confirmed, cured, and new cases in each city in China.

To contain this coronavirus, Wuhan was locked down on January 23, 2020, with residents not being allowed to leave the city. This was immediately prior to the Spring festival of the Chinese New Year (January 25, 2020). As firms normally shut down for the Chinese New Year (CNY), electricity consumption tends to be much lower during this annual holiday. We restrict our sample to the specific period of December 1, 2019, to January 31, 2020. To eliminate the Spring festival effect, the seventh day of the first lunar month (January 31, 2020), which is the first day of returning to work after the holiday, is set up as the cutoff date for capturing the panic effects on a firm's performance before and after the outbreak of the disease (see Figure 1).

2.2. Descriptive Statistics

We construct our dataset by merging the three databases. The matched dataset has a panel of 34,040 firms and a total of around 4.2 million observations, with detailed firm characteristics during this period of 2019–2020. Electricity consumption in the comparable period for 2018–19 is pre-determined for before our sample period. Matched by the lunar calendar date, data for the period from December 12, 2018, to April 10, 2019, are collected for tracking firms' performances prior to the COVID-19 pandemic. Both the mean and standard deviation of the main variables are reported in Table 1.

To distinguish between different types of firms, we set unique identification codes for all sample firms according to the "Industrial classification for national economic activities[2]" sourced from China's Standardization Administration and General Administration of Quality Supervision, Inspection, and Quarantine. The electricity consumption by 18 industry categories is presented in Table 2. Since the

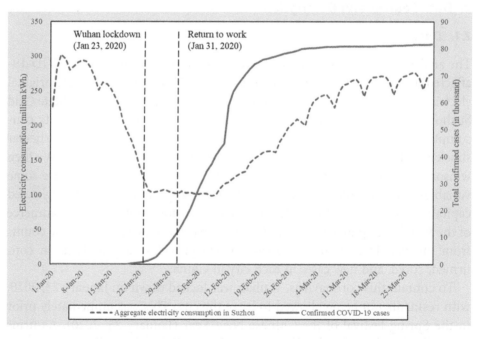

Figure 1. The development trend of COVID-19 in China and the response of Suzhou by electricity consumption. This graph reports the cumulative number of confirmed cases of COVID-19 in China and the total electricity consumption of Suzhou enterprises from January 1, 2020, to March 31, 2020. The horizontal axis is the Gregorian Calendar date, the main vertical axis is the total electricity consumption of Suzhou enterprises ('000,000 kWh), and the secondary axis is the cumulative number of confirmed cases in China ('000).

Table 1. Descriptive statistics of the main variables.

Main Variables	Dec 12, 2018–Apr 10, 2019		Dec 1, 2019–Mar 31, 2020		Difference
	Mean	SD	Mean	SD	
Electricity consumption	7.32	62.78	6.63	80.48	−0.69***
Numbers of daily new cases in Suzhou	0	0	1.26	2.25	1.26***
Numbers of total cured cases in Suzhou	0	0	27.81	35.98	27.81***

This table reports the descriptive statistics of the main variables used in the regression in the control group and the treatment group, including the average value and standard error of electricity consumption ('000 kWh) and new and cured cases of COVID-19. The control group represents the samples from December 12, 2018 to April 10, 2019, and the treatment group represents the samples from December 1, 2019 to March 31, 2020. Difference refers to the difference of the mean value between the control group and the treatment group. * $p < 0.1$, ** $p < 0.05$, *** $p < 0.01$.

COVID-19 outbreak, there has been a large decline in electricity usage for the sample firms in Suzhou, with the magnitude of the decline ranging from 0.4% to 74.3% across industries during the period from January 31, 2020, to March 31, 2020. The macroeconomic impact of COVID-19 is found to be a peak loss of 87.1%. The response slowly recovered to 8.8% by March 31, 2020, a 95.9% improvement over the lowest point.

3. Empirical Strategy

The DID estimate strategy is employed by comparing different treatment and control groups (Liu and Qiu 2016; Viard and Fu 2015). Specifically, we exploit two sources of variations: time variation (before and after a critical date for

Table 2. Descriptive statistics of electricity consumption at the industry level.

Industry Categories	Sample Number	Dec 12, 2018–Apr 10, 2019		Dec 1, 2019–Mar 31, 2020		Difference
		Mean	SD	Mean	SD	
Agriculture (A)	39,772	1.26	3.43	1.19	3.56	−0.07**
Mining and quarrying (B)	1,464	3.69	2.90	2.71	2.72	−0.98***
Manufacturing (C)	6,746,884	8.00	68.92	7.18	88.55	−0.82***
Utilities (D)	56,120	17.41	56.28	17.28	57.34	−0.13
Construction (E)	292,312	1.99	18.63	2.24	16.98	0.25***
Wholesale and retail trades (F)	300,120	3.77	8.66	3.20	7.78	−0.57***
Transport, storage and postal services (G)	170,312	4.88	36.47	5.51	48.14	0.63***
Accommodation and catering (H)	144,692	3.25	5.46	2.46	4.44	−0.79***
Information transfer, computer services and software (I)	17,324	7.31	23.6	18.91	73.55	11.60***
Finance (J)	6,100	9.03	11.73	8.55	11.38	−0.48*
Real estate (K)	165,188	6.38	15.28	5.35	13.25	−1.03***
Leasing and commercial services (L)	130,052	4.64	13.10	4.02	12.05	−0.62***
Scientific research and polytechnic services (M)	49,776	5.82	21.39	5.21	15.01	−0.61***
Administration of water environment and public facilities (N)	73,688	3.59	14.83	4.18	17.40	0.59***
Resident, repairing and other services (O)	60,268	2.91	13.63	2.46	12.26	−0.45***
Education (P)	13,420	5.43	9.59	5.41	9.43	−0.02
Health care and social work (Q)	4,148	2.48	3.50	3.06	3.75	0.58***
Culture, sports and entertainment (R)	34,160	3.92	8.10	3.32	7.26	−0.60***

This table reports the average electricity consumption ('000 kWh) of enterprises at the industrial level in Suzhou. Industries are marked by capital letters from A to R. The control group represents the samples from December 12, 2018 to April 10, 2019, and the treatment group represents the samples from December 1, 2019 to March 31, 2020. Difference refers to the difference of the mean value between the control group and the treatment group. * $p < 0.1$, ** $p < 0.05$, *** $p < 0.01$.

COVID-19) and cross-sectional variation (firm performance during the period 2019–20 as the treatment group and firm performance during the period 2018–19 as the control group). We compare the firm's performance during the period 2019–20 to *itself* in the same matched lunar calendar period 2018–19.

3.1. Aggregate-level Analysis

We begin our analysis by examining the impact of COVID-19 on firm performance at the aggregate level. The DID specification can be described as follows:

$$Y_{f,t} = \beta_0 + \beta_1 Treat_f \times Post_t + \alpha_f + \psi_t + \varepsilon_{f,t} \tag{1}$$

where $Y_{f,t}$ is the logarithm of the electricity consumption of firm f at the date t; $Treat_f$ is a dummy variable which is equal to one for the period from December 1, 2019, to March 31, 2020, and zero otherwise; $Post_t$ is an indicator of return to work after the New Year holiday, which is equal to one after the seventh day of the first lunar month, and zero otherwise; α_f is a firm-fixed effect (FE) that absorbs time-invariant firm heterogeneity; ψ_t is the date FE that eliminates the time-specific impact and $\varepsilon_{f,t}$ is an error term. We also control the Chinese New Year-FE by counting the days before and after the new year. β_1 is our main interest coefficient which captures the overall impact of COVID-19 on firm performance. A negative sign on β_1 indicates that the COVID-19 pandemic decreases the business activity of a firm, while a positive sign indicates an increase in activity.

3.2. Disaggregate-level Analysis

The impact of the COVID-19 pandemic on firms' business activities depends on a firm's characteristics. To assess the differences in the responses of heterogeneous firms, we further add an interaction term to Equation (1) as follows:

$$Y_{f,t} = \beta_0 + \beta_1 Treat_f \times Post_t + \beta_2 Treat_f \times Post_t \times Type_f + \alpha_f + \psi_t + \varepsilon_{f,t} \tag{2}$$

where $Type_f$ is a dummy representing different firm types, which is equal to one if the firm f possesses the specific type, and zero otherwise. There are three main types: industry, ownership, and business condition. Our main interest is on parameter β_1 and β_2, where β_2 captures the extra average impact of COVID-19 on the group defined by the interactive term, relative to the benchmark group, while $\beta_1 + \beta_2$ captures the impact of COVID-19 on the sub-sample defined by $Type_f$.

3.3. Dynamic Responses to COVID-19

Firms have behaved differently with respect to the pandemic, depending on the nature of their business activities. After the event date (January 31, 2020) there are nine weeks in the post-period in our sample. To further capture the dynamic evolution of the impact of COVID-19, we estimate the following specified regression:

$$Y_{f,t} = \beta_0 + \sum_{j=0}^{K} \beta_j Treat_f \times Post_j + \alpha_f + \psi_t + \varepsilon_{f,t} \tag{3}$$

where the post-period after the event date (the seventh day of the lunar month) is divided into a continuum of subsequent weeks after the event date indexed by $j \in [1, 9]$. Especially, $Post_j$ represents the number of weeks after January 31, 2020. β_j captures the responses of firms to the pandemic during the corresponding week.

4. Estimation Results and Discussions

4.1. Aggregate-level Analysis

We examine the aggregate response of firms to the pandemic based on our DID specification (1) in Table 3. In column (1) the COVID-19 shock reduced a firm's production by 57% ($= 1 - \exp(-0.85)$), relative to the unaffected period in 2018–19. We also observe a statistically significant panic effect for a firm's activities. The coefficients of the number of new confirmed cases and cured cases are reported to be significantly negative and significantly positive in columns 2 and 3, respectively.

4.2. Disaggregate-level Analysis

An analysis at the disaggregate level is conducted since it can handle firm heterogeneity. In Table 4, we report the results from three sets of regressions specified according to Equation (2) by industry, ownership, and business condition. We implement the models that differ in the estimation sample and the definition of the variable *Type*.

4.3. Industrial Classification

All sample firms are categorized into 18 industries according to the "Industrial classification for national economic activities." The estimated coefficients $(\beta_1 + \beta_2)$ provide an estimate of the sum of the lockdown and the virus effects. As we show in Panel A, most firms have suffered a sizable and unexpected negative external shock. The firms belonging to the mining and quarrying,

Table 3. The aggregate-level results.

	ln $electricity\,consumption_{ft}$		
	(1)	(2)	(3)
$treat_f \times post_t$	−0.85***	−0.60***	−2.93***
	(0.00)	(0.00)	(0.00)
$treat_f \times post_t$		−0.64***	
$\times \ln(1 + confirm_t)$		(0.00)	
$treat_f \times post_t$			0.58***
$\times \ln(1 + cure_t)$			(0.00)
Constant	4.49***	4.51***	4.51***
	(0.00)	(0.00)	(0.00)
Firm FE	Y	Y	Y
Day-of-week FE	Y	Y	Y
Distance-to-CNY FE	Y	Y	Y
Observations	8,305,760	8,305,760	8,305,760
R-squared	0.22	0.23	0.25

This table reports the regression results of COVID-19's impact on electricity consumption of the enterprises at an aggregated level. The dependent variable is the logarithm of electricity consumption. We include fixed effects for firm, day of week and distance to CNY in the regressions. Y = Yes and N = No. p-values in parentheses, * $p < 0.1$, ** $p < 0.05$, *** $p < 0.01$.

manufacturing, hospitality, and culture, sports, and entertainment industries suffered more than other industries. Manufacturing experiences the sharpest decline due to the joint impact. The estimated coefficients for industries such as construction, information transfer, computer services and software, and health care and social work are positive. It indicates that firms in these industries have had a positive response to the COVID-19 shock.

4.4. Ownership

In terms of ownership, we classified firms into three main types: state-owned enterprises (SOEs), domestic private firms, and foreign-invested enterprises (FIEs). FIEs include Sino-foreign joint ventures and wholly foreign-owned enterprises. The results in Panel B suggest that all types of firms reduced their economic activities significantly in response to the COVID-19 shock. The negative effect on the SOEs is the weakest. The effect on private firms is the strongest which suggests that they may be more affected by the lockdown effect on their production workers' mobility.

4.5. Business Conditions

Furthermore, we examine the firms' responses by three business conditions: international trading firms and non-trading firms; listed firms and non-listed firms; and firm size (registered capital). Based on Equation (2), we use three dummies representing whether firms satisfy these conditions to measure the interactive term – $Type_f$. The results suggest that the COVID-19 crisis has affected international trading firms less than non-trading firms; its impact on

Table 4. The disaggregate-level results.

	\ln electricity consumption$_{ft}$								
	(1)	(2)	(3)	(4)	(5)	(6)	(7)	(8)	(9)
	A	B	C	D	E	F	G	H	I
Panel A: by industry category									
treat$_f$ × post$_t$	-0.85***	-0.85***	-0.47***	-0.85***	-0.89***	-0.85***	-0.85***	-0.84***	-0.85***
	(0.00)	(0.00)	(0.00)	(0.00)	(0.00)	(0.00)	(0.00)	(0.00)	(0.00)
treat$_f$ × post$_t$ × Type$_f$	0.26***	-0.30***	-0.46***	0.44***	1.36***	0.01	0.29***	-0.16***	0.77***
	(0.00)	(0.00)	(0.00)	(0.00)	(0.00)	(0.14)	(0.00)	(0.00)	(0.00)
Firm FE	Y	Y	Y	Y	Y	Y	Y	Y	Y
Day-of-week FE	Y	Y	Y	Y	Y	Y	Y	Y	Y
Distance-to-CNY FE	Y	Y	Y	Y	Y	Y	Y	Y	Y
Constant	4.49***	4.49***	4.49***	4.49***	4.49***	4.49***	4.49***	4.49***	4.49***
	(0.00)	(0.00)	(0.00)	(0.00)	(0.00)	(0.00)	(0.00)	(0.00)	(0.00)
Observations	8,305,760	8,305,760	8,305,760	8,305,760	8,305,760	8,305,760	8,305,760	8,305,760	8,305,760
R-squared	0.22	0.22	0.22	0.22	0.22	0.22	0.22	0.22	0.22

	(10)	(11)	(12)	(13)	(14)	(15)	(16)	(17)	(18)
	J	K	L	M	N	O	P	Q	R
treat$_f$ × post$_t$	-0.85***	-0.85***	-0.85***	-0.85***	-0.85***	-0.85***	-0.85***	-0.85***	-0.85***
	(0.00)	(0.00)	(0.00)	(0.00)	(0.00)	(0.00)	(0.00)	(0.00)	(0.00)
treat$_f$ × post$_t$ × Type$_f$	0.45***	0.32***	0.10***	0.30***	0.40***	0.16***	0.29***	0.78***	-0.03
	(0.00)	(0.00)	(0.00)	(0.00)	(0.00)	(0.00)	(0.00)	(0.00)	(0.10)
Firm FE	Y	Y	Y	Y	Y	Y	Y	Y	Y
Day-of-week FE	Y	Y	Y	Y	Y	Y	Y	Y	Y
Distance-to-CNY FE	Y	Y	Y	Y	Y	Y	Y	Y	Y
Constant	4.49***	4.49***	4.49***	4.49***	4.49***	4.49***	4.49***	4.49***	4.49***
	(0.00)	(0.00)	(0.00)	(0.00)	(0.00)	(0.00)	(0.00)	(0.00)	(0.00)

(Continued)

Table 4. (Continued).

	(19)	(20)	(21)	(22)	(23)	(24)	(25)
Observations	8,305,760	8,305,760	8,305,760	8,305,760	8,305,760	8,305,760	8,305,760
R-squared	0.22	0.22	0.22	0.22	0.22	0.22	0.22
				ln $electricity\,consumption_{it}$			
Sample	SOEs	Private	Foreign	Hong Kong, Macao, Taiwan regions, China	Tradable	Listed firms	Size
Panel B: by ownership nature and basic business conditions							
$treat_f \times post_t$	−0.85***	−0.79***	−0.86***	−0.85***	−0.85***	−0.85***	−0.67***
	(0.00)	(0.00)	(0.00)	(0.00)	(0.00)	(0.00)	(0.00)
$treat_f \times post_t \times Type_f$	0.43***	−0.07***	0.14***	0.12***	0.02***	0.33***	−0.36***
	(0.00)	(0.00)	(0.00)	(0.00)	(0.00)	(0.00)	(0.00)
Firm FE	Y	Y	Y	Y	Y	Y	Y
Day-of-week FE	Y	Y	Y	Y	Y	Y	Y
Distance-to-CNY FE	Y	Y	Y	Y	Y	Y	Y
Constant	4.49***	4.49***	4.49***	4.49***	4.49***	4.49***	4.49***
	(0.00)	(0.00)	(0.00)	(0.00)	(0.00)	(0.00)	(0.00)
Observations	8,305,760	8,305,760	8,305,760	8,305,760	8,305,760	8,305,760	8,305,760
R-squared	0.22	0.22	0.22	0.22	0.22	0.22	0.22

This table reports the regression results of industry and enterprise heterogeneity. Please refer to Table 2 for details of sample classification. The dependent variable is the logarithm of electricity consumption. We include fixed effects for firm, day of week and distance to CNY in regressions. Y = Yes and N = No. p-values in parentheses, * $p < 0.1$, ** $p < 0.05$, *** $p < 0.01$.

listed firms is smaller than on non-listed firms; and smaller firms experienced an additional 30% decline in their business activity compared to larger firms. A possible reason for international trading firms being less affected is the level of risk aversion caused by the spread of the pandemic internationally at the same time as firms in China gradually restarted production.

4.6. The Dynamics of Firms' Response

We studied the dynamic pattern of firms' responses to COVID-19. Figure 2 presents the dynamic path of the percentage change in firms' daily electricity consumption. We observe a pattern with a sudden decline in the first two weeks and a rapid recovery in the subsequent seven weeks. For the first two weeks, the percentage changes in daily electricity consumption are – 79% and – 87%. Starting from the third week after the seventh day of the first lunar month, the percentage changes of each week are – 80%, – 65%, – 38%, – 17%, – 10%, 25%, and 9%, respectively. The real activities of many firms had recovered to a certain extent since March 20, 2020 (the eighth week after the event date).

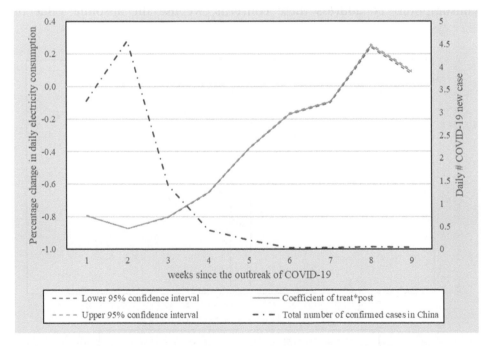

Figure 2. The dynamic changes in electricity consumption after the outbreak of COVID-19. This graph reports the dynamic changes in the average electricity consumption of firms in the nine weeks after the outbreak of COVID-19 and the changes of the number of newly confirmed cases in China. The horizontal axis represents the number of weeks and the 0 point represents the seventh day of the Chinese New Year in 2020. The main vertical axis represents the change level (%) of electricity consumption compared with the same period in the previous year. The secondary vertical axis represents the number of newly confirmed cases in China ('000).

5. Robustness Checks

In this section, we conduct a series of robustness checks. The results are reported in Figure 3 and Table 5.

5.1. Parallel Trend Test

The validity of the DID estimation hinges on the assumption that the time trends of the treatment and control groups are parallel before the treatment occurs. To check whether the parallel trend holds for the treatment and control groups in our estimation, the weekly average electricity consumption for both the pre- and post-periods is calculated and the results are reported in Figure 3.

5.2. Different Measures of the Dependent Variable

One may be concerned that the different measures of the dependent variable may affect the validity of the estimated coefficient and that the logarithmic variable cannot directly reflect the change in the quantity of electricity consumption. To address these concerns, we use the absolute value of

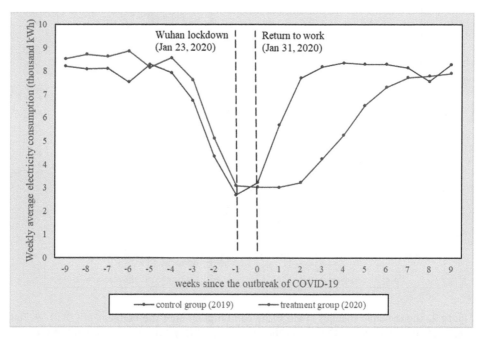

Figure 3. The time trends of the weekly average electricity consumption ('000 kWh). This graph reports the results of the parallel trend test. The horizontal axis represents the number of weeks from the event date (January 31, 2020). The vertical axis represents the weekly average electricity consumption ('000 kWh) of the control group (December 12, 2018, to April 10, 2019) and the treatment group (December 31, 2019, to March 31, 2020).

Table 5. Robustness checks.

	(1)	(2)	(3)	(4)	(5)
	Absolute value	ln electricity consumption$_{ft}$	ln electricity consumption$_{ft}$	ln electricity consumption$_{ft}$	ln electricity consumption$_{ft}$
	All	Alternative control group	Mixed effect	FWLS	Two period
treat$_t$ × post$_t$	-2.30***	-0.40***	-0.85***	-0.84***	-0.35***
	(0.00)	(0.00)	(0.00)	(0.00)	(0.00)
Constant	2.38***	3.93***	2.03***	2.01***	7.01***
	(0.00)	(0.00)	(0.00)	(0.00)	(0.00)
Firm FE	Y	Y	N	N	Y
Day-of-week FE	Y	Y	Y	Y	N
Distance-to-CNY FE	Y	Y	Y	Y	N
Industry FE	N	N	Y	Y	N
Observations	8,305,760	7,875,885	8,305,760	8,305,760	136,160
R-squared	0.01	0.16	0.14	0.14	0.03

This table reports the results of the robustness test. The dependent variable in column (1) is the absolute value of electricity consumption ('000 kWh), and in the other columns, it is the logarithm of electricity consumption. We include one or more fixed effects for firm, day of week, distance to CNY and industry in regressions. Y = Yes and N = No. p-values in parentheses, * $p < 0.1$, ** $p < 0.05$, *** $p < 0.01$.

electricity consumption ('000 kWh) as the dependent variable. The estimation result is reported in column (2) of Table 5. The negative shock caused by COVID-19 on the firms' performance is still robust and statistically significant.

5.3. Alternative Control Group

Selecting the same enterprises in the previous year as the control group may ignore differences between the years themselves. To solve this problem, we selected samples from December 23, 2017, to April 23, 2018 (matched by the same Chinese Year Calendar) to form a new control group. The results in column (3) of Table 5 still show that COVID-19 has a large negative impact on the electricity consumption of enterprises, which confirms the insensitivity of our results.

5.4. Alternative Estimation Method

To alleviate the concern of the existence of the heteroscedasticity, we employed two alternative estimation methods to replace the Generalized Least Squares (GLS) method in our main model by the pooled ordinary least squares and the feasible weighted least squares estimators. The new results are reported in columns (3) and (4) of Table 5. We find that our estimated results are robust to these two regression methods.

5.5. Two-period Estimation

The accuracy of the standard errors dominates both the validity of the DID estimation and, crucially, the resulting statistical inference. Following Liu and Qiu (2016), we employed another method to compute the standard errors, which divided the panel structure into pre- and post-treatment periods, and then calculated the White-robust standard errors. Column (5) of Table 5 illustrates the new regression result, which supports our conclusion that results from the main regression are robust.

6. Conclusion

How did firms' business activities respond to the initial stage of the COVID-19 pandemic? To shed empirical light on this question, we use DID analysis to capture firms' reactions to the COVID-19 shock based on the daily electricity consumption data. We employ an extensive firm-level sample that contains 34,040 enterprises in Suzhou, China. We have three main findings. First, at the aggregate level, firms' electricity consumption was hit hard across the board and dropped by an average of 57%. Second, at the disaggregate level, manufacturing firms were adversely affected, while firms in industries such as construction, information transfer, computer services and software, and health care and social work had a positive response to the COVID-19 shock. The pandemic-induced decline in private firms' business activities is larger than that of the SOEs and FIEs. Third, firms' business activities plummeted in line with the increase in the severity of the public health crisis during the first two weeks after the treatment began, but the real activities of firms were recovering, to a certain extent, by March 20, 2020 (the eighth week after the event date).

Our results have some important implications. First, all firms had a sudden drop in economic activity in response to the official outbreak of the COVID-19 pandemic, but the resulting economic outcome differed across industries. Our results help justify the scope for policymaking in terms of providing appropriate Chinese government assistance to industries and firms. Resources should be allocated to those firms that face difficulty in recovering and whose impacted activities would be more disruptive for the industrial value chains. Second, during such urgent and critical times, large financing policy decisions should be made and implemented quickly. Industries adversely affected by the COVID-19 pandemic such as manufacturing, hospitality, and culture, sports, and entertainment are worthy of assistance ahead of less affected industries. Third, governments need to consider how to allocate resources over time. The quick recovery of firms' production in our sample period does not necessarily indicate that the economic uncertainty created by this pandemic has diminished. Governments will need to assess the long-term economic impact of the pandemic.

Notes

1. A database which provides time series data on stocks, bonds, funds, derivatives, indices, and the macroeconomy in China.
2. Version No. GB/T 4754–2017.

Funding

This work was supported by the National Natural Science Foundation of China [71873029]; Statistical Analysis Project of State Grid Corporation of China in Suzhou [ZXGS-2020-SZ -A-03-130]; Jiangsu Social Science Foundation [18JD008]; Fundamental Research Funds for the Central Universities [22420202520057].

ORCID

Xin Gu ⓘ http://orcid.org/0000-0001-7343-6903

References

Ali, M., N. Alam, and S. A. R. Rivzi. 2020. Coronavirus (COVID-19) — An epidemic or pandemic for financial markets. *Journal of Behavioral and Experimental Finance* 27. doi:10.1016/j.jbef.2020.100341.

Apergis, E., and N. Apergis. 2020. Can the COVID-19 pandemic and oil prices drive the US Partisan conflict index? *Energy Research Letters* 1 (1):13144. doi:10.46557/001c.13144.

Bloom, E. A., V. de Wit, and M. J.-S. J. Carangal. 2005. Potential Economic Impact of an Avian Flu Pandemic on Asia. ERD Policy Brief No. 42. Economics and Research Department, Asian Development Bank, Malina, Philippines. Accessed May 25, 2020. https://www.adb.org/sites/default/files/publication/28082/pb042.pdf.

Ding, W., R. Levine, C. Lin, and W. Xie. 2020. Corporate immunity to the COVID-19 pandemic. NBER Working Paper No. 27055. National Bureau of Economic Research, Cambridge, MA. Accessed May 25, 2020. https://www.nber.org/papers/w27055.pdf.

Eaton, J., K. Samuel, N. Brent, and R. John. 2016. Trade and the global recession. *American Economic Review* 106 (11):3401–38. doi:10.1257/aer.20101557.

Fan, V. Y., D. T. Jamison, and L. H. Summers. 2016. The inclusive cost of pandemic influenza risk. NBER Working Paper No. 22137. National Bureau of Economic Research, Cambridge, MA. Accessed June 9, 2020. https://www.nber.org/papers/w22137.pdf.

Fu, M., and H. Shen. 2020. COVID-19 and corporate performance in the energy industry. *Energy Research Letters* 1 (1):12967. doi:10.46557/001c.12967.

Gil-Alana, L. A., and M. Monge. 2020. Crude oil prices and COVID-19: Persistence of the shock. *Energy Research Letters* 1 (1):13200. doi:10.46557/001c.13200.

Guerrieri, V., G. Lorenzoni, L. Straub, and I. Werning. 2020. Macroeconomic implications of COVID-19: Can negative supply shocks cause demand shortages? NBER Working Paper No. 26918. National Bureau of Economic Research, Cambridge, MA. Accessed June 1, 2020. https://www.nber.org/papers/w26918.pdf.

Haroon, O., and S. A. R. Rizvi. 2020. COVID-19: Media coverage and financial markets behavior—a sectoral inquiry. *Journal of Behavioral and Experimental Finance* 27. doi:10.1016/j.jbef.2020.100343.

Hepburn, C., B. O'Callaghan, N. Stern, J. Stiglitz, and D. Zenghelis. 2020. Will COVID-19 fiscal recovery packages accelerate or retard progress on climate change? *Oxford Review of Economic Policy* 36. doi:10.1093/oxrep/graa015.

James, S., and T. Sargent. 2002. The economic impact of an influenza pandemic. *Archives of Virology* 159 (1):103–16. doi:10.1007/s00705-013-1787-3.

Keogh-Brown, M. R., and R. D. Smith. 2008. The economic impact of SARS: How does the reality match the predictions? *Health Policy (Amsterdam, Netherlands)* 88 (1):0–120. doi:10.1016/j.healthpol.2008.03.003.

Lee, G. O. M., and M. Warner. 2005. The consequences of the SARS epidemic for China's employment and human resources. *Journal of Comparative Asian Development* 4 (1):9–28. doi:10.1080/15339114.2005.9678408.

Liu, L., E. Z. Wang, and C. C. Lee. 2020. Impact of the COVID-19 pandemic on the crude oil and stock markets in the US: A time-varying analysis. *Energy Research Letters* 1 (1):13154. doi:10.46557/001c.13154.

Liu, Q., and L. D. Qiu. 2016. Intermediate input imports and innovations: Evidence from Chinese firms' patent filings. *Journal of International Economics* 103 (Nov.):166–83. doi:10.1016/j.jinteco.2016.09.009.

Narayan, P. K. 2020. Oil price news and COVID-19—Is there any connection? *Energy Research Letters* 1 (1):13176. doi:10.46557/001c.13176.

Potter, C. W. 2001. A history of influenza. *Journal of Applied Microbiology* 91 (4):572. doi:10.1046/j.1365-2672.2001.01492.x.

Qin, M., Y. C. Zhang, and C. W. Su. 2020. The essential role of pandemics: a fresh insight into the oil market. *Energy RESEARCH LETTERS* 1 (1):13166. doi:10.46557/001c.13166.

Qiu, Y., X. Chen, and W. Shi. 2020. Impacts of social and economic factors on the transmission of coronavirus disease 2019 (COVID-19) in China. *Journal of Population Economics* 1–46. doi:10.1007/s00148-020-00778-2.

Reinhart, C. M. 2020. This time truly is different. Accessed May 25, 2020. https://www.project-syndicate.org/commentary/covid19-crisis-has-no-economicprecedent-by-carmen-reinhart-2020-03.

Verikios, K., J. McCaw, J. McVernon, and A. Harris. 2010. H1N1 influenza in Australia and its macroeconomic effects. COPS Working Paper No. G-212. Centre of Policy Studies/ IMPACT Centre, Melbourne, Australia. Accessed June 4, 2020. https://www.copsmodels.com/ftp/workpapr/g-212.pdf.

Viard, V. B., and S. Fu. 2015. The effect of Beijing's driving restrictions on pollution and economic activity. *Journal of Public Economics* 125:98–115. doi:10.1016/j.jpubeco.2015.02.003.

COVID–19's Impact on Stock Prices Across Different Sectors— An Event Study Based on the Chinese Stock Market

Pinglin He, Yulong Sun, Ying Zhang ⓘⒹ, and Tao Li

ABSTRACT

In this article, we use an event study approach to empirically study the market performance and response trends of Chinese industries to the COVID-19 pandemic. The study found that transportation, mining, electricity & heating, and environment industries have been adversely impacted by the pandemic. However, manufacturing, information technology, education and health-care industries have been resilient to the pandemic.

1. Introduction

The year 2020 is destined to be recorded in history because of extraordinary turn of events. The outbreak and spread of novel coronavirus (COVID-19) disease across the world have seriously affected people's production and life in general. Economies around the world are presently facing severe challenges due to the COVID-19 outbreak. According to real-time statistical data released by Johns Hopkins University, as of June 5, 2020, globally there have been 6,601,349 diagnosed cases of and 389,620 deaths from COVID-19. There are already clear signs of a recession in the global economy. In the "Global Economic Outlook" report in April 2020, the International Monetary Fund predicted that global gross domestic product (GDP) would fall by 3% throughout the year, while the World Trade Organization predicted that global trade could decline by as much as 32% in 2020. The impact of COVID-19 on the economy is not a cyclical fluctuation in the traditional economic development process. The short-term disasters generated by the pandemic also surpass any endogenous and extreme events in the past. Assessing and understanding the economic impact of COVID-19 has become an important issue. The purpose of this article is to evaluate the impact of COVID-19 on stock prices.

The traditional economic and financial theory holds that stock prices are mainly affected by market and firm characteristic-based factors. Companies in the same industry face the same regulatory and policy environment and similar macroeconomic conditions. When faced with changes in the economic environment, the operating conditions of companies in the same industry are highly correlated (Moskowitz and Grinblatt 1999). According to the theory of behavioral finance, in addition to the basic value of stocks, emergencies will have an impact on investors' psychological and behavioral factors, which in turn will have an important impact on stock prices. Lee and Jiang (2002) believe that investor optimism will reduce earnings volatility, while investor pessimism will increase earnings volatility. Therefore, the outbreak of COVID-19 will have an impact on the economic environment, which will affect investor sentiment, causing stock price changes.

The COVID-19 pandemic, as a public health emergency, is not only causing human infections and deaths, it is also disrupting the stock market. According to the China Health Committee, as of June 5th, the cumulative number of COVID-19 diagnoses in China was 84,617, with a cumulative death of 4,645. As the first country to respond to COVID-19, China made great efforts to resume work and production. When COVID-19 was declared, the Chinese government called for greater macro-policy adjustments and an active fiscal and taxation policy (Li, Zhang, and Zhao 2020). Yang, Chen, and Zhang (2020) found that the outbreak of the pandemic caused a sharp rise in risks in the financial sector, which transmitted to other industries. However, different industries are affected by the pandemic to varying degrees, and their responsiveness also varies. To comprehensively evaluate the impact of COVID-19 on stock prices of various Chinese industries, we adopted an event study approach. We examine the stock prices of industries that react to the pandemic.

The empirical results show that the COVID-19 pandemic has a severe impact on China's traditional industries, such as transportation, mining, electricity and heating, and environment. In contrast, it created opportunities for the development of high-tech fields. The manufacturing, information technology, education, and health industries responded positively to the pandemic. Our study contributes to the literature as follows. First, we explore the impact of the pandemic on the stock prices of various subsectors and explored the responsiveness of each industry to the pandemic. Secondly, our research is the first to employ the event study method to examine the effects on COVID-19 at the industry level. Our study therefore contributes to a small but growing literature on COVID-19 and its repercussions on different aspects of the economic and financial system (see, inter alia, Ali, Alam, and Rizvi 2020; Apergis and Apergis 2020; Fu and Shen 2020; Gil-Alana and Monge 2020; Narayan 2020). We contribute from the stock market reaction point of view.

The article proceeds as follows. Section 2 presents the literature review. Section 3 outlines the sample, variables, and models. Section 4 presents the empirical results and analysis. Section 5 presents further analysis, while Section 6 concludes the article.

2. Literature Review

In the capital market, emergencies often affect investor behavior by affecting investor sentiment, which ultimately affects stock prices. The earliest event study proposed by Fama et al. (1969) can be used to understand whether market security prices are related to specific events. In recent years, event study has been widely used in the field of accounting and financial practice and has gradually become a common research method in business studies. The existing research literature on the relationship between emergencies and stock prices mainly focuses on terrorist attacks, natural disasters, political behavior, and financial crises. Kalra, Henderson, and Raines (1993) studied the catastrophe of the Soviet Chernobyl nuclear power plant. Nikkinen et al. (2008) found that the "911" incident caused a significant drop in global stock prices, but they quickly recovered. Al-Rjoub (2011) and Al Rjoub and Azzam (2012) studied the Mexican tequila crisis in 1994, the Asian-Russian financial crisis from 1997 to 1998, the American "911" attack in 2001, the Iraq war in 2004, the financial crisis of November 2005, and the global financial crisis of 2008–2009. These authors explored whether these periods have an impact on the stock compensation behavior of the Jordan Stock Exchange.

Righi and Ceretta (2011) found that the European debt crisis of 2010 changed the risk of major European markets, particularly the volatility of the German, French, and British markets. Schwert (2011) studied the fluctuation of US stock prices during the financial crisis. Rengasamy (2012) studied the impact of Eurozone sovereign debt-related policy announcements and development rewards, as well as the stock market volatility of the BRIC countries (i.e., Brazil, Russia, India, China, and South Africa). Bai et al. (2019) applied rare disasters to a general equilibrium model and found that the capital asset pricing model (CAPM) considering emergencies can better reflect the stock price. Lanfear, Lioui, and Siebert (2018) studied the impact of US hurricanes on stock returns and found that emergencies affecting consumer growth will impact the stock market. Yin, Lu, and Pan (2020) studied the impact of the Sino-US trade war on the Chinese stock market and found that negative events have a longer-lasting impact on the stock market than positive events. There are also studies that focus on industry segments. Kaplanski and Levy (2010) discuss the impact of aviation accidents on stock prices and believe that unstable stock prices are more vulnerable to this effect. Ragin and Halek (2016) studied the 43 largest disasters in the insurance industry since 1970 and found that insurance brokers received abnormal stock returns on the day of the incident. Al Rjoub (2009) analyzed the impact of the financial crisis on the stock market.

The literature on the impact of emergencies on stock markets is quite broad but few studies examine the negative impact of major public health events on stock markets. Existing studies mainly focus on influenza and SARS pandemic s. A representative study by Goh and Law (2002) found that the 1997 Asian financial crisis and the 1998 Hong Kong avian influenza outbreak had a significant negative impact on tourism. Mctier, Tse, and Wald (2011) studied the impact of flu on the US stock market and found that an increase in the flu rate would reduce the enthusiasm of trading activities and stock returns. Chen, Jang, and Kim (2007) studied the impact of SARS on the hotel industry in Taiwan and found that SARS caused the stock price of the hotel industry to plummet. Chen, Jang, and Kim (2007) studied the long-term impact of the SARS pandemic on four major stock markets in China and Asia and found it has a significant impact on the financial integration of the stock market. In general, there is no comprehensive analysis of the impact of emergencies on the stock price of the entire industry in the literature.

As a public health incident of international concern, COVID-19 has a huge and sustained negative impact on the global economy (Iyke 2020a). Mei-Ping et al. (2018) studied the impact of SARS on Asian financial markets. Narayan and Phan (2020) studied the impact of COVID-19 on the stock market and the response of countries. Sobieralski (2020) analyzed the impact of COVID-19 on the aviation industry and employment. Many stock prices in China's A-share market have fallen to historical low levels, and the US stock market has four unprecedented nosedives. The negative COVID-19 impact on the stock market has increased the difficulty of risk prevention and control (Guidolin, Hansen, and Pedio 2019; Laura, Barbara, and Ana 2016). However, there is limited industry-level research on the effect of COVID-19 on stock prices in the existing literature, and there are industry limitations on the economic level of COVID-19 (Iyke 2020b; Reilly 2020; Saadat, Rawtani, and Hussain 2020). Qin et al. (2020) analysed the impact of the pandemic on oil markets. Ali, Alam, and Rizvi (2020) studied the impact of COVID-19 on different financial securities and compared the situation of China and other countries but paid less attention to industry heterogeneity. Liu et al. (2020) discussed the impact of COVID-19 on crude oil prices and stock prices in the US. In this context, we delved into the different changes in the stock prices of various industries during the pandemic window period in order to discover the ability of different industries to respond to the pandemic.

3. Samples, Variables and Models

3.1. Research Model

Event study mainly examines the abnormal changes of sample stock prices (or abnormal returns) after a specific event occurs. Han and Ming (2018) made a systematic study of the event method. We used event study in this article to examine the impact of the COVID-19 pandemic on the stock market. There are three main models for calculating abnormal returns: the average adjusted return rate model; the market index adjusted return rate model; and the market model.

The average adjusted rate of return model has a large deviation, when a bull or bear market occurs on the event day (Klein and Rosenfeld 1987). The market index adjusted return model has a strong relationship assumption, which is not applicable in most cases (Huang and Li 2018). Market models are the most commonly used and have good predictive power (Brenner 1979). In this article, we used the market model, which is outlined as follows.

Calculate the normal rate of return:

$$R_{i,t} = \alpha_i + \beta_i R_{i,M_{i,t}} \tag{1}$$

Calculate the average abnormal rate of return:

$$AR_{i,t} = R_{i,t} - (\alpha_i + \beta_i R_{i,M_{i,t}}) \tag{2}$$

Calculate the cumulative abnormal rate of return:

$$CAR_{i(t_1,t_2)} = \sum_{t_2}^{t=t_1} AR_{i,t} \tag{3}$$

where, $R_{i,t}$ is the return rate of stock i on the trading day t, $R_{i,M_{i,t}}$ is the market return rate of the trading market, α_i and β_i are the regression coefficients of the daily return rate of the stock i and the market return rate. The expected normal return of individual stock i can be calculated, if α_i and β_i remain stable during the estimation period. $AR_{i,t}$ is the average abnormal return rate of stock i on the trading day t, obtained by subtracting the expected return from the actual return. $CAR_{i(t_1,t_2)}$ is the cumulative abnormal return rate of stock i in the event window period (t_1, t_2).

3.2. Event Window and Sample Selection

From December 30, 2019, news about the COVID-19 outbreak in the southern China seafood market in Wuhan started circulating online, and this began causing crowd panic. We took the closure of Wuhan on January 23, 2020, as reported by the official media such as People's Daily and Xinhuanet, as the event day of the COVID-19 outbreak. If the estimation window is too short, the results will be biased. If the estimation window is too long, the forecast structure may change. In order to improve the forecast accuracy as much as possible, we selected 160 trading days before the event date as the forecast period. We choose every five trading days around the event occurrence date as the event window period. Figure 1 shows the event window.

The sample selected in this article comes from the Shanghai and Shenzhen A-share market and consists a total of 2,895 listed companies. The time interval is from June 3, 2019, to March 13, 2020. The companies' individual stock returns and comprehensive market returns come from the CSMAR database. We used the T-test to observe the abnormal return rate during the window period.

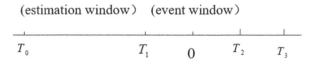

Figure 1. Event window. The T0-T1 segment is the estimation window, the T1-T2 segment is the event window and the T2-T3 segment is the post-event window.

4. Empirical Results and Analysis

4.1. Industry-wide Analysis in the Event Windows

We first drew on the research method of He et al. (2019), divided the market into different markets, and analyzed the market value of Shanghai and Shenzhen A-shares before and after the outbreak of COVID-19. The regression results showed that on the day COVID-19 broke out, the overall stock value of the Shanghai and Shenzhen A-share markets did not significantly fluctuate. However, as the pandemic intensified, from the 15th trading day after the event, the market value of Shanghai and Shenzhen A shares significantly dropped and continued along that path for a long time. Breakdown of the Shenzhen Stock Exchange and Shanghai Stock Exchange samples, we observed that both markets responded quickly to COVID-19. The abnormal returns of listed companies on the Shanghai Stock Exchange significantly dropped, whereas the excess returns of listed companies on the Shenzhen Stock Exchange rose.

To explore the reasons behind these heterogenous reactions, we analyzed the industry characteristics of listed companies on the Shanghai and Shenzhen markets. The main service entities of the Shanghai Stock Exchange are mainly Chinese central enterprises and state-owned enterprises, which are mostly traditional industries, whereas the listed companies on the Shenzhen Stock Exchange are mostly high-tech enterprises. In summary, the outbreak of COVID-19 had a serious negative impact on China's traditional industries, but created opportunities for the development of high-tech industries. To further explore the impact of the COVID-19 outbreak, we conducted in-depth research on 18 sub-sectors in China.

4.2. Analysis of Various Industries in the Event Window

Tables 2–4 show the impact of the COVID-19 pandemic on the market value of 18 sub-sectors in China. It can be seen from Table 2 that, on the day of the COVID-19 outbreak, the stock prices of the agriculture, mining, electric and heating, and construction industries all significantly declined, and the value of companies in other industries except agriculture continued to decline during the window period. However, the manufacturing industry continued to rise on the day of the outbreak and subsequent days, and the wholesale and retail industries were not significantly affected.

As can be seen from Table 3, the market value of companies in transportation, real estate, and environmental industries significantly decreased on the day of the outbreak and subsequent days, and lodging and catering, and business service industries were also affected to a certain extent. The stock price of the information technology industry significantly increased on the day of the outbreak, and again markedly increased during the (0, +20) window period.

It can be seen from Table 4 that the education and health industries were significantly hit when the pandemic broke out, but rebounded in the subsequent event window. The financial services, scientific research, sports and entertainment, and public management industry have been significantly affected by the pandemic.

Table 1. Results of the impact of COVID-19 shock on the stock market value.

	Shanghai A-share		Shenzhen A-share		Shanghai & Shenzhen	
Event window	CAR	t value	CAR	t value	CAR	t value
(−30, 0)	−0.0026***	−8.3631	0.0010***	3.2400	−0.0008***	−3.6554
(−25, 0)	−0.0023***	−8.6949	0.0011***	3.7277	−0.0007***	−3.4667
(−20, 0)	−0.0019***	−6.5061	0.0011***	3.4741	−0.0005**	−2.0991
(−15, 0)	0.0020***	−6.0126	0.0015***	4.0150	−0.0003	−1.2748
(−10, 0)	0.0015***	−3.5329	0.0012***	2.6477	−0.0002	−0.5711
(−5, 0)	−0.0014**	−2.2324	0.0020***	2.9782	0.0003	0.5756
(0, 0)	−0.0023	−1.1299	0.0048**	2.0413	0.0011	0.7257
(0, +5)	−0.0025***	−3.3820	0.0019***	2.2955	−0.0004	−0.6548
(0, +10)	−0.0020***	−4.1906	0.0017**	2.1853	−0.0004	−1.3138
(0, +15)	−0.0024***	−6.2579	0.0015***	3.4582	−0.0005***	−1.7924
(0, +20)	−0.0026***	−7.9244	0.0016***	4.4673	−0.0005***	−2.1927
(0, +25)	−0.0024***	−8.2220	0.0013***	3.9040	−0.0006***	−2.8623
(0, +30)	−0.0024***	−6.8778	0.0014***	3.5839	−0.0006***	−2.1401

CAR stands for cumulative abnormal return. The ordinate represents the event window. ***, **, and * are significant at 1%, 5%, and 10% confidence levels, respectively.

Table 2. Results of the impact of COVID-19 in various industries.

Event window	Agriculture	Mining	Manufacturing	Electric& heating	Construction	Wholesale & retail
(−30, 0)	−0.0062***	−0.0121***	0.0011***	−0.0079***	−0.0051***	0.0006
	(−2.43)	(−8.27)	(3.75)	(−10.86)	(−5.35)	(0.65)
(−20, 0)	−0.0011	−0.0099***	0.0010***	−0.0075***	−0.0025**	0.0013
	(−0.46)	(−6.99)	(3.55)	(−10.34)	(−2.49)	(1.45)
(−10, 0)	−0.0145***	−0.0175***	0.0018***	−0.0059***	−0.0030**	0.0026*
	(−4.84)	(−9.37)	(4.24)	(−5.65)	(−2.04)	(1.83)
(0, 0)	−0.0316**	−0.0389***	0.0063***	−0.0262***	−0.0155**	0.0056
	(−2.40)	(−3.95)	(3.06)	(−4.76)	(−2.07)	(0.74)
(0, +10)	0.0045	−0.0096***	0.0010	−0.0070***	−0.0082***	−0.0002
	(1.28)	(−5.02)	(2.01)	(−6.12)	(−5.05)	(−0.10)
(0, +20)	0.0012	−0.0105***	0.0007**	−0.0068***	0.0001	−0.0014
	(0.55)	(−7.67)	(2.12)	(−8.43)	(0.11)	(−1.38)
(0, +30)	0.0024	−0.0112***	0.0007*	−0.0059***	−0.0008	0.0001
	(1.09)	(−8.23)	(1.91)	(−6.74)	(−0.58)	(0.10)

CAR stands for cumulative abnormal return. The abscissa represents the industry, and the ordinate represents the event window. ***, **, and * are significant at 1%, 5%, and 10% confidence levels, respectively.

Table 3. Results of the impact of COVID-19 in various industries-Continued Table 1.

Event window	Transportation	Lodging & catering	Business service	Real estate	Environment	Information technology
(−30, 0)	−0.0016*	−0.0033	0.0023	−0.0050***	−0.0141***	0.0006
	(−1.86)	(−1.03)	(1.21)	(−5.73)	(−9.34)	(0.47)
(−20, 0)	−0.0019**	−0.0032	0.0037**	−0.0025***	−0.0151***	0.0019*
	(−2.19)	(−0.97)	(2.06)	(−2.80)	(−9.94)	(1.68)
(−10, 0)	0.0016	−0.0026	0.0006	−0.0040	−0.0113***	0.0000
	(1.17)	(−0.61)	(0.25)	(−3.36)	(−5.06)	(0.01)
(0, 0)	−0.0109*	−0.0016	0.0096	−0.0270***	−0.0219**	0.0246***
	(−1.73)	(−0.06)	(0.96)	(−4.41)	(−2.39)	(3.69)
(0, +10)	−0.0032**	−0.0051	0.0003	−0.0038***	−0.0087***	0.0022
	(−2.28)	(−0.93)	(0.11)	(−2.73)	(−3.25)	(1.33)
(0, +20)	−0.0047***	0.0005	−0.0008	−0.0013	−0.0080***	0.0040***
	(−4.97)	(0.12)	(−0.46)	(−1.34)	(−4.13)	(3.30)
(0, +30)	−0.0033***	−0.0011	−0.0003	−0.0014	−0.0073***	0.0019
	(−3.17)	(−0.26)	(−0.18)	(−1.33)	(−3.59)	(1.44)

CAR stands for cumulative abnormal return. The abscissa represents the industry, and the ordinate represents the event window. ***, **, and * are significant at 1%, 5%, and 10% confidence levels, respectively.

Table 4. Results of the impact of COVID-19 in various industries—Continued Table 2.

Event window	Scientific research	Education	Health	Sports&Entertainment	Public management	Information technology
(−30, 0)	−0.0032*	−0.0107***	−0.0016	0.0005	0.0014	−0.0076***
	(−1.83)	(−2.89)	(−0.39)	(0.26)	(0.47)	(−7.24)
(−20, 0)	−0.0034*	−0.0091**	−0.0018	0.0013	0.0015	−0.0081***
	(−1.93)	(−2.55)	(−0.44)	(0.69)	(0.53)	(−8.86)
(−10, 0)	0.0035	−0.0213***	0.0024	−0.0083***	0.0018	−0.0030**
	(1.36)	(−4.48)	(0.37)	(−3.28)	(0.40)	(−2.46)
(0, 0)	−0.0003	−0.0305	−0.0276***	0.0111	0.0402	−0.0065
	(−0.02)	(−1.05)	(−4.65)	(0.79)	(1.56)	(−1.16)
(0, +10)	−0.0009	−0.0058	0.0051	0.0023	0.0022	−0.0038***
	(−0.30)	(−0.74)	(0.83)	(0.73)	(0.46)	(−2.82)
(0, +20)	−0.0044**	0.0104*	−0.0028	−0.0023	−0.0014	−0.0049***
	(−2.18)	(1.81)	(−0.64)	(−1.18)	(−0.51)	(−4.76)
(0, +30)	−0.0021	0.0031	0.0021	−0.0029	−0.0007	−0.0065***
	(−0.95)	(0.51)	(0.40)	(−1.45)	(−0.22)	(−6.39)

CAR stands for cumulative abnormal return. The abscissa represents the industry, and the ordinate represents the event window. ***, **, and * are significant at 1%, 5%, and 10% confidence levels, respectively.

4.3. Impact of COVID-19 on the Whole Industry

In the context of economic globalization, the large-scale spread of the pandemic has forced most countries and regions to adopt strict control measures, which will inevitably affect the normal operation of the globalized production system, as well as the industrial and capital chains. It is worth noting that, in the current and near future, the pandemic situation in other countries would intensify, resulting in further disruption in the global economy. Currently, China is in a golden period of full-scale recovery and production. Order reduction is another severe challenge for these industries and enterprises after suffering the winter. To discuss, in depth, the impact of COVID-19 on various industries, we produced a graph (as shown in Figure 2) of the average daily stock price movement across the industries during the event window. The industry's stock price performance on the day of the COVID-19 outbreak

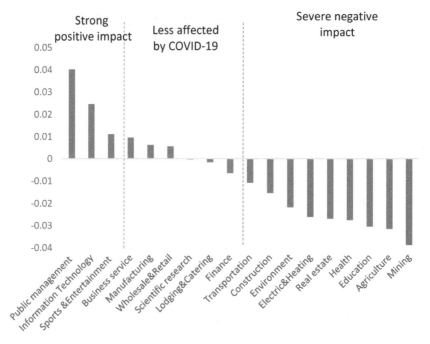

Figure 2. The average change of stock prices in various industries on the event day. The data in the table refer to the stock price fluctuations of various industries on the event day, which can be divided into strong positive impact, less affected by COVID-19, and severe negative impact according to the size of the fluctuation.

can be divided into three categories: mildly affected industries, severely positively affected industries, and severely negatively affected industries.

Overall, most industries suffered strong negative impacts, among which the mining industry and agriculture were the most severely impacted. As the COVID-19 pandemic intensified globally, mining companies took measures to protect extractors and communities, postponed projects, and closed mines. Some companies closed their headquarters and implemented the home office to help curb the spread of the virus. Judging from the agricultural situation, the spread of the pandemic caused the country to halt large-scale assembly activities, which hindered agricultural activities and caused severe damage to the agricultural economy. The pandemic quickly swept across the country and had a major impact on agricultural production, migrant workers, and rural investment. These were quickly reflected in the capital market. The business service, manufacturing, retail, and other industries are less affected by COVID-19. The public management, information technology, and sports and entertainment industries did not only withstand the negative impact on the day of the incident, but also showed a strong coping ability – stock prices increased, to a certain extent, across these industries.

We further divided the event window and selected the process of the entire industry affected by the pandemic. The detailed results are shown in

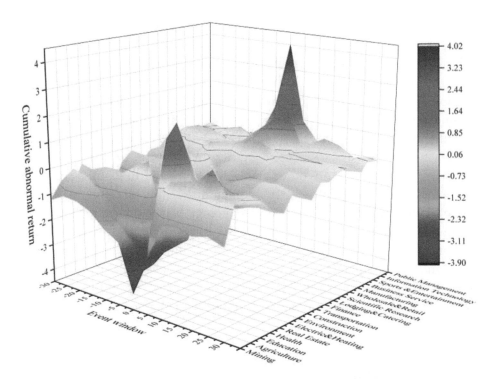

Figure 3. Curved surface curve of stock price changes of industries in each event window. The data in the table are the trends of CARs in different industries following different event windows. The X-axis is the industry, the Y-axis is the event window, and the Z-axis is CAR.

Figure 3. When the COVID-19 broke out, China took quarantine measures to prevent the spread of the virus. The first industry to be hit was transportation. The share price of the transportation industry continued to fall after several event windows. The share price of the mining industry, which is closely related to the transportation industry, plummeted after the outbreak, and, in turn, the average daily abnormal return rate fell below 0.0389. This was the largest decline in the industry's average daily abnormal return rate on the China's A-share market that day; the decline continued for the next six event windows. The main reason behind this decline is that the mining industry is highly dependent on logistics and transportation. When the COVID-19 broke out, roads were closed, and product transportation is stagnated, which affected investor sentiment and, in turn, caused stock prices to fall. At the same time, the electric and heating, and environmental industries, which mainly rely on infrastructure construction, often required substantial labor support. Following the COVID-19 outbreak, these industries encountered labor shortages, and their stock prices also fell.

Despite the overall decline of the China's stock market, some industries went against the trend, showing a strong immunity to the COVID-19 outbreak. In multiple event windows on and after the COVID-19 outbreak, the excess return rate of the manufacturing and information technology industries was always positive, whereas the average abnormal return rate of the education and health industries was negative on the event day. After multiple event window fluctuations, the cumulative excess return rate became positive, and the stock price steadily rebounded. The reason for this phenomenon may be that the COVID-19 outbreak incentivized the manufacturing industry to respond quickly by stepping up the production of masks, ventilators, and other medical equipment to fight against the pandemic, which then boosted the momentum of the stock market. In the case of crowd isolation, information technology played an important role in the timely sharing of information and the spread of digital pandemic prevention and control; with the success of the Chinese medical team's anti-pandemic war, the pandemic situation is gradually controllable. "Suspended classes and non-stop learning" and the comprehensive promotion of online classes gradually restored investors' confidence in the health and education industry.

5. Further Research

Companies with different equity types often have different abilities to cope with external shocks. To explore the mechanism underlying COVID-19's impact on the stock market, we further conducted group research on companies with different equity properties. It can be seen from Table 5 that, on the day of the outbreak and various incident windows, the cumulative abnormal returns of Chinese state-owned enterprises were significantly negative, and non-state-owned enterprises showed a small increase. This shows that COVID-19 has a significant impact on state-owned

Table 5. Results of the impact of COVID-19 on the market value with different equity types.

Event window	State-owned enterprise		Non-State-owned	
	CAR	t value	CAR	t value
(−30, 0)	−0.0044***	−13.6065	0.0016***	5.4283
(−25, 0)	−0.0043***	−14.8563	0.0017***	6.2801
(−20, 0)	−0.0037***	−11.7272	0.0017***	5.5661
(−15, 0)	−0.0038***	−10.4429	0.0019***	5.3276
(−10, 0)	−0.0031***	−6.6895	0.0014***	3.3328
(−5, 0)	−0.0022***	−3.2951	0.0014***	2.1533
(0, 0)	−0.0023	−0.9852	0.0029	1.3897
(0, +5)	−0.0038***	−4.6013	0.0017**	2.3049
(0, +10)	−0.0029***	−5.3999	0.0009*	1.8206
(0, +15)	−0.0032***	−7.5579	0.0011***	2.7569
(0, +20)	−0.0028***	−7.8893	0.0009***	2.6301
(0, +25)	−0.0029***	−9.1710	0.0008***	2.7968
(0, +30)	−0.0029***	−7.4830	0.0009**	2.4385

CAR stands for cumulative abnormal return. The ordinate represents the event window. ***, **, and * are significant at 1%, 5%, and 10% confidence levels, respectively.

enterprises. State-owned enterprises are mostly traditional industries, and this conclusion is consistent with the one for the Shanghai Stock Exchange and Shenzhen Stock Exchange samples. This strengthened our finding that the COVID-19 outbreak has a serious impact on China's traditional industries, such as transportation, mining, electric and heating, and environment industries. The estimates also strengthened our finding that the pandemic created opportunities for the development of high-tech industries such as information technology, education, health, manufacturing, and other industries.

6. Conclusions and Recommendations

We used an event study approach to empirically explore the impact of the COVID-19 outbreak on the stock prices of various Chinese industries. We found that the pandemic negatively impacted stock prices on the Shanghai Stock Exchange, whereas it positively impacted the stock prices on the Shenzhen Stock Exchange. COVID-19 hit the traditional industries of China negatively and more seriously but created opportunities for the development of high-tech industries. The pandemic greatly affected the transportation, mining, electric and heating, and environmental industries. However, the manufacturing, information technology, education, and health industries strongly responded to the pandemic in a positive fashion, providing a boost to confidence on the stock market. China's large economy, complete infrastructure and industrial chain, and strong supporting capabilities helped the country to quickly overcome the adverse effects of COVID-19.

At the same time, the "new infrastructure" that the Chinese government is strongly supporting, including manufacturing, information technology, and other industries, can quickly boost effective investment now, thereby boosting effective market demand and consumption. Taking 5 G network construction as an example, it cannot only drive the research and development and production of related equipment, but can also foster the growth of online education, smart home, immersive gaming, and other consumption. COVID-19 is also forcing the upgrading of China's industrial chain. Digital technologies such as big data and cloud computing can transform the industrial chain, realize precise perception, online processing, and intelligent decision-making, and help to break through the industry bottleneck of China.

COVID-19 is a typical black swan event, and its occurrence, development, and even disappearance, as well as the depth, breadth, and intensity of its impact, are all unknown. The stock market is a barometer of the economy, and the capital market reflects the overall situation of a country's economy to a certain extent. This article discussed the market performance of all industries in China under the influence of COVID-19 and analyzed, in detail, the response trends and capabilities of industries that are hard hit. The article expanded the research field of COVID-19 and explored the heterogenous reaction of industries to major emergencies. The conclusions of this article also provided reference for countries across the world in their fight against the pandemic and resume economic production.

Funding

The National Social Science Fund of China (17BGL051), the Fundamental Research Funds for the Central Universities (2018QN068), the Fundamental Research Funds for the Central Universities (2019FR005), and the Beijing Social Science Fund (18GLB017) supported this work.

ORCID

Ying Zhang ⓘ http://orcid.org/0000-0001-8198-7289

References

Al Rjoub, S. A. (2011). Business cycles, financial crises, and stock volatility in Jordan stock exchange. *International Journal of Economic Perspectives*, 5(1).

Al Rjoub, S. A., and H. Azzam. 2012. Financial crises, stock returns and volatility in an emerging stock market: The case of Jordan. *Journal of Economic Studies* 39 (2):178–211. doi:10.1108/01443581211222653.

Al Rjoub, S. A. M. 2009. Business cycles, financial crises, and stock volatility in Jordan stock exchange. *Social Science Electronic Publishing* 31 (1):127–32. doi:10.2139/ssrn.1461819.

Ali, M., N. Alam, and S. A. R. Rizvi. 2020. Coronavirus (COVID-19) – An epidemic or pandemic for financial markets. *Journal of Behavioral and Experimental Finance* 100341. doi:10.1016/j.jbef.2020.100341.

Apergis, N., and E. Apergis. 2020. Can the COVID-19 pandemic and oil prices drive the US Partisan conflict index. *Energy Research Letters* 1 (1):13144. doi:10.46557/001c.13144

Bai, H., K. Hou, H. Kung, E. X. N. Li, and L. Zhang. 2019. The CAPM strikes back? An equilibrium model with disasters. *Journal of Financial Economics* 131 (2):269–98. doi:10.2139/ssrn.2568352.

Brenner, M. 1979. The sensitivity of the efficient market hypothesis to alternative specifications of the market model. *Journal of Finance* 34 (4):915–29. doi:10.1111/j.1540-6261.1979.tb03444.x.

Chen, M. H., S. C. Jang, and W. G. Kim. 2007. The impact of the SARS outbreak on Taiwanese hotel stock performance: An event-study approach. *International Journal of Hospitality Management* 26 (1):0–212. doi:10.1016/j.ijhm.2005.11.004.

Fama, E. F., L. Fisher, and M. Jensen. 1969. The adjustment of stock price to new information. *International Economic Review* 10:1–21. doi:10.2139/ssrn.321524.

Fu, M., and H. Shen. 2020. COVID-19 and corporate performance in the energy industry. *Energy Research Letters* 1 (1):12967. doi:10.46557/001c.12967

Gil-Alana, L. A., and M. Monge. 2020. Crude oil prices and COVID-19: Persistence of the shock. *Energy Research Letters* 1 (1):13200. doi:10.46557/001c.13200

Goh, C., and R. Law. 2002. Modeling and forecasting tourism demand for arrivals with stochastic nonstationary seasonality and intervention. *Tourism Management* 23 (5):499–510. doi:10.1016/S0261-5177(02)00009-2.

Guidolin, M., E. Hansen, and M. Pedio. 2019. Cross-asset contagion in the financial crisis: A bayesian time-varying parameter approach. *Journal of Financial Markets* 45:83–114. doi:10.1016/j.finmar.2019.04.001.

Han, H., and L. Ming. 2018. An overview of event study methodology. *Statistics & Decision* 34 (13):66–71. doi:10.13546/j.cnki.tjyjc.2018.13.015.

He, P. L., Y. L. Sun, Y. R. Chen, and J. Ning. 2019. Analyst following, overseas background of directors and quality of information. *Scientific Decision Making* 9:1–27. doi:10.3773/j..1006-4885.

Huang, H., and Li, M. (2018). An overview of event study methodology. *Statistics & Decision* 34 (13):66–71.

Iyke, B. N. 2020a. The disease outbreak channel of exchange rate return predictability: Evidence from COVID-19. *Emerging Markets Finance and Trade* 56 (10), 2277–2297. doi:10.1080/1540496X.2020.1784718

Iyke, B. N. 2020b. COVID-19: The reaction of US oil and gas producers to the pandemic. *Working Paper.*

Kalra, R., G. V. Henderson, and G. A. Raines. 1993. Effects of the chernobyl nuclear accident on utility share prices. *Quarterly Journal of Business & Economics* 32:52–77.

Kaplanski, G., and H. Levy. 2010. Sentiment and stock prices: The case of aviation disasters. *Journal of Financial Economics* 95 (2):174–201. doi:10.1016/j.jfineco.2009.10.002.

Klein, A., and J. Rosenfeld. 1987. The influence of market conditions on event-study residuals. *Journal of Financial and Quantitative Analysis* 22 (3):345–51. doi:10.2307/2330968.

Lanfear, M. G., A. Lioui, and M. G. Siebert. 2018. Market anomalies and disaster risk: Evidence from extreme weather events. *Journal of Financial Markets* 46:100–477. doi:10.1016/j.finmar.2018.10.003.

Laura, B., C. Barbara, and G.-U. Ana. 2016. Bank fragility and contagion: Evidence from the bank CDS market. *Journal of Empirical Finance* 38:394–416. doi:10.1016/j.jempfin.2016.01.011.

Lee, W. Y., C. X. Jiang, and D. C. Indro. 2002. Stock market volatility, excess returns, and the role of investor sentiment. *Journal of Banking & Finance* 26 (12):2277–99. doi:10.1016/S0378-4266(01)00202-3.

Li, M., X. X. Zhang, and J. Z. Zhao. 2020. The active fiscal policy trend and the finance-taxation system reform in China after the epidemic. *Management World* 4:26–34. doi:10.19744/j.cnki.11-1235/f.2020.0050.

Liu, L., E.-Z. Wang, and -C.-C. Lee. 2020. Impact of the COVID-19 pandemic on the crude oil and stock markets in the US: A time-varying analysis. *Energy Research Letters* 1 (1):13154. doi:10.46557/001c.13154

Mctier, B. C., Y. Tse, and J. K. Wald. 2011. Do stock markets catch the flu? *Journal of Financial & Quantitative Analysis* 48 (3):979–1000. doi:10.1017/S0022109013000239.

Mei-Ping, C., L. Chien-Chiang, L. Yu-Hui, and C. Wen-Yi. 2018. Did the S.A.R.S. epidemic weaken the integration of Asian stock markets? Evidence from smooth time-varying cointegration analysis. *Economic Research-Ekonomska Istraivanja* 31 (1):908–26. doi:10.1080/1331677X.2018.1456354.

Moskowitz, T. J., and M. Grinblatt. 1999. Do Industries Explain Momentum? *The Journal of Finance* 54 (4):1249–90. doi:10.1111/0022-1082.00146.

Narayan, P. K. 2020. Oil price news and COVID-19—is there any connection? *Energy Research Letters* 1 (1):2138–2150. doi:10.1080/1540496X.2020.1784719.

Narayan, P. K., and D. H. B. Phan. 2020. Country responses and the reaction of the stock market to COVID-19—A preliminary exposition. *Emerging Markets Finance and Trade* 56 (10):2138–2150. doi:10.1080/1540496X.2020.1784719.

Nikkinen, J., M. M. Omran, and M. P. Sahlstr. 2008. Stock returns and volatility following the september 11 attacks: Evidence from 53 equity markets. *International Review of Financial Analysis* 17 (1):27–46. doi:10.1016/j.irfa.2006.12.002.

Qin, M., Y.-C. Zhang, and C.-W. Su. 2020. The essential role of pandemics: A fresh insight into the oil market. *Energy Research Letters* 1 (1):13166. doi:10.46557/001c.13166

Ragin, M. A., and M. Halek. 2016. Market expectations following catastrophes: An examination of insurance broker returns. *The Journal of Risk and Insurance* 83 (4):849–76. doi:10.1111/jori.12069.

Reilly, J. (2020). Treatment considerations for coronavirus (COVID-19). *Hospital Practice.* doi:10.1080/21548331.2020.1754618

Rengasamy, E. 2012. Sovereign debt crisis in the euro zone and its impact on the BRICS's stock index returns and volatility. *Economics and Finance Review* 2 (2):37–46.

Righi, M. B., and P. S. Ceretta. 2011. Analyzing the structural behavior of volatility in the major European markets during the Greek crisis. *Economics Bulletin* 31 (4):3016–29. doi:10.1016/S0169-8141(02)00133-6.

Saadat, S., D. Rawtani, and C. M. Hussain. 2020. Environmental perspective of COVID-19. *Science of the Total Environment* 728:138–870. doi:10.1016/j.scitotenv.2020.138870.

Schwert, G. W. 2011. Stock volatility during the recent financial crisis. *European Financial Management* 17 (5):789–805. doi:10.1111/j.1468-036X.2011.00620.x.

Sobieralski, J. B. 2020. Covid-19 and airline employment: Insights from historical uncertainty shocks to the industry. *Transportation Research Interdisciplinary Perspectives* 5:100–23. doi:10.1016/j.trip.2020.100123.

Yang, Z. H., Y. T. Chen, and P. M. Zhang. 2020. Macroeconomic shock, financial risk transmission and governance response to major public emergencies. *Management World* 5:13–35. doi:10.19744/j.cnki.11-1235/f.2020.0067.

Yin, Z. C., H. Z. Lu, and B. X. Pan. 2020. The impact of the Sino-US trade war on China's stock market: An event-based analysis. *Journal of Management* 33 (1):18–28. doi:10.19808/j.cnki.41-1408/F.2020.01.003.

The Impact of the COVID-19 Pandemic on Firm Performance

Huayu Shen (ID), Mengyao Fu, Hongyu Pan, Zhongfu Yu, and Yongquan Chen

ABSTRACT

Using the financial data of listed Chinese companies, we study the impact of COVID-19 on corporate performance. We show that COVID-19 has a negative impact on firm performance. The negative impact of COVID-19 on firm performance is more pronounced when a firm's investment scale or sales revenue is smaller. We show, in an additional analysis, that the negative impact of COVID-19 on firm performance is more pronounced in serious-impact areas and industries. These findings are among the first empirical evidence of the association between pandemic and firm performance.

1. Introduction

The outbreak of the novel coronavirus (COVID-19) brought seriously affected health care, economy, transportation, and other fields in different industries and regions. Population mobility sharply dropped, as a result of the quarantine policy, which led to weakened spending power and a stagnant economy. At the macro level, the COVID-19 outbreak caused the worst global recession since 1930, when the economy got absolutely creamed. The gross domestic product of China fell by 6.8% in the first quarter compared with the same period last year,[1] and many countries suffered severe corporate bankruptcies and job losses (Fu and Shen 2020). At the firm-level, the COVID-19 outbreak may affect the stock market (Iyke 2020a; Liu, Wang, and Lee 2020; Narayan and Phan 2020), firm performance in the energy industry (Fu and Shen 2020) and other aspects (Hagerty and Williams 2020). It is necessary to evaluate the impact of such major public health emergencies on corporate performance in these tough economic times, as the listed companies are the base component of national economy. Investigations suggest that internal factors of the financial system may be the main causes of the economic decline in the recent years (Zubair, Kabir, and Huang 2020). For instance, the economic "stagflation" of the 1970s was caused by the soaring oil prices during this period and the economic depression of 2008 was caused by subprime mortgage crisis (Zubair,

Kabir, and Huang 2020). Nevertheless, the recent recession is due to external factors, mostly resulting from the mandatory policy of lockdowns following the COVID-19 pandemic. Therefore, the methods for analyzing and measuring the economic impact of financial crises cannot be applied under the COVID outbreak. At present, there are limited methodologies for assessing the impact of emergencies, especially the impact of the COVID-19 pandemic, on the economy, industries, and firms.

This paper is divided into two parts: performance forecasting and quantifying the impact of COVID-19. Firstly, we use the financial data of listed Chinese companies from 2013 to 2019 to predict their performance in the first quarter of 2020. The forecast results are compared with the actual value to chart the pandemic impact on firm-level performance in different industries. Further, we use the financial data of the first quarter of 2014–2020 to quantify the pandemic impact. We use investment growth and total revenue as moderating variables to investigate the mechanism of the pandemic impact. Finally, we divide the listed companies into high- and low-affected groups by region and industry dimensions. We then use a Differences-in-Differences (DID) model to quantify the impact of COVID-19 on firm performance along the two dimensions. We find that the COVID-19 outbreak resulted in a decline in corporate performance, both by industry and region dimensions. More investment and income would effectively reduce the negative impact of the pandemic. In the robustness tests, we considered alternative dependent variables and used the propensity score matching (PSM) method. We also performed a contractual test as part of the robustness tests. The results in the robustness tests are consistent with the main ones.

The paper contributes to the literature as follows. Firstly, we investigated the impact of COVID-19 on corporate performance in different regions and industries for the first time. Studies on the impact of the COVID pandemic on the economy mostly focused on the macro level. Extant studies investigated the connection between COVID-19 and oil price (Gil-Alana and Monge 2020; Narayan 2020), COVID-19 and exchange rates (Iyke 2020b), and the impact of COVID-19 on US partisan conflict index (Apergis and Apergis 2020). In this paper, we shifted the perspective to corporate performance at the regional, industry, and firm levels, quantifying the impact of COVID-19 using the DID method. Secondly, we explored the mechanisms through which COVID-19 affects corporate performance. We found that the COVID-19 outbreak reduced corporate revenues, which ultimately led to lower performance, implying that increasing investment and income will reduce the negative impact of the pandemic. Thirdly, this paper enriches the literature measuring the impact of major public health emergencies on economy. Country responses and the reaction of the stock market to COVID-19 are previously discussed (Liu, Wang, and Lee 2020; Narayan and Phan 2020). Our analysis is novel in that we examine how COVID-19 influences corporate performance.

This paper also proposes an empirical method to evaluate the impact of the pandemic on corporate performance in different Chinese industries at the provincial level.

The remainder of this paper is arranged as follows. Section 2 presents the theoretical analysis and research hypotheses. Section 3 outlines the samples and methods. Sections 4 and 5, respectively, present the empirical results and robustness tests. Section 6 concludes the paper.

2. Theoretical Analysis and Research Hypotheses

2.1. COVID-19 and Firm Performance

COVID-19 is a major health emergency worldwide. More than seven million people have been diagnosed worldwide, since January 2020,[2] and several countries and regions are affected by the pandemic. Countries are forced to adopt quarantine measures because of the highly infectiousness nature of COVID-19. These measures have a great negative impact on aggregate demand, especially on consumption and exports. On the one hand, people were asked to go out less, and crowded places such as shopping malls were shut down. On the other hand, several countries imposed restrictions on import to prevent viral transmission, which greatly hit export-oriented businesses in China. Consequently, gross domestic product of China decreased by 6.8% in the first quarter of 2020. Extant studies investigated the connection between COVID-19 and oil price (Gil-Alana and Monge 2020; Narayan 2020), while few studies examined the impact of COVID-19 on the performance of public companies. Based on this analysis, we proposed the following research hypothesis:

H_{1-1}: *Ceteris paribus*, COVID-19 has a negative impact on the performance of listed companies.

Via which channel, however, does the COVID-19 affect corporate performance? According to the real options theory, managers tend to defer investment when uncertainties rise, which may lead to miss profitable projects (Zeng et al. 2016). COVID-19 brings higher external risks, which lead managers to increase their cash holdings in case of emergencies. More cash retention takes up the investment funds and reduces enterprises' momentum of sustainable development. In the short term, based on Maslow's hierarchy of needs, Consumers' demand for health and safety is more urgent than that for social contact during the pandemic, resulting in a shrinking demand (Hagerty and Williams 2020). These factors lead to a decline in corporate revenue, and ultimately a decline in corporate performance. The companies' productivity and revenue declined sharply due to the implementation of the quarantine measures, which inevitably led to performance decline. Based on this analysis, we hypothesized that:

H_{1-2}: *Ceteris paribus*, when the firm's investment scale is smaller, the negative impact of COVID-19 on firm performance is more pronounced.

H_{1-3}: *Ceteris paribus*, the negative impact of COVID-19 on firm performance is more pronounced, if a firm's sales revenue is less.

2.2. The Impact of COVID-19 on the Sector Dimension

A sector refers to the detailed division of the organizational structure system of business units or individuals engaged in homogenous production in the national economy (Phan, Sharma, and Narayan 2015). Sector classification can explain the development stage of the industry itself and its status in the national economy. Previous studies investigated that country responses and the reaction of the stock market to COVID-19 (Narayan and Phan 2020), and the impact of COVID-19 on US partisan conflict index (Apergis and Apergis 2020). The drawback of investigating the impact of the pandemic at the aggregate market level is that such an investigation assumes a homogeneous impact on sectorial performance – which implies that COVID-19 has the same impact for all sectors. Narayan and Sharma (2011) argue that sectors are heterogenous and therefore are likely to react to market shocks differently. Phan, Sharma, and Narayan (2015) also found strong evidence that return predictability has links to certain industry characteristics. Therefore, the supply–demand relationship varies with the characteristics of the industry during the pandemic.

Which sectors are hard hit by the outbreak? Tourism, film and TV entertainment, catering retail, and transportation sectors are the most affected industries in China (Fu and Shen 2020). Following the restrictions, civil aviation during the 2020 Spring Festival travel rush period decreased by 29.5%.[3] Many countries canceled Chinese flights and imposed immigration controls on international routes following the COVID-19 outbreak, which greatly and negatively impacted China's transportation industry in the first quarter. In addition, the highly anticipated movies in the Chinese Spring Festival season pulled from the shelves before their release, and cinemas closed for a short time to prevent people from gathering in confined space. Based on historical data, the box office of Chinese New Year movies accounted for about 21% to 32% of the annual box office.[4] However, the withdrawal of Chinese New Year movies this year caused loss in production costs, marketing costs, and other expenses, which is difficult to be estimated. Tourism has also been seriously affected by the pandemic. The winter holiday and Spring Festival are the peak seasons for Chinese tourism, which were shut down during the pandemic. The tourism industry has been hit by the closure of many scenic spots in China under the quarantine policy, as well as the cancellation of international flights and immigration controls. Based on this analysis, we hypothesized that:

H_2: *Ceteris paribus*, the COVID-19 pandemic has a negative impact on the performance of enterprises in serious-impact industries. That is, the enterprises in serious-impact industries have lower performance than those in other industries, following the pandemic.

2.3. Pandemic Impact in the Regional Dimension

A common feature of all recent studies on COVID-19's economic impacts is that they focus on the aggregate market. Gil-Alana and Monge (2020) investigated the relationship between crude oil prices and COVID-19, finding a persistent shock on oil prices. Narayan and Phan (2020) also discussed the country responses and the reaction of the stock market to COVID-19. In other words, these studies take a macro perspective in analyzing the role of COVID-19 in determining the fluctuations in economies. However, extant research found that the incremental impact of the degree and speed of operations within a given region, is greater for regions exhibiting faster economic growth than others exhibiting slower growth (Demirbag, Glaister, and Sengupta 2019). This means the impact of COVID-19 on corporate performance has obvious regional heterogeneity, since the growth rate is different across regions. Therefore, the region where the enterprise operates plays a crucial role in strategic selection and operation management.

After China began its comprehensive fight against the pandemic, seven provinces – Henan, Hunan, Jiangxi, Anhui, Zhejiang, Guangdong, and Hubei – implemented tight restrictions on labor and delayed the resumption of work.[5] In contrast, for those cities located far away from the epicenter with a low rate of staff turnover, the time for resumption will be significantly earlier. By the end of February, the resumption of work in 31 provinces reached more than 50%, while Hubei province was still in line.[6] According to the signal theory, early resumption of work gives managers a signal of reduced risk (Fu and Shen 2020). These companies will end their cash crisis earlier and invest more capital in profitable projects. In addition, lenders in these regions, such as banks and investment institutions, will also be affected by risk reduction signals, thus reducing the financing constraints on enterprises in these regions. Early resumption provides these companies more time and capital to cope with the decline in corporate performance, which may make a great difference. To sum up, we hypothesized that:

H₃: *Ceteris paribus*, the COVID-19 pandemic has a negative impact on corporate performance in the serious-impact regions. That is, corporate performance in the serious-impact regions is lower than in other regions.

3. Data and Model

We used the financial data of listed Chinese companies from 2013 to 2019 to predict corporate performance in t + 1 period, i.e. 2014–2020. Then, we selected data for the first quarter from 2014 to 2020 as the research sample to investigate the pandemic impact on corporate performance. We excluded the following data to make it more comparable: (1) ST, *ST, and other financially distressed companies, and kept the data for companies in normal operation; (2) data for companies in the banking, securities, and other financial industries due to the incomparability; (3) companies with missing data. In order to reduce the impact of outliers, we winsorized the continuous variables at 1% and 99% levels. All data are from the China Stock Market & Accounting Research (CSMAR) database.

We adopted the following model to predict corporate performance:

$$NROA_{it+1} = \beta_0 + \beta_1 SIZE_{it} + \beta_2 LEV_{it} + \beta_3 GROWTH_{it} + \beta_4 HF10_{it} + \beta_5 LIQ_{it} + \beta_6 INDUSTRY + \beta_7 YEAR + \varepsilon_{it}$$

(1)

In order to test the impact of the COVID-19 pandemic on corporate performance and the mechanism underlying this impact, we used the following models:

$$NROA_{it} = \beta_0 + \beta_1 CNCA_{it} * Period_{it} + \beta_2 CNCA_{it} + \beta_3 Period_{it} + \beta_4 SIZE_{it} + \beta_5 LEV_{it} + \beta_6 GROWTH_{it} + \beta_7 HF10_{it} + \beta_8 FCF_{it} + \beta_9 TR_{it} + \beta_{10} INDUSTRY + \beta_{911} YEAR + \varepsilon_{it}$$

(2)

$$NROA_{it} = \beta_0 + \beta_1 REV_{it} * Period_{it} + \beta_2 REV_{it} + \beta_3 Period_{it} + \beta_4 SIZE_{it} + \beta_5 LEV_{it} + \beta_6 GROWTH_{it} + \beta_7 HF10_{it} + \beta_8 FCF_{it} + \beta_9 TR_{it} + \beta_{10} INDUSTRY + \beta_{11} YEAR + \varepsilon_{it}$$

(3)

To further explore the dimensions impact of the COVID-19 pandemic, we adopted the following DID model:

$$NROA_{it} = \beta_0 + \beta_1 treated_i * period_{it} + \beta_2 treated_i + \beta_3 period_{it} + \beta_4 SIZE_{it} + \beta_5 LEV_{it} + \beta_6 GROWTH_{it} + \beta_7 HF10_{it} + \beta_8 FCF_{it} + \beta_9 TR_{it} + \beta_{10} INDUSTRY + \beta_{11} YEAR + \varepsilon_{it}$$

(4)

where the dependent variable, *NROA*, is the net profit return rate, which represents the company's performance status; *period* is a dummy variable of the outbreak point; *treated* is a dummy variable of "pandemic impact degree". Investment growth rate (*CNCA*) and total revenue (*REV*) are moderating variables in the pandemic–performance relationship. When the research is carried out in an industry dimension, the classification criteria for the *treated* are as follows. According to the China securities regulatory commission's 2012 industry classification guidelines, all listed companies are divided into 18 categories. We have identified the following eight industries as high-impact groups, which are tourism, film and television entertainment, catering retail, transportation, realty business, construction, accommodation, and export manufacturing industries. These industries, which are characterized by personnel intensity, social interaction, and cross-border trade, have been greatly affected by the policies implemented in response to the COVID-19 outbreak; for instance, there was a sharp drop in demand. Other industries are classified as low-impact industries. The place of incorporation is the basic data of grouping when taking region as the research dimension. According to the number of confirmed cases in all provinces on March 26, 2020,[7] the areas with a cumulative number of confirmed cases of more than 500 people were considered as high-impact areas, and others as low-impact areas. The following provinces and cities were listed as high-impact areas: Hubei, Guangdong, Henan, Zhejiang, Hunan, Anhui, Jiangxi, Shandong, Jiangsu, Chongqing, Sichuan, and Beijing. We believe that the first quarter will be the main period affected by COVID-19, since the outbreak of the pandemic (i.e. since January to February 2020) in China.

This paper focuses on the regression coefficient of *treated ∗ period*. If the coefficient is negative, it means that the pandemic has a negative effect on the performance of the enterprises; otherwise, it has a positive effect. Following the studies on factors affecting corporate performance (see, example, Fu and Shen 2020), we include, as controls, enterprise size (*SIZE*), asset-liability ratio (*LEV*), revenue growth rate (*GROWTH*), the share held by the top 10 shareholders (*HF*10), free cash flow (*FCF*), and trade receivable turnover (*TR*). In addition, we control for industry and annual-fixed effects. The main variables and related definitions used in the model are shown in Table 1.

4. Empirical Results

4.1. Performance Forecast

Granziera and Sekhposyan (2019) found that business cycle indicators, financial conditions, uncertainty, and measures of past relative performances are generally useful for explaining models' relative forecasting performances. Through the comparison of performance forecast and actual data, information

Table 1. Variable definitions.

Variables	Descriptions
NROA	Net profit margin on total assets, net profit/ending balance on total assets
Treated	The dummy variable of "outbreak impact degree" is 1 if the enterprise belongs to the high-impact region/industry, otherwise it is 0.
Period	The dummy variable of "outbreak time" is 1 after the outbreak, or 0 otherwise.
CNCA	Growth rate of fixed assets is measured as: (ending value of net fixed assets for the current period – initial value of net fixed assets for the current period)/(initial value of net fixed assets for the current period)
REV	The logarithm of total revenue for the current period
SIZE	The size of an enterprise is measured by the logarithm of its total assets
LEV	The asset-liability ratio is the total liabilities/total assets measure
GROWTH	Growth rate of operating income, i.e. (current operating income – previous operating income)/ previous operating income
HF10	The Herfindahl index 10, or the share held by the top 10 shareholders
FCF	Free cash flow, EBITDA + depreciation and amortization – working capital increase – capital expenditure
TR	Trade receivable turnover/1000, Trade receivable turnover = operating revenue/average trade receivable balance
INDUSTRY	Used to control industry fixed effect
YEAR	Used to control the fixed effect of year

This table introduces all the variables used in the above four models and their definition descriptions.

users will have a more convenient and intuitive understanding of the impact of COVID-19 on the performance of listed companies, which are the basic component of national economy.

We predicted the performance of various industries in the first quarter of 2020 using Model (1), and predicted values are presented in Figure 1. The horizontal (i.e. x) axis corresponds to the industry names, as shown in Table 2. The results show that all sectors were affected by the COVID-19 pandemic, with the actual performance 0.005 below the predicted performance and thus supporting hypothesis H_1. The hardest-hit sectors by the pandemic were accommodation and catering, followed by education. Under the impact of the outbreak, the net profit margin of total assets in the accommodation and catering industry was −0.02, which was significantly lower than other industries. This sector was virtually shut down in the first quarter due to the emergency quarantine measures implemented across the entire country. Meanwhile, the winter vacation, during which extracurricular tutoring is usually carried out, was wasted, and the education industry lost most revenue in the first quarter.

4.2. Descriptive Statistics

Table 3 reports the descriptive statistics of the main variables studied in this paper, which are based on the financial data from 2014 to 2020. The average value of NROA is 0.008, and the median value is 0.006, indicating that the overall profitability of listed companies is not high or these companies are on the edge of profitability. The average value of CNCA is −0.0039; thus, enterprises have reduced the investment in fixed assets on average. The income

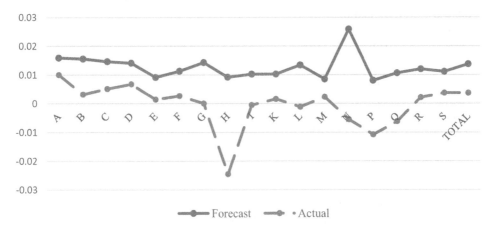

Figure 1. Forecast and actual value of industry performance in 2020 Q1. Calculated and plotted according to the financial data of China's listed companies from 2013 to 2020.

Table 2. Industry code descriptions.

Code	Descriptions
A	Agriculture, forestry, animal husbandry and fishery
B	The mining industry
C	Manufacturing
D	Electricity, heat, gas and water production and supply industries
E	Construction
F	Wholesale and retail
G	Transportation, warehousing and postal services
H	Accommodation and catering
I	Information transmission, software and information technology services
K	Leasing and business services
L	Scientific research and technical services
M	Water, environment and utilities management
N	Residential services, repairs and other services
P	Education
Q	Health and social work
R	Culture, sport and entertainment
S	Comprehensive

This table reports the descriptions of Industry code. The information comes from the industry code issued by China securities regulatory commission in 2012.

levels of listed companies vary greatly, with a standard deviation of 1.5456. After logarithmic calculation, the standard deviation of enterprise scale is 1.280, with a maximum value of 26.231 and a minimum value of 19.917, which reflects the large difference in the size of listed enterprises. The average asset-liability ratio is 0.417, which is kept at a reasonable level and plays a good leverage role. The average growth rate of operating income is −0.194, and the median is −0.195, which reflects the trend of the decline of the overall operating income. The average value of the Herfindahl index 10 is 0.156, which means the average equity concentration is not high; the associated standard deviation is 0.112. Free cash flow reflects the cash flow strain of the enterprise, and the average value of −0.162 reflects a relatively tight cash flow. The trade

Table 3. Descriptive statistics.

Variables	N	Mean	SD	Min	Max	P50
NROA	11,921	0.008	0.013	−0.023	0.056	0.006
CNCA	11,921	−0.0039	0.0596	−0.1348	0.3906	−0.0147
REV	11,921	20.0648	1.5456	16.2403	24.2174	19.9649
SIZE	11,921	22.364	1.280	19.917	26.231	22.189
LEV	11,921	0.417	0.206	0.051	0.893	0.405
GROWTH	11,921	−0.194	0.349	−0.881	1.278	−0.195
HF10	11,921	0.156	0.112	0.015	0.551	0.124
FCF	11,921	−0.162	1.642	−9.437	6.397	−0.027
TR	11,921	0.007	0.023	0.00004	0.181	0.001

This table reports the result of descriptive statistics; all variables are provided in Table 1.

receivable turnover rate shows large standard deviation, which reflects the different efficiency of different enterprises in the operation of assets.

4.3. Unit Root and Parallel Trend Tests

In order to ensure the reliability of the results, we carried out unit root and parallel trend tests. These also ensure the stability of the data. All variables passed the unit root test at the 1% level, and the data were stable. According to the results of parallel trend test, the performance variation trend of the high-impact group and the low-impact group was similar before the pandemic outbreak in early 2020, which could be further modeled. The parallel trend test results are presented in Figures 2 and 3.

4.4. Regression Results

We first considered the impact of COVID-19 on corporate performance and the mechanisms underlying this impact. We took operating investment growth rate (*CNCA*) and total revenue (*REV*) as the moderating variables. The empirical results are shown in Table 4. Panel A reports the pandemic's impact on corporate performance. The coefficient of *period* is −0.0044 and is significant at 1% level. COVID-19 has a negative impact on performance, which leads to the decline of the profit margin, thus supporting hypothesis H_{1-1}. Panels B and C report results for investment and revenue moderating effect, respectively. In Panel B, the regression coefficient of the core variable *period* is −0.0042, which is significant at the 1% level, indicating that the COVID-19 pandemic has a great negative impact on the corporate performance. The coefficient of *CNCA* * *period* is 8.8008, which is significant at the 5% level. The signs of the two variables are different, indicating that high fixed asset investment will weaken the negative impact of the pandemic on corporate performance. In Panel C, the coefficient of *REV* * *period* is 0.0009 and is significant at the 1% level. This is contrary to the *period* coefficient of −0.0030, indicating that an increase in corporate income will weaken the negative

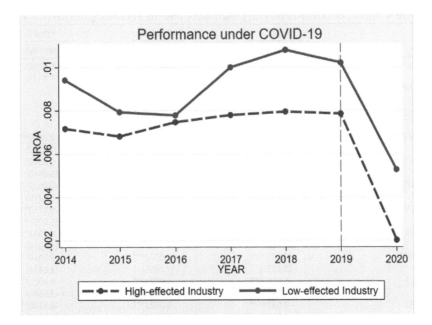

Figure 2. Parallel trend test in industry dimension. Calculated and plotted according to the financial data of China's listed companies from 2014 to 2020.

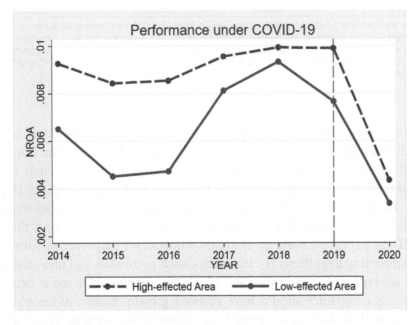

Figure 3. Parallel trend test in region dimension. Calculated and plotted according to the financial data of China's listed companies from 2013 to 2020.

impact of the pandemic. The results support hypotheses H_{1-2} and H_{1-3}, respectively.

Table 4. Impact of COVID-19 on firm performance and the influencing mechanism test.

	Panel A	Panel B	Panel C
	Baseline	Investment	Revenue
Period	−0.0044***	−0.0042***	−0.0030***
	(−13.9575)	(−13.4412)	(−9.8444)
CNCA*Period		8.8008**	
		(2.0625)	
CNCA		2.8315*	
		(1.9356)	
REV*Period			0.0009***
			(3.8237)
REV			0.0062***
			(35.0446)
SIZE	0.0026***	0.0026***	−0.0037***
	(17.3273)	(17.2104)	(−15.8219)
LEV	−0.0235***	−0.0235***	−0.0250***
	(−31.5029)	(−31.5544)	(−35.0957)
GROWTH	0.0074***	0.0074***	0.0041***
	(24.7820)	(24.7087)	(13.6314)
HF10	0.0072***	0.0072***	0.0049***
	(5.1331)	(5.1655)	(3.6431)
FCF	−0.0002***	−0.0002***	−0.0002***
	(−4.5577)	(−4.6000)	(−3.6845)
TR	0.0324***	0.0322***	0.0140***
	(6.0869)	(6.0564)	(2.7502)
Constant	−0.0413***	−0.0408***	−0.0238***
	(−11.8996)	(−11.7881)	(−7.0254)
IND	Yes	Yes	Yes
YEAR	Yes	Yes	Yes
N	11,914	11,914	11,914
Adj-R^2	0.3758	0.3780	0.3825

The mechanism of pandemic's impact on corporate performance. This table reports the results of the regressions by investment and revenue moderating effects. The dependent variable is net return on assets. Columns (1) shows the pandemic impact. Columns (2) and Columns (3) shows the moderating effect of investment and revenue. Significance levels of 10%, 5%, and 1% are denoted by *, **, and ***, respectively.

Further, we grouped the enterprises using the degree of COVID-19 impact by industry and region for our analysis. The DID estimates of the impact of COVID-19 on corporate performance are shown in Table 5. Panels D and E show the results for high-impact industries and high-impact regions, respectively. In Panel D, the regression coefficient of the core variable *treated * period* is −0.0011, which is significant at the 5% level, indicating that the COVID-19 pandemic has a great negative impact on corporate performance, thus supporting hypothesis H_2. Industries, such as tourism and film entertainment, are typically service-oriented, which are influenced by social networking. These companies should have realized growth mostly, as people have more spare time during the Spring Festival and winter holiday. However, the ban on overseas travel and the withdrawal of films drove revenues downward, leading to a negative impact of COVID-19 on performance in these industries. The pandemic is the decisive factor that caused a significant decline in the performance of high-impact industries.

Table 5. Impact of COVID-19 on firm performance between serious impact industry and region.

	Panel D	Panel E
	Industry	Region
Treated*period	−0.0011**	−0.0011**
	(−2.5058)	(−2.1782)
Treated	−0.0012***	0.0017***
	(−2.6339)	(3.8288)
Period	−0.0040***	−0.0035***
	(−11.3798)	(−6.9329)
SIZE	0.0026***	0.0026***
	(17.3459)	(17.3910)
LEV	−0.0234***	−0.0232***
	(−31.4776)	(−31.2051)
GROWTH	0.0073***	0.0074***
	(24.5227)	(24.7822)
HF10	0.0070***	0.0072***
	(4.9580)	(5.1005)
FCF	−0.0002***	−0.0002***
	(−4.5411)	(−4.5273)
TR	0.0319***	0.0332***
	(5.9898)	(6.2480)
Constant	−0.0414***	−0.0424***
	(−11.9230)	(−12.2156)
IND	Yes	Yes
YEAR	Yes	Yes
N	11,921	11,921
Adj-R^2	0.3779	0.3793

The impact of COVID-19 on corporate performance. This table reports the original regression results both in industry dimension and regional dimension. The dependent variable is net return on assets. Columns (1) shows the original regression results in industry dimension. Columns (2) show the regression results in regional dimension. Significance levels of 10%, 5%, and 1% are denoted by **, and ***, respectively.

In Panel E, the regression coefficient of the core variable *treated * period* is −0.0011 and significant at the 5% level, as shown by the results without the PSM method. Taking the region as the criterion, the pandemic has a significant negative impact on the serious-impact regions, which is reflected by the decline in corporate performance. To curb the spread of the pandemic, governments of these regions adopted policies that restricted the movement of people. This led to lower consumption levels and the shutdown of many firms in the high-impact areas. Both consumption and production decreased or stagnated, while fixed costs remained at the same level. As a result, corporate performance in high-impact regions declined, which supports hypothesis H$_3$.

5. Robustness Tests

In order to ensure the credibility of the results by reducing the deviation caused by errors, we used the PSM method, alternative dependent variables, and a counterfactual test. This forms our robustness tests. The test results are shown in Tables 6 and 7.

5.1. Estimates Using the PSM Method

We used the PSM method to shrink the sample size along two dimensions. The results presented in the first column of Table 6 suggest that the coefficient of the interaction term after the PSM is −0.0014 and is significant at the 1% level, which supports hypothesis H_2 that the pandemic has a significant negative effect on the high-impact industry. We repeated the analysis for the regional dimension. The results suggest that, after the PSM, the coefficient of the interaction term is −0.0019 and is significant at the 1% level, which supported hypothesis H_3 that the pandemic has a significant negative effect on the high-impact areas.

5.2. Estimates Based on Alternative Dependent Variables

We measured corporate performance using the return on equity (ROE), and established the following model:

$$ROE_{it} = \beta_0 + \beta_1 treated_i * period_{it} + \beta_2 treated_i + \beta_3 period_{it} + \beta_4 SIZE_{it}$$
$$+ \beta_5 LEV_{it} + \beta_6 GROWTH_{it} + \beta_7 HF10_{it} + \beta_8 FCF_{it} + \beta_9 TR_{it}$$
$$+ \Sigma INDUSTRY + \Sigma YEAR + \varepsilon_{it} \tag{5}$$

Table 6. Robustness test.

	Panel D	Panel E	Panel F	
	PS Matched	PS Matched	Industry	Regional
Treated*period	−0.0014***	−0.0019***	−0.0029***	−0.0022**
	(−2.7914)	(−2.6371)	(−3.2028)	(−2.1598)
Treated	−0.0012**	0.0011**	−0.0011	0.0037***
	(−2.4402)	(2.2414)	(−1.3556)	(4.6900)
Period	−0.0033***	−0.0037***	−0.0063***	−0.0056***
	(−7.1919)	(−6.1599)	(−9.2014)	(−5.6206)
SIZE	0.0025***	0.0030***	0.0052***	0.0051***
	(15.0676)	(14.9585)	(18.5482)	(18.5777)
LEV	−0.0230***	−0.0295***	−0.0308***	−0.0304***
	(−27.0570)	(−28.3515)	(−21.8226)	(−21.5304)
GROWTH	0.0081***	0.0090***	0.0140***	0.0141***
	(22.3192)	(19.3332)	(24.0244)	(24.2705)
HF10	0.0070***	0.0037**	0.0153***	0.0155***
	(4.5069)	(2.0037)	(5.9114)	(6.0212)
FCF	−0.0001***	−0.0001*	−0.0005***	−0.0005***
	(−2.7228)	(−1.8196)	(−5.2885)	(−5.2909)
TR	0.0345***	0.0171***	0.0626***	0.0657***
	(6.4002)	(4.6247)	(6.1643)	(6.4801)
Constant	−0.0391***	−0.0481***	−0.0916***	−0.0935***
	(−10.4418)	(−10.9685)	(−14.5804)	(−14.9020)
IND	Yes	Yes	Yes	Yes
YEAR	Yes	Yes	Yes	Yes
N	8,316	5,446	11,900	11,900
Adj-R^2	0.3758	0.3649	0.3190	0.3253

The impact of COVID-19 on corporate performance. This table reports the results of the regressions of original regression results, results after propensity score matched method and results of alternative dependent variable test. The dependent variable is net return on assets in Columns (1) and (2), and returns on equity in Columns (3) and Columns (4). Columns (1) shows the regression results after PS-matched in industry dimension. Columns (2) show the regression results after PS-matched in regional dimension. Columns (3) reports regression results in industry dimension and Columns (4) reports results in regional dimension. Significance levels of 10%, 5%, and 1% are denoted by *, **, and ***, respectively.

Table 7. Placebo test.

	Panel G	
	Industry	Regional
Treated*period	−0.0005	−0.0003
	(−1.2033)	(−0.6815)
Treated	−0.0012**	0.0015***
	(−2.3202)	(2.9773)
Period	−0.0044***	−0.0043***
	(−11.0524)	(−8.2611)
SIZE	0.0030***	0.0030***
	(17.3977)	(17.4315)
LEV	−0.0261***	−0.0260***
	(−30.4105)	(−30.1757)
GROWTH	0.0082***	0.0082***
	(23.1464)	(23.3905)
HF10	0.0068***	0.0070***
	(4.2646)	(4.4160)
FCF	−0.0003***	−0.0003***
	(−4.3330)	(−4.3500)
TR	0.0386***	0.0398***
	(6.2336)	(6.4330)
Constant	−0.0475***	−0.0484***
	(−12.2568)	(−12.4761)
IND	Yes	Yes
YEAR	Yes	Yes
N	11,921	11,921
Adj-R^2	0.3694	0.3703

The impact of COVID-19 on corporate performance. This table reports the results of the regressions of original regression results both in industry dimension and regional dimension. The dependent variable is net return on assets. Columns (1) shows the original regression results in industry dimension. Columns (2) show the regression results in regional dimension. Significance levels of 10%, 5%, and 1% are denoted by **, and ***, respectively.

We estimated this regression and reported the results in Panel F of Table 6. The first column reflects the impact of the pandemic on different industries. The interaction term coefficient is −0.0029 and is significant at the 1% level, indicating that the pandemic has a significant negative effect on corporate performance in the high-impact industries. The second column reflects the pandemic's impact along the regional dimension. The coefficient of the interaction term is −0.0022 and is significant at the 5% level, indicating that corporate performance in the high-impact regions is greatly affected by the negative impact of the pandemic. The pandemic had a significant restricting effect on production and sales, which eventually led to the decline of corporate performance. This analysis proves that the results are robust.

5.3. Placebo Test

We used a placebo experiment to perform the counterfactual analysis. To do this, we replaced the DID time point year 2020 with 2019, 2018, and 2017,[8] and the results are shown in Table 7 (see Guariso and Verpoorten 2018). The effect of the pandemic on corporate performance is neither significant in the industry dimension nor in the regional dimension, indicating that the main results are robust.

6. Conclusion

Focusing on firm-level performance, this paper comprehensively discusses the impact of the COVID-19 pandemic on corporate performance and its mechanism. We also make a further discussion on the pandemic impact along two dimensions: serious-impact industries and serious-impact regions. Our study found that the COVID-19 outbreak has a significant negative impact on the performance of listed Chinese companies by decreasing investment scales and reducing the total revenue. For the industries affected by the pandemic, such as tourism, catering, and transportation, there is a significant decline in corporate performance in the first quarter of 2020. The pandemic has a negative impact on the production, operation, and sales of these industries, which is eventually reflected in the negative return rate. Along the regional dimension, the negative impact is much more pronounced in high-affected areas as strict quarantine measures limit consumptions and productions, sending a negative signal to managers and its stakeholders. Financial constraints may make the operation even harder in the pandemic (COVID-19).

Compared with the SARS pandemic of 2003, the development of transportation infrastructure increased the speed of population flow, which led to a faster spread of COVID-19. From the perspective of COVID-19 pandemic prevention, the quarantine measures across the country effectively hindered the spread of the pandemic. However, the production and consumption are limited at the same time, leading to a sluggish market and declining corporate performance in the first quarter. The pandemic exerted great downward pressure on China's macroeconomy. Fortunately, the impact has a large scope but with a short duration. If the pandemic can be effectively controlled, the fluctuations of the first quarter's performance will not change the positive trend of global economy in a long time.

The negative impact of the pandemic on the global economy is severe, while the prevention and control of the COVID-19 pandemic are at a crucial stage. Focusing on corporate performance, there will be great fluctuations in the first and second quarters of 2020. Key industries, such as tourism and catering, may become the "epicenter" of the pandemic's impact. In addition to preventing and controlling the spread of the pandemic, countries should gradually give support to the industries that are likely to be severely affected by the pandemic, offering various subsidies and preferential policies to the enterprises in the worst-hit areas, so as to enable them to smoothly weather the pandemic storm. Managers should pay attention to the changing environment outside and adjust their business strategies in time. It is vital to make the production and operation meet the consumption trend of "post-pandemic era," to promptly restore the operation.

For investors, they should correctly view the fluctuation of returns during the COVID-19 pandemic and accordingly control the risks associated with their financial assets.

Notes

1. Data from China's monetary policy implementation report for the first quarter of 2020. http://www.pbc.gov.cn/goutongjiaoliu/113456/113469/4021012/index.html.
2. https://coronavirus.jhu.edu/map.html.
3. Data from the ministry of transport, http://www.mot.gov.cn/.
4. http://firstreport.acmr.com.cn/rpdetail.aspx?f1=A01&rpcode=R000016245.
5. https://www.sohu.com/a/371741371_120011488.
6. https://baijiahao.baidu.com/s?id=1659324100357368892&wfr=spider&for=pc.
7. https://news.sina.cn/2020-03-26/detail-iimxyqwa3254791.d.html.
8. We just list the results of year 2019, if you need results for 2018 and 2017, please contact the authors.

Acknowledgments

Thank you very much for the supports from the Beijing Social Science Foundation Project (19GLC074) and Fundamental Research Funds for the Central Universities (2020MS044).

Funding

This work was supported by the Beijing Social Science Fund [19GLC074]; and Fundamental Research Funds for the Central Universities [2020MS044].

ORCID

Huayu Shen 🆔 http://orcid.org/0000-0003-4093-1515

References

Apergis, N., and E. Apergis. 2020. Can the COVID-19 pandemic and oil prices drive the US partisan conflict index. *Energy Research Letters* 1 (1):13144. doi:10.46557/001c.13144

Demirbag, M., K. Glaister, and A. Sengupta. 2019. Which regions matter for MNEs? The role of regional and firm level differences. *Journal of World Business* 55 (1):101026. doi:10.1016/j.jwb.2019.101026.

Fu, M., and H. Shen. 2020. COVID-19 and corporate performance in the energy industry - Moderating effect of goodwill impairment. *Energy Research Letters* 1 (1):12967. doi:10.46557/001c.12967

Gil-Alana, L. A., and M. Monge. 2020. Crude oil prices and COVID-19: Persistence of the shock. *Energy Research Letters* 1 (1):13200. doi:10.46557/001c.13200

Granziera, E., and T. Sekhposyan. 2019. Predicting relative forecasting performance: An empirical investigation. *International Journal of Forecasting* 35 (4):1636–57. doi:10.1016/j.ijforecast.2019.01.010.

Guariso, A., and M. Verpoorten. 2018. Armed conflict and schooling in rwanda: Digging deeper. *Nephron. Clinical Practice* 25 (1):634–62.

Hagerty, S. L., and L. M. Williams. 2020. The impact of COVID-19 on mental health: The interactive roles of brain biotypes and human connection. *Brain, Behavior, & Immunity – Health* 5:100078. doi:10.1016/j.bbih.2020.100078.

Iyke, B. N. (2020a). COVID-19: The reaction of US oil and gas producers to the pandemic. Working Paper.

Iyke, B. N. 2020b. The disease outbreak channel of exchange rate return predictability: Evidence from COVID-19. *Emerging Markets Finance and Trade.* 56 (10):2277–2297. doi:10.1080/1540496X.2020.1784718.

Liu, L., E.-Z. Wang, and C. C. Lee. 2020. Impact of the COVID-19 pandemic on the crude oil and stock markets in the US: A time-varying analysis. *Energy Research Letters* 1 (1):13154. doi:10.46557/001c.13154

Narayan, P., and S. Sharma. 2011. New evidence on oil price and firm returns. *Journal of Banking & Finance* 35 (12):3253–62. doi:10.1016/j.jbankfin.2011.05.010.

Narayan, P. K. 2020. Oil price news and COVID-19 - Is there any connection? *Energy Research Letters* 1 (1):13176. doi:10.46557/001c.13176

Narayan, P. K., and D. H. B. Phan. 2020. Country responses and the reaction of the stock market to COVID-19 – A preliminary exposition. *Emerging Markets Finance and Trade.* 56 (10):2138–2150. doi:10.1080/1540496X.2020.1784719

Phan, D. H. B., S. S. Sharma, and P. K. Narayan. 2015. Stock return forecasting: Some new evidence. *International Review of Financial Analysis* 40:38–51. doi:10.1016/j.irfa.2015.05.002.

Zeng, M., P. Zhang, S. Yu, and G. Zhang. 2016. Decision-making model of generation technology under uncertainty based on real option theory. *Energy Conversion and Management* 110:59–66. doi:10.1016/j.enconman.2015.12.005.

Zubair, S., R. Kabir, and X. Huang. 2020. Does the financial crisis change the effect of financing on investment? Evidence from private SMEs. *Journal of Business Research* 110:456–63. doi:10.1016/j.jbusres.2020.01.063.

Which Firm-specific Characteristics Affect the Market Reaction of Chinese Listed Companies to the COVID-19 Pandemic?

Hao Xiong, Zuofeng Wu, Fei Hou, and Jun Zhang

ABSTRACT

This paper investigates market reaction to the novel corona virus (COVID-19) pandemic. Using a sample of Chinese listed firms, we find that market reaction to the COVID-19 outbreak is more intense in firms within the industries that are vulnerable to the virus, and those with high institutional investors. Furthermore, firms with larger scale, better profitability and growth opportunity, higher combined leverage, and less fixed assets experience less adverse impact of the COVID-19 outbreak than other firms.

1. Introduction

It is widely recognized that the COVID-19 pandemic is not only an extreme public health event, but it is also an unprecedented shock to the economy (Fu and Shen 2020; Narayan 2020). The influence of the COVID-19 pandemic on the financial market attracted great attention (Ali, Alam, and Rizvi 2020; Haroon and Rizvi 2020). In this paper, we seek to investigate the reactions of the financial market to the COVID-19 pandemic. Specially, we empirically establish the firm-specific characteristics that make some firms more vulnerable to the COVID-19 pandemic than others.

COVID-19 was identified in China on 31 December 2019, and after this date the virus spread rapidly across the country. According to the notification of China's National Health Commission, approximately 82,877 people were infected by COVID-19 virus, and 4,633 people died from the virus in China by May 2nd (see Figure 1). Meanwhile, more than 3.3 million COVID-19 infections and over 230,000 deaths from COVID-19 are recorded worldwide (excluding China, Figure 2). In response, the World Health Organization declared that the COVID-19 outbreak evolved into a full-blown global pandemic. It is certain that COVID-19 is highly contagious, spreads quickly, and has enormously negative impact on both lives and economies. In order to stem the further spread of this virus, many countries took a series of emergency measures, including entire

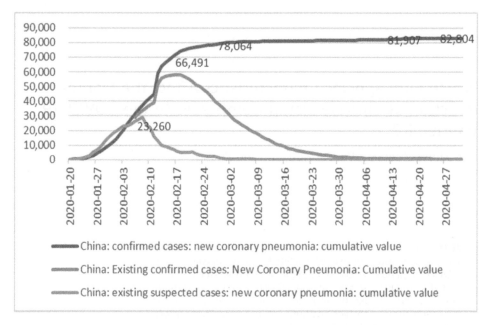

Figure 1. COVID-19 confirmed cases in China. This figure demonstrates the cumulative number of COVID19 cases in China until May 2nd. (Source: the database of China Stock Market and Accounting Research).

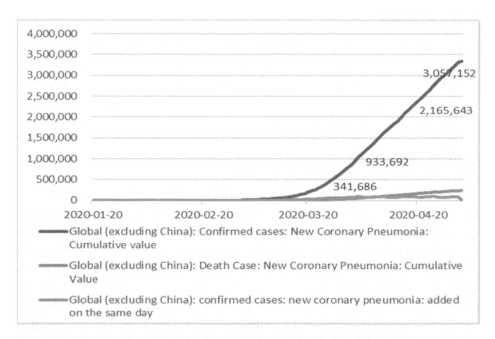

Figure 2. COVID-19 confirmed and death cases of the world excluding China. This figure presents the cumulative number of COVID19 confirmed and death cases of the world excluding China until May 2nd. (Source: the database of China Stock Market and Accounting Research).

regions lockdown, travel restrictions, and workplace closures, which impair both the demand and supply sides of economies because people are locked down in their homes and workers are laid off and lost income (Park et al. 2020).

The COVID-19 pandemic seriously restricted global economic activity. As Baker et al. (2020) point out, no previous infectious disease outbreak, including Spanish Flu, impacted the stock market as powerfully as the COVID-19 pandemic. It is estimated that two-thirds of the global impact is in China, where the outbreak is concentrated (Abiad et al. 2020). The extreme event of the COVID-19 pandemic caused great fluctuations in China's capital market, but a limited number of studies empirically examined the capital market reaction to the COVID-19 pandemic. Accordingly, we fill this void by tackling the link between firm-specific characteristics and China's capital market reaction to the COVID-19 pandemic.

Based on a sample of Chinese listed firms, we examine the investors' response to the COVID-19 pandemic using the event study method. Our empirical results show that firms in the industries that are sensitive to the impact of the COVID-19 pandemic have significantly lower cumulative abnormal return (CAR) around the outbreak. Meanwhile, firms with good financial conditions (larger scale, better profitability and growth opportunity, higher combined leverage, and less fixed assets) will experience less adverse impact of the COVID-19 pandemic. In addition, the institutional investors are significantly negatively related to CAR around the COVID-19 outbreak. The above results are still valid after adopting alternative measurement of dependent variable and event estimation window.

The main contributions of this paper are as follows. First, to our knowledge and literature in hand, this study is the first to investigate the relationship between firm-specific characteristics and China's capital market reactions to the COVID-19 pandemic. Existing studies examined the impacts of extreme events such as Spanish Flu and SARS on the capital market. This study provides the first look at the impact of the COVID-19 pandemic, which will expand the scope of the literature focusing on market reaction to extreme events. Moreover, this study contributes to the limited but growing literature on the economic consequences of the COVID-19 pandemic (Apergis and Apergis 2020; Gil-Alana and Monge 2020; Liu, Wang, and Lee 2020). Second, prior studies showed that firm characteristics have important effects on market reaction (Akron 2011). Our paper verifies that firm-specific characteristics indeed influence market reaction to the COVID-19 outbreak, adding to the existing literature. Third, a branch of studies in accounting and finance stress the role of institutional investors in China (Jiang and Kim 2015). Our study shows that institutional investors have significantly negative impact on market reaction to the COVID-19 outbreak, providing additional support to the evidence that institutional investors in China are buy-and-sell speculators and not buy-and-hold investors.

2. Research Design

2.1. Event Study Method of the COVID-19 Pandemic

In applying the event study method to the COVID-19 pandemic, we first identify the event day that Wuhan went into lockdown, which is on January 23rd, 2020. All buses, subways, and ferries were shut down, schools were suspended, and businesses and shops were closed to stop the COVID-19 virus from spreading further across the nation (Park et al. 2020). The assessment of an event's impact on stock prices requires estimating abnormal returns using the market model method (see Mackinlay 1997). This is as follows:

$$R_{i,t} = \alpha_0 + \alpha_1 R_{m,t} + \mu \qquad (1)$$

where $R_{i,t}$ represents the actual stock return at time t without considering reinvestment of cash dividend; $R_{m,t}$ is the return of the market index at time t. The estimation window, containing observations prior to the lockdown announcement ($t \in [-120, -21]$), consists of 100 trading days. In the model (1), α_0 and α_1 are parameters to be estimated, which represent the risk-free return rate and how much individual stocks are correlated with market return, respectively.

We calculate the daily abnormal returns of each company around the event date using the following model:

$$AR_{i,t} = R_{i,t} - \hat{\alpha}_0 - \hat{\alpha}_1 R_{m,t} \qquad (2)$$

where $AR_{i,t}$ is the abnormal return for firm i at time t. In order to draw overall inferences for the event of interest, the abnormal return measures must be aggregated over time into a measure of cumulative abnormal returns. Thus, the market reaction to the COVID-19 pandemic can be obtained by taking CAR[-τ, +τ] measured as the cumulative abnormal return (CAR) over an interval starting -τ and ending +τ trading days around the event day that Wuhan went into lockdown.

2.2. Data Source and Model Design

In this study, we explore the influence of firm-specific characteristics on market reaction to the COVID-19 pandemic from the following aspects: industrial characteristics, financial conditions, and external and internal governance. Our sample consists of all Chinese A-share listed firms after excluding firms with several missing observations on the variables used in our empirical analysis, and all data are from the China Stock Market and Accounting Research (CSMAR) database, which is the most frequently used database for China finance and accounting studies. Also, we winsorize the top and bottom 1% of each variable's distribution to alleviate the influence of extreme observations, and finally obtain 3,518 firm samples. In order to establish the firm-specific characteristics important to market reaction to the COVID-19 pandemic, we estimate the following model:

$$
\begin{aligned}
CAR_{i,t}[-\tau, +\tau] = \ & \alpha_0 + \alpha_1 VIND_{i,t} + \alpha_2 SIZE_{i,t} \\
& + \alpha_3 ROA_{i,t} + \alpha_4 TOBINQ_{i,t} + \alpha_5 OCAP_{i,t} \\
& + \alpha_6 CLEV_{i,t} + \alpha_7 CASH_{i,t} + \alpha_8 FIX_{i,t} \qquad (3) \\
& + \alpha_9 BIG4_{i,t} + \alpha_{10} IHOLD_{i,t} + \alpha_{11} BOARD_{i,t} \\
& + \alpha_{12} INDP_{i,t} + \varepsilon_{i,t}
\end{aligned}
$$

where the dependent variable, $CAR_{i,t}$ $[-\tau, +\tau]$ measures the CAR for firm i over an interval starting $-\tau$ and ending $+\tau$ trading days around the event day. So, $CAR_{i,t}$ $[-1, +1]$ is the 3 days (-1 to $+1$) CAR for firm i around the day of the COVID-19 outbreak, and $AR_{i,t}$ ($\tau = 0$) is the abnormal return for firm i at the day of the COVID-19 outbreak.

Following the literature (Kong and Su 2019; Shen et al. 2020), we incorporate a set of variables, including vulnerable industry (VIND), firm size (SIZE), return on assets (ROA), growth opportunity (TOBINQ), operating capacity (OCAP), combined leverage (CLEV), cash flow (CASH), fixed assets (FIX), big-4 external auditor (BIG4), institutional investors holding shares (IHOLD), board size (BOARD), and the proportion of independent directors (INDP), which could affect the relation between COVID-19 pandemic and the market reaction of the listed companies. The detailed definitions of variables are in Table 1.

3. Empirical Results and Analysis

3.1. Descriptive Statistics

Table 2 reports the descriptive statistics of the variables used in this study. As shown in Table 2, the median values of AR, and CAR [−1, +1] are −0.001 and −0.013, respectively, revealing the basic characteristics of CAR around the COVID-19 outbreak. The variable VIND has a mean value of 0.186, suggesting that 18.6% of the firms are vulnerable to the COVID-19 pandemic. The average firm size (SIZE), returns on total assets (ROA), growth opportunity (TOBINQ), total revenue to total assets (OCAP), degree of combined leverage (CLEV), total cash flow to total assets (CASH), and fixed assets to total assets (FIX) are about 4.99 billion Chinese Yuan, 2.4%, 1.864, 59.1%, 1.389, 14.3%, 19.5%, respectively. The descriptive statistics of governance variables reveal that the auditor is a big-4 external auditor in 6.2% of firms (BIG4), the average percentage of ownership held by institutional investors (IHOLD) is 3.6%, the number of directors in the boardroom

Table 1. Variable definitions.

Variable type	Variable name	Measurement
Dependent variables	AR	The abnormal return at the day of Wuhan went into lockdown.
	CAR[−1, +1]	Three days (−1 to +1) cumulative abnormal returns (CAR) around the day of Wuhan went into lockdown.
Independent variables and control variables	VIND	A dummy variable, equaling 1 if the industry is transportation, food and beverage retail, hotel and tourism, postal warehouse, real estate, video entertainment, and construction, which are vulnerable to the COVID-19 pandemic, and 0 otherwise (Ali, Alam, and Rizvi 2020; Fu and Shen 2020; Haroon and Rizvi 2020).
	SIZE	Firm size, measured by the natural logarithm of total assets.
	ROA	Return on assets, computed as the net profit scaled by total assets.
	TOBINQ	A firm's growth opportunity, measured as book value of assets less the book value of equity, plus the market value of equity, scaled by the book value of assets.
	OCAP	Operating capacity, measured as the ratio of total revenue to total assets.
	CLEV	Degree of combined leverage, measured as the leverage ratio that sums up the combined effect of the degree of operating leverage and the degree of financial leverage has on the Earning per share.
	CASH	Cash flow, measured as the ratio of total cash flow to total assets.
	FIX	Fixed assets, measured as the ratio of fixed assets to total assets.
	BIG4	A dummy variable, equaling 1 if the auditor is a big-4 external auditor, and 0 otherwise.
	IHOLD	Institutional investors holding shares, measured as the percentage of ownership in the firm held by institutional investors.
	BOARD	Board size, measured as the natural logarithm of the number of directors in the boardroom.
	INDP	The proportion of independent directors, measured as the number of independent directors to the total number of directors in the boardroom.

Table 2. Descriptive statistical results.

Variables	N	MEAN	SD	MIN	MEDIAN	MAX
AR	3,518	0.001	0.029	−0.101	−0.001	0.153
CAR[−1, +1]	3,518	−0.005	0.070	−0.295	−0.013	0.449
VIND	3,518	0.186	0.389	0.000	0.000	1.000
SIZE	3,518	22.330	1.464	19.770	22.110	27.290
ROA	3,518	0.024	0.101	−0.549	0.035	0.205
TOBINQ	3,518	1.864	1.222	0.819	1.480	8.246
OCAP	3,518	0.591	0.397	0.023	0.516	2.272
CLEV	3,518	1.389	0.855	0.597	1.125	6.837
CASH	3,518	0.143	0.110	0.008	0.113	0.545
FIX	3,518	0.195	0.156	0.001	0.163	0.675
BIG4	3,518	0.062	0.241	0.000	0.000	1.000
IHOLD	3,518	0.036	0.048	0.000	0.018	0.239
BOARD	3,518	2.225	0.165	1.792	2.226	2.708
INDP	3,518	0.380	0.050	0.308	0.375	0.571

(BOARD) is nine on average, and the average ratio of independent directors (INDP) is 38.0%.

3.2. Univariate Tests

Table 3 reports the Pearson and Spearman correlation analysis of variables. The following findings are noteworthy: (1) Both AR and CAR[−1, +1] are significantly positively correlated with SIZE, ROA, and CLEV; (2) Both AR and CAR[−1, +1] are significantly negatively correlated with VIND, FIX, and

Table 3. Results of Pearson and Spearman correlation coefficients.

Variables		(1)	(2)	(3)	(4)	(5)	(6)	(7)
AR	(1)	1.000	0.677***	−0.033**	0.088***	0.026	0.002	−0.033*
CAR[−1, +1]	(2)	0.755***	1.000	−0.004**	0.034*	0.044**	−0.078***	−0.051**
VIND	(3)	−0.051**	−0.027**	1.000	0.235***	−0.090***	−0.268***	−0.030
SIZE	(4)	0.048**	0.006**	0.227***	1.000	−0.157***	−0.599***	−0.069***
ROA	(5)	0.027**	0.039*	−0.027	−0.022	1.000	0.271***	0.273***
TOBINQ	(6)	0.008	−0.022	−0.137***	−0.399***	0.015	1.000	0.102***
OCAP	(7)	−0.018	−0.029	0.078***	−0.062***	0.137***	0.020	1.000
CLEV	(8)	0.031**	0.032**	0.023	0.165***	−0.189***	−0.133***	−0.034*
CASH	(9)	0.019	0.012	−0.028	−0.198***	0.195***	0.226***	0.049**
FIX	(10)	−0.056***	−0.024**	−0.136***	0.027	0.007	−0.098***	0.051**
BIG4	(11)	0.048**	0.023	0.074***	0.383***	0.051**	−0.077***	−0.031
IHOLD	(12)	−0.011**	−0.066***	0.027	0.359***	0.077***	0.079***	0.001
BOARD	(13)	0.008	0.014	0.034*	0.317***	0.018	−0.135***	−0.058***
INDP	(14)	−0.004	−0.017	0.009	0.011	−0.015	0.039*	0.002
Variables		(8)	(9)	(10)	(11)	(12)	(13)	(14)
AR	(1)	0.022	0.040*	−0.098***	0.071***	−0.001	0.037*	−0.019
CAR[−1,+1]	(2)	0.030**	0.007	−0.037*	0.042*	−0.084***	0.045**	−0.033*
VIND	(3)	0.071***	−0.028	−0.199***	0.074***	0.031	0.026	0.003
SIZE	(4)	0.297***	−0.202***	−0.008	0.278***	0.418***	0.234***	−0.029
ROA	(5)	−0.679***	0.328***	0.026	0.010	0.133***	−0.021	−0.036*
TOBINQ	(6)	−0.309***	0.249***	−0.050**	−0.153***	−0.022	−0.160***	0.035*
OCAP	(7)	−0.127***	0.127***	0.181***	−0.058***	0.024	−0.048**	−0.015
CLEV	(8)	1.000	−0.493***	0.109***	0.026	−0.003	0.050**	0.037*
CASH	(9)	−0.275***	1.000	−0.240***	−0.027	0.000	−0.024	−0.024
FIX	(10)	0.123***	−0.265***	1.000	−0.087***	−0.050**	0.033	−0.025
BIG4	(11)	−0.013	−0.012	−0.061***	1.000	0.148***	0.134***	−0.002
IHOLD	(12)	−0.005	−0.011	−0.042*	0.138***	1.000	0.096***	−0.004
BOARD	(13)	0.050**	−0.036*	0.048**	0.164***	0.119***	1.000	−0.711***
INDP	(14)	0.016	−0.014	−0.013	0.024	0.010	−0.567***	1.000

$* p < 10\%$; $** p < 5\%$; $*** p < 1\%$. The lower left triangle is the Pearson correlation coefficient, the upper right triangle is the Spearman correlation coefficients.

IHOLD; (3) The coefficients of the pair-wise correlation among variables are generally low (<0.50), and all of the variance inflation factors (VIFs) are less than 10, suggesting that no serious multi-collinearity problem exists when these variables are simultaneously included in the regression.

3.3. Empirical Results

Table 4 presents the regression estimates regarding the influence of firm-specific characteristics on market reaction to the COVID-19 pandemic. As shown in Columns (1)–(4) of Table 4, the coefficients for VIND are negative and significant across all cases (i.e. from −0.013 with t = −4.00 to −0.002 with t = −1.89). This suggests that VIND is negatively associated with CAR, and thus providing strong and consistent evidence that firms within the transportation, food and beverage retail, hotel and tourism, postal warehouse, real estate, video entertainment, and construction industries are vulnerable to the COVID-19 pandemic. As for the signs and significance of the other corporate characteristics in Table 4, we note the following aspects: (1) The coefficients for SIZE are significantly positive in Columns (1) and (2), and insignificant in Columns (3) and (4), respectively. These results show that the influence of

Table 4. Influence of firm-specific characteristics on the market reaction to COVID-19 pandemic.

Variables	(1) CAR[−1,+1]	(2) CAR[−1,+1]	(3) AR	(4) AR
VIND	−0.013*** (−4.00)	−0.013*** (−4.15)	−0.002* (−1.67)	−0.002* (−1.89)
SIZE	0.003** (3.80)	0.004*** (3.96)	−0.000 (−0.11)	0.001 (1.25)
ROA	0.025** (2.02)	0.027** (2.16)	0.014*** (2.89)	0.016*** (3.15)
TOBINQ	0.001 (1.18)	0.002* (1.74)	−0.001 (−1.49)	−0.000 (−0.39)
OCAP	−0.002 (−0.49)	−0.001 (−0.46)	−0.002* (−1.77)	−0.002* (−1.66)
CLEV	0.001** (2.42)	0.001** (2.36)	0.001** (2.48)	0.001** (2.31)
CASH	0.007 (0.62)	0.007 (0.59)	0.003 (0.53)	0.002 (0.44)
FIX	−0.033*** (−4.03)	−0.032*** (−3.98)	−0.007** (−2.06)	−0.007** (−2.15)
BIG4		0.008 (1.40)		0.002 (1.07)
IHOLD		−0.073*** (−2.67)		−0.048*** (−4.32)
BOARD		−0.010 (−1.05)		−0.000 (−0.07)
INDP		−0.027 (−0.92)		−0.010 (−0.81)
CONSTANT	−0.079*** (−3.69)	−0.068** (−2.05)	0.004 (0.46)	−0.005 (−0.34)
Observations	3,518	3,518	3,518	3,518
Adj R^2	0.0137	0.0166	0.0065	0.0124

* $p < 10\%$; ** $p < 5\%$; *** $p < 1\%$. All reported t-statistics are based on standard errors adjusted for White (1980).

corporate scale on CAR is inconsistent during different time windows. Corporate scale has a positive influence on CAR [−1, +1], and insignificant influence on the abnormal return (AR) on the day of the Wuhan lockdown; (2) The coefficients for ROA are positive and significant in Columns (1)–(4), implying that profitability positively influences CAR [−1, +1] and AR; (3) CLEV has significantly positive coefficients in Columns (1)–(4), suggesting that higher degree of combined leverage positively influences CAR [−1,+1] and AR; (4) The coefficients for FIX are all significantly negative in Columns (1)–(4), revealing that firms with more fixed assets have significantly lower CAR around the outbreak of COVID-19. Moreover, as shown of governance variables in Table 4, only IHOLD has significantly negative coefficients in Columns (1)–(4), meaning that firms with a higher percentage of institutional investors share lower CAR[−1,+1] and AR.

4. Robustness Tests

4.1. Robustness Tests Using Other Measures of CAR [-t, +t]

Table 5 reports the regression results for the influence of firm-specific characteristics on market reaction to the COVID-19 pandemic using CAR [−5, +5] and CAR [−10, +10], respectively. As shown Columns (1)–(4) of Table 5, the coefficients for VIND, FIX, and IHOLD are negative and significant, implying that vulnerable industries, fixed assets, and institutional investors have a negative impact on CAR[−5,+5] and CAR[−10,+10]. In addition, the coefficients for SIZE, ROA, TOBINQ, and CLEV are positive and significant in Columns (1)–(4), suggesting that firms with larger scale, better profitability and growth opportunity, and higher degree of combined leverage have significantly higher CAR around the outbreak of COVID-19.

Table 5. Robustness tests using other measures of CAR[-t, +t].

Variables	(1) CAR[−5,+5]	(2) CAR[−5,+5]	(3) CAR[−10,+10]	(4) CAR[−10,+10]
VIND	−0.027*** (−5.88)	−0.027*** (−5.86)	−0.041*** (−6.31)	−0.041*** (−6.29)
SIZE	0.010*** (7.14)	0.010*** (5.56)	0.012*** (6.66)	0.013*** (5.49)
ROA	0.109*** (6.01)	0.108*** (5.93)	0.267*** (10.66)	0.266*** (10.60)
TOBINQ	0.006*** (3.59)	0.005*** (3.28)	0.007*** (3.27)	0.006*** (2.79)
OCAP	0.001 (0.28)	0.001 (0.22)	0.008 (1.29)	0.007 (1.15)
CLEV	0.001** (2.06)	0.001** (2.06)	−0.001 (−0.89)	−0.001 (−0.79)
CASH	0.018 (1.03)	0.019 (1.06)	0.026 (1.06)	0.029 (1.17)
FIX	−0.013** (−2.06)	−0.011*** (−2.93)	−0.003** (−2.18)	−0.001** (−2.04)
BIG4		0.008 (1.00)		−0.004 (−0.34)
IHOLD		−0.018** (−2.45)		−0.078** (−2.40)
BOARD		−0.016 (−1.17)		−0.037* (−1.91)
INDP		−0.027 (−0.62)		0.014 (0.22)
CONSTANT	−0.245*** (−7.72)	−0.194*** (−3.94)	−0.319*** (−7.20)	−0.251*** (−3.67)
Observations	3,518	3,518	3,518	3,518
Adj R²	0.0345	0.0352	0.0599	0.0623

* $p < 10\%$; ** $p < 5\%$; *** $p < 1\%$. All reported t statistics are based on standard errors adjusted for White (1980).

These results are qualitatively similar to the main ones, suggesting that our findings are robust.

4.2. Robustness Tests Using Other Measures of the Event Estimation Window

Table 6 provides the results for the effect of firm-specific characteristics on market reaction to the COVID-19 pandemic using other event windows. To ensure that the results in Table 4 are robust, we adopt the event estimation window, containing observations prior to the Wuhan lockdown announcement ($t \in [-170, -21]$), which consists of 150 trading days to compute CAR [−1, +1] and AR. As shown in Table 6, VIND and FIX coefficients in Columns (1)–(4) are significantly negative. Similarly, the coefficients for IHOLD are

Table 6. Robustness tests using other measures of the event estimation window.

Variables	(1) CAR[−1,+1]	(2) CAR[−1,+1]	(3) AR	(4) AR
VIND	−0.014*** (−4.43)	−0.014*** (−4.59)	−0.002* (−1.81)	−0.003** (−2.04)
SIZE	0.002** (1.97)	0.003** (2.43)	−0.001 (−1.31)	0.000 (0.22)
ROA	0.019* (1.89)	0.021* (1.74)	0.012** (2.52)	0.014*** (2.77)
TOBINQ	0.001 (0.78)	0.002 (1.38)	−0.001 (−1.59)	−0.000 (−0.48)
OCAP	0.001 (0.48)	0.002 (0.51)	−0.001 (−0.94)	−0.001 (−0.83)
CLEV	0.001*** (2.61)	0.001** (2.54)	0.001*** (2.61)	0.001** (2.45)
CASH	0.013 (1.15)	0.013 (1.13)	0.003 (0.56)	0.002 (0.48)
FIX	−0.026*** (−3.26)	−0.025*** (−3.18)	−0.005** (−2.45)	−0.005** (−2.49)
BIG4		0.010** (1.97)		0.004* (1.66)
IHOLD		−0.082*** (−3.13)		−0.051*** (−4.64)
BOARD		−0.010 (−1.09)		−0.001 (−0.17)
INDP		−0.015 (−0.51)		−0.008 (−0.64)
CONSTANT	−0.039* (−1.89)	−0.032 (−0.99)	0.014 (1.61)	0.006 (0.46)
Observations	3,464	3,464	3,464	3,464
Adj R²	0.0111	0.0154	0.0057	0.0130

* $p < 10\%$; ** $p < 5\%$; *** $p < 1\%$. All reported t statistics are based on standard errors adjusted for White (1980).

negative and significant in Columns (2) and (4), while ROA and CLEV have significantly positive coefficients in all Columns. Overall, the findings are unchanged using the 150-trading-days event window to re-estimate model (1), which means that they are robust.

5. Conclusions

In this study, we investigate what firm-specific characteristics affect the market reaction of listed companies to the COVID-19 pandemic. We find that firms in vulnerable industries, with more fixed assets, and higher percentage of institutional investors have significantly lower CAR around the outbreak of COVID-19. Meanwhile, we also provide systematic evidence that the firms' scale, profitability, growth opportunity, and combined leverage have positive impacts on CAR. Using the Chinese context, we first investigate market reaction to the COVID-19 pandemic and explore the role of corporate characteristics and governance systems in explaining the pandemic effects on CAR, which has several practical implications for the literature on extreme events and investor behavior.

First, our findings establish that firm-specific characteristics affect market reactions to the COVID-19 outbreak by showing significantly positive and negative influence on CAR of the outbreak, echoing the typical event study (Mackinlay 1997). That is, our study pinpoints the firm-specific characteristics the investors should take into account when valuing a firm following an extremely infectious disease outbreak.

Second, we provide strong evidence that firms within the industries that are vulnerable to the pandemic have significantly lower CAR around the outbreak of COVID-19. This result lends support to arguments that the firms in the transportation, food and beverage retail, hotel and tourism, postal warehouse, real estate, video entertainment, and construction industries are vulnerable to the COVID-19 pandemic (Hassan et al. 2020).

Third, our findings reveal that corporate financial conditions have a significant impact on CAR around the outbreak of COVID-19. The firms with larger scale, better profitability and growth opportunity, higher combined leverage, and less fixed assets will experience less adverse impact than otherwise identical firms. These findings echo studies emphasizing that corporate financial conditions exert a powerful influence on market reaction (Akron 2011).

Forth, our findings show that market reaction to the COVID-19 outbreak does not vary systematically with the features of corporate governance, except for institutional investors. This supports the contention that institutional investors in China are buy-and-sell speculators and not buy-and-hold investors (Jiang and Kim 2015). That is, institutional investors do not have the incentive and power to exert oversight over firms in the context of China.

Funding

This work was supported by the Beijing Social Science Fund [19GLC074]; Initiation Project of Preventing the COVID-19 Pandemic for Scientific Research of Guizhou University of Finance and Economics [2020YQ11]; Fundamental Research Funds for the Central Universities [2020MS044].

References

Abiad, A., M. Arao, S. Dagli, B. Ferrarini, I. Noy, P. Osewe, J. Pagaduan, D. Park, and R. Platitas. 2020. The economic impact of the COVID-19 outbreak on developing Asia Asian Development Bank Briefs. No.128.

Akron, S. 2011. Market reactions to dividend announcements under different business cycles. *Emerging Markets Finance and Trade* 47 (5):72–85. doi:10.2753/REE1540-496X4706S505.

Ali, M., N. Alam, and S. A. R. Rizvi. 2020. Coronavirus (COVID-19) – An epidemic or pandemic for financial markets. *Journal of Behavioral and Experimental Finance* 27:100341. doi:10.1016/j.jbef.2020.100341.

Apergis, E., and N. Apergis. 2020. Can the COVID-19 pandemic and oil prices drive the US partisan conflict index. *Energy Research Letters* 1 (1):13144. doi:10.46557/001c.13144

Baker, S. R., N. Bloom, S. J. Davis, K. J. Kost, M. C. Sammon, and T. Viratyosin. 2020.The unprecedented stock market impact of COVID-19. Working Paper 26945. National Bureau of Economic Research. doi:10.3386/w26945.

Fu, M., and H. Shen. 2020. COVID-19 and corporate performance in the energy industry. *Energy Research Letters* 1 (1):12967. doi:10.46557/001c.12967

Gil-Alana, L. A., and M. Monge. 2020. Crude oil prices and COVID-19: Persistence of the shock. *Energy Research Letters* 1 (1):13200. doi:10.46557/001c.13200

Haroon, O., and S. A. R. Rizvi. 2020. COVID-19: Media coverage and financial markets behavior – A sectoral inquiry. *Journal of Behavioral and Experimental Finance* 27:100343. Advance online publication. doi:10.1016/j.jbef.2020.100343.

Hassan, T. A., S. Hollander, L. Lent, and A. Tahoun. 2020. Firm-level exposure to epidemic diseases Covid-19, SARS, and H1N1. Working Paper 26971, National Bureau of Economic Research. doi: 10.3386/w26971.

Jiang, F., and K. A. Kim. 2015. Corporate governance in China: A modern perspective. *Journal of Corporate Finance* 32:190–216. doi:10.1016/j.jcorpfin.2014.10.010.

Kong, L., and H. Su. 2019. On the market reaction to capitalization of R&D expenditures: Evidence from ChiNext. *Emerging Markets Finance and Trade*. 1–12. Advance online publication. doi:10.1080/1540496X.2019.1668769.

Liu, L., E.-Z. Wang, and -C.-C. Lee. 2020. Impact of the COVID-19 pandemic on the crude oil and stock markets in the US: A time-varying analysis. *Energy Research Letters* 1 (1):13154. doi:10.46557/001c.13154

Mackinlay, A. C. 1997. Event studies in economics and finance. *Journal of Economic Literature* 35 (1):13–39.

Narayan, P. K. 2020. Oil price news and COVID-19 – Is there any connection? *Energy Research Letters* 1 (1):13176. doi:10.46557/001c.13176

Park, C. Y., J. Villafuerte, A. Abiad, B. Narayanan, E. Banzon, J. Samson, A. Aftab, and M. C. Tayag. 2020. An updated assessment of the economic impact of COVID-19. Asian Development Bank Briefs No.133.

Shen, H., S. Zheng, H. Xiong, W. Tang, and J. Dou. 2020. Stock market mispricing and firm innovation based on path analysis. *Economic Modelling*. Advance online publication. doi:10.1016/j.econmod.2020.03.001.

White, H. 1980. A heteroskedasticity-consistent covariance matrix estimator and a direct test for heteroskedasticity. *Econometrica* 48 (4):817–38. doi:10.2307/1912934.

COVID-19 Pandemic and Firm-level Cash Holding—Moderating Effect of Goodwill and Goodwill Impairment

Xiuhong Qin, Guoliang Huang, Huayu Shen ⓘD, and Mengyao Fu

ABSTRACT

The COVID-19 outbreak seriously affected all economies, especially the operations of listed companies, around the world. This article studies the impact of COVID-19 on firm-level cash holdings using the difference-in-differences method. It finds that COVID-19 has a significant positive impact on cash holdings in serious-impact industries. Goodwill and goodwill impairment can weaken this positive impact, which may be related to higher business risks in these firms. Therefore, managers should raise firms' cash holding level during the pandemic to protect firms against contingencies. Managers should also be aware of financing constraints due to risks.

1. Introduction

The novel coronavirus (COVID-19) outbreak seriously affected economies and brought challenges to firms and individuals. The performance of companies across various industries fluctuated sharply, following the COVID-19 outbreak—most companies suffered declining performance (Fu and Shen 2020), falling stock prices (Narayan and Phan 2020), and other serious problems (Gil-Alana and Monge 2020). While some Chinese provinces gradually resumed work and production, Hubei province, which is worst hit, is still being delayed. Sharp reduction in production levels alongside slow turnover led to complete stagnation in sectors, such as tourism and catering, in the first quarter of 2020. On the one hand, these enterprises, which are characterized by service, social contact, and population mobility, are unable to carry out operations and obtain income and cash inflow. On the other hand, the necessary fixed costs, and personnel expenses drive the cash-out. A long-term "cash deficit" leads to huge cash flow pressure for firms in industries seriously affected by the pandemic.

The catering industry, for example, which greatly drives China's consumption, was pressured from both sides—drop in operating revenue and high-fixed cost. The restaurant industry suffered an 80% drop in revenue in the first quarter of 2020, due to a ban on crowd gathering,[1] leading to the shutdown of many restaurants. Meanwhile, the high cost of rent and employee wages made the situation in the catering industry even worse. In order to cope with the operational risks caused by COVID-19 and ensure that firms can smoothly survive the pandemic, managers tend to increase firms' cash holding level in the short term through bank loans or equity financing to ease the cash flow pressures. However, the financing capacity of the firms is different, so it is debatable whether the companies can raise the cash in time.

The literature on the economic impact of COVID-19 is limited. We add to the limited literature by studying the impact of COVID-19 on corporate cash holdings. Specifically, we contribute to the literature as follows. First, this article studies, for the first time, the impact of COVID-19 on cash holding levels across firms in different industries. Holding a reasonable level of cash is essential for firms to control risks and improve profitability. Previous studies investigated the country responses and the reaction of the stock market to COVID-19 (Narayan and Phan 2020), the connection between COVID-19 and oil price news (Gil-Alana and Monge 2020; Narayan 2020), and the impact of COVID-19 on US Partisan conflict index (Apergis and Apergis 2020). There are few studies on the impact of COVID-19 on corporate performance. In this article, we used the difference-in-differences (DID) model to quantify the fluctuation of cash holding level before and after the pandemic, revealing the impact of this major health emergency on cash holding level. Second, this article provides a methodological guidance for measuring the cash prevention motivation of enterprises. In the case of major emergencies, the change in cash held by enterprises is mainly affected by precautionary motives. Therefore, this article quantifies the influence of prevention motivation on cash holding level to some extent (Narayan and Phan 2020). Third, this article proposes a mechanism for changing the level of cash holdings under the pandemic situation. Following the occurrence of major emergencies, enterprises will increase their cash holdings. However, high goodwill and goodwill impairment, as a kind of risk warning signals, hold back the increase in cash level (Harford, Humphery-Jenner, and Powell 2012). Fourth, our results serve as guidelines for the selection of methods for corporate managers to relieve cash flow pressures during the pandemic. Since goodwill and goodwill impairment will reduce the financing capacity of firms, managers should pay more attention to the cash level and keep the cash flow risk under control, so as to prevent the rupture of the cash flow caused by financing constraints (Fu and Shen 2020).

In this article, we take the cash holding level of listed companies in China in the first quarters of 2014–2020 as the research object, and the industries affected by the pandemic as the measurement standard. We divided the industries into high-affected and low-affected industries. We use two moderators, namely whether the firm has goodwill or not and whether the firm has goodwill impairment or not, to measure the moderating effect between COVID-19 and cash holding level. The article finds that COVID-19 has a positive impact on the cash holding level of firms in industries seriously affected by the pandemic. In other words, compared with firms slightly affected, these firms may choose to hold more cash in order to resist the risks associated with the pandemic. After introducing the moderators, we found that goodwill and goodwill impairment weakened the positive effect of the pandemic on the cash holding level. That is, firms with goodwill and goodwill impairment would increase their cash holding level less. We believe that this is related to the fact that firms with goodwill and goodwill impairment have high financial risks and are subject to financing constraints from banks and creditors.

The remainder of this article is arranged as follows. Section 2 presents the theoretical framework and hypotheses. Section 3 explains the data and method used to examine the relationship between the COVID-19 outbreak and cash holding level, as well as the moderating effect of goodwill and goodwill impairment on this relationship. Section 4 reports the empirical results. Section 5 reports the robustness tests, while Section 6 concludes our study.

2. Theoretical Framework and Research Hypotheses

2.1. The Impact of COVID-19 on Cash Holdings

Cash is often regarded as the "blood" of an enterprise and the necessary support for its daily operations (Opler et al. 1999). There are three motives for companies to hold cash, namely the motive of prevention, of transaction, and of speculation (Opler et al. 1999). Acharya, Davydenko, and Strebulaev (2012) found a significant positive correlation between future cash fluctuations and corporate cash holdings. During the COVID-19 outbreak, with the implementation of the quarantine policy, the operational activities of enterprises were forced to stop, leading to a significant decline in their income level. Meanwhile, some fixed expenditures were increasing. These factors worsened the cash flow state of enterprises during the pandemic.

So why do managers need to rapidly increase cash holdings? On the one hand, managers must maintain the necessary liquidity level of the enterprises to cover fixed costs and expenses, since COVID-19 brought short-term uncertainties into their operations. Holding a certain level of cash would help the enterprises to maintain liquidity for emergencies, thereby avoiding the need for external financing (Opler et al. 1999). On the other hand, due to different external financing capacity of enterprises, managers must increase the level of cash holdings in advance to prevent the cash gap caused by loan restrictions. Companies can reduce refinancing risks by increasing cash holdings and saving cash from cash flow, and cash reserves can help alleviate the problem of underinvestment (Harford, Klasa, and Maxwell 2014). Thus, our first research hypothesis is:

H_1: *Ceteris paribus*, COVID-19 has a positive impact on the cash holding level of firms. That is, firms in sensitive industries will have a higher cash holding level.

2.2. Moderating Effect of Goodwill and Goodwill Impairment

Goodwill refers to the potential economic value that can bring excess profits to the business operation in the future, or the capitalized value that the expected profitability of a business exceeds the normal profitability of identifiable assets, such as the average rate of return on investment (Godfrey and Koh 2001). Goodwill is a unique accounting asset generated by mergers and acquisitions (Fu and Shen 2020). When consideration paid is higher than the fair value of the target's net asset, the difference between them will be recognized as goodwill, which can be reflected in the merged financial statements of the acquirer. Previous studies found that goodwill can significantly increase the value of a company; the capitalization of goodwill, especially, will cause widespread concern in the capital market after merger and acquisition (Godfrey and Koh 2001; Jennings, LeClere, and Thompson 2001). However, in recent years, it is found that executives tend to use M&As to increase their own remuneration, and, consequently, goodwill fails to bring value enhancement to enterprises (Harford, Humphery-Jenner, and Powell 2012). According to the principal–agent theory, the agency problem between the management and shareholders, due to the inconsistency of objectives and information asymmetry, causes the management to pay more attention to short-term benefits. M&As without careful analysis often cause business conflicts, increasing the risks of enterprises, and damage the interests of shareholders.

However, through which channels does goodwill affect cash holdings? This is mainly reflected in the risk brought by goodwill, which leads to higher financing constraints for enterprises. High goodwill recognition reflects the huge risk of business integration. Enterprises with large goodwill will have more non-systematic risks than other enterprises, and banks and other credit institutions will impose more loan restrictions on them. Based on the above reasoning, our second research hypothesis is:

H_2: *Ceteris paribus*, goodwill will weaken the positive effect of COVID-19 on corporate cash holdings.

Goodwill impairment refers to the recognition of the corresponding impairment loss after the impairment test of the goodwill formed in the merger of the enterprise, which is a way for the executives to empty the listed companies (Fu and Shen 2020). An overestimation of the acquired party's net assets leads to an exaggeration of synergies, while there will be bubbles in the goodwill. When performance is poor, goodwill impairment will be recognized. According to the signal theory, an enterprise can release the signal of its operating status to investors and the market through public information (Fu and Shen 2020). As an accounting treatment, goodwill impairment is usually considered as a feature of poor management (Harford, Humphery-Jenner, and Powell 2012). Enterprises fail to realize the promised performance of M&As, thus sending a bad business signal to the market and stakeholders. Therefore, in the case of the pandemic, the bank, as the main lender, will integrate multiple information to control the loan limit for these goodwill impaired companies. To sum up, our third research hypothesis is:

H₃: *Ceteris paribus*, the occurrence of goodwill impairment will weaken the positive effect of the pandemic on the corporate cash holding level.

3. Data and Model

We selected listed companies on the Shanghai and Shenzhen stock exchanges. We collected their cash holdings and relevant financial data from the period of 2014 to 2020. Since the pandemic mainly affected the first quarter of 2020, we collected the financial data for the first quarter of 2014–2020. The following samples were excluded to ensure the comparability of research objects: (1) Special treatment (ST), *ST, and other financially distressed companies[2]; (2) Data on banks, securities, and other financial companies; (3) Companies with significant missing data.[3] After screening, a total of 1,663 companies were included in the study. In order to reduce the impact of extreme values, we winsorized the data at 0.01 and 0.99 level. The data is from the China Stock Market & Accounting Research (CSMAR) database.

In general, the pandemic's impact is unique, and, thus, it is difficult to guarantee the complete randomness of sample distribution between the high-impact group and the low-impact group. Zhu, Qian, and Wei (2020) investigate the effects and mechanisms of high speed-railway on urban land expansion in China using the DID model. There may be differences in corporate performance before and after the COVID-19 outbreak. A single or lateral comparison method to compare and contrast corporate performance following the COVID-19 outbreak will ignore these differences, and, in turn, lead to biased estimates of the effect of the outbreak of pandemic. The DID model is exactly based on the data obtained from the natural experiment. The DID model can effectively control the ex-ante differences among research subjects (i.e. treated and controlled groups/firms) and effectively separate the real effect of the COVID-19 outbreak.

To test the first hypothesis, H_1, we used the following model:

$$
\begin{aligned}
Cashholdings_{it} = {} & \beta_0 + \beta_1 Treated_{it}*Period_{it} + \beta_2 Treated_{it} + \beta_3 Period_{it} \\
& + \beta_4 SIZE_{it} + \beta_5 LEV_{it} + \beta_6 GROWTH_{it} + \beta_7 NROA_{it} \\
& + \beta_8 HF10_{it} + \beta_9 FCF_{it} + \beta_{10} TR_{it} + \beta_{11} IND + \beta_{12} YEAR + \varepsilon_{it}
\end{aligned}
$$

$$(1)$$

where the dependent variable, *Cashholdings*, is the ratio of cash to current operating income, which represents the cash holding level of the enterprise. *Treated* is a dummy variable indicating the degree of pandemic impact and *Period* is a dummy variable indicating the pandemic period. This article focuses on the regression coefficient of *Treated * Period*, which reflects the impact of the pandemic on the cash holding level of enterprises. If the value of β_1 is positive, then the pandemic has a positive impact on the cash holding level of enterprises; hence, the pandemic urges enterprises to improve their cash holding level, and vice versa. Following prior study (Opler et al. 1999), Model (1) includes variables to control for firms' normal cash holdings required to meet operational, investment, and financing needs. Specifically, we set the following variables to reduce the interference, those are: enterprise-scale (*SIZE*) measured as the log value of total assets. We believe that larger companies have better access to financing, leading to higher levels of cash holdings (Gao, Harford, and Li 2013). Asset–liability ratio (*LEV*) is included as companies need to hold more cash to cope with interest and principal on their debts (Gao, Harford, and Li 2013). The growth rate of revenue (*GROWTH*) is included because companies with high growth characteristics prefer holding more cash for investment in new projects (Gao, Harford, and Li 2013). We include the total assets net profit margin (*NROA*) as a control variable because holding cash leads to missing out on profitable projects, resulting in lower profitability (Clarkson, Gao, and Herbohn 2020). The top 10 shareholders' equity holdings (*HF10*) measures the voice of corporate shareholders, which may contribute to less information asymmetry, transparency, and greater access to external financing and low cost of capital (Gao, Harford, and Li 2013). Free cash flow (*FCF*) and trade receivable turnover (*TR*) measure the cash flow status and working capital management of the enterprise, respectively. If the enterprise has abundant cash flow and effective working capital management, the managers will decrease the cash holding level (Gao, Harford, and Li 2013). We controlled the annual and industry fixed effects.

In accordance with the China securities regulatory commission's 2012 industry classification guidelines, we identified the following eight industries as high-impact group, namely tourism, film and television entertainment, catering retail, transportation, realty business, construction, accommodation, and export

Table 1. Variables definitions.

Variables	Definitions
Cash holdings	Enterprise cash holding level, the calculation method is: monetary capital/current operating income.
Treated	The dummy variable of "outbreak impact degree" is 1 if the enterprise belongs to the high-impact region/industry, otherwise it is 0.
Period	The dummy variable of "outbreak time" is 1 after the outbreak, or 0 otherwise.
GW	Whether the enterprise has goodwill, the existence is 1, otherwise is 0.
GWIM	Whether the enterprise has goodwill impairment, it is 1; otherwise, it is 0.
SIZE	The size of an enterprise is measured by the logarithm of its total assets.
LEV	The asset-liability ratio is the total liabilities/total assets measure.
GROWTH	Growth rate of operating income, i.e. (current operating income – previous operating income)/previous operating income.
NROA	Net profit margin on total assets, net profit/ending balance on total assets.
HF10	The Herfindahl index 10, or the share held by the top 10 shareholders.
FCF	Free cash flow, EBITDA + depreciation and amortization – working capital increase – capital expenditure.
TR	Trade receivable turnover/1000, Trade receivable turnover = Revenue/average trade receivable balance.
IND	Used to control industry fixed effect.
YEAR	Used to control the fixed effect of year.

This table introduces all the variables of this article and their definition descriptions.

manufacturing industries. The business that the companies carried out are characterized by personnel intensive, social interaction, and cross-border trade, which are shut down during the pandemic period. Other industries are classified as low-impact industries. As for the dummy variable *Period*, we are convinced that the performance in the first quarter of 2020 should be recognized as affected-period, since the pandemic occurred between January and February 2020.

We test the second and third hypotheses H_2 and H_3 using Models (2) and (3), respectively. That is,

$$
\begin{aligned}
Cashholdings_{it} = {} & \beta_0 + \beta_1 GW_{it} * Treated_{it} * Period_{it} + \beta_2 Treated_{it} * Period_{it} \\
& + \beta_3 Treated_{it} + \beta_4 Period_{it} + \beta_5 GW_{it} + \beta_6 SIZE_{it} + \beta_7 LEV_{it} \\
& + \beta_8 GROWTH_{it} + \beta_9 NROA_{it} + \beta_{10} HF10_{it} + \beta_{11} FCF_{it} \\
& + \beta_{12} TR_{it} + \beta_{13} IND + \beta_{14} YEAR + \varepsilon_{it}
\end{aligned}
$$

$$(2)$$

$$
\begin{aligned}
Cashholdings_{it} = {} & \beta_0 + \beta_1 GWIM_{it} * Treated_{it} * Period_{it} + \beta_2 Treated_{it} * Period_{it} \\
& + \beta_3 Treated_{it} + \beta_4 Period_{it} + \beta_5 GWIM_{it} + \beta_6 SIZE_{it} \\
& + \beta_7 LEV_{it} + \beta_8 GROWTH_{it} + \beta_9 NROA_{it} + \beta_{10} HF10_{it} \\
& + \beta_{11} FCF_{it} + \beta_{12} TR_{it} + \beta_{13} IND + \beta_{14} YEAR + \varepsilon_{it}
\end{aligned}
$$

$$(3)$$

where *GW* is a dummy variable indicating "whether there is goodwill" and *GWIM* is a dummy variable indicating "whether there is goodwill impairment." The variables and their definitions are shown in Table 1.

4. Empirical Results

4.1. Descriptive Statistics

Descriptive statistics were conducted on the variables involved in the models, and the results are shown in Table 2. The average cash holding level of the dependent variable was 2.1538, and the median is 1.1499. The average cash holding level is low. In the sample, the maximum value is 22.2866, the minimum value is 0.1152, and the standard deviation is 3.1905, indicating that the cash holding level of enterprises is greatly different. The average value of enterprise size is 22.3694 and the standard deviation is 1.2814. As the variable of enterprise size is the logarithm of the actual value, the overall scale of listed companies is large. The average asset–liability ratio is 0.4166 and the median is 0.4042, indicating that the balance between liabilities and equity accounts is basically maintained, with slightly lower liabilities and a relatively reasonable leverage level. The growth rate of main business income is adopted as the enterprise development index. The average growth rate is −0.1954 and median growth rate is −0.1964, indicating that the overall enterprise income was in a declining trend in the first quarter. Using the net profit margin of total assets to measure the profitability of different enterprises, the statistical results show that the mean value is 0.0080 and the median value is 0.0062. The overall listed companies are in a break-even state with low profitability. The average shareholding ratio of the top 10 shareholders is 0.1563, which means low concentration among listed companies. The cash flow status is fragile, and the independent "hematopoietic" function of the enterprise is weak with a mean-free cash flow value of −0.1619. The standard deviation of trade receivable turnover rate is 0.0236, indicating a large gap in trade receivable turnover speed between different industries. To sum up, the listed companies are characterized by large scale, moderate leverage, low profitability, slightly declining operating income, low equity concentration, and fragile cash flow.

4.2. Unit Root Test and Parallel Trend Test

Before estimating the panel regressions, we subjected the variables to a unit root test to ensure stability. The parallel trend test can ensure that the study

Table 2. Descriptive statistics.

Variables	N	MEAN	SD	MIN	MAX	P50
Cash Holdings	11,641	2.1538	3.1905	0.1152	22.2866	1.1499
SIZE	11,641	22.3694	1.2814	19.9792	26.2424	22.1903
LEV	11,641	0.4166	0.2057	0.0506	0.8883	0.4042
GROWTH	11,641	−0.1954	0.3474	−0.8799	1.2580	−0.1964
NROA	11,641	0.0080	0.0127	−0.0231	0.0557	0.0062
HF10	11,641	0.1563	0.1125	0.0164	0.5545	0.1241
FCF	11,641	−0.1619	1.6433	−9.4023	6.4390	−0.0270
TR	11,641	0.0067	0.0236	0.00004	0.1882	0.0012

This table reports the results of all variables descriptive statistics, including mean value, minimum value, median value and maximum value.

samples are in the same trend without being impacted by the pandemic, and the experimental group and the control group are comparable. The unit root test results are shown in Table 3. All variables passed the unit root test at the 1% level, and, hence, are stable.

We proceeded to carry out the parallel trend test. Figure 1, which displays the parallel trend test, shows that the high-affected industries and low-affected industries have the same variation in trends before the pandemic outbreak, which means that the DID model is suitable for our analysis.

4.3. Regression Results

We estimate the DID model and report the results in Table 4. Column (1) reports the influence of the pandemic on the cash holding level of enterprises

Table 3. Unit root test.

Variables	Levin, Lin & Chu t*	Im-Pesaran-Shin t*	Stationarity
Cash Holdings	−2.0e+03***	−2.0937***	Stable
SIZE	−1.2e+02***	−35.6905***	Stable
LEV	−1.5e+02***	−1.8421***	Stable
GROWTH	−3.0e+02***	−2.1930***	Stable
NROA	−98.1854***	−1.8088***	Stable
HF10	−3.7e+03***	−7.8884***	Stable
FCF	−4.1e+02***	−2.6835***	Stable
TR	−3.3e+05***	−43.0748***	Stable

This table reports the results of the unit root test. * $p < 10\%$; ** $p < 5\%$; *** $p < 1\%$ (two-tailed). All reported t statistics are based on standard errors adjusted for Huber-White (White 1980).

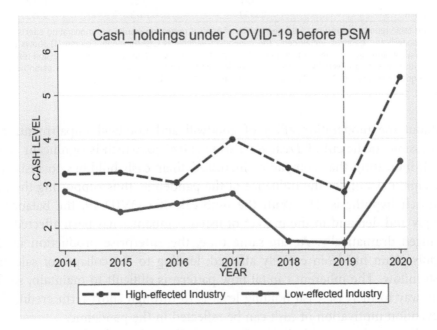

Figure 1. Parallel trend test before propensity score matching. Note: Calculated and plotted according to the financial data of China's listed energy companies from 2014 to 2020.

Table 4. The empirical results. The impact of COVID-19 on cash holdings.

	(1) Baseline	(2) GW	(3) GWIM
Treated*Period	0.4336***	0.8519***	0.5420***
	(3.6611)	(5.0973)	(4.1422)
GW*Treated*Period		−0.6887***	
		(−3.5498)	
GW		−0.2304**	
		(−2.1483)	
GWIM*Treated*Period			−0.4223*
			(−1.9516)
GWIM			−0.1197
			(−1.0283)
Treated	0.0257	0.0365	0.0283
	(0.2045)	(0.2904)	(0.2249)
Period	−0.1650*	−0.1849**	−0.1694*
	(−1.7939)	(−2.0075)	(−1.8421)
SIZE	−0.0353	−0.0133	−0.0322
	(−0.8598)	(−0.3214)	(−0.7841)
LEV	−3.8972***	−3.9039***	−3.9024***
	(−18.8964)	(−18.9293)	(−18.9090)
GROWTH	−1.3123***	−1.3126***	−1.3146***
	(−16.1685)	(−16.1799)	(−16.1957)
NROA	−27.9904***	−27.8269***	−28.0489***
	(−11.5367)	(−11.4682)	(−11.5580)
HF10	0.0342	−0.0939	−0.0152
	(0.0916)	(−0.2502)	(−0.0407)
FCF	−0.0503***	−0.0499***	−0.0500***
	(−3.7517)	(−3.7176)	(−3.7296)
TR	−5.5591***	−5.6839***	−5.6123***
	(−4.1071)	(−4.1957)	(−4.1435)
Constant	4.6799***	4.3367***	4.6615***
	(5.0101)	(4.6238)	(4.9896)
IND	YES	YES	YES
YEAR	YES	YES	YES
N	11,641	11,641	11,641
Adj-R^2	0.2950	0.2973	0.2955

This table reports the results of the regressions of original regression results and moderating effects by goodwill and goodwill impairment. The dependent variable is Cash/Revenue. Column (1) shows the original regression results without moderating effects. Columns (2) and (3) show the regression results with moderating effects by goodwill and goodwill impairment. Z-statistics is reported in parenthesis. Significance levels of 10%, 5%, and 1% are denoted by *, **, and ***, respectively.

without the moderating effect of goodwill and goodwill impairment. The regression coefficient of *Treated* ∗ *Period* is 0.4336, which is significant at 1% level, indicating that companies increased their cash holdings to resist the systemic risks under the influence of the pandemic, thus supporting the first research hypothesis, H$_1$. With the outbreak of COVID-19, the balance of supply and demand in the market of listed companies has been affected and changed dramatically. At the same time, the enterprise production in the supply chain has been entirely affected, leading to the collapse of sale and cash inflow. The inherent capital flow pattern is difficult to maintain, so the only way to increase cash holding level is to through short-term credit. The prevention motivation of cash can be reflected in the pandemic.

Column (2) reported the moderating effect of goodwill on changes in corporate cash holdings during the COVID-19 pandemic. The coefficient of

*Treated * Period* is 0.8519 and is significant at the 1% level, indicating that the cash holding level of the enterprise significantly increased during the pandemic. The interaction term of *GW * Treated * Period* is significant at the 1% level, with a coefficient of −0.6887, indicating that the presence of goodwill weakened the positive effect of the pandemic on cash holding level and supported the second research hypothesis, H_2. Enterprises with goodwill have higher non-systematic risks than others without it, and their financing costs and risks are higher. For the lending entities during the pandemic, banks and credit institutions appropriately reduced their credit line. For enterprises, their debt financing channels, and scale are hindered, and the level of cash holdings that management can increase is limited.

Column (3) reported the moderating effect of goodwill impairment on the cash holding level of enterprises during the pandemic. The main effect term (coefficient) is 0.5420, which is significant at 1%, indicating that the level of cash holding increased significantly under the influence of the pandemic. The coefficient of *GWIM * Treated * Period* is −0.4223, which is significant at the 10% level and contrary to the coefficient of the main effect, indicating that the impairment of goodwill plays a negative regulating role. This supported the third research hypothesis, H_3, that the increase in cash holding level of enterprises during the pandemic is hindered by the goodwill impairment. The goodwill impairment highlighted the mistakes made in the budget consideration of the merger and acquisition—the inability to reach the targeted performance. With the gradual bursting of the goodwill bubble, the sustainable development of the company is questioned. In this case, the lending institution needs to evaluate the credit level of the enterprise to control bad debts, which limits the financing channels and scale of the enterprise.

5. Robustness Tests

We chose propensity score matching (PSM) method and alternative dependent variables for the robustness tests. The results are consistent with the baseline results, and, hence, our conclusions are robust.

5.1. Using Alternative Dependent Variables

First, we performed the regression analysis using alternative dependent variables (Shen, Xia, and Zhang 2018). We expanded cash to cash and equivalents, including highly liquid, and interest-earning investments with financing maturities of 3 months or less. Then, we used the ratio of cash and cash equivalents to current operating income as the corporate cash holding level. The results are shown in Table 5. The first column is the influence of the pandemic on the cash holding level of enterprises without controlling goodwill and goodwill impairment effects. The regression coefficient of the interaction

Table 5. Robustness test by replacing dependent variable.

	(1)	(2)	(3)
	Baseline	GW	GWIM
Treated*Period	0.4546***	0.9964***	0.5829***
	(3.4261)	(5.3230)	(3.9771)
GW*Treated*Period		−0.8918***	
		(−4.1051)	
GW		−0.2601**	
		(−2.2067)	
GWIM*Treated*Period			−0.5003**
			(−2.0643)
GWIM			−0.1582
			(−1.2366)
Treated	0.0187	0.0315	0.0219
	(0.1347)	(0.2275)	(0.1582)
Period	0.4065***	0.3827***	0.4008***
	(3.9518)	(3.7157)	(3.8951)
SIZE	−0.0851*	−0.0589	−0.0811*
	(−1.8724)	(−1.2805)	(−1.7812)
LEV	−4.5063***	−4.5132***	−4.5141***
	(−19.6151)	(−19.6506)	(−19.6369)
GROWTH	−1.3964***	−1.3964***	−1.3995***
	(−15.3926)	(−15.4033)	(−15.4255)
NROA	−31.3060***	−31.1189***	−31.3676***
	(−11.5492)	(−11.4811)	(−11.5696)
HF10	0.3943	0.2410	0.3317
	(0.9524)	(0.5793)	(0.7989)
FCF	−0.0568***	−0.0562***	−0.0564***
	(−3.7811)	(−3.7439)	(−3.7570)
TR	−5.3562***	−5.4970***	−5.4275***
	(−3.5492)	(−3.6400)	(−3.5942)
Constant	5.9766***	5.5599***	5.9523***
	(5.7854)	(5.3615)	(5.7619)
IND	YES	YES	YES
YEAR	YES	YES	YES
N	11,641	11,641	11,641
Adj-R^2	0.2948	0.2977	0.2957

The Impact of COVID-19 on cash holdings. This table reports the results of the regressions of original regression results and moderating effects by goodwill and goodwill impairment. The dependent variable is Cash and cash equivalents/Revenue. Column (1) shows the original regression results without moderating effects. Columns (2) and (3) show the regression results with moderating effects by goodwill and goodwill impairment. Z-statistics is reported in parenthesis. Significance levels of 10%, 5%, and 1% are denoted by *, **, and ***, respectively.

term *Treated * Period* is 0.4546, which is significant at a 1% level, indicating that the pandemic has a positive effect on the cash holding level of enterprises. That is, the cash holding level significantly increased, following the pandemic, and this is consistent with the baseline results. Columns (2) and (3), respectively, report the moderating effect of goodwill and goodwill impairment on cash holding level, and their coefficients are, respectively, −0.8918 and −0.5003, proving that both goodwill and goodwill impairment could weaken the positive effect of the pandemic on cash holding level.

5.2. Estimates Based on the PSM Method

To ensure covariate balance, we re-estimate the regression after screening the variables using the PSM method. First, the parallel trend test result following

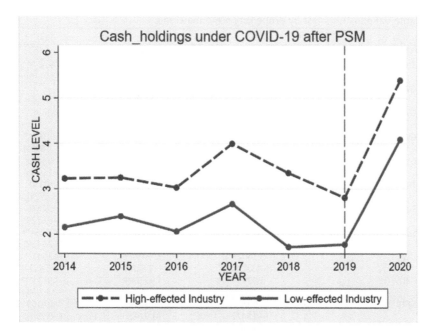

Figure 2. Parallel trend test after propensity score matching. Note: Calculated and plotted according to the financial data of China's listed energy companies from 2014 to 2020.

the PSM is shown in Figure 2. The DID regression estimates, following the PSM are reported in Table 6. We report results for the main effect, goodwill moderating effect, and goodwill impairment moderating effect. The interaction coefficient of the main effect, goodwill moderating effect, and goodwill impairment moderating effect is, respectively, 0.5053, 0.9063, and 0.6032, which were all significant at the 1% level. The moderator coefficient of goodwill is −0.6616, indicating that goodwill weakened the positive effect of the pandemic on the cash holding level. The moderator coefficient of goodwill impairment is −0.3827. This means that the occurrence of goodwill impairment also hindered the positive impact of the pandemic on the cash holding level, which is consistent with the baseline results.

6. Conclusion

This article analyzes the changes in the cash holding level of listed Chinese companies before and after the COVID-19 pandemic. By probing into the impact of the pandemic on the cash holding level of these firms, we discuss the moderating effect on cash holding level of goodwill and goodwill impairment. Our study found that the COVID-19 pandemic has a significant positive effect on the cash holding level of the listed companies. It highlights the prevention motive of holding cash, and that more enterprises choose to increase the level of cash holding to prevent systemic risks. Goodwill, to some extent,

Table 6. Robustness test by propensity score matching.

	(1)	(2)	(3)
		PS Matched	
Treated*Period	0.5053***	0.9063***	0.6032***
	(3.5385)	(4.8024)	(3.9110)
GW*Treated*Period		−0.6616***	
		(−3.2597)	
GW		−0.3065***	
		(−2.7452)	
GWIM*Treated*Period			−0.3827*
			(−1.6906)
GWIM			−0.1313
			(−1.0806)
TREAT	0.0319	0.0476	0.0350
	(0.2480)	(0.3698)	(0.2721)
Period	−0.0791	−0.1072	−0.0846
	(−0.6288)	(−0.8520)	(−0.6729)
SIZE	−0.0993**	−0.0686	−0.0954**
	(−2.2103)	(−1.5020)	(−2.1159)
LEV	−3.1602***	−3.1819***	−3.1681***
	(−13.4390)	(−13.5277)	(−13.4534)
GROWTH	−1.9099***	−1.9072***	−1.9138***
	(−18.7315)	(−18.7242)	(−18.7680)
HF10	−0.3562	−0.5409	−0.4169
	(−0.8472)	(−1.2792)	(−0.9880)
FCF	−0.0345**	−0.0340**	−0.0343**
	(−2.4062)	(−2.3726)	(−2.3908)
TR	−6.7837***	−7.0011***	−6.8555***
	(−4.2046)	(−4.3368)	(−4.2463)
Constant	5.4129***	4.9377***	5.3793***
	(5.3175)	(4.8251)	(5.2825)
IND	YES	YES	YES
YEAR	YES	YES	YES
N	8,148	8,148	8,148
Adj-R^2	0.2736	0.2766	0.2742

The Impact of COVID-19 on cash holdings. This table reports the results of the regressions of original regression results and moderating effects by goodwill and goodwill impairment. The dependent variable is Cash/Revenue. All samples are treated by propensity score matching. Column (1) shows the original regression results without moderating effects. Columns (2) and (3) show the regression results with moderating effects by goodwill and goodwill impairment. Z-statistics is reported in parenthesis. Significance levels of 10%, 5%, and 1% are denoted by *, **, and ***, respectively.

reflects the potential operating risks of enterprises. Furthermore, the goodwill impairment is a direct reflection of worse performance after the merger and reorganization, which warns the stakeholders, especially the creditors, of the risks. The systemic risk increases, and creditors will be more cautious in the measurement of loan risk under COVID-19. Therefore, the existence of goodwill or impairment of goodwill will exert a constraint on the financing capacity of enterprises and hinder the increase in cash holding level of enterprises in the special period.

Cash holding level has always been an important research topic in the field of corporate finance. This is because it plays a significant role in the operation of enterprises. In this period of COVID-19 outbreak, sudden financial crises occur from time to time across enterprises due to the associated economic shutdowns in some industries, imbalance of market supply and demand, and sudden cash gap of enterprises, among others. At the firm-level, cash flow disruption is the most fatal factor that would directly lead to bankruptcy. From the perspective of the supply chain, the business reputation between enterprises will be greatly affected due to the uncontrollable bad debts. The cash flow from operational activities would shrink as well. In response to the COVID-19 pandemic, the increased cost of pandemic prevention will also become an important source of cash flow pressure. Management must raise the level of cash holdings in order to ensure that the company can survive during the tough times and cope with the rising rigid costs. However, unsystematic risks, such as excessive mergers and acquisitions, have reduced enterprise credit capacity, leading to difficulties to maintain cash holding level and liquidity.

At present, the pandemic situation (prevention and control) is still severe. Enterprises should change their business strategies in time, while facing this turbulent economic situation and tense cash flow. The corporate should focus on changes in cash holding level, as well as cost control and the expansion of financing sources. In terms of cash flow, companies should pay attention to the level of cash holdings in a timely manner and rely on financing activities to obtain cash support in case of business shutdown and shrinking cash inflow. As for cost control, enterprises should change to the cost leadership strategy as soon as possible and reduce the daily operating costs to get liquidity. The strict control of cash cost, especially, will help enterprises alleviate the shortage of cash flow. Finally, enterprises should expand financing sources appropriately. Based on the pecking order theory, the cost of equity capital will be lower than the cost of equity financing due to the tax shield effect of debt capital, which becomes the preference of the management. In the case of the COVID-19 pandemic, however, the sources and scale of debt financing will be limited by the lenders, and there may be insufficient and untimely financing. Therefore, managers should communicate with shareholders in time to obtain cash flow support, and then maintain a high level of cash holdings to cope with sudden risks.

Notes

1. https://www.sohu.com/a/392112155_732165.
2. Special treatment deals with the special treatment of the stock transactions of listed companies with abnormal financial or other conditions because of "special treatment". *ST refers to the listed companies' loss for three consecutive years, whereby the exchange gives an early warning of delisting.
3. Missing data refers to the lack of data in some years of a listed company's dependent and independent variables, as well as control variables. The main reason for the missing data is that the listed companies have not published relevant data.

Funding

This work was supported by the Beijing Social Science Fund [19GLC074]; Fundamental Research Funds for the Central Universities [2020MS044].

ORCID

Huayu Shen ⑩ http://orcid.org/0000-0003-4093-1515

References

Acharya, V., S. A. Davydenko, and I. A. Strebulaev. 2012. Cash holdings and credit risk. *Review of Financial Studies* 25 (12):3572–609. doi:10.1093/rfs/hhs106.

Apergis, E., and N. Apergis. 2020. Can the COVID-19 pandemic and oil prices drive the US Partisan conflict index? *Energy Research Letters* 1 (1):13144. doi:10.46557/001c.13144

Clarkson, P., R. Gao, and K. Herbohn. 2020. The relationship between a firm's information environment and its cash holding decision. *Journal of Contemporary Accounting & Economics* 16 (2):100201. doi:10.1016/j.jcae.2020.100201.

Fu, M., and H. Shen. 2020. COVID-19 and corporate performance in the energy industry. *Energy Research Letters* 1 (1):12967. doi:10.46557/001c.12967

Gao, H., J. Harford, and K. Li. 2013. Determinants of corporate cash policy: Insights from private firms. *Journal of Financial Economics* 109 (3):623–39. doi:10.1016/j.jfineco.2013.04.008.

Gil-Alana, L. A., and M. Monge. 2020. Crude oil prices and COVID-19: Persistence of the shock. *Energy Research Letters* 1 (1):13200. doi:10.46557/001c.13200

Godfrey, J., and P. S. Koh. 2001. The relevance to firm valuation of capitalizing intangible assets in total and by category. *Australian Accounting Review* 11 (2):39–48. doi:10.1111/j.1835-2561.2001.tb00186.x.

Harford, J., M. Humphery-Jenner, and R. Powell. 2012. The sources of value destruction in acquisitions by entrenched managers. *Social Science Electronic Publishing* 106 (2):247–61.

Harford, J., S. Klasa, and W. F. Maxwell. 2014. Refinancing risk and cash holdings. *Journal of Finance* 69 (3):975–1012. doi:10.1111/jofi.12133.

Jennings, H., M. LeClere, and R. B. Thompson II. 2001. Goodwill amortization and the usefulness of earnings. *Financial Analysts Journal* 57 (5):20–28. doi:10.2469/faj.v57.n5.2478.

Narayan, P. K. 2020. Oil price news and COVID-19—Is there any connection? *Energy Research Letters* 1 (1):13176. doi:10.46557/001c.13176

Narayan, P. K., and D. H. B. Phan. 2020. Country responses and the reaction of the stock market to COVID-19—A preliminary exposition. *Emerging Markets Finance and Trade* 56 (10):2138–2150. doi:10.1080/1540496X.2020.1784719.

Opler, T. C., L. Pinkowitz, R. M. Stulz, and R. Williamson. 1999. The determinants and implications of corporate cash holdings. *Journal of Financial Economics.* 52 (1):3–46. doi:10.1016/S0304-405X(99)00003-3.

Shen, H., N. Xia, and J. Zhang. 2018. Customer-based concentration and firm innovation. *Asia Pacific Journal of Financial Studies* 47 (2):248–79. doi:10.1111/ajfs.12210.

White, H. 1980. A heteroskedasticity-consistent covariance matrix estimator and a direct test for heteroskedasticity. *Econometrica*, 48 (4):817-838. doi:10.2307/1912934.

Zhu, X., X. Qian, and Y. Wei. 2020. Do high-speed railways accelerate urban land expansion in China? A study based on the multi-stage difference-in-differences model. *Socio-economic Planning Sciences* 71:100846. in press. doi:10.1016/j.seps.2020.100846.

Is the Chinese Economy Well Positioned to Fight the COVID-19 Pandemic? the Financial Cycle Perspective

Ding Liu, Weihong Sun, and Xuan Zhang

ABSTRACT

This paper conducts a time-frequency analysis of the macro-financial variables in China to assess its resilience in fighting the coronavirus pandemic (COVID-19). We find that the Chinese business and financial cycles over the short, medium, and long terms all are in, or close to, the contraction phase before the COVID-19 outbreak. Meanwhile, the Chinese economy has decoupled from the global financial cycle since 2015. These results suggest that China may be better positioned than other emerging economies to win the war against the pandemic. However, extraordinary macroeconomic policies are still needed to mitigate the pandemic-induced economic meltdown.

1. Introduction

Assessing the economic impact of the coronavirus pandemic (COVID-19) is essential for policymakers, yet challenging because of huge uncertainty surrounding COVID-19 as well as a lack of timely data. According to the World Health Organization (WHO), by June 4 2020, COVID-19 has led to more than 6 million confirmed infections and nearly 0.4 million deaths in 213 countries. These numbers are increasing rapidly. High human costs that are still rising require necessary containment measures. However, these measures are severely derailing the world economy. In the World Economic Outlook report recently released by the International Monetary Fund (IMF), the global economy is projected to contract by 3% in 2020 as quarantines and lockdowns cripple output, much worse than during the 2008–09 financial crisis. Hence, it is imperative for policymakers to assess the size of the economic damage, so that effective policies can be designed to mitigate the pandemic-induced economic meltdown. However, doing so is challenging. Besides lack of data, macroeconomic policy is operating under massive uncertainty given that it is difficult to know the duration of COVID-19, the duration of containment measures being taken to flatten the infection curve, and the effect all of these will have on the economy. This paper offers a new perspective on tackling this challenge. Specifically, we study how resilient the Chinese economy is in fighting COVID-19 from the financial cycle perspective.

Our idea is simple and hinges on an established regularity: recessions that coincide with the contraction phase of a financial cycle are especially severe (Borio 2014; Reinhart and Rogoff 2011). If the Chinese financial cycle is in, or close to, the contraction phase before COVID-19, then it is possible that the pandemic-induced recession will be far worse. Accordingly, stronger macroeconomic policies, than those required otherwise, are needed to mitigate the negative impacts. Borio (2014) defines the financial cycle as "self-reinforcing interactions between perceptions of value and risk, attitudes towards risk, and financing constraints, which translate into booms followed by busts." COVID-19 has dealt an unprecedented blow to financial markets: financial conditions have tightened abruptly, with risk asset prices dropping sharply as investors have rushed to safety and liquidity (IMF 2020). The financial accelerator and related mechanisms may amplify economic fluctuations, trigger imbalance, lead to macroeconomic destabilization, and threaten financial stability (Bernanke, Gertler, and Gilchrist 1999; Kiyotaki and Moore 1997).

Our exploration is worthwhile for at least two reasons. First, as the largest emerging economy, China has been the engine of global growth for the past two decades. Hence, it is important to evaluate whether the Chinese economy is well positioned to fight COVID-19. A deeper and longer contraction in China is definitely not good for the world economy. The National Bureau of Statistics of China reported on April 17, 2020 that the Chinese gross domestic product has plunged 6.8% year on year in the first quarter of 2020, as the virus has forced factories and businesses to close. This is the first time in four decades that China has seen its economy shrinking. Our assessment offers a new perspective, which can aid policymakers in designing effective policies to prevent the public health crisis from turning into a deep, long-lasting slump. Second, COVID-19 poses unprecedented health, economic, and financial stability challenges. Financial conditions have tightened sharply amid rising uncertainty about the spread of COVID-19 and an expected drop-off in economic activity due to containment measures. Stock prices have fallen, volatility has surged, and credit spreads have widened (Baldwin and Weder Di Mauro 2020; IMF 2020). To prevent the emergence of adverse macro-financial feedback loops, it is important to look through the financial cycle lens.

For this purpose, we explore where China stands in the business and financial cycles before COVID-19. To do so, we use wavelet-based techniques to extract business and financial cycles from the Chinese macro-financial data, and quantify how these cycles are related to the global financial cycle in the time-frequency domain. This analysis is informative in assessing the severity of the economic effects of COVID-19 on the Chinese economy, in designing possible policy actions. and in gauging measures that have been taken.

Two key findings emerge from our analysis. First, time-frequency decomposition from the wavelet analysis shows that the short, medium, and long-term Chinese business and financial cycles are in, or close to, the contraction phase before COVID-19. Moreover, the downturn has become worse in the first quarter of 2020. Hence, according to the financial cycle view, extraordinary macroeconomic policies are required to mitigate the economic meltdown. This is consistent with the policy decisions in the government work report delivered by Premier Li Keqiang to the opening of the National People's Congress on Friday, May 22, 2020.[1] Among them, a variety of monetary policy tools, such as required reserve ratio reductions, interest rate cuts, and re-lending will be used to enable the M2 money supply and aggregate financing to grow at notably higher rates than 2019. On the fiscal front, the deficit-to-GDP ratio in 2020 is projected at more than 3.6%, with a deficit increase of 1 trillion yuan over last year. 1 trillion yuan of special government bonds will be issued for COVID-19 control.

Second, the Chinese business and financial cycles co-move with the global financial cycle represented by the market fear (the VIX) index before 2015.[2] The correlations are notably significant during the 2008 global financial crisis. However, this is not the case after 2015. This suggests that to fight COVID-19 and restart the economy, Chinese policymakers should pay more attention to domestic factors relative to external shocks. In this sense, China may be better positioned than other emerging economies to win the war against the pandemic. To be clear, we are not saying that a global recession will not hurt China; rather, we are suggesting that negative global spillovers are not the major threat to the current Chinese economy.

Our paper is closely related to the financial cycle literature. Financial cycle and its interaction with the business cycle has been a central policy issue since the 2008 global financial crisis. Claessens, Kose, and Terrones (2011, 2012)), Drehmann, Borio, and Tsatsaronis (2012), and Aikman, Haldane, and Nelson (2015), among others, analyze macro-financial variables such as credit and asset prices and show that financial cycles are longer and larger than business cycles, and that recessions are more severe when they coincide with financial downturns.[3] Building on these works, this paper extracts business and financial cycles from the latest Chinese macro-financial data, and quantifies how these cycles are related to global financial cycle. Then, we assess the resilience of the Chinese economy in the time of COVID-19 from the financial cycle perspective.

In terms of empirical methods, three main approaches have been used to analyze the characteristics of the financial cycle: (1) turning points algorithms (Drehmann, Borio, and Tsatsaronis 2012), (2) frequency-based filter methods (Aikman, Haldane, and Nelson 2015), and (3) spectral analysis (Strohsal, Proano, and Wolters 2019). However, these approaches have limitations. The turning point algorithms assume a fixed rule to locate local maxima and minima, while frequency-based filter methods require a pre-specified frequency band (Strohsal, Proano, and Wolters 2019). The Fourier transform only provides information regarding how much of each frequency exists in the time series. This method provides no information on how the frequency content evolves over time (Verona 2016). Wavelet analysis overcomes the aforementioned shortcomings of the alternative methods. This is because wavelet analysis allows us to consider both the frequency and time variations of a time series, without imposing a priori assumption of the frequency range at which the financial cycle is assumed to operate. Therefore, in this paper, we adopt wavelet analysis to decompose Chinese financial and business cycles. In addition, we use wavelet coherence to analyze the relationship between Chinese financial and business cycles, and the global financial cycle in the time-frequency domain, as a way to assess whether external shocks will inhibit the war against COVID-19 in China.

Our paper also contributes to the emerging COVID-19 literature. Taking the dynamics of COVID-19 as given, several papers use New Keynesian models to assess the effects of the pandemic and policy responses. Interpreting the pandemic as a large negative shock to the utility of consumption, Faria-e Castro (2020) studies different forms of fiscal policy. Fornaro and Wolf (2020) consider the pandemic as a negative shock to the productivity growth rate and show that COVID-19 may lead to stagnation traps. Guerrieri et al. (2020) show that when the negative supply shock triggered by COVID-19 asymmetrically affects different sectors of the economy, this shock can produce an even larger contraction in demand, leading to deflationary pressures.

Our work shares the same message from these papers, that is, drastic and well-designed policies are needed to minimize the economic effects of COVID-19. However, our reasons are different. There are papers that integrate epidemiological models of contagion into macroeconomic settings and study how to contain the pandemic in cost-effective ways.[4] One prominent example is Eichenbaum, Rebelo, and Trabandt (2020), who study the interaction between economic decisions and rates of infection. They consider optimal Pigouvian policy to internalize the infection externality. There are also some empirical studies seeking to determine the real-time effects of COVID-19.[5] All the papers mentioned are exclusively focusing on the US. In contrast, few papers focus on the largest emerging economy, that is, China (Fu and Shen 2020). More importantly, our paper is the first one to assess the economic impact of COVID-19 from the financial cycle perspective. This new angle generates fresh insights which may inform Chinese policymakers in their responses to COVID-19.

In the following sections of the paper, Section 2 describes the wavelet methods and data, Section 3 outlines the empirical results and policy implications, and Section 4 presents the conclusions.

2. Methods and Data

2.1. Wavelet Analysis

This subsection presents a very brief introduction to wavelet analysis. Interested readers can refer to Aguiar-Conraria and Soares (2014) for technical details. We use continuous wavelet transforms (CWT) to analyze how the Chinese financial and business cycles have evolved over time, and their lead-lag relationship with global financial cycle. Given a time series $x(t)$, its CWT with respect to the wavelet ψ is defined by the following function:

$$W_{x;\psi}(\tau, s) = \int_{-\infty}^{\infty} x(t) \frac{1}{\sqrt{|s|}} \psi^* \left(\frac{t-\tau}{s} \right) dt \qquad (1)$$

where $*$ denotes complex conjugation, s is a scaling or dilation factor that controls the width of the wavelet and τ is a translation parameter controlling its location. By mapping the original series into a function of τ and s, the wavelet transform gives us information simultaneously in the time and frequency domain.

Since wavelet transforms preserve the energy of the original time series $x(t)$, it is possible to recover $x(t)$ from its wavelet transform. We use the inverse CWT implemented in the Wavelet Toolbox of MATLAB to get the different cycle components of $x(t)$, as reported in Figures 1 and 2. Complex-valued analytic wavelets are natural choices to extract information on both amplitude and phase of cycles. Hence, this paper uses a Morlet wavelet with $\omega_0 = 6$. Further details can be found in Aguiar-Conraria and Soares (2014).

In analogy with the terminology used in Fourier analysis, the local wavelet power spectrum (WPS) is defined as

$$\text{WPS}_x(\tau, s) = |W_x(\tau, s)|^2 \qquad (2)$$

which gives us a measure of the variance distribution of the time-series in the time-frequency plane. After averaging over all times, we obtain the global wavelet power spectrum (GWPS):

$$\text{GWPS}_x(s) = \int_{-\infty}^{\infty} |W_x(\tau, s)|^2 d\tau \qquad (3)$$

We use cross-wavelet power, wavelet coherency and phase difference to deal with the time–frequency dependencies between two time-series. The cross-wavelet transform W_{xy} of two time-series, $x(t)$ and $y(t)$, is defined as

$$W_{xy}(\tau, s) = W_x(\tau, s) W_y^*(\tau, s) \qquad (4)$$

where W_x and W_y are the wavelet transforms of $x(t)$ and $y(t)$, respectively. The cross-wavelet power is then defined as $|W_{xy}(\tau, s)|$, which depicts the local

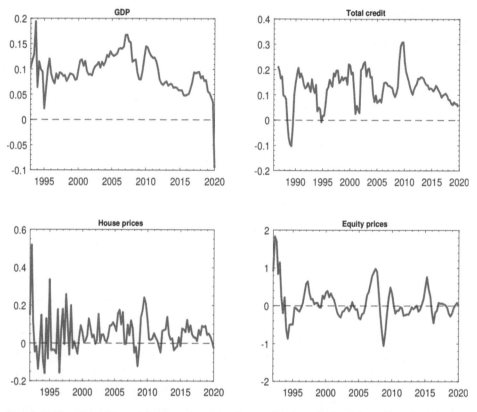

Figure 1. The data this graph plots the annual growth rates obtained by taking four-quarter differences for real GDP (1993:Q1-2020:Q1), real total credit (1986Q4-2019Q4), real house prices (1992:Q1-2020:Q1) and real equity prices (1992:Q1-2020:Q1).

covariance between two time-series at each time and frequency. The wavelet coherency R_{xy} is a normalized version of the cross-wavelet power:

$$R_{xy}(\tau, s) = \frac{\left|S\big(W_{xy}(\tau,s)\big)\right|}{\sqrt{S(|W_{xx}(\tau,s)|)S\big(\left|W_{yy}(\tau,s)\right|\big)}} \tag{5}$$

where S denotes a smoothing operator in both time and scale.

With a complex-valued wavelet coherency, we can compute the phase-difference $\phi_{x,y}$ from the cross-wavelet transform by the following formula:

$$\phi_{x,y}(\tau, s) = arctan\left(\frac{\Im\big(W_{xy}(\tau,s)\big)}{\Re\big(W_{xy}(\tau,s)\big)}\right) \tag{6}$$

where arctan is the inverse tangent function; $\Re\big(W_{xy}(\tau, s)\big)$ and $\Im\big(W_{xy}(\tau, s)\big)$ are the real and imaginary part of $W_{xy}(\tau, s)$, respectively. We have $\phi_{x,y} \in [-\pi, \pi]$. A phase difference of zero indicates that the time series $x(t)$ and $y(t)$ move together at the specified frequency. If $\phi_{x,y} \in (0, \pi/2)$, then the two series move in phase, but the time-series $x(t)$ leads $y(t)$; if

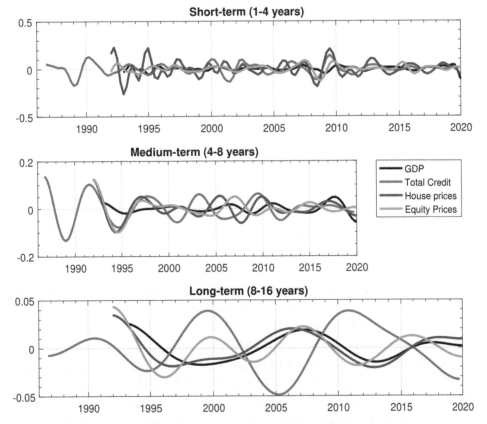

Figure 2. Chinese business and financial cycles in different frequencies. This graph plots short-, medium- and long-term cycles for the growth rate of real GDP (black solid), total credit (red solid), house prices (blue solid) and equity prices (green solid).

$\phi_{x,y} \in (-\pi/2, 0)$, then $y(t)$ leads; a phase difference of π (or $-\pi$) indicates an antiphase relation; if $\phi_{x,y} \in (\pi/2, \pi)$, then $y(t)$ is leading, while $x(t)$ is leading if $\phi_{x,y} \in (-\pi, -\pi/2)$.

2.2. Data and Descriptive Statistics

In this subsection, we describe the data used in our wavelet analyzes. We use data for three of the most common proxies for the financial cycle: (1) total credit to the private, non-financial sector; (2) residential property prices; and (3) equity prices.[6] The Chinese financial system is dominated by a banking sector with large state-owned banks. These banks have played a critical role in financing the state sectors, and the investment-driven economic growth (Allen, Qian, and Gu 2017). The real estate market has systemic importance to the Chinese economy, since local governments, firms, and households use real estate as collateral for debt financing (Liu and Xiong 2018). This induces pro-cyclicality of credit and real estate prices. Meanwhile, credit-to-GDP ratio is predictive of financial crises (Schularick and Taylor 2012). Intuitively, credit-to-GDP ratio, as an approximate measure of leverage in the macro-economy, can be used as an indirect indicator of the absorptive capacity of the financial system. Finally, the stock market in China now has more than 3000 firms listed and traded in the Shanghai and Shenzhen exchanges. The domestic A-share market is the second largest in the world in terms of total market capitalization, trailing only the US equity markets (Allen, Qian, and Gu 2017).

Accordingly, we collect the following indicators as representative variables of the Chinese financial cycle. The time series of total credit to the private, non-financial sector is taken from the credit statistics compiled by the Bank for International Settlements (BIS). Residential property prices are represented by the average commercial housing sales price, which in turn is equal to the total revenue of housing sales divided by the floor area of housing sales. The Shanghai Stock Exchange Composite Index is taken as a representative indicator of the Chinese stock market. GDP serves as the representative variable for the business cycle. Following Rey (2015) and Cerutti, Claessens, and Rose (2019), we use the VIX index as a proxy for the global financial cycle. All data except the total credit come from the Wind Economic Database.[7] All of the variables are quarterly with the sample period being as long as possible: GDP (1993: Q1-2020: Q1), total credit (1986:Q4-2019:Q4), house prices (1992:Q1-2020:Q1), equity prices (1992:Q1-2020:Q1) and the VIX (1991:Q2-2020:Q1). All series except the VIX are seasonally adjusted, deflated by the consumer price index and measured in logs. Then, annual growth rates are obtained by taking four-quarter differences for each time series. Figure 1 reports the time series of the four Chinese macro-financial variables.

Table 1 contains descriptive statistics of all variables. The real GDP growth in China is quite high and relatively stable. The average real GDP growth rate is about 9.5%, while the standard deviation is 3.6%. The growth rates of equity prices are far more volatile than those of total credit, and house prices. The average growth rate of stock prices is 6.7%, but the standard deviation is as high as 43.7%. Overall, Chinese financial cycles are more pronounced than business cycles as they exhibit larger changes over the cycle and tend to be more violent. Moreover, the correlation coefficients return positive signs.

Table 1. Descriptive statistics for the data. This table reports the means, standard deviations and correlation coefficients for the data. Note that the variables are annual growth rate obtained by taking four-quarter differences for real GDP (1993:Q1-2020:Q1), real total credit (1986Q4-2019Q4), real house prices (1992:Q12020:Q1), real equity prices (1992:Q1-2020:Q1) and the VIX (1991Q2-2020Q1).

	Mean	Standard deviation	Correlation with GDP	Correlation with VIX
GDP	0.095	0.036	1.000	−0.175
Total credit	0.127	0.068	0.144	−0.059
House prices	0.051	0.094	0.063	−0.082
Stock prices	0.067	0.437	0.224	−0.124
VIX	0.045	0.358	−0.175	1.000

Consistent with the financial cycle literature, total credit, house prices, and equity prices are procyclical, and the Chinese macro-financial variables are all negatively correlated with the VIX. This is quite intuitive: higher VIX growth implies higher levels of global market fear which have adverse spillover effects on the economic and financial activities in China. The results below show that these negative spillover effects from the global financial cycle to the Chinese business and financial cycles are pronounced during some sub-sample periods only before 2015.

3. Empirical Analysis and Policy Implications

3.1. Where China Is Standing over the Business and Financial Cycles?

We use the inverse continuous wavelet transforms to isolate different cycle components of the Chinese macro-financial variables. Figure 2 shows the results. We group the cycle components into three categories, that is "short-term" (1–4 years), "medium-term" (4–8 years), and "long-term'" (8–16 years).[8] The short-term and medium-term cycles capture high frequency fluctuations which correspond to traditional business cycle frequencies, while the long-term category obtains low frequency fluctuations. Consistent with the literature, the Chinese financial cycles, particularly in terms of total credit, are much longer and larger than business cycles. However, we do not emphasize this pattern here. Similarly, we choose not to relate these cycles to events like the 2008 global financial crisis that have occurred during the sample period, since this is not our focus. In this respect, interested readers can refer to Wang and Li (2019) for some discussions. For this paper, the main message is clear: the short, medium, and long-term Chinese business and financial cycles are in, or close to, the contraction phase before COVID-19.

Claessens, Kose, and Terrones (2011, 2012) and Drehmann, Borio, and Tsatsaronis (2012) show that recessions are deeper when they coincide with the contraction phase of the financial cycle. In addition, Drehmann, Borio, and Tsatsaronis (2012) use the average of the medium-term cycle in credit and house prices to construct a synthetic financial cycle, and then contrast it with the business cycle identified by the short-term frequency filter. These considerations motivate us to use Figure 3 to highlight whether the current Chinese financial cycle is in the contraction phase and coinciding with the downturn induced by COVID-19. It is appealing to proxy the financial cycle by the average of total credit and house prices here, since the stock market in China is not as important as the banking system in funding economic activities (Allen, Qian, and Gu 2017). Figure 3 clearly tells us that the present economic meltdown in China coincides with the contraction phase of the financial cycle.

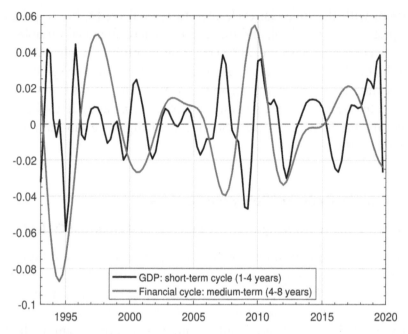

Figure 3. Chinese short-term business cycle versus medium-term financial cycle. This graph plots short-term business cycle (black solid) and medium-term financial cycle (red solid). The latter is calculated as the average of the medium-term cycles for the growth rate of total credit and house prices.

3.2. Synchronization with Global Financial Cycle

In this subsection, we present the coherence and phase differences between each pair of Chinese macro-financial variables and the global financial cycle. The phase-difference is represented by a thick red line. The green line represents the phase of the Chinese macro-financial variables, and the blue line represents the phase of the VIX. Our tools give quantified indications of co-movement between time series, and a measure of the lead-lag relationship of their oscillations at each frequency and each point in time.

3.2.1. Total Credit

First, we take total credit as the indicator of the Chinese financial cycle. China has been increasingly integrated into the world economy and opening up its financial markets. Thus, we expect total credit to relate significantly with the VIX, at least during some sub-sample periods. The results are presented in Figure 4, which include the coherency, the phases, and the phase differences for the total credit-VIX pair.[9]

For cycles of 1–4 years, the coherency is significant from 1997 to 2003. For cycles in the frequency bands of 4–8 years, there is a large region of significant coherency between total credit and the VIX between 2003 and 2015. There is also a significant coherency for cycles of 8–16 years, but this turns non-

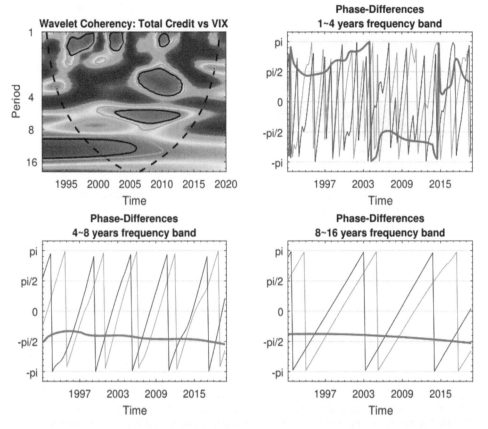

Figure 4. Chinese financial cycle and global financial cycle: total credit vs VIX. This graph plots the coherency at each time-frequency region and the phase differences between the total credit and the VIX. The green line represents the phase of the total credit, and the blue line represents the phase of the VIX.

significant around 2010. The phase differences provide evidence that the VIX is not an important predictor for total credit in China since 2015. At the 4–8 years band, until 2015, an increase in the VIX preceded an increase in total credit. The timing of these results is consistent with the occurrence of the 1997 Asian financial crisis and the 2008 global financial crisis. The main message is that the Chinese financial cycle, in terms of total credit, has been decoupled from the global one since 2015.

3.2.2. House Prices

We now take the house prices as an indicator of the Chinese financial cycle and assess its relation to the VIX, which serves as the proxy for the global financial cycle. We expect the house prices to relate significantly with the VIX, at least during some important sub-sample periods. The results are presented in Figure 5. For cycles of 4–8 years, there is a large region of significant coherency between house prices and the VIX between 2007 and 2013. There is also

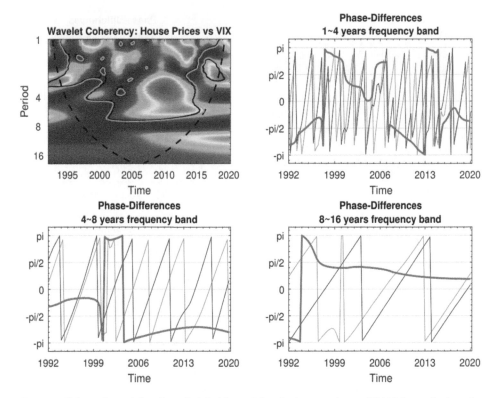

Figure 5. Chinese financial cycle and global financial cycle: house prices vs VIX. This graph plots the coherency at each time-frequency region and the phase differences between the house prices and the VIX. The green line represents the phase of the house prices, and the blue line represents the phase of the VIX.

a significant coherency for cycles of 1–4 years since 2018. The phase differences show that at the 4–8 years band, the VIX index is negatively correlated with Chinese property prices, which are leading. However, the VIX is positively correlated with, and leads the Chinese financial cycle at higher frequency in terms of house prices since 2018. This suggests that the housing market in China is affected by the global cycle in the short run, though the evidence is not strong.

3.2.3. Equity Prices

As the last indicator of the Chinese financial cycle, we consider equity prices and assess its relation to the VIX. We expect the equity prices to also relate significantly with the VIX index, at least during some important sub-sample periods. The results are presented in Figure 6. Relative to total credit and house prices, the Chinese stock market is less correlated with the global financial cycle. Only cycles of 1–4 years during the Asian and global financial crises show short-lived regions of significant coherency. Hence, the stock market and

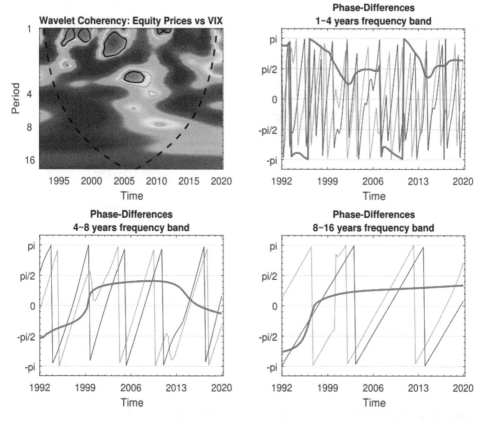

Figure 6. Chinese financial cycle and global financial cycle: stock prices vs VIX. This graph plots the coherency at each time-frequency region and the phase differences between the stock prices and the VIX. The green line represents the phase of the stock prices, and the blue line represents the phase of the VIX.

total credit convey the same message that the Chinese financial cycle has been decoupled from the global one since 2015.

3.2.4. Business Cycle

Finally, we explore how the business cycle in China is correlated with the global financial cycle over time. China has grown into the largest exporting country in the world. Thus, we expect output to relate significantly with the VIX, at least during some sub-sample periods. The results are presented in Figure 7. For cycles in the frequency bands of 1–4 and 4–8 years, there is a large region of significant coherency between output and the VIX between 2005 and 2015. The phase differences suggest that the VIX is an important predictor for output growth in China during the period covering the 2008 global financial crisis. An increase in the fear index precedes a decrease in Chinese economic growth. However, this co-movement has been broken or at least has become far weaker since 2015.

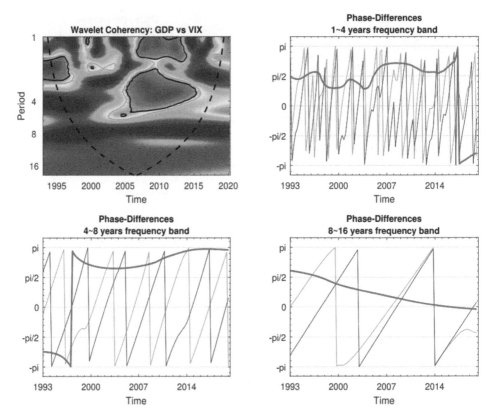

Figure 7. Chinese business cycle and global financial cycle: output vs VIX. This graph plots the coherency at each time-frequency region and the phase differences between the Chinese real GDP and the VIX. The green line represents the phase of the real GDP, and the blue line represents the phase of the VIX.

3.3. Policy Implications

COVID-19 is a large negative demand shock and an adverse supply shock that creates new policy challenges for Chinese policymakers. In the short run, the priority is to contain the spread of the virus and to adopt emergency relief measures that mitigate economic and financial impacts of COVID-19. The macroeconomic policy goal in the near term is not to stimulate the economy, but rather to support those affected by the containment measures. As Gourinchas (2020, 32) puts it, "flattening the infection curve inevitably steepens the macroeconomic recession curve." After the spread of the pandemic has been controlled and containment measures relaxed, macroeconomic policy can turn to stimulating aggregate demand and hence boost the economic recovery.

These principles suggest that monetary policy measures should lean against the tightening of financial conditions and maintain the flow of credit to the real economy. Unlike major advanced economies, policy rates in China are not near or below zero. Therefore, a variety of monetary policy tools such as required reserve ratio reductions, interest rate cuts, and re-lending are available to preserve the stability of the financial system and support the economy. One major finding in this paper is that the Chinese business and financial cycles over the short, medium, and long term all are in, or close to, the contraction phase before COVID-19. Hence, monetary policy is advised to be forward-looking and decisive when needed, and to monitor likely financial sector vulnerabilities in the near term. After all, financial conditions play an important role in determining the distribution of economic growth (Adrian, Boyarchenko, and Giannone 2019).

COVID-19 has led to a series of unprecedented fiscal interventions by governments worldwide (Baldwin and Weder Di Mauro 2020). The fiscal policy response in China to COVID-19 also has been both robust and timely. Given the nature of COVID-19, large, timely and targeted fiscal measures are necessary to ensure that a temporary shutdown of economic activity does not lead to permanent damage to the productive capacity of the economy, and to avoid a deep, long-lasting slump (Fornaro and Wolf 2020; Guerrieri et al. 2020). One thing to be cautious about is that declining tax revenue plus large fiscal expenditures including fee exemptions, cost reductions, and subsidies will lead to sharp increases in both public and private debt in the near future. The resulting debt burden may impact both economic recovery and medium term growth prospects.

In summary, the outlook for COVID-19 and economic activity is uncertain. Macroeconomic policies for coping with COVID-19 can be divided into relief measures and recovery policies, which are appropriate at different stages. The scale, scope, and timing of the monetary and fiscal policy responses in China to COVID-19 are extraordinary and certainly cushion the unprecedented shock. However, additional support from both macroeconomic policies may be needed, depending on the course of COVID-19, and the depth and duration of the downturn it causes. As indicated by the main findings of this paper, the upside is that for the Chinese economy, external shocks may be less concerning relative to domestic factors. However, policy responses are urged to consider the phase of the current financial cycle.

4. Conclusion

COVID-19 has led to an economic meltdown in China – the largest emerging economy and the engine of global growth for the past two decades. Hence, it is important to evaluate the resilience of the Chinese economy in the time of COVID-19. For this purpose, we use wavelet-based techniques to identify where China stands with regards to the business and financial cycles, as well as to quantify how these cycles are related to the global financial cycle in the time-frequency domain before COVID-19. Two main findings emerge. First, the short, medium, and long term Chinese business and financial cycles are in, or close to, the contraction phase before COVID-19. Second, the Chinese business and financial cycles are basically decoupled from the global financial cycle since 2015. These results suggest that domestic factors are probably far more important than external shocks in fighting COVID-19 and restarting the Chinese economy. In this sense, China may be better positioned than other emerging economies to win the war against COVID-19. However, extraordinary macroeconomic policies may be still required to mitigate the pandemic-induced economic meltdown.

Two directions for future research are worth pursuing. One is applying the same methodology to other emerging economies like India or Brazil which are suffering from COVID-19, and assessing whether these countries have the same resilience as China does. The other is incorporating financial cycles into the New Keynesian DSGE framework with SIR or SIER models of contagion. This will allow us to conduct counterfactual experiments in quantifying the effects of COVID-19 on both financial and macroeconomic stability.

Notes

1. The report can be accessed via http://english.www.gov.cn/2020special/govtworkreport2020.
2. The VIX index reflects the forward-looking volatility implied by options on the S&P 500 index.
3. See Borio (2014) for an excellent summary of the stylized facts of financial cycles.
4. Atkeson (2020) provides a useful overview of the susceptible-infectious-recovered (SIR) models and their implications in the current COVID-19 pandemic.
5. see Apergis and Apergis (2020) and Baker et al. 2020) for examples.
6. The survey paper by Borio (2014) concludes that the most parsimonious description of the financial cycle is in terms of credit and property prices.
7. The official introduction of this database can be accessed via https://www.wind.com.cn/en/edb.html.
8. The growth rates of equity prices are much higher relative to those of other variables, so we rescale them by
   dividing by 10 in the plot.
9. Wavelet coherency ranges from blue (low coherency) to red (high coherency). The dark lines represent regions of statistically significant powers at 5%, while gray lines delimit regions significant at 10%. A black dashed line indicates the cone of influence which is affected by edge effects, and where caution should be applied when interpreting the evidence. The phase-difference is represented by a thick red line. The same interpretation applies to other similar figures.

Acknowledgments

We thank the editor and two anonymous referees for helpful suggestions. We also thank the participants of 2020 EMFT Online Symposium on the Pandemics for comments. However, all errors remain our own.

Funding

Ding Liu would like to gratefully acknowledge the financial support from the Collaborative Innovation Center of Financial Security at SWUFE (Grant No. JRXT202005). Xuan Zhang would like thank the financial support from National Natural Science Foundation of China (Grant No. 71801117). This work was supported by the National Natural Science Foundation of China [No. 71801117]; CICFDSC [No. JRXT202005].

References

Adrian, T., N. Boyarchenko, and D. Giannone. 2019. Vulnerable growth. *American Economic Review* 109 (4):1263–89.

Aguiar-Conraria, L., and M. J. Soares. 2014. The continuous wavelet transform: Moving beyond uni- and bivariate analysis. *Journal of Economic Surveys* 28 (2):344–75.

Aikman, D., A. G. Haldane, and B. D. Nelson. 2015. Curbing the credit cycle. *The Economic Journal* 125 (585):1072–109.

Allen, F., J. Qian, and X. Gu. 2017. An overview of China's financial system. *Annual Review of Financial Economics* 9:191–231.

Apergis, E., and N. Apergis. 2020. Can the COVID-19 pandemic and oil prices drive the US partisan conflict index? *Energy Research Letters* 1:1.doi:10.46557/001c.13144. doi:10.46557/001c.12967.

Atkeson, A. 2020. What will be the economic impact of COVID-19 in the US? Rough estimates of disease scenarios. *NBER Working Paper No. 26867.*

Baker, S. R., N. Bloom, S. J. Davis, and S. J. Terry. 2020. COVID-induced economic uncertainty, *NBER Working Paper No. 26983.*

Baldwin, R., and E. Weder Di Mauro. 2020. *Mitigating the COVID economic crisis: Act fast and do whatever it takes*. London, UK: Centre for Economic Policy Research Press.

Bernanke, B. S., M. Gertler, and S. Gilchrist. 1999. The financial accelerator in a quantitative business cycle framework. Chapter 21 in *Handbook of macroeconomics, Vol. 1*, ed. J. B. Taylor and M. Woodford, 1341–93. Amsterdam: North Holland.

Borio, C. 2014. The financial cycle and macroeconomics: What have we learnt? *Journal of Banking & Finance* 45:182–98.

Cerutti, E., S. Claessens, and A. K. Rose. 2019. How important is the global financial cycle? evidence from capital flows. *IMF Economic Review* 67 (1):24–60.

Claessens, S., M. A. Kose, and M. E. Terrones. 2011. Financial cycles: What? how? when? In. *NBER International Seminar on Macroeconomics* 7:303–44.

Claessens, S., M. A. Kose, and M. E. Terrones. 2012. How do business and financial cycles interact? *Journal of International Economics* 87 (1):178–90.

Drehmann, M., C. E. Borio, and K. Tsatsaronis. 2012. Characterizing the financial cycle: Don't lose sight of the medium term! *BIS Working Papers No. 380.*

Eichenbaum, M. S., S. Rebelo, and M. Trabandt. 2020. The macroeconomics of epidemics, *NBER Working Paper No. 26882.*

Faria-e Castro, M. 2020. Fiscal policy during a pandemic. *FRB St. Louis Working Paper 2020-006E.*

Fornaro, L., and M. Wolf. 2020. COVID-19 coronavirus and macroeconomic policy. *CEPR Working Paper No. 14529.*

Fu, M., and H. Shen. 2020. COVID-19 and corporate performance in the energy industry. *Energy Research Letters* 1:1.

Gourinchas, P.-O. 2020. Flattening the pandemic and recession curves. Unpublished note.

Guerrieri, V., G. Lorenzoni, L. Straub, and I. Werning. 2020. Macroeconomic implications of COVID-19: Can negative supply shocks cause demand shortages? *NBER Working Paper No. 26918.*

IMF. 2020. Global financial stability report: Markets in the time of COVID-19, April.

Kiyotaki, N., and J. Moore. 1997. Credit cycles. *Journal of Political Economy* 105:211–48.

Liu, C., and W. Xiong. 2018. China's real estate market, *NBER Working Paper No. 25297.*

Reinhart, C., and K. Rogoff. 2011. *This time is different.* Princeton: Princeton University Press.

Rey, H. 2015. Dilemma not trilemma: The global financial cycle and monetary policy independence, *NBER Working Paper No. 21162.*

Schularick, M., and A. M. Taylor. 2012. Credit booms gone bust: Monetary policy, leverage cycles, and financial crises, 1870-2008. *American Economic Review* 102 (2):1029–61.

Strohsal, T., C. R. Proano, and J. Wolters. 2019. Characterizing the financial cycle: Evidence from a frequency domain analysis. *Journal of Banking & Finance* 106:568–91.

Verona, F. 2016. Time–frequency characterization of the US financial cycle. *Economics Letters* 144:75–79.

Wang, B., and H. Li. 2019. The time-varying characteristics of the Chinese financial cycle and impact from the United States. *Applied Economics* 52 (11):1200–18.

The Disease Outbreak Channel of Exchange Rate Return Predictability: Evidence from COVID-19

Bernard Njindan Iyke

ABSTRACT

We provide novel evidence that disease outbreaks contain valuable information that can be used to enhance exchange rate return and volatility predictions. Our analysis exploits the novel coronavirus (COVID-19) outbreak as a good experimental setup to test our intuition. Data show that the COVID-19 outbreak has been rapid and deadly. Using the total number of infections per million, we demonstrate that COVID-19 has better predictive power over volatility than over returns for a one-day ahead forecast horizon. Conversely, COVID-19 tends to shape returns more than volatility over a five-day ahead forecast horizon. Our findings remain intact over the two forecast horizons using the total number of deaths per million as an alternative COVID-19 measure. This evidence supports a new channel of exchange rate return predictability, namely the disease outbreak channel.

1. Introduction

We test the intuition that disease outbreaks contain important information that can enhance exchange rate return and volatility predictions. Our test exploits daily data on the recent COVID-19 outbreak. We show that the information contained in the COVID-19 outbreak can be used to predict returns and volatility of specific currencies. We specifically document two sets of findings. First, considering a one-day ahead forecast horizon, the COVID-19 pandemic can predict, at best, two exchange rate returns, USD–CLP and USD–SEK, and six exchange rate return volatility, USD–CHF, USD–CNY, USD–ILS, USD–JPY, USD–PEN, and USD–KRW. Second, considering a 5-day ahead forecast horizon, the pandemic can predict eight returns, namely USD–CAD, USD–CHF, USD–EUR, USD–INR, USD–PLN, USD–SEK, USD–GBP, and GBP–USD, and four return volatility, USD–CAD, USD–EUR, USD–SEK, and USD–GBP.[1] These results are robust to a competing measure of COVID-19 outbreak and to a competing model.[2]

The empirical analysis is stepwise. First, we utilize the COVID-19 outbreak as a unique experimental setup to test our intuition. That is, we retrieve a unique dataset that contains information on the number of cases (infections) and deaths, new cases and deaths, and total cases and deaths per million, compiled by Our World in Data.[3] Following, Narayan and Phan (2020), we focus on the 25 most affected countries by COVID-19 based on the number of infections and deaths.[4] Ten out of the 25 countries, namely Brazil (BRA), Chile (CHL), China (CHN), India (IND), Israel (ISR), Korea (KOR), Peru (PER), Poland (POL), Russia (RUS), and Turkey (TUR), are generally classified as emerging markets, whereas the remaining 15 are advanced economies.[5] Second, we combine the COVID-19 dataset with an exchange rate return dataset covering 17 bilateral exchange rates.[6] Thus, the sample selection provides a comprehensive picture regarding the reaction of a broad spectrum of exchange rates to the COVID-19 outbreak. The sample is from 31/12/2019 to 08/05/2020 – the start date chosen to mark the first recorded COVID-19 case.

Third, we examine key properties of the data and document evidence of heteroskedasticity and persistency, in line with prior studies (see, e.g., Narayan, Sharma, and Phan 2019; Sharma, Phan, and Narayan 2019). Fourth, to properly handle our moderate sample setup, we estimate bivariate generalized autoregressive conditional heteroskedasticity models of order one, GARCH(1,1). In this setup, we explore the impact of COVID-19 on return volatility by introducing an indicator of COVID-19 in the variance equation.

The efficient market hypothesis assumes that economic agents are rational and optimize their utility rationally. This means that agents consider all relevant information when buying or selling assets (see Iyke 2019). Hence, asset prices reflect all available information. An important implication of this theory is that asset prices (returns) follow a random walk process, so that analysts can only consistently outperform the market by taking higher risks or by exploiting inside information (Iyke 2019). Central to this theory is that agents are rational, and information is symmetric. In the real world, these conditions are rarely met, and, hence, asset prices/returns do not follow a random walk process. Information flow becomes critical to asset price or return discovery.

Along this line of thought, and contrary to Meese and Rogoff (1983), several studies show that anomalies in the foreign exchange market can be exploited to develop exchange rate frameworks/strategies that outperform a random walk framework.[7] In a stochastic model of exchange rate determination, for example, Edwards (1983) demonstrates that unanticipated news plays an important role in the spot rate discovery, and that new information explains the market forecasting error of exchange rates. A related argument has been earlier made by Frenkel (1981), who shows that exogenous news (events) spur exchange rate volatility and deviations from purchasing power parity. Similarly, Hodrick (1989) shows that unanticipated macroeconomic events – exogenous swings in the conditional variances of income growth, and monetary and fiscal policies –

affect risk premia, which influence the first- and second-order exchange rate moments. Rime, Sarno, and Sojli (2010) show that order flow can explain and forecast exchange rates, if order flow mirrors agents' heterogeneous expectations regarding macroeconomic fundamentals, and foreign exchange markets slowly digest macroeconomic news.

Recent studies find support for the role of unanticipated information in the prediction of exchange rate returns and/or volatility. For example, Narayan et al. (2018) and Sharma, Phan, and Narayan (2019) find that unanticipated events like terrorism and government shutdowns contain valuable information that enhances exchange rate return prediction. We draw inspirations from these studies and test whether unanticipated events can help us better understand exchange rates. The novelty of our study is that, unlike existing studies, we provide an empirical evidence that disease outbreaks may contain valuable information to understanding exchange return and volatility. Disease outbreaks are often unexpected and even when expected, the magnitude of their impact (rate of infections and deaths) cannot be predicted with certainty. The negative sentiments or panics associated with them could have a substantial impact on financial markets (Ali, Alam, and Rizvi, 2020; Fu and Shen 2020; Gil-Alana and Monge 2020; Liu, Wang, and Lee 2020; Narayan 2020). Haroon and Rizvi (2020) show that sentiments generated by COVID-19 related news lead to stock market fluctuations. We exploit the information contained in the COVID-19 outbreak to predict exchange rate return and volatility across emerging and advanced markets.

Our analysis is an extension of the broad literature on exchange rate determination (Iyke 2018). This literature mainly emphasizes fundamental macroeconomic indicators, such as foreign interest rates, government spending, terms of trade, and net assets, among others, as key determinants of equilibrium exchange rates (Iyke 2018). We identify disease outbreaks as an alternative channel of exchange rate behavior. Particularly, we demonstrate that disease outbreaks can explain and forecast exchange rate return and volatility. Our empirical exploit seeks to spur theoretical development on the connection between disease outbreaks and exchange rate determination.

We proceed as follows: Section II presents the descriptive analysis and the results. Section III concludes the paper.

2. Descriptive Analysis and Results

2.1. Descriptive Analysis

Figure 1 shows the mean number of COVID-19 cases and deaths recorded between 31/12/2019 and 08/05/2020. Following Narayan and Phan (2020), we focus on the 25 most affected countries by COVID-19 based on the number of infections and deaths, and the cutoff date for this ranking is 16/04/2020. Panel

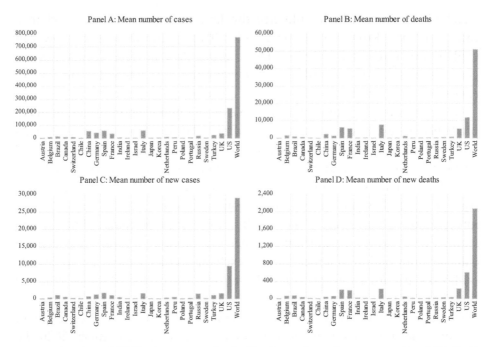

Figure 1. Number of COVID-19 cases and deaths. The figure shows the mean number of COVID-19 cases and deaths recorded between 31/12/2019 and 08/05/2020. For consistency with our empirical analysis, these plots exclude weekend observations. Panels A, B, C, and D show, respectively, the mean number of cases, deaths, new cases, and new deaths.

A shows that, on average, the US recorded the highest number of people infected by COVID-19 per day, i.e., approximately 229,253 cases per day, followed by Italy 59,525, Spain 58,297, China 56,241, and Germany 43,136 cases per day. During the same period, Poland recorded, on average, the least number of infections per day, i.e., 2,773 cases per day, followed by Japan 3,095, Chile 3,427, Israel 3,975, and Ireland 4,284 cases per day, in that order. The average number of COVID-19 infections recorded per day worldwide during the same period is 770,582.

The mean number of COVID-19 infections/cases translates to the mean number of deaths per day, as shown in Panel B. The US leads, in terms of the average number of deaths from COVID-19 per day, recording approximately 11,727 deaths per day, which is trailed by Italy, 7,552, Spain 6,133, France 5,371, and the UK 5,307 deaths per day. Chile recorded the lowest average number of deaths per day from the pandemic, reporting approximately 41 deaths per day, followed by Israel 45, Japan 80, Korea 87, and Poland 115 deaths per day. During the same period, approximately 50,812 deaths per day were recorded worldwide.

With regards to new infections, on average, the US leads, recording approximately 9,328 infections per day. This is followed by Spain, Italy, the UK, and Russia, which recorded approximately 1,729, 1,580, 1,536, and 1,423 new infections per day, respectively. On average, Korea, Japan, Poland, Israel, and Austria recorded the least number of infections per day, equivalent of 75, 100, 115, 122, and 124 infections per day, respectively. In terms of new deaths per day, the US again leads, recording approximately 595 new deaths per day, followed by the UK (226), Italy (222), Spain (203), and France (191). Israel, Korea, and Chile recorded the least number of new deaths per day (i.e. approximately two deaths per day), followed by Japan (4) and Austria (5). Over the same period, approximately 28,909 and 62,064 mean number of new infections and deaths per day, respectively, were recorded worldwide.

Figure 1 clearly shows that the COVID-19 outbreak has been rapid and deadly. The sheer impact of this pandemic is reflected in the swift policies, including lockdowns and stimulus packages, implemented by countries across the globe.[8] Naturally, financial markets reacted to the panic associated with the pandemic – in this regard, foreign exchange markets are no different. Figure 2 shows the reaction of two different exchange rates, the US dollar–British pound (GBP–USD) and the Indian rupee–US dollar (USD–INR) exchange rates, to COVID-19 between 31/12/2019 and 08/05/2020. The US dollar reacted by appreciating against the British pound, while the Indian rupee reacted by depreciating against the US dollar.[9] Note that the reaction of these currencies is consistent across currency pairs. For instance, the Indian rupee depreciated against the Australian dollar, British pound, and the Canadian dollar, as well, while the US dollar appreciated against these currencies.[10]

Table 1 shows summary statistics for exchange returns, and the total number of COVID-19 cases and deaths per million. Note that TCM_ and TDM_ denote, respectively, the total number of COVID-19 cases and deaths per million (see Table A1 in appendix for details). We use direct quotes of the exchange rates as one US dollar to units of the domestic currencies. To examine the US exchange rate return and volatility predictability, we quoted the British pound in US dollar units (i.e. GBP–USD). We utilize the closing price of the exchange rate, and a decrease in the exchange rate indicates a depreciation of the domestic currency against the US dollar. We calculate exchange rate returns (EXR_t) as $ln(EX_t/EX_{t-1})x100$, where EX_t is the exchange rate at time t. We collected the exchange rate and COVID-19 datasets from the Global Financial Data and Our World in Data, respectively.

Since the exchange rates are direct quotes, positive returns imply a depreciation of the local currency against the US dollar – the exception being the GBP–USD, which implies a depreciation of the US dollar against the British pound. The statistics suggest that all currencies, except USD–JPY and GBP–USD, have positive mean values. These exchange rates have, therefore, depreciated over the period of the COVID-19 pandemic. The two returns (USD–JPY and GBP–USD) recorded negative mean values and, hence, these currencies appreciated over the sample period. In practice, the JPY and USD

Table 1. Summary statistics.

Variable	Mean	SD	Skewness	Kurtosis	JB	ADF	AR	ARCH
USD–BRL	0.3817	1.1502	-0.0806	3.8355	0.2459	-10.1737(0.0000)	-0.0877(0.4143)	0.3652(0.8328)
USD–CAD	0.0751	0.6495	0.5357	4.8273	0.0002	-9.2887(0.0000)	0.0191(0.8568)	0.1065(0.9799)
USD–CHF	0.0031	0.5535	0.1810	4.6503	0.0040	-7.7717(0.0000)	0.1959(0.0616)	0.5904(0.6705)
USD–CLP	0.1007	0.8939	0.0047	3.3575	0.7805	-10.8324(0.0000)	-0.1459(0.1713)	1.2044(0.3152)
USD–CNY	0.0171	0.3139	1.0424	5.2582	0.0000	-11.0784(0.0001)	-0.1549(0.1407)	0.5433(0.7043)
USD–EUR	0.0364	0.5825	0.2928	4.5917	0.0038	-8.1025(0.0000)	0.1564(0.1367)	0.4989(0.7366)
USD–INR	0.0609	0.5017	-0.2254	5.2933	0.0000	-10.3925(0.0000)	-0.0936(0.3760)	0.3471(0.8453)
USD–ILS	0.0176	0.7834	0.3039	7.8413	0.0000	-8.8646(0.0000)	0.0678(0.5208)	0.9620(0.4328)
USD–JPY	-0.0196	0.8209	0.8149	8.2714	0.0000	-11.6046(0.0001)	-0.1999(0.0564)	0.1057(0.9802)
USD–KRW	0.0594	0.7162	-0.7448	6.3300	0.0000	-10.4809(0.0000)	-0.0993(0.3462)	1.1165(0.3543)
USD–PEN	0.0307	0.5372	-1.3226	7.6893	0.0000	-8.5642(0.0000)	0.1017(0.3348)	0.3865(0.8177)
USD–PLN	0.1074	0.8345	0.6046	6.9621	0.0000	-7.7128(0.0000)	0.2030(0.0526)	1.3155(0.2710)
USD–RUB	0.1817	1.6823	1.7751	11.1571	0.0000	-11.8986(0.0001)	-0.2248(0.0316)	0.4493(0.7726)
USD–SEK	0.0437	0.7358	1.2009	8.3722	0.0000	-7.5746(0.0000)	0.2173(0.0383)	3.7092(0.0079)
USD–TRY	0.1877	0.6860	-0.2110	4.4322	0.0133	-8.9082(0.0000)	0.0581(0.5838)	0.0633(0.9925)
USD–GBP	0.0720	0.8726	0.6149	6.5510	0.0000	-6.7796(0.0000)	0.3225(0.0017)	0.0633(0.9925)
GBP–USD	-0.0714	0.8719	-0.6141	6.4387	0.0000	-6.7952(0.0000)	0.3204(0.0019)	0.0872(0.9862)
TCM_AUT	529.1084	712.8600	0.7708	1.7558	0.0005	-0.4145(0.9011)	1.0118(0.0000)	0.1080(0.9794)
TCM_BEL	972.8031	1522.5169	1.2536	2.9418	0.0000	-3.9831(0.0023)	1.0257(0.0000)	0.0362(0.9974)
TCM_BRA	70.4649	145.4177	2.3607	7.7864	0.0000	-0.1054(0.9447)	1.0912(0.0000)	0.1035(0.9810)
TCM_CAN	292.5606	503.5894	1.6018	4.1992	0.0000	-1.5169(0.5205)	1.0437(0.0000)	0.2429(0.9132)
TCM_CHE	1005.9419	1372.9724	0.8446	1.9257	0.0004	0.9152(0.9953)	1.0136(0.0000)	5.7802(0.0004)
TCM_CHL	179.2970	319.7873	1.8907	5.6804	0.0000	3.6231(1.0000)	1.0687(0.0000)	2.1030(0.0876)
TCM_CHN	39.0746	24.5874	-0.7758	1.7412	0.0004	-1.9011(0.3305)	0.9877(0.0000)	0.4929(0.7410)
TCM_DEU	514.8440	739.8339	0.9894	2.2470	0.0002	-0.4404(0.8964)	1.0188(0.0000)	0.1034(0.9810)
TCM_ESP	1246.8705	1792.4913	0.9796	2.2103	0.0002	-0.3992(0.9037)	1.0179(0.0000)	0.1886(0.9437)
TCM_FRA	523.2816	760.1330	1.0406	2.3684	0.0001	-1.4554(0.5514)	1.0210(0.0000)	0.4370(0.7815)
TCM_IND	4.6191	9.6082	2.2956	7.3926	0.0000	2.3628(1.0000)	1.0845(0.0000)	0.2893(0.8842)
TCM_IRL	867.6324	1472.0922	1.4916	3.6316	0.0000	-0.9568(0.7654)	1.0322(0.0000)	0.0121(0.9997)
TCM_ISR	459.2078	694.8414	1.1073	2.5054	0.0000	-2.7354(0.0722)	1.0201(0.0000)	0.0683(0.9913)
TCM_ITA	984.5006	1304.9542	0.8727	2.0904	0.0005	0.6836(0.9911)	1.0180(0.0000)	0.0451(0.9961)
TCM_JPN	24.4745	39.7074	1.4926	3.6311	0.0000	-2.3755(0.1516)	1.0308(0.0000)	1.2492(0.2966)
TCM_KOR	98.6022	93.5322	0.0283	1.1461	0.0012	-1.0063(0.7481)	1.0001(0.0000)	2.3864(0.0575)
TCM_NLD	563.2945	848.5655	1.1715	2.7360	0.0000	-2.4833(0.1230)	1.0240(0.0000)	3.2651(0.0154)
TCM_PER	187.5988	411.2352	2.4425	8.0800	0.0000	-0.7152(0.8365)	1.0886(0.0000)	0.3461(0.8460)

(Continued)

Table 1. (Continued).

Variable	Mean	SD	Skewness	Kurtosis	JB	ADF	AR	ARCH
TCM_POL	73.2624	121.5863	1.4673	3.6733	0.0000	-3.1043(0.0298)	1.0378(0.0000)	4.9954(0.0012)
TCM_PRT	585.5520	905.3135	1.1880	2.7485	0.0000	-2.9201(0.0471)	1.0250(0.0000)	0.1333(0.9697)
TCM_RUS	121.7972	278.4980	2.5283	8.4887	0.0000	1.8562(0.9998)	1.0920(0.0000)	0.2780(0.8914)
TCM_SWE	454.4420	726.5974	1.4718	3.7640	0.0000	-4.0859(0.0017)	1.0401(0.0000)	0.2552(0.9057)
TCM_TUR	286.8672	505.2283	1.5250	3.7293	0.0000	-2.2444(0.1925)	1.0347(0.0000)	2.3657(0.0593)
TCM_UK	527.6099	903.5105	1.5501	3.9548	0.0000	2.0874(0.9999)	1.0418(0.0000)	0.8766(0.4816)
TCM_US	692.6019	1161.4014	1.4719	3.6891	0.0000	0.4258(0.9830)	1.0381(0.0000)	0.4119(0.7996)
TCM_WLD	98.8586	147.3348	1.3725	3.4491	0.0000	3.2333(1.0000)	1.0370(0.0000)	0.1633(0.9564)
TDM_AUT	14.3692	23.3348	1.3035	3.0545	0.0000	-3.6770(0.0061)	1.0262(0.0000)	0.1104(0.9786)
TDM_BEL	130.8820	232.9684	1.5293	3.7030	0.0000	-1.3883(0.5845)	1.0340(0.0000)	0.0991(0.9825)
TDM_BRA	4.5822	9.9492	2.4228	7.9779	0.0000	-2.7410(0.0715)	1.0899(0.0000)	4.0406(0.0048)
TDM_CAN	14.3620	29.8550	2.1461	6.4132	0.0000	-1.5480(0.5047)	1.0679(0.0000)	0.0239(0.9989)
TDM_CHE	37.4514	59.7805	1.2759	2.9946	0.0000	-3.1160(0.0290)	1.0268(0.0000)	0.0315(0.9981)
TDM_CHL	2.1704	4.1848	1.8819	5.2244	0.0000	-2.4012(0.1444)	1.0511(0.0000)	0.0334(0.9978)
TDM_CHN	1.6016	1.1737	-0.1993	1.6123	0.0169	-0.3937(0.9049)	0.9964(0.0000)	0.0178(0.9994)
TDM_DEU	15.2342	26.8305	1.5599	3.8904	0.0000	3.8012(1.0000)	1.0382(0.0000)	0.6999(0.5941)
TDM_ESP	131.1658	199.4737	1.1252	2.5749	0.0000	-0.7597(0.8250)	1.0228(0.0000)	2.3106(0.0644)
TDM_FRA	82.2855	136.5265	1.3351	3.0911	0.0000	-2.2785(0.1812)	1.0268(0.0000)	0.1944(0.9407)
TDM_IND	0.1495	0.3182	2.3762	7.8577	0.0000	1.7073(0.9996)	1.0876(0.0000)	0.0255(0.9987)
TDM_IRL	42.1973	82.3432	1.9050	5.1930	0.0000	-1.6078(0.4744)	1.0458(0.0000)	0.0508(0.9951)
TDM_ISR	5.1794	9.1267	1.4941	3.5899	0.0000	-1.9616(0.3032)	1.0316(0.0000)	0.1219(0.9743)
TDM_ITA	124.9081	175.3364	0.9976	2.3426	0.0002	1.2599(0.9983)	1.0215(0.0000)	0.0528(0.9947)
TDM_JPN	0.6357	1.1677	2.1168	6.2942	0.0000	6.1700(1.0000)	1.0566(0.0000)	0.2272(0.9224)
TDM_KOR	1.7021	1.9404	0.5921	1.6565	0.0019	-2.0760(0.2548)	1.0111(0.0000)	3.8182(0.0067)
TDM_NLD	62.4967	101.5362	1.3348	3.1883	0.0000	-0.8559(0.7975)	1.0303(0.0000)	0.1560(0.9598)
TDM_PER	5.1359	11.4464	2.5032	8.3607	0.0000	-6.0866(0.0000)	1.0891(0.0000)	0.3382(0.8514)
TDM_POL	3.0439	5.7259	1.7981	4.8339	0.0000	-1.7264(0.4143)	1.0482(0.0000)	2.0628(0.0929)
TDM_PRT	20.4728	34.8116	1.4646	3.5940	0.0000	-2.1343(0.2320)	1.0332(0.0000)	6.3915(0.0002)
TDM_RUS	1.1118	2.6013	2.5516	8.4986	0.0000	-9.0704(0.0000)	1.0887(0.0000)	0.7115(0.5863)
TDM_SWE	46.8962	87.0557	1.7384	4.5724	0.0000	-2.0658(0.2589)	1.0473(0.0000)	1.0741(0.3746)
TDM_TUR	7.0587	13.0264	1.6952	4.3762	0.0000	-0.8450(0.8006)	1.0415(0.0000)	3.0407(0.0216)
TDM_UK	78.1737	138.8991	1.5723	3.9348	0.0000	1.7934(0.9997)	1.0386(0.0000)	0.0428(0.9965)
TDM_US	35.4274	66.3058	1.7394	4.5515	0.0000	-0.4011(0.9034)	1.0467(0.0000)	0.1313(0.9705)
TDM_WLD	6.5187	10.5418	1.4786	3.6936	0.0000	-0.2611(0.9252)	1.0377(0.0000)	0.3994(0.8085)

The table reports summary statistics for exchange returns, and total number of COVID-19 cases and deaths per million. TCM_ and TDM_ denote, respectively, total number of COVID-19 cases and deaths per million. SD, JB, ADF, AR, and ARCH denote, respectively, standard deviation, Augmented Dickey–Fuller statistic, coefficients of the autoregressive process of order one, and the Lagrange multiplier test for autoregressive conditional heteroskedasticity. Note that p-values associated with the ADF, AR, and ARCH tests are in the parentheses. The sample is from 31/12/2019 to 08/05/2020, and the returns are in percentages.

Panel A: GBP–USD reaction

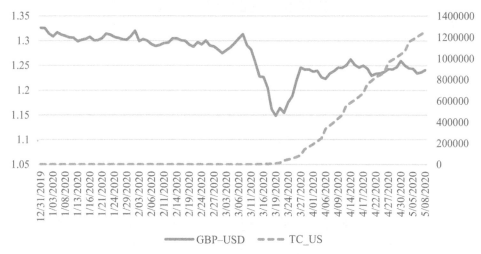

Panel B: USD–INR reaction

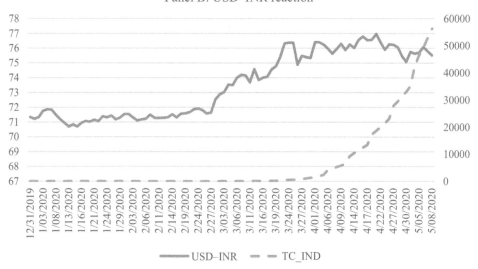

Figure 2. Exchange rate reaction to COVID-19. The figure shows the reaction of two exchange rates, GBP–USD and USD–INR, to COVID-19 between 31/12/2019 and 08/05/2020. The US dollar reacts by appreciating against the British pound, while the Indian rupee reacted by depreciating against the US dollar. TC_US and TC_IND denote, respectively, the total number of COVID-19 cases recorded in the US and India.

could be safe-haven currencies as they tend to increase in value in times of distress. USD–RUB is the most volatile return (with a standard deviation of 1.68%), whereas USD–RUB is the least volatile return (with a standard deviation of 0.58%).

Six exchange rates, namely USD–BRL, USD–INR, USD–KRW, USD–PEN, USD–TRY, and GBP–USD, are more likelihood to appreciate, whereas the remaining 11 are more likely to depreciate, as indicated by the negative and positive skewness statistics, respectively. The returns also exhibit fat tails with high and sharp central peaks as indicated by the kurtoses – this feature is unique to high-frequency exchange rate returns. Although obvious from the skewness and kurtosis statistics, the Jarque–Bera (JB) test results show that the returns are non-normally distributed. We find weak or no evidence of return persistency and heteroskedasticity as indicated by the results of the Augmented Dickey–Fuller (ADF), the first-order autoregression (AR(1)), and the autoregressive conditional heteroscedastic (ARCH) Lagrange multiplier test results. For the COVID-19 indicators (TCM_ and TDM_), we find evidence of persistency and heteroskedasticity, and, hence, our empirical model is motivated by these features.

2.2. Results

2.2.1. Main Results

We document two sets of results. First, we estimate and report the predictive impact of COVID-19 on returns and volatility based on a one-day ahead forecast horizon. Second, we repeat this analysis, considering a five-day ahead forecast horizon, in line with prior studies (see, e.g., Sharma, Phan, and Narayan 2019). With regards to the one-day ahead forecast horizon, we estimate the following GARCH(1,1) model of exchange rate return.

$$EXR_t = \gamma_0 + \gamma_1 \Delta TCM_{t-1} + \epsilon_t \tag{1}$$

where EXR and ΔTCM denote, respectively, exchange rate returns and the first difference of total number of COVID-19 infections per million; γ_0 and γ_1 are parameters of the model, and ϵ_t is the zero mean error term with a conditional variance, σ_t^2, which has the functional form

$$\sigma_t^2 = \bar{\rho} + \alpha_0 \left(\epsilon_{t-1}^2 - \bar{\rho} \right) + \alpha_1 \left(\sigma_{t-1}^2 - \bar{\rho} \right) + \alpha_2 \Delta TCM_{t-1} \tag{2}$$

where α_0, α_1, and α_2 are parameters of the conditional variance function.

The total number of COVID-19 infections per million enters Equations (1) and (2) in first difference because the variable is non-stationary or is persistent. We estimate Equations (1) and (2) and report the results in Table 2. The COVID-19 outbreak contains valuable information to enhancing return and volatility predictions, if we reject the null hypothesis that γ_1 and α_2 are zero. The results suggest that COVID-19 has a negative predictive impact on two currencies, USD–CLP and USD–SEK. For volatility, COVID-19 negatively predicts the currencies USD–CHF, USD–CNY, USD–ILS, USD–JPY, and USD–PEN, and positively predicts USD–KRW. These estimates imply that COVID-19 has better predictive power over return volatility when compared with its predictive power over returns for a one-day ahead forecast horizon.

Table 2. One-day ahead predictive impact of COVID-19.

Countries (exchange rates)	A: Mean equation		B: Variance equation	
	γ_1	P-value	α_2	P-value
Austria (USD–EUR)	−0.0015	(0.5451)	−0.0016	(0.0443)
Belgium (USD–EUR)	−0.0008	(0.3122)	−0.0001	(0.6823)
Brazil (USD–BRL)	−0.0064	(0.6671)	0.0215	(0.4853)
Canada (USD–CAD)	−0.0027	(0.4401)	−0.0010	(0.1495)
Switzerland (USD–CHF)	−0.0006	(0.5417)	−0.0005	(0.0767)
Chile ((USD–CLP)	−0.0060	(0.0981)	0.0002	(0.9154)
China ((USD–CNY)	0.0120	(0.4807)	−0.0078	(0.0125)
Germany (USD–EUR)	−0.0019	(0.3923)	−0.0004	(0.3576)
Spain (USD–EUR)	−0.0006	(0.4697)	−0.0002	(0.3810)
France (USD–EUR)	−0.0010	(0.5796)	−0.0003	(0.4074)
India (USD–INR)	−0.0467	(0.4896)	−0.0088	(0.5823)
Ireland (USD–EUR)	−0.0004	(0.5514)	−0.0000	(0.7382)
Israel (USD–ILS)	−0.0007	(0.7725)	−0.0032	(0.0001)
Italy (USD–EUR)	−0.0009	(0.4737)	−0.0001	(0.6798)
Japan (USD–JPY)	−0.0252	(0.5322)	−0.0417	(0.0027)
Korea (USD–KRW)	−0.0296	(0.2518)	0.0092	(0.0000)
Netherlands (USD–EUR)	−0.0010	(0.5024)	−0.0002	(0.5970)
Peru (USD–PEN)	0.0002	(0.9052)	−0.0009	(0.0044)
Poland (USD–PLN)	−0.0084	(0.4090)	−0.0033	(0.2853)
Portugal (USD–EUR)	−0.0014	(0.3321)	−0.0001	(0.6110)
Russia (USD–RUB)	−0.0029	(0.6065)	−0.0008	(0.9001)
Sweden (USD–SEK)	−0.0034	(0.0137)	−0.0006	(0.1049)
Turkey (USD–TRY)	0.0017	(0.5451)	0.0004	(0.7634)
United Kingdom (USD–GBP)	−0.0006	(0.5746)	0.0004	(0.6625)
United States (GBP–USD)	0.0008	(0.4063)	0.0003	(0.6381)

The table shows the one-day ahead impact of COVID-19 on exchange rate returns and volatility. We estimate Equations (1) and (2) and report the coefficients (γ_1 and α_2) and their p-values for the COVID-19 indicator ΔTCM. The sample period is from 31/12/2019 to 08/05/2020

Consistent with Figure 2, we expected that the predictive power of COVID-19 over returns is positive, so that as the number of infections rise, exchange rates will depreciate. That is, we expected the predictability to be positive. Instead, we find it to be negative when considering the one-day ahead forecast horizon. It could be that the direction of predictability varies over time. Sharma, Phan, and Narayan (2019) show that unexpected news, such as government shutdowns, has a time-varying predictive impact on exchange rate returns. Hence, we examine a five-day ahead predictability of return and volatility by including four additional lags into the mean and variance equations as follows

$$EXR_t = \gamma_0 + \sum_{i=1}^{5} \gamma_i \Delta TCM_{t-i} + \epsilon_t \qquad (3)$$

The conditional variance, σ_t^2, has the functional form

$$\sigma_t^2 = \bar{\rho} + \alpha_0 \left(\epsilon_{t-1}^2 - \bar{\rho} \right) + \alpha_1 \left(\sigma_{t-1}^2 - \bar{\rho} \right) + \sum_{i=1}^{5} \alpha_{i+1} \Delta TCM_{t-i} \qquad (4)$$

We estimate Equations (3) and (4) and report the results in Table 3. The COVID-19 outbreak predicts return and volatility, if we reject the null

Table 3. Five-day ahead predictive impact of COVID-19.

Countries (exchange rates)	A: Mean equation						B: Variance equation					
	γ_1	γ_2	γ_3	γ_4	γ_5	$\sum_{i}^{5}\gamma_i$	a_2	a_3	a_4	a_5	a_6	$\sum_{i}^{5}a_{i+1}$
Austria (USD–EUR)	-0.0054	0.0030	0.0015	-0.0030	0.0009	-0.0030	0.0018	0.0007	0.0009	-0.0014	-0.0019	-0.0000
	(0.1593)	(0.4068)	(0.5223)	(0.4797)	(0.8556)	(0.1656)	(0.6779)	(0.8800)	(0.8215)	(0.7540)	(0.6329)	(0.9876)
Belgium (USD–EUR)	-0.0017	0.0009	0.0006	-0.0004	0.0002	-0.0004	-0.0003	-0.0002	0.0000	-0.0004	-0.0004	-0.0013
	(0.0006)	(0.1201)	(0.2536)	(0.4122)	(0.7206)	(0.6186)	(0.5163)	(0.7039)	(0.9856)	(0.1263)	(0.3375)	(0.0993)
Brazil (USD–BRL)	-0.0441	0.0001	0.0388	-0.0095	0.0297	0.0150	0.0000	0.0000	0.0000	0.0000	0.0000	0.0000
	(0.2444)	(0.9967)	(0.6386)	(0.8704)	(0.8339)	(0.8253)	(1.0000)	(1.0000)	(1.0000)	(1.0000)	(1.0000)	(1.0000)
Canada (USD–CAD)	-0.0018	0.0044	-0.0070	0.0013	-0.0024	-0.0055	-0.0018	0.0023	-0.0013	-0.0007	-0.0006	-0.0021
	(0.6185)	(0.0518)	(0.0193)	(0.6078)	(0.4526)	(0.0094)	(0.2136)	(0.0577)	(0.6318)	(0.7186)	(0.8145)	(0.1702)
Switzerland (USD–CHF)	-0.0016	0.0007	0.0002	-0.0005	0.0007	-0.0005	0.0003	0.0002	0.0002	-0.0002	-0.0005	-0.0001
	(0.0642)	(0.6248)	(0.7945)	(0.5654)	(0.6383)	(0.6599)	(0.6552)	(0.8975)	(0.8643)	(0.7928)	(0.3380)	(0.8527)
Chile ((USD–CLP)	-0.0041	0.0032	-0.0036	-0.0072	0.0012	-0.0104	-0.0014	-0.0015	-0.0015	-0.0016	-0.0024	-0.0084
	(0.6929)	(0.5401)	(0.6902)	(0.7632)	(0.9060)	(0.4751)	(0.9235)	(0.9109)	(0.9468)	(0.9585)	(0.9471)	(0.8034)
China ((USD–CNY)	-0.0124	-0.0227	0.0245	0.0150	0.0195	0.0239	-0.0042	-0.0037	-0.0035	-0.0033	-0.0037	-0.0183
	(0.8723)	(0.7138)	(0.8186)	(0.8040)	(0.7416)	(0.6495)	(0.9182)	(0.9214)	(0.9183)	(0.9252)	(0.7592)	(0.2113)
Germany (USD–EUR)	-0.0041	0.0021	-0.0009	-0.0011	0.0021	-0.0019	-0.0003	-0.0002	-0.0002	-0.0005	-0.0010	-0.0023
	(0.0310)	(0.3351)	(0.4586)	(0.6827)	(0.5744)	(0.4427)	(0.9492)	(0.9347)	(0.8253)	(0.7616)	(0.5950)	(0.0580)
Spain (USD–EUR)	-0.0018	0.0007	0.0000	-0.0003	0.0007	-0.0006	-0.0000	-0.0000	0.0001	-0.0003	-0.0004	-0.0006
	(0.0210)	(0.4658)	(0.9908)	(0.8186)	(0.7003)	(0.5513)	(0.9948)	(0.7762)	(0.8283)	(0.7593)	(0.6251)	(0.3010)
France (USD–EUR)	-0.0029	0.0027	-0.0004	-0.0013	0.0015	-0.0003	0.0009	0.0008	0.0015	-0.0021	-0.0011	-0.0001
	(0.2015)	(0.4960)	(0.8380)	(0.6576)	(0.7285)	(0.8763)	(0.6590)	(0.7464)	(0.6182)	(0.2929)	(0.6376)	(0.8850)
India (USD–INR)	0.0201	0.0505	-0.1348	-0.0044	-0.0158	-3.2332	-0.0171	0.0123	-0.0214	0.0010	-0.0449	-2.2030
	(0.8091)	(0.3940)	(0.0313)	(0.9553)	(0.9382)	(0.6829)	(0.9046)	(0.9145)	(0.7406)	(0.9829)	(0.3700)	(0.1986)
Ireland (USD–EUR)	-0.0006	0.0009	0.0006	-0.0013	0.0003	-0.0001	-0.0002	-0.0002	-0.0002	-0.0003	-0.0003	-0.0012
	(0.4676)	(0.5921)	(0.6790)	(0.6834)	(0.8186)	(0.9440)	(0.7667)	(0.8317)	(0.8169)	(0.4717)	(0.5907)	(0.0002)
Israel (USD–ILS)	-0.0016	0.0013	-0.0005	-0.0002	-0.0021	-0.0032	-0.0013	-0.0013	-0.0011	-0.0011	-0.0011	-0.0059
	(0.6399)	(0.7301)	(0.9350)	(0.9726)	(0.3987)	(0.5767)	(0.7363)	(0.5971)	(0.8317)	(0.7917)	(0.4215)	(0.0794)
Italy (USD–EUR)	-0.0020	0.0015	-0.0004	-0.0006	0.0010	-0.0005	0.0006	0.0007	0.0003	-0.0008	-0.0008	-0.0001
	(0.1091)	(0.4662)	(0.7141)	(0.6417)	(0.2391)	(0.7792)	(0.0244)	(0.6763)	(0.8989)	(0.6448)	(0.3952)	(0.9074)
Japan (USD–JPY)	-0.0087	0.0057	0.0250	-0.0100	0.0014	0.0134	-0.0185	-0.0186	-0.0179	-0.0172	-0.0171	-0.0892
	(0.8568)	(0.9426)	(0.6041)	(0.8264)	(0.9860)	(0.8908)	(0.7591)	(0.5648)	(0.4262)	(0.7714)	(0.7443)	(0.0920)
Korea (USD–KRW)	-0.0363	0.0124	0.0154	-0.0054	0.0250	0.0111	0.0044	-0.0146	-0.0002	0.0015	0.0104	0.0016
	(0.4620)	(0.7733)	(0.5706)	(0.8797)	(0.2983)	(0.7424)	(0.9338)	(0.8337)	(0.9945)	(0.9212)	(0.5651)	(0.9144)

(Continued)

Table 3. (Continued).

Countries (exchange rates)	A: Mean equation						B: Variance equation					
	γ_1	γ_2	γ_3	γ_4	γ_5	$\sum^5 \gamma_i$	α_2	α_3	α_4	α_5	α_6	$\sum^5 \alpha_{i+1}$
Netherlands (USD–EUR)	-0.0024	0.0022	0.0015	-0.0017	0.0007	0.0003	-0.0002	-0.0002	-0.0002	-0.0006	-0.0006	-0.0018
	(0.0039)	(0.1976)	(0.1358)	(0.3535)	(0.5612)	(0.8967)	(0.7636)	(0.8346)	(0.8387)	(0.6309)	(0.6382)	(0.0567)
Peru (USD–PEN)	-0.0008	0.0003	-0.0005	0.0003	0.0011	0.0004	-0.0002	-0.0003	-0.0003	-0.0003	-0.0004	-0.0015
	(0.7312)	(0.8784)	(0.9325)	(0.9438)	(0.8560)	(0.9268)	(0.9331)	(0.8601)	(0.9191)	(0.9064)	(0.9175)	(0.2547)
Poland (USD–PLN)	-0.0198	0.0176	0.0059	-0.0243	0.0081	-0.0125	-0.0012	-0.0058	-0.0097	-0.0087	-0.0047	-0.0301
	(0.0266)	(0.3000)	(0.5667)	(0.0463)	(0.4612)	(0.5300)	(0.8787)	(0.7442)	(0.2663)	(0.3961)	(0.6870)	(0.1282)
Portugal (USD–EUR)	-0.0029	0.0018	0.0007	-0.0012	0.0007	-0.0008	-0.0004	-0.0004	-0.0004	-0.0006	-0.0009	-0.0026
	(0.0148)	(0.1711)	(0.2480)	(0.4023)	(0.5815)	(0.6965)	(0.5928)	(0.7153)	(0.4618)	(0.4040)	(0.1278)	(0.0112)
Russia (USD–RUB)	-0.0049	0.0001	-0.0022	-0.0022	-0.0033	-0.0126	-0.0056	-0.0059	-0.0058	-0.0060	-0.0074	-0.0308
	(0.7560)	(0.9967)	(0.8588)	(0.8834)	(0.9560)	(0.6876)	(0.8831)	(0.8537)	(0.8011)	(0.8625)	(0.8772)	(0.3653)
Sweden (USD–SEK)	-0.0023	0.0017	-0.0042	0.0002	0.0022	-0.0024	0.0011	-0.0001	-0.0013	0.0005	-0.0010	-0.0008
	(0.2106)	(0.4686)	(0.0340)	(0.9086)	(0.3973)	(0.1660)	(0.5036)	(0.9608)	(0.0000)	(0.7722)	(0.7049)	(0.1943)
Turkey (USD–TRY)	0.0015	0.0038	-0.0035	0.0003	-0.0004	0.0017	0.0001	0.0015	0.0005	-0.0017	-0.0019	-0.0016
	(0.5801)	(0.1035)	(0.1727)	(0.9215)	(0.8730)	(0.5065)	(0.9167)	(0.7244)	(0.9474)	(0.8037)	(0.6618)	(0.5127)
United Kingdom (USD–GBP)	0.0000	0.0008	-0.0013	-0.0003	-0.0006	-0.0014	-0.0002	-0.0008	-0.0008	-0.0016	-0.0004	-0.0038
	(0.9777)	(0.0033)	(0.2628)	(0.8012)	(0.6820)	(0.4815)	(0.9092)	(0.7100)	(0.5936)	(0.0435)	(0.8001)	(0.1250)
United States (GBP–USD)	0.0006	-0.0009	0.0021	-0.0006	0.0006	0.0018	0.0003	-0.0003	-0.0008	-0.0011	-0.0005	-0.0024
	(0.6057)	(0.4397)	(0.0313)	(0.5271)	(0.6760)	(0.2078)	(0.8542)	(0.8710)	(0.5430)	(0.2043)	(0.8123)	(0.0033)

The table shows the five-day ahead impact of COVID-19 on exchange rate returns and volatility. We estimate Equations (3) and (4) and report the coefficients (γ_i and α_{i+1}) and their p-values (in parentheses) for the COVID-19 indicator ΔTCM. The last column of Panels A and B reports the sum of the coefficients and their p-values. The sample period is from 31/12/2019 to 08/05/2020.

hypothesis that γ_i and α_{i+1} are zero (for $i = 1, \ldots, 5$). We observe that COVID-19 negatively predicts five returns, namely USD–CHF, USD–EUR, USD–INR, USD–PLN, and USD–SEK, and positively predicts USD–GBP and GBP–USD returns; the predictability oscillates from positive to negative with regards to USD–CAD. In terms of volatility, we find positive predictability for USD–CAD and USD–EUR, and negative predictability for USD–SEK and USD–GBP.

Thus, consistent with our argument, the direction of return predictability changes over the five-day period. This is intuitive given that the numeraire currency (USD) is also affected by the COVID-19 outbreak. Bad news in the US could lead to a transitory appreciation of the domestic currency relative to the USD, and this reverses quickly as the US market assimilates the bad news (see, e.g., Figure 2). Over a five-day period, COVID-19 tends to affect returns more than volatility.

2.2.2. Robustness Tests
We subject our results to robustness checks. To do this, we replace ΔTCM with the first difference of the total number of deaths from COVID-19 per million (ΔTDM) and reproduce the estimates. Table 4 shows that COVID-19 has better predictive power over volatility than over returns using a one-day ahead forecast horizon. Table 5 shows that, over a five-day ahead forecast horizon, COVID-19 tends to influence returns more than volatility. These estimates are consistent with the main results.

2.2.3. Additional Tests
The traditional GARCH(1,1) models, in Equations (1)-(4), assume linearity in the impact of COVID-19 on exchange rate return volatility. Yet, in reality, foreign exchange markets are known to react differently to positive and negative news. For example, Iyke and Ho (2019) argue that negative news induces higher exchange rate volatility because it is associated with a higher likelihood of speculative attacks. Speculative attacks are episodes during which forex investors sell their currency assets in large quantities, inducing sharp depreciation in the local currency (Iyke 2017; Iyke and Ho 2020). The exponential GARCH (EGARCH) model can better accommodate this feature of the forex market (Iyke and Ho 2019). We use the GARCH(1,1) model for our baseline analysis mainly to sidestep the small sample size property of the data, as stated in Section I.

Against this backdrop, we take the analysis a step further by examining the impact of COVID-19 on returns and volatility within an EGARCH model. Table A2 shows that COVID-19 has identical predictive power over returns and volatility using a one-day ahead forecast horizon. Table A3 shows that, over a five-day ahead forecast horizon, COVID-19 tends to influence returns more than volatility, consistent with the main results.

Table 4. One-day ahead predictive impact of COVID-19 using ΔTDM.

Countries (exchange rates)	A: Mean equation		B: Variance equation	
	γ_1	P-value	a_2	P-value
Austria (USD–EUR)	−0.0585	(0.2276)	−0.0036	(0.7199)
Belgium (USD–EUR)	−0.0036	(0.3829)	−0.0003	(0.6991)
Brazil (USD–BRL)	−0.0936	(0.6547)	0.2209	(0.5410)
Canada (USD–CAD)	−0.0264	(0.5448)	−0.0102	(0.2628)
Switzerland (USD–CHF)	−0.0089	(0.6229)	−0.0011	(0.7137)
Chile ((USD–CLP)	−0.2643	(0.3014)	−0.4313	(0.0610)
China ((USD–CNY)	−0.0043	(0.9949)	−0.1232	(0.0000)
Germany (USD–EUR)	−0.0282	(0.4473)	−0.0024	(0.7257)
Spain (USD–EUR)	−0.0069	(0.3166)	−0.0008	(0.5419)
France (USD–EUR)	−0.0104	(0.1899)	−0.0008	(0.6137)
India (USD–INR)	−0.7456	(0.7130)	−0.2682	(0.6771)
Ireland (USD–EUR)	−0.0006	(0.9892)	0.0000	(1.0000)
Israel (USD–ILS)	−0.0103	(0.9145)	−0.1564	(0.0065)
Italy (USD–EUR)	−0.0059	(0.5221)	−0.0010	(0.6018)
Japan (USD–JPY)	−0.1327	(0.9317)	−1.0420	(0.0034)
Korea (USD–KRW)	−1.6349	(0.3299)	−0.0082	(0.9863)
Netherlands (USD–EUR)	−0.0091	(0.4149)	−0.0010	(0.6278)
Peru (USD–PEN)	0.0062	(0.9023)	−0.0315	(0.0000)
Poland (USD–PLN)	−0.1400	(0.3527)	−0.0454	(0.3677)
Portugal (USD–EUR)	−0.0243	(0.3608)	−0.0013	(0.8387)
Russia (USD–RUB)	−0.2540	(0.6999)	−0.0837	(0.9059)
Sweden (USD–SEK)	−0.0254	(0.0174)	−0.0046	(0.1128)
Turkey (USD–TRY)	0.0523	(0.5632)	0.0168	(0.6702)
United Kingdom (USD–GBP)	−0.0069	(0.3473)	0.0021	(0.6751)
United States (GBP–USD)	0.0095	(0.5069)	0.0055	(0.5922)

The table shows the one-day ahead impact of COVID-19 on exchange rate returns and volatility. We estimate Equations (1) and (2) and report the coefficients and their p-values for the COVID-19 indicator ΔTDM. The sample period is from 31/12/2019 to 08/05/2020.

Overall, we note a significant improvement in predictability over a five-day ahead forecast horizon using the EGARCH(1,1) model relative to the GARCH(1,1) model.

3. Concluding Remarks

We test whether disease outbreaks contain valuable information to enhancing the prediction of exchange rate return and volatility. Disease outbreaks are often unexpected and even when expected, the magnitude of their impact (rate of infections and deaths) cannot be predicted with certainty. The negative sentiments or panics associated with them could have a substantial impact on financial markets. The COVID-19 outbreak provides a good experimental setup to test our intuition. Using the total number of infections as our measure of COVID-19 information, we show that COVID-19 has better predictive power over volatility than over returns for a one-day ahead forecast horizon, whereas for a five-day ahead forecast horizon, the reverse is true – COVID-19 tends to shape returns more than volatility. The results remain intact for these forecast horizons using an alternative COVID-19 measure, the total number of deaths from COVID-19 per million. This

Table 5. Five-day ahead predictive impact of COVID-19 using ΔTDM.

Countries (exchange rates)	A: Mean equation						B: Variance equation					
	γ_1	γ_2	γ_3	γ_4	γ_5	$\sum_{i}^{5}\gamma_i$	α_2	α_3	α_4	α_5	α_6	$\sum_{i}^{5}\alpha_{i+1}$
Austria (USD–EUR)	-0.1175 (0.0551)	0.0489 (0.4230)	0.0573 (0.0005)	-0.0217 (0.8064)	-0.0242 (0.6397)	-0.0572 (0.3024)	0.0019 (0.9767)	0.0116 (0.7154)	0.0137 (0.8448)	-0.0187 (0.6353)	-0.0196 (0.6309)	-0.0111 (0.5594)
Belgium (USD–EUR)	-0.0058 (0.4776)	0.0054 (0.2117)	0.0046 (0.3257)	-0.0071 (0.1689)	0.0026 (0.7046)	-0.0003 (0.9719)	-0.0015 (0.6772)	-0.0015 (0.6076)	-0.0015 (0.4935)	-0.0015 (0.6761)	-0.0015 (0.7645)	-0.0074 (0.0000)
Brazil (USD–BRL)	-0.5276 (0.0080)	-0.0757 (0.7875)	0.4697 (0.4377)	-0.1036 (0.7026)	0.5928 (0.3844)	0.3556 (0.1736)	0.0932 (0.8793)	0.6779 (0.2011)	-0.3792 (0.6744)	-0.1637 (0.7662)	-0.2982 (0.8893)	-0.0701 (0.8937)
Canada (USD–CAD)	-0.0278 (0.6542)	0.0430 (0.1819)	-0.0747 (0.2207)	0.0204 (0.7040)	-0.0126 (0.8559)	-0.0517 (0.2317)	-0.0144 (0.7164)	0.0389 (0.1858)	-0.0017 (0.9846)	-0.0244 (0.5943)	-0.0095 (0.7065)	-0.0111 (0.3944)
Switzerland (USD–CHF)	-0.0382 (0.0089)	-0.0044 (0.8282)	0.0317 (0.0742)	-0.0149 (0.4745)	0.0224 (0.2488)	-0.0034 (0.8655)	0.0009 (0.9289)	-0.0058 (0.5696)	0.0036 (0.7369)	-0.0066 (0.2744)	-0.0107 (0.1709)	-0.0187 (0.0181)
Chile ((USD–CLP)	-0.1415 (0.7700)	0.1144 (0.7050)	-0.3635 (0.3536)	-0.5838 (0.0566)	0.2187 (0.6503)	-0.7558 (0.0574)	-0.0964 (0.0000)	-0.0921 (0.7496)	-0.2309 (0.6321)	-0.1240 (0.9046)	-0.1443 (0.8299)	-0.6877 (0.5258)
China ((USD–CNY)	-0.0668 (0.9177)	0.2249 (0.8477)	-0.2521 (0.6688)	-0.3217 (0.7421)	0.1865 (0.7948)	-0.2292 (0.8487)	-0.1223 (0.3593)	-0.0966 (0.3144)	-0.0881 (0.4801)	-0.0841 (0.2508)	-0.0858 (0.0036)	-0.4769 (0.0001)
Germany (USD–EUR)	-0.0169 (0.8512)	0.0267 (0.7938)	0.0572 (0.5404)	-0.0958 (0.5959)	-0.0147 (0.9272)	-0.0434 (0.4460)	0.0117 (0.7983)	0.0175 (0.7473)	0.0125 (0.8847)	-0.0405 (0.6497)	-0.0052 (0.5739)	-0.0040 (0.7025)
Spain (USD–EUR)	-0.0179 (0.0001)	0.0096 (0.0004)	-0.0005 (0.9246)	-0.0021 (0.7983)	0.0060 (0.7318)	-0.0050 (0.6082)	-0.0013 (0.8157)	-0.0014 (0.7068)	-0.0009 (0.6201)	-0.0027 (0.5207)	-0.0034 (0.4797)	-0.0097 (0.1272)
France (USD–EUR)	-0.0192 (0.2806)	0.0091 (0.5572)	0.0032 (0.7030)	-0.0045 (0.8242)	0.0085 (0.6597)	-0.0029 (0.8297)	-0.0026 (0.7433)	-0.0026 (0.8124)	-0.0028 (0.6917)	-0.0029 (0.5076)	-0.0027 (0.7983)	-0.0136 (0.3510)
India (USD–INR)	1.6722 (0.7474)	-0.3157 (0.9339)	-3.9825 (0.3802)	0.5570 (0.9112)	-1.1642 (0.9326)	-3.2232 (0.6829)	-0.3626 (0.8892)	-0.4041 (0.8704)	-0.3825 (0.8574)	-0.4859 (0.8482)	-0.5678 (0.8499)	-2.2030 (0.1986)
Ireland (USD–EUR)	0.0012 (0.9695)	-0.0000 (0.9999)	-0.0098 (0.6598)	-0.0048 (0.8956)	0.0124 (0.7028)	-0.0009 (0.9700)	-0.0028 (0.7695)	-0.0031 (0.6734)	-0.0030 (0.7706)	-0.0028 (0.5127)	-0.0033 (0.7448)	-0.0149 (0.3339)
Israel (USD–ILS)	-0.0715 (0.8195)	0.1413 (0.7386)	-0.0516 (0.9192)	-0.0165 (0.9765)	-0.1982 (0.6884)	-0.1965 (0.4496)	-0.0669 (0.7885)	-0.0676 (0.7165)	-0.0727 (0.0061)	-0.0995 (0.7371)	-0.0649 (0.7992)	-0.3717 (0.2477)
Italy (USD–EUR)	-0.0117 (0.1617)	0.0070 (0.5424)	0.0016 (0.7571)	-0.0074 (0.4151)	0.0087 (0.4091)	-0.0018 (0.8744)	0.0012 (0.6112)	0.0006 (0.9417)	0.0008 (0.8689)	-0.0037 (0.7499)	-0.0063 (0.4592)	-0.0073 (0.2712)
Japan (USD–JPY)	-0.2843 (0.9664)	-0.3023 (0.9145)	0.0213 (0.9951)	0.2077 (0.9308)	0.5769 (0.9249)	0.2193 (0.9604)	-0.3953 (0.7796)	-0.3964 (0.8143)	-0.4009 (0.8269)	-0.4121 (0.7367)	-0.4448 (0.8309)	-2.0495 (0.0030)
Korea (USD–KRW)	-2.0224 (0.3467)	0.4224 (0.8304)	-0.7178 (0.6788)	-0.0325 (0.9877)	1.2255 (0.4410)	-1.1248 (0.3800)	1.2073 (0.5232)	0.8886 (0.8187)	-0.0638 (0.9747)	0.2548 (0.9323)	0.9810 (0.0000)	3.2679 (0.1508)

(Continued)

Table 5. (Continued).

Countries (exchange rates)	A: Mean equation						B: Variance equation					
	γ_1	γ_2	γ_3	γ_4	γ_5	$\sum_{1}^{5}\gamma_i$	a_2	a_3	a_4	a_5	a_6	$\sum_{1}^{5}a_{i+1}$
Netherlands (USD–EUR)	−0.0264	0.0225	0.0097	−0.0171	0.0063	−0.0050	−0.0024	−0.0034	0.0000	−0.0069	−0.0065	−0.0192
	(0.0113)	(0.0313)	(0.2458)	(0.1040)	(0.6048)	(0.7102)	(0.7429)	(0.0313)	(0.9987)	(0.3811)	(0.4496)	(0.1316)
Peru (USD–PEN)	−0.0495	0.0024	−0.0186	0.0187	0.0444	−0.0027	−0.0087	−0.0094	−0.0090	−0.0154	−0.0133	−0.0558
	(0.7024)	(0.9782)	(0.8313)	(0.9003)	(0.7768)	(0.9794)	(0.9639)	(0.9140)	(0.9512)	(0.9036)	(0.9331)	(0.4357)
Poland (USD–PLN)	−0.4196	0.1942	−0.1179	−0.1887	0.2958	−0.2362	−0.1189	−0.1036	−0.1157	−0.1214	−0.1244	−0.5841
	(0.2267)	(0.6580)	(0.7862)	(0.6680)	(0.7162)	(0.6042)	(0.6361)	(0.7845)	(0.9077)	(0.8457)	(0.7017)	(0.0000)
Portugal (USD–EUR)	−0.0261	0.0298	−0.0117	−0.0400	0.0386	−0.0095	−0.0036	−0.0033	−0.0041	−0.0273	−0.0129	−0.0511
	(0.3618)	(0.3154)	(0.5756)	(0.0240)	(0.0434)	(0.7730)	(0.8803)	(0.8699)	(0.8217)	(0.0509)	(0.4565)	(0.0143)
Russia (USD–RUB)	−0.4366	0.4588	0.0459	−0.6064	−0.0788	−0.6171	−0.2993	−0.1451	−0.4896	−0.5307	−0.7531	−2.2179
	(0.6642)	(0.6550)	(0.9682)	(0.6169)	(0.9774)	(0.7246)	(0.9258)	(0.9272)	(0.8036)	(0.8797)	(0.8055)	(0.0645)
Sweden (USD–SEK)	−0.0083	0.0140	0.0070	−0.0175	−0.0182	−0.0230	0.0001	−0.0072	0.0010	−0.0013	−0.0101	−0.0176
	(0.8249)	(0.7480)	(0.8937)	(0.5628)	(0.5107)	(0.3333)	(0.9959)	(0.7877)	(0.9486)	(0.9328)	(0.7218)	(0.2012)
Turkey (USD–TRY)	0.0742	−0.0023	−0.1658	0.0686	0.0031	−0.0222	0.0083	0.0468	0.0123	−0.0823	−0.0432	−0.0581
	(0.3793)	(0.9796)	(0.0917)	(0.3509)	(0.9810)	(0.8053)	(0.9822)	(0.7227)	(0.9470)	(0.6890)	(0.8940)	(0.5603)
United Kingdom (USD–GBP)	−0.0010	−0.0016	−0.0124	0.0040	−0.0094	−0.0204	0.0076	0.0003	0.0011	−0.0079	−0.0040	−0.0029
	(0.9218)	(0.8660)	(0.2189)	(0.6849)	(0.4106)	(0.0118)	(0.5315)	(0.9467)	(0.8954)	(0.2132)	(0.6662)	(0.5424)
United States (GBP–USD)	0.0075	−0.0188	0.0074	0.0158	0.0006	0.0125	0.0000	0.0000	0.0000	0.0000	0.0000	0.0000
	(0.9489)	(0.9076)	(0.9637)	(0.9405)	(0.9977)	(0.9141)	(1.0000)	(1.0000)	(1.0000)	(1.0000)	(1.0000)	(1.0000)

The table shows the five-day ahead impact of COVID-19 on exchange rate returns and volatility. We estimate Equations (3) and (4) and report the coefficients (γ_i and a_{i+1}) and their p-values (in parentheses) for the COVID-19 indicator ΔTDM. The last column of Panels A and B reports the sum of the coefficients and their p-values. The sample period is from 31/12/2019 to 08/05/2020.

evidence supports a new channel of exchange rate predictability, namely the disease outbreak channel.

Notes

1. The currencies are Chilean peso per US dollar (USD–CLP), Swedish krona per US dollar (USD–SEK), Swiss franc per US dollar (USD–CHF), Chinese yuan per US dollar (USD–CNY), Israeli new shekel per US dollar (USD–ILS), Japanese yen per US dollar (USD–JPY), Peruvian new sol per US dollar (USD–PEN), Korean won per US dollar (USD–KRW), Canadian dollar per US dollar (USD–CAD), Euro per US dollar (USD–EUR), Indian rupee per US dollar (USD–INR), Poland złoty per US dollar (USD–PLN), Great Britain pound per US dollar (USD–GBP), and US dollar per Great Britain pound (GBP–USD).
2. See Table A1 in appendix for full names of these currencies.
3. See https://ourworldindata.org/coronavirus-source-data for details.
4. These countries are Austria (AUT), Belgium (BEL), Brazil (BRA), Canada (CAN), Chile (CHL), China (CHN), France (FRA), Germany (DEU), India (IND), Ireland (IRL), Israel (ISR), Italy (ITA), Japan (JPN), Korea (KOR), Netherlands (NLD), Peru (PER), Poland (POL), Portugal (PRT), Russia (RUS), Spain (ESP), Sweden (ESP), Switzerland (CHE), Turkey (TUR), United Kingdom (UK), and United States (US).
5. We classify these countries following the MSCI market classification, the International Monetary Fund's classification, and others. See https://www.msci.com/market-classification and https://en.wikipedia.org/wiki/Emerging_market for details on emerging market economies.
6. These exchange rates are USD–BRL, USD–CAD, USD–CHF, USD–CLP, USD–CNY, USD–EUR, USD–INR, USD–ILS, USD–JPY, USD–KRW, USD–PEN, USD–PLN, USD–RUB, USD–SEK, USD–TRY, USD–GBP, and GBP–USD (Table A1 in the appendix for details)
7. See Ince, Molodtsova, and Papell (2016).
8. See Narayan and Phan (2020) for a commentary.
9. Note that, when quoting the US dollar, we use the British pound as the base currency (numeraire). We quote all other currencies using the US dollar as the base currency.
10. We do not show these plots, to preserve space. See, for instance, https://www.cnbc.com/2020/02/24/as-coronavirus-fuels-market-panic-some-experts-say-the-dollar-is-the-only-safe-currency.html.

References

Ali, M., N. Alam, and S. A. R. Rizvi. 2020. Coronavirus (COVID-19) – An epidemic or pandemic for financial markets. *Journal of Behavioral and Experimental Finance* 100341. doi:10.1016/j.jbef.2020.100341.

Edwards, S. 1983. Floating exchange rates, expectations and new information. *Journal of Monetary Economics* 11 (3):321–36. doi:10.1016/0304-3932(83)90022-3.

Frenkel, J. A. 1981. Flexible exchange rates, prices and the role of "news": Lessons from the 1970s. *Journal of Political Economy* 89:665–705. doi:10.1086/260998.

Fu, M., and H. Shen. 2020. COVID-19 and corporate performance in the energy industry. *Energy Research Letters* 1 (1):12967. doi: 10.46557/001c.12967.

Gil-Alana, L. A., and M. Monge. 2020. Crude oil prices and COVID-19: Persistence of the shock. *Energy Research Letters* 1 (1):13200. doi: 10.46557/001c.13200.

Haroon, O., and S. A. R. Rizvi. 2020. COVID-19: Media coverage and financial markets behavior—A sectoral inquiry. *Journal of Behavioral and Experimental Finance* 100343. doi:10.1016/j.jbef.2020.100343.

Hodrick, R. J. 1989. Risk, uncertainty and exchange rates. *Journal of Monetary Economics* 23 (3):433–59. doi:10.1016/0304-3932(89)90041-X.

Ince, O., T. Molodtsova, and D. H. Papell. 2016. Taylor rule deviations and out-of-sample exchange rate predictability. *Journal of International Money and Finance* 69:22–44. doi:10.1016/j.jimonfin.2016.06.002.

Iyke, B. N. 2017. The Penn effect revisited: New evidence from Latin America. *Review of Development Economics* 21 (4):1364–79. doi:10.1111/rode.12328.

Iyke, B. N. 2018. Macro determinants of the real exchange rate in a small open small island economy: Evidence from Mauritius via BMA. *Buletin Ekonomi Moneter Dan Perbankan* 21 (1):57–80. doi:10.21098/bemp.v21i1.922.

Iyke, B. N. 2019. A test of the efficiency of the foreign exchange market in Indonesia. *Buletin Ekonomi Moneter Dan Perbankan* 21:439–64. doi:10.21098/bemp.v0i0.976.

Iyke, B. N., and S. Y. Ho. 2019. Consumption and exchange rate uncertainty: Evidence from selected Asian countries. *The World Economy*. doi:10.1111/twec.12900.

Iyke, B. N., and S. Y. Ho (2020). Global uncertainty, exchange rate returns and volatility in Africa. *Working Paper*.

Liu, L., E.-Z. Wang, and C. C. Lee. 2020. Impact of the COVID-19 pandemic on the crude oil and stock markets in the US: A time-varying analysis. *Energy Research Letters* 1 (1):13154. doi: 10.46557/001c.13154.

Meese, R. A., and K. Rogoff. 1983. Empirical exchange rate models of the seventies: Do they fit out of sample? *Journal of International Economics* 14 (1–2):3–24. doi:10.1016/0022-1996(83) 90017-X.

Narayan, P. K. 2020. Oil price news and COVID-19—Is there any connection? *Energy Research Letters* 1 (1):13176. doi: 10.46557/001c.13176.

Narayan, P. K., S. Narayan, S. Khademalomoom, and D. H. B. Phan. 2018. Do terrorist attacks impact exchange rate behavior? New international evidence. *Economic Inquiry* 56 (1):547–61. doi:10.1111/ecin.12447.

Narayan, P. K., and D. H. B. Phan. 2020. Country responses and the reaction of the stock market to COVID-19—A preliminary exposition. *Emerging Markets Finance and Trade* 56 (10):2138–2150. doi:10.1080/1540496X.2020.1784719.

Narayan, P. K., S. S. Sharma, and D. Phan. 2019. Predicting exchange rate returns. *Emerging Markets Review*. doi:10.1016/j.ememar.2019.100668.

Rime, D., L. Sarno, and E. Sojli. 2010. Exchange rate forecasting, order flow and macroeconomic information. *Journal of International Economics* 80 (1):72–88. doi:10.1016/j.jinteco.2009.03.005.

Sharma, S. S., D. H. B. Phan, and P. K. Narayan. 2019. Exchange rate effects of US government shutdowns: Evidence from both developed and emerging markets. *Emerging Markets Review* 40:100626. doi:10.1016/j.ememar.2019.100626.

Appendix

Table A1. Variables and countries.

Panel A: Variables			Panel B: Countries
Variable	Full name	Source	Austria
USD–BRL	Brazilian per US dollar	Global Financial Data (GFD)	Belgium
USD–CAD	Canadian dollar per US dollar	GFD	Brazil
USD–CHF	Swiss franc per US dollar	GFD	Canada
USD–CLP	Chilean peso per US dollar	GFD	Chile
USD–CNY	Chinese yuan per US dollar	GFD	China
USD–EUR	Euro per US dollar	GFD	France
USD–INR	Indian rupee per US dollar	GFD	Germany
USD–ILS	Israeli new shekel per US dollar	GFD	India
USD–JPY	Japanese yen per US dollar	GFD	Ireland
USD–KRW	Korean won per US dollar	GFD	Israel
USD–PEN	Peruvian new sol per US dollar	GFD	Italy
USD–PLN	Polish złoty per US dollar	GFD	Japan
USD–RUB	Russian ruble per US dollar	GFD	Korea
USD–SEK	Swedish krona	GFD	Netherlands
USD–TRY	Turkish new lira per US dollar	GFD	Peru
USD–GBP	Great Britain pound per US dollar	GFD	Poland
GBP–USD	US dollar per Great Britain pound	GFD	Portugal
TC	Total cases	Our World in Data (OWD)	Russia
TD	New cases	OWD	Spain
NC	Total deaths	OWD	Sweden
ND	New deaths	OWD	Switzerland
TCM	Total cases per million	OWD	Turkey
TDM	total deaths per million	OWD	United Kingdom
			United States of America

The table shows the full names and sources of the variables as well as the countries included in our sample.

Table A2. One-day ahead predictive impact of COVID-19 using an EGARCH(1,1) model.

Countries (exchange rates)	A: Mean equation		B: Variance equation	
	γ_1	P-value	a_2	P-value
Austria (USD–EUR)	−0.0043	(0.0137)	−0.0001	(0.9611)
Belgium (USD–EUR)	−0.0006	(0.3770)	−0.0004	(0.5293)
Brazil (USD–BRL)	−0.0059	(0.7019)	0.0015	(0.7725)
Canada (USD–CAD)	−0.0027	(0.3930)	−0.0012	(0.3965)
Switzerland (USD–CHF)	−0.0012	(0.0857)	−0.0002	(0.7669)
Chile ((USD–CLP)	−0.0057	(0.1316)	0.0003	(0.9340)
China ((USD–CNY)	0.0090	(0.5767)	−0.0503	(0.3296)
Germany (USD–EUR)	−0.0023	(0.1191)	−0.0006	(0.6060)
Spain (USD–EUR)	−0.0009	(0.1362)	−0.0003	(0.5348)
France (USD–EUR)	−0.0017	(0.2581)	−0.0011	(0.3487)
India (USD–INR)	−0.0583	(0.3933)	0.1706	(0.5730)
Ireland (USD–EUR)	−0.0002	(0.7478)	−0.0005	(0.3490)
Israel (USD–ILS)	−0.0002	(0.8814)	−0.0012	(0.5877)
Italy (USD–EUR)	−0.0013	(0.1516)	−0.0006	(0.4274)
Japan (USD–JPY)	−0.0085	(0.4968)	−0.0565	(0.0000)
Korea (USD–KRW)	−0.0279	(0.0292)	0.0454	(0.2192)
Netherlands (USD–EUR)	−0.0008	(0.5192)	−0.0010	(0.3225)
Peru (USD–PEN)	−0.0003	(0.8289)	0.0000	(0.9861)
Poland (USD–PLN)	−0.0027	(0.7866)	−0.0139	(0.0002)
Portugal (USD–EUR)	−0.0012	(0.2787)	−0.0005	(0.5810)
Russia (USD–RUB)	−0.0047	(0.3541)	−0.0003	(0.8694)
Sweden (USD–SEK)	−0.0039	(0.0029)	−0.0016	(0.0483)
Turkey (USD–TRY)	0.0012	(0.6109)	−0.0016	(0.4388)
United Kingdom (USD–GBP)	−0.0006	(0.5193)	−0.0005	(0.6821)
United States (GBP–USD)	0.0007	(0.3571)	−0.0005	(0.5951)

The table shows the one-day ahead impact of COVID-19 on exchange rate returns and volatility based on an EGARCH(1,1). We estimate an exponential GARCH version of Equations (1) and (2) and report the coefficients (γ_1 and a_2) and their p-values for the COVID-19 indicator ΔTCM. The sample period is from 31/12/2019 to 08/05/2020.

Table A3. Five-day ahead predictive impact of COVID-19 using an EGARCH(1,1) model.

Countries (exchange rates)	A: Mean equation						B: Variance equation					
	γ_1	γ_2	γ_3	γ_4	γ_5	$\sum_{i=1}^{5}\gamma_i$	α_2	α_3	α_4	α_5	α_6	$\sum_{i=1}^{5}\alpha_{i+1}$
Austria (USD–EUR)	−0.0075 (0.0420)	0.0035 (0.4292)	0.0030 (0.5547)	−0.0021 (0.4117)	0.0021 (0.6239)	−0.0012 (0.6321)	0.0064 (0.6689)	−0.0168 (0.5429)	0.0261 (0.3687)	−0.0231 (0.3950)	0.0060 (0.6368)	−0.0015 (0.3835)
Belgium (USD–EUR)	−0.0014 (0.0857)	0.0011 (0.3978)	0.0002 (0.8988)	−0.0005 (0.4794)	0.0003 (0.8446)	−0.0003 (0.8053)	−0.0025 (0.5999)	0.0001 (0.9889)	0.0045 (0.7116)	−0.0077 (0.4808)	0.0050 (0.0745)	−0.0005 (0.5267)
Brazil (USD–BRL)	−0.0381 (0.2348)	0.0491 (0.1685)	0.0319 (0.0859)	−0.0425 (0.2921)	0.0141 (0.3379)	0.0146 (0.6002)	0.0774 (0.2555)	0.0426 (0.6167)	−0.0916 (0.1636)	0.0288 (0.7898)	−0.0962 (0.2881)	−0.0390 (0.1886)
Canada (USD–CAD)	−0.0025 (0.3307)	0.0029 (0.4847)	−0.0056 (0.0587)	0.0025 (0.4350)	−0.0009 (0.9294)	−0.0036 (0.4065)	−0.0246 (0.0057)	0.0138 (0.3934)	−0.0141 (0.4675)	0.0026 (0.8889)	0.0220 (0.1747)	−0.0004 (0.8243)
Switzerland (USD–CHF)	−0.0042 (0.0001)	0.0009 (0.1054)	0.0027 (0.0751)	−0.0003 (0.4659)	0.0009 (0.0202)	0.0000 (0.9945)	0.0140 (0.0233)	−0.0088 (0.3487)	0.0172 (0.0155)	−0.0115 (0.0410)	−0.0110 (0.0113)	−0.0002 (0.9327)
Chile ((USD–CLP)	−0.0032 (0.0461)	0.0057 (0.0568)	−0.0026 (0.4414)	−0.0100 (0.0000)	0.0046 (0.6537)	−0.0054 (0.4649)	−0.0522 (0.0423)	0.0497 (0.1790)	−0.0892 (0.0986)	0.0105 (0.8561)	0.0838 (0.0281)	0.0025 (0.6557)
China ((USD–CNY)	0.0078 (0.0000)	−0.0252 (0.0000)	0.0235 (0.0000)	0.0098 (0.0000)	0.0300 (0.0000)	0.0460 (0.0000)	−2.0167 (0.0017)	−0.0581 (0.8970)	0.0241 (0.9522)	0.5331 (0.1005)	−0.0803 (0.7738)	−1.5979 (0.0004)
Germany (USD–EUR)	−0.0055 (0.0023)	0.0027 (0.1495)	−0.0000 (0.9901)	−0.0006 (0.7567)	0.0020 (0.6491)	−0.0015 (0.5375)	−0.0072 (0.5494)	−0.0041 (0.8118)	0.0245 (0.3426)	−0.0184 (0.3857)	0.0041 (0.6340)	−0.0011 (0.4590)
Spain (USD–EUR)	−0.0029 (0.0000)	0.0009 (0.3205)	0.0001 (0.9516)	−0.0001 (0.9229)	0.0008 (0.0014)	−0.0011 (0.0488)	−0.0001 (0.9811)	0.0069 (0.1414)	0.0103 (0.0535)	−0.0061 (0.1676)	−0.0133 (0.0003)	−0.0023 (0.3548)
France (USD–EUR)	−0.0051 (0.0063)	0.0040 (0.2148)	0.0040 (0.3364)	−0.0024 (0.2425)	−0.0005 (0.8749)	−0.0001 (0.9664)	−0.0109 (0.4474)	0.0009 (0.9637)	0.0228 (0.2770)	−0.0212 (0.3861)	0.0069 (0.5805)	−0.0015 (0.3022)
India (USD–INR)	−0.0004 (0.9859)	−0.1177 (0.3485)	−0.2426 (0.0006)	0.3600 (0.0004)	−0.0539 (0.1159)	−0.0545 (0.4161)	1.3458 (0.0058)	1.4360 (0.0552)	−0.9143 (0.4576)	0.2954 (0.7731)	−3.2139 (0.0000)	−1.0509 (0.0000)
Ireland (USD–EUR)	−0.0013 (0.0000)	0.0011 (0.0000)	0.0012 (0.0006)	−0.0013 (0.0000)	0.0000 (0.5915)	−0.0002 (0.0541)	0.0072 (0.1763)	−0.0118 (0.1330)	0.0108 (0.1759)	−0.0220 (0.0031)	0.0128 (0.0139)	−0.0030 (0.0146)
Israel (USD–ILS)	−0.0001 (0.9565)	0.0009 (0.6266)	−0.0006 (0.4663)	0.0004 (0.7883)	−0.0021 (0.0945)	−0.0015 (0.2907)	−0.0124 (0.1621)	0.0070 (0.5623)	−0.0151 (0.1254)	−0.0053 (0.6694)	0.0221 (0.0156)	−0.0037 (0.0071)
Italy (USD–EUR)	−0.0022 (0.0944)	0.0017 (0.0000)	0.0004 (0.0000)	−0.0012 (0.0000)	0.0008 (0.5353)	−0.0005 (0.3380)	0.0089 (0.1253)	−0.0041 (0.0233)	0.0103 (0.3173)	−0.0094 (0.2494)	−0.0051 (0.4137)	0.0005 (0.7580)
Japan (USD–JPY)	−0.0284 (0.0944)	0.0171 (0.3253)	0.0306 (0.2110)	−0.0175 (0.1968)	−0.0106 (0.4296)	−0.0089 (0.7340)	−0.5106 (0.0000)	−0.4242 (0.6102)	0.2127 (0.3621)	−0.3530 (0.1693)	0.8733 (0.0000)	−0.2017 (0.0362)
Korea (USD–KRW)	−0.1235 (0.0000)	0.0240 (0.0001)	0.0827 (0.0270)	−0.0123 (0.1969)	0.0506 (0.0015)	0.0215 (0.3524)	0.1918 (0.0028)	−0.1179 (0.1585)	−0.0270 (0.8069)	−0.2522 (0.0001)	−0.0458 (0.7470)	−0.2511 (0.0484)

(Continued)

Table A3. (Continued).

Countries (exchange rates)	A: Mean equation						B: Variance equation					
	γ_1	γ_2	γ_3	γ_4	γ_5	$\sum_5 \gamma_i$	α_2	α_3	α_4	α_5	α_6	$\sum_5 \alpha_{t+1}$
Netherlands (USD–EUR)	−0.0004	0.0021	−0.0009	−0.0021	0.0007	−0.0006	0.0023	−0.0077	0.0160	−0.0237	0.0119	−0.0012
	(0.8280)	(0.1774)	(0.7188)	(0.0135)	(0.6853)	(0.7419)	(0.7763)	(0.4520)	(0.3561)	(0.1119)	(0.0239)	(0.4671)
Peru (USD–PEN)	−0.0002	0.0029	−0.0017	−0.0010	0.0011	0.0011	0.0131	0.0632	−0.0303	−0.0149	−0.0897	−0.0586
	(0.0275)	(0.0000)	(0.0000)	(0.0196)	(0.0000)	(0.0005)	(0.5958)	(0.0042)	(0.0725)	(0.4663)	(0.0010)	(0.0001)
Poland (USD–PLN)	−0.0099	0.0209	0.0056	−0.0230	0.0037	−0.0028	0.0926	0.0036	−0.0174	−0.0363	−0.0740	−0.0314
	(0.3865)	(0.3117)	(0.5716)	(0.0039)	(0.3779)	(0.8249)	(0.0244)	(0.9368)	(0.7576)	(0.6719)	(0.3258)	(0.3154)
Portugal (USD–EUR)	−0.0033	0.0020	0.0010	−0.0013	0.0011	−0.0006	−0.0014	0.0041	0.0093	−0.0115	−0.0027	−0.0022
	(0.0024)	(0.2340)	(0.4661)	(0.0929)	(0.0460)	(0.5429)	(0.8760)	(0.5916)	(0.4796)	(0.2881)	(0.7089)	(0.4028)
Russia (USD–RUB)	−0.0100	0.0116	−0.0028	−0.0035	−0.0040	−0.0086	−0.0110	0.1076	−0.0721	0.0067	−0.1183	−0.0871
	(0.0000)	(0.0000)	(0.0000)	(0.4639)	(0.0000)	(0.0000)	(0.4666)	(0.0001)	(0.0040)	(0.7380)	(0.0000)	(0.0000)
Sweden (USD–SEK)	−0.0022	0.0018	−0.0022	−0.0028	0.0015	−0.0039	0.0111	−0.0049	−0.0107	0.0153	−0.0135	−0.0028
	(0.3414)	(0.0000)	(0.0844)	(0.0921)	(0.4728)	(0.0233)	(0.3514)	(0.7333)	(0.5964)	(0.3008)	(0.1986)	(0.0181)
Turkey (USD–TRY)	0.0031	0.0043	−0.0036	−0.0006	−0.0017	0.0015	−0.0327	0.0351	0.0007	−0.0195	0.0151	−0.0013
	(0.2134)	(0.3330)	(0.3397)	(0.7718)	(0.7055)	(0.4554)	(0.0027)	(0.0386)	(0.9728)	(0.3339)	(0.2179)	(0.7248)
United Kingdom (USD–GBP)	−0.0006	0.0010	−0.0015	0.0001	−0.0005	−0.0014	0.0026	−0.0028	−0.0001	−0.0032	0.0018	−0.0017
	(0.7493)	(0.3174)	(0.2290)	(0.9450)	(0.7230)	(0.2982)	(0.8236)	(0.7775)	(0.9914)	(0.7127)	(0.9096)	(0.6027)
United States (GBP–USD)	0.0006	−0.0008	0.0021	−0.0007	0.0000	0.0013	0.0024	−0.0017	−0.0011	−0.0004	−0.0008	−0.0015
	(0.5980)	(0.4582)	(0.0423)	(0.5302)	(0.9699)	(0.2179)	(0.7691)	(0.8207)	(0.8673)	(0.9601)	(0.9481)	(0.5781)

The table shows the five-day ahead impact of COVID-19 on exchange rate returns and volatility. We estimate an exponential GARCH version of Equations (3) and (4) and report the coefficients (γ_i and α_{t+1}) and their p-values (in parentheses) for the COVID-19 indicator ΔTCM. The last column of Panels A and B reports the sum of the coefficients and their p-values. The sample period is from 31/12/2019 to 08/05/2020.

Fear Sentiment, Uncertainty, and Bitcoin Price Dynamics: The Case of COVID-19

Conghui Chen, Lanlan Liu, and Ningru Zhao

ABSTRACT

This paper studies the impact of fear sentiment caused by the coronavirus pandemic on Bitcoin price dynamics. We construct a new proxy for coronavirus fear sentiment using hourly Google search queries on coronavirus-related words. The results show that market volatility has been exacerbated by fear sentiment as the result of an increase in search interest in coronavirus. Moreover, we find that negative Bitcoin returns and high trading volume can be explained by fear sentiment regarding the coronavirus. Our results also show that Bitcoin fails to act as a safe haven during the pandemic.

1. Introduction

Bitcoin, the first and most well-known cryptocurrency, has attracted great attention in recent years. Due to its extreme volatility, Bitcoin has been classified as a speculative investment rather than a currency (Cheah and Fry 2015; Yermack 2015). Previous studies have extensively examined the main drivers of changes in Bitcoin prices. It is widely acknowledged that a fundamental supply and demand factor (Kristoufek 2015); investors' interest (Ciaian, Rajcaniova, and Kancs 2016); macroeconomic and financial developments (Panagiotidis, Stengos, and Vravosinos 2019); and technological factors (Adjei 2019) are the main determinants of bitcoin prices. In relation to macroeconomic and financial developments, the expanding literature has examined the relationship between some macroeconomic indicators and Bitcoin prices. Panagiotidis, Stengos, and Vravosinos (2019) find that external shocks, such as changes in interest rates or exchange rates, seem to have an impact on Bitcoin's price. Moreover, Bitcoin is found to be uncorrelated or negatively correlated with other financial asset classes, such as gold, the US dollar, and major stock market indices, so it can be viewed as a hedge to reduce portfolio risk (Dyhrberg 2016; Guesmi et al. 2019) or hailed as "digital gold" with safe-haven properties against extreme downside risks of global stock markets (Shahzad et al. 2019).

During the coronavirus outbreak, Bitcoin was hit hard and lost half its value within days, decreasing from 9,000 USD on March 7 to around 4,000 USD on March 13.[1] However, the plunge in Bitcoin price may not be explained by the literature. The purpose of our study is to investigate how Bitcoin's price reacts in the wake of the coronavirus pandemic, since it is the first significant global turmoil to occur while Bitcoin is actively being traded. In particular, we examine how fear sentiment affects Bitcoin price dynamics. Our research is inspired by one strand of the literature on behavioral finance that analyzes the impact of investor sentiment on asset price dynamics (Baker and Wurgler 2006; Da, Engelberg, and Gao 2015; Tetlock 2007), and demonstrates that low asset returns can be explained by high sentiment. Da, Engelberg, and Gao (2015) construct a fear index by aggregating the Google search volume of words with negative tones and suggest that negative sentiment is associated with return reversals. Because the number of new confirmed cases and mortality rates are increasing dramatically, negative sentiment induced by the coronavirus crisis is the dominant emotion in financial markets. Recent empirical studies intensively discuss the impact of COVID-19 on the financial markets and suggest that it is associated with a decrease in asset prices and an increase in market volatility (Ali, Alam, and Rizvi 2020; Apergis and Apergis 2020; Gil-Alana and Monge 2020). Moreover, several studies highlight the impact of negative sentiment and find that it leads to liquidity dry-ups and higher market volatility (Baig et al. 2020; Zaremba et al. 2020). Mamaysky (2020) show that sentiment related to coronavirus news drives changes in asset prices in the markets.

Following Da, Engelberg, and Gao (2015), we adopt internet search-based measures of investors' sentiment, since the frequency of sentiment measure is available on an hourly basis. In addition, people who search for information on the coronavirus are more concerned about the pandemic, so the search volume of coronavirus-related keywords can well represent a fearful attitude toward the virus. Therefore, we aggregate hourly search volume of terms such as "Coronavirus" and "COVID-19" from Google Trends to construct a proxy for fear sentiment. First, we explore the relationship between coronavirus fear sentiment and market uncertainty. Our results show that fear sentiment driven by coronavirus is positively correlated with uncertainty, as measured by the VIX. This indicates that the degree of market uncertainty is higher when fear sentiment is strong. We then examine the lead-lag relationship between fear sentiment, Bitcoin returns, and Bitcoin trading volume during the outbreak period using vector autoregressive (VAR) models. Our findings show that an increase in fear sentiment will lead to lower Bitcoin returns and higher Bitcoin trading volume.

The paper's contributions are twofold. First, we construct a new proxy of fear sentiment induced by the coronavirus using high-frequency Google search data. The results imply that our fear sentiment measure is appropriate by exploiting its comovement with the VIX, which is widely used as an investor fear gauge (Mele, Obayashi, and Shalen 2015; Whaley 2000). Second, our paper extends the literature by examining Bitcoin price dynamics in the case of extreme events. In line with Ali, Alam, and Rizvi (2020) and Gil-Alana and Monge (2020), our research provides evidence that negative Bitcoin returns can be explained by fear sentiment during the coronavirus crisis. In addition, our study shows that Bitcoin returns are adversely affected by market downturn, in contrast to earlier empirical studies (Bouri et al. 2017; Corbet et al. 2018; Shahzad et al. 2019). Based on our results, Bitcoin exhibits patterns similar to traditional financial assets, and its safe-haven properties are highly questionable. Our results suggest that Bitcoin may not be suitable for portfolio management or risk management, because it cannot be viewed as a safe haven during times of extreme crisis.

The rest of the paper is organized as follows. Section 2 describes the data and presents a preliminary analysis. Section 3 outlines the econometric model used to analyze the dynamic linkages between investor sentiment, uncertainty, and Bitcoin price dynamics during the coronavirus pandemic. Section 4 presents the results and our discussion. Section 5 performs robustness checks to validate our findings, and Section 6 concludes.

2. Data and Preliminary Analysis

2.1. Data and Variables

The data used in this paper are sourced from CryptoCompare, Bloomberg, and Google Trends. We first obtain hourly data on Bitcoin prices in US dollars (BTC/USD) and Bitcoin trading volume from the CryptoCompare website through the application programming interface (API).[2] Specifically, hourly Bitcoin prices are the Bitcoin trading volume-weighted average prices across more than 250 cryptocurrency exchanges. Bitcoin hourly trading volume is the total number of Bitcoins (BTC) traded on those exchanges.

Next, we obtain hourly data on the Cboe Volatility Index (VIX) from Bloomberg to measure investors' expectations on short-term market volatility. The VIX is calculated based on real-time S&P 500 Index call and put options, which reflect the short-term expected volatility of the US equity market. It is widely followed by a variety of global investors as an indicator of financial market uncertainty (Mele, Obayashi, and Shalen 2015).

For the measurement of investors' fear sentiment regarding the coronavirus pandemic, we employ internet search–based data from Google Trends, in line with prior studies (Da, Engelberg, and Gao 2015). Google provides hourly search volume for search queries through Google Trends, which are scaled by the time-series maximum during the specific period.[3] In order to develop an accurate measure of fear sentiment, it is paramount to identify the proper search terms in Google Trends. The term 'Coronavirus' has experienced the biggest increase in search frequency of all search queries since 15 January 2020.[4] To capture the variation of households' search interest over time, we include the term 'COVID-19', which became the leading search term in Google after the WHO announced on 11 February that would be the official name for the virus. Finally, we download hourly search volume data on the two terms – 'Coronavirus' and 'COVID-19' – using the Python 'gtrendsR' package and choose worldwide search trends to represent the fear sentiment of households across different countries. We aggregate the hourly search volume of the two items to measure the evolution of fear sentiment related to the coronavirus outbreak.

Time-series data on Bitcoin price dynamics, the VIX, and Google Trends cover the period from 15 January 2020 to 24 April 2020, because the first confirmed case of COVID-19 was detected outside of China on 14 January 2020, according to WHO Disease Outbreak News.[5]

2.2. Preliminary Analysis

Table 1 reports descriptive statistics for the data used in this study, including the fear sentiment proxy, the VIX, Bitcoin prices, and Bitcoin trading volume. The fear sentiment has a minimum value of zero during the first two hours on 15 January 2020, which indicates that the coronavirus had not attracted attention before that period. The standard deviation of the fear sentiment is 48.070, which suggests a large variation in search volume data. The mean of the VIX is 35.891, with a historical high of 83.830 on 17 March. The excess skewness and kurtosis of the VIX shows a high degree of market uncertainty during this period. Bitcoin prices have a maximum value of 10,466.600 on 13 February and decrease to a minimum value of 4,240.690 as a result of the continued spread of coronavirus. In addition, Bitcoin's average trading volume is 2309.507 BTC per hour and the kurtosis is 37.842, which reflects the high liquidity of the Bitcoin market.

In Figure 1, we plot the dynamics of hourly Bitcoin prices (BTC/USD) and fear sentiment with 2,424 observations for each series. As can be seen, the two series move negatively over the sample period, with a negative correlation of −0.90. As fear sentiment increased to its peak value on 16 March, Bitcoin's price simultaneously plunged. In light of this, we would expect a possible correlation between fear sentiment and Bitcoin price movements.

Table 1. Descriptive statistics.

	Mean	Std.Dev	Min	Max	Skew	Kurtosis
Sentiment	49.403	48.070	0.000	164.356	0.431	1.702
VIX	35.891	19.803	11.790	83.830	0.402	2.013
Bitcoin prices ($)	8,041.190	1,455.874	4,240.690	10,466.600	−0.243	1.881
Bitcoin trading volume (BTC)	2309.507	2910.273	244.600	38,290.150	4.814	37.842

This table reports descriptive statistics of the data, including the fear sentiment proxy, the VIX, Bitcoin prices, and Bitcoin trading volume. The fear sentiment proxy is calculated as the sum of Google search volume for "Coronavirus" and "COVID-19" from 15 January 2020 to 24 April 2020.

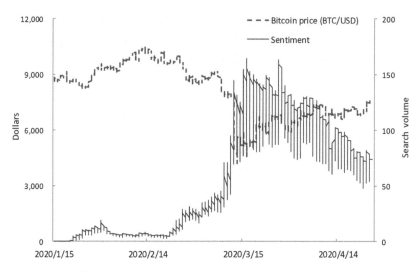

Figure 1. Evolution of fear sentiment (Level) and Bitcoin prices. This graph plots hourly data on the fear sentiment proxy (right y-axis) and Bitcoin prices (BTC/USD, left y-axis) from 15 January 2020 to 24 April 2020.

We employ augmented Dickey-Fuller tests (ADF) to examine the stationarity of time-series data. The results reported in the appendix (Table 1) show that a unit root is present in both the Bitcoin price and fear sentiment. Then we normalize and detrend both series by taking first differences (logarithm difference for Bitcoin prices) and perform additional stationarity tests. As shown in the appendix (Table 2), we can reject the null hypothesis that the series of the fear sentiment (first difference), VIX, Bitcoin returns, and Bitcoin trading volume are not stationary. In Figure 2, we present the dynamics of the sentiment, VIX, Bitcoin returns, and Bitcoin trading volume.

3. Methodology

Following Urquhart (2018), we employ vector autoregressive (VAR) models to investigate the relationship between fear sentiment, uncertainty, and Bitcoin returns and trading volume. VAR is used to capture more complex dynamics of multiple time series. Specifically, it is an appropriate estimation technique to examine the interdependence dynamic relationships among our variables (Tantaopas, Padungsaksawasdi, and Treepongkaruna 2016).

Let X_t be a vector of variables of interest; then a VAR (p) model will have the following structure:

$$X_t = \alpha + \sum_{j=1}^{p} \beta_j X_{t-j} + \varepsilon_t \tag{1}$$

Table 2. VAR estimations for fear sentiment, uncertainty (VIX), and Bitcoin price dynamics.

	Panel A: VAR Estimation					
	Model 1		Model 2		Model 3	
	V_t	S_t	R_t	S_t	VOL_t	S_t
S_{t-1}	−0.0937*	0.2994***	−0.0001	0.7265***	61.2383***	0.7269***
S_{t-2}	0.1613***	−0.1958 ***	0.00019*	−0.1316***	−33.6227*	−0.1372***
S_{t-3}			−0.00035***	0.0331	7.5371	0.0473**
S_{t-4}			0.00022**	0.0207		
V_{t-1}	0.9421***	0.0159				
V_{t-2}	0.0425	0.0803***				
R_{t-1}			−0.0707***	−3.2772		
R_{t-2}			−0.0538***	0.1919		
R_{t-3}			−0.0122	9.4368**		
R_{t-4}			0.0448**	5.8806		
VOL_{t-1}					0.5853***	0.000015
VOL_{t-2}					0.0444*	0.000048
VOL_{t-3}					0.1637***	−0.000035
	Panel B: Granger Causality Test					
S_t does not Granger cause V_t	12.090***		V_t does not Granger cause S_t		189.740***	
S_t does not Granger cause R_t	12.285**		R_t does not Granger cause S_t		5.901	
S_t does not Granger cause VOL_t	17.764***		VOL_t does not Granger Cause S_t		4.829	

Panel A shows estimation results for three VAR models. Model 1 reports results for fear sentiment and the VIX; Model 2 for fear sentiment and Bitcoin returns; and Model 3 for fear sentiment and Bitcoin trading volume. Panel B reports test statistics of the Granger causality test for Model 1, Model 2, and Model 3. The sample period is from 15 January 2020 to 24 April 2020.
*** indicates 1% level significance, ** indicates 5% level significance, and * indicates 10% level significance.

where α is a vector of constants, β_j is a vector of coefficients, and ε_t is a vector of independent white noise innovations. p denotes the number of optimal lags determined by several information criteria, including the Akaike information criterion (AIC), Hannan–Quinn information criterion (HQIC), Schiwarz-Bayesian information criteria (SBIC), and final prediction error (FPE).

We employ three models to explore the dynamics among fear sentiment, uncertainty, and Bitcoin returns and trading volume. Model 1 studies the relationship between fear sentiment and uncertainty (VIX) $(X_t = S_t, V_t)$; Model 2 examines the dynamics between fear sentiment and Bitcoin returns $(X_t = S_t, R_t)$; and Model 3 investigates the interactions between fear sentiment and Bitcoin trading volume $(X_t = S_t, VOL_t)$.

We also employ Granger causality tests (Granger 1969) to further investigate the causal relationships between fear sentiment and the other variables discussed above. We reject the null hypothesis using the statistic of χ^2-test.[6] The lags of each null hypothesis are based on the best optimal lags in VAR models.

4. Empirical Results

4.1. Fear Sentiment and VIX

Table 2 presents the estimates of the impact of fear sentiment on market uncertainty. As expected, we find that an increase in uncertainty can be driven

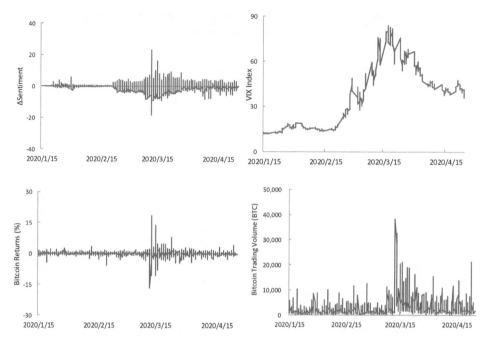

Figure 2. Evolution of the fear sentiment (difference), VIX, Bitcoin returns, and Bitcoin trading volume. This graph plots hourly data on the first difference of fear sentiment proxy (upper left), VIX (upper right), Bitcoin returns (lower left), and Bitcoin dollar trading volume (lower right) from 15 January 2020 to 24 April 2020. In particular, Bitcoin returns are the first differences of log Bitcoin prices.

by fear of the coronavirus, as indicated by a significant and positive relationship between fear sentiment and the VIX. Our results are consistent with those of Baig et al. (2020), who suggest that negative sentiment generated by coronavirus news is associated with market volatility. In addition, the results suggest that market uncertainty is attributable to fear sentiment, which indicates that a higher degree of market uncertainty can induce Bitcoin investors to obtain more information regarding the pandemic, leading to increased search volume on the coronavirus. Based on the results of Granger causality tests shown in Panel B of Table 2, we can confirm the existence of a bidirectional causality relationship between the VIX and fear sentiment.

4.2. Fear Sentiment and Bitcoin Returns

Next, we explore the relationship between fear sentiment and Bitcoin returns. As our results demonstrate in Table 2, there is strong evidence that fear sentiment has a significantly negative impact on Bitcoin returns at lag 3, with a significance level of 1%. In line with Baker and Wurgler (2006), negative Bitcoin returns are attributed to mounting fears related to the coronavirus. Investors may put more selling pressure on Bitcoin if they become more pessimistic as a result of increased search activity for coronavirus information. We then find a significant and positive relationship between fear sentiment and Bitcoin returns at lag 4. Our findings are consistent with those of Da, Engelberg, and Gao (2015), who argue that fear sentiment leads to return reversal. As Bitcoin can rebound quickly, this indicates that Bitcoin prices are extremely volatile during the outbreak of the coronavirus (Cheah and Fry 2015). Granger causality tests support our findings that fear sentiment has a causal effect on Bitcoin returns. However, the reverse causality from fear sentiment to Bitcoin returns seems to be insignificant, as indicated by the results in Panel B of Table 2. In addition, our results indicate that Bitcoin cannot serve as a safe haven, because Bitcoin returns do not respond independent of the market turmoil caused by the coronavirus. As market conditions deteriorated, Bitcoin returns exhibited the positive correlation with the markets (Conlon and Mcgee 2020; Corbet, Larkin, and Lucey 2020).

4.3. Fear Sentiment and Bitcoin Trading Volume

We further examine the relationship between fear sentiment and Bitcoin trading volume. As can be seen in Table 2, fear sentiment has a significantly positive effect on Bitcoin trading volume at lag 1. Consistent with Tetlock (2007), our findings suggest that the stronger the fear sentiment, the higher the Bitcoin trading volume. As fear sentiment was amplified through increased search volume for relevant coronavirus terms, Bitcoin investors may trade more frequently and make irrational decisions based on contemporaneous information on the coronavirus. To further justify our results, we performed Granger causality tests on the relationship between fear sentiment and Bitcoin trading volume. Our results are supported by the tests in Panel B of Table 2, since we can reject the null hypothesis that fear sentiment does not Granger cause Bitcoin trading volume at the 1% level.

5. Robustness Tests

To ensure the reliability of our results, we split our sample into two subsamples to conduct several robustness tests.[7] We select 11 February as the breakpoint, which is when the WHO announced that the new disease had been named COVID-19. Since that day, the search volume of COVID-19 is included to construct our proxy for fear sentiment. Therefore, the first subsample runs from 15 January 2020 to 10 February 2020 while the second subsample covers the period from 11 February 2020 to 24 April 2020.

Table 3 displays the estimation results for the second subsample. Consistent with our main results, we find that fear sentiment is positively correlated with uncertainty. The relationship between fear sentiment and Bitcoin returns remain significant and negative at lag 3 and then return reversal appears at lag 4. We also

Table 3. VAR estimations for fear sentiment, uncertainty, and Bitcoin price dynamics (Subsample 2).

	Panel A: VAR Estimation					
	Model 1		Model 2		Model 3	
	V_t	S_t	R_t	S_t	VOL_t	S_t
S_{t-1}	0.0224	0.2975***	−0.00012	0.7291***	60.4313 ***	0.7294***
S_{t-2}	0.0834***	−0.1990***	0.0002	−0.1328 ***	−33.0992	−0.1385 ***
S_{t-3}			−0.0004 ***	0.0336	7.6242	0.0475 **
S_{t-4}			0.0002 **	0.0203		
V_{t-1}	0.9356***	−0.0916				
V_{t-2}	0.0442	0.1642***				
R_{t-1}			−0.0730***	−3.3721		
R_{t-2}			−0.0569**	0.0853		
R_{t-3}			−0.0150	9.8157 *		
R_{t-4}			0.0451*	6.1212		
VOL_{t-1}					0.5949 ***	0.00002
VOL_{t-2}					0.0345	0.00005
VOL_{t-3}					0.1629***	−0.00004
	Panel B: Granger Causality Test					
S_t does not Granger cause V_t	9.9472***		V_t does not Granger cause S_t		111.02***	
S_t does not Granger cause R_t	9.528**		R_t does not Granger cause S_t		4.469	
S_t does not Granger cause VOL_t	13.747***		VOL_t does not Granger cause S_t		3.702	

Panel A presents estimation results for three VAR models. Model 1 reports results for fear sentiment and the VIX; Model 2 for fear sentiment and Bitcoin returns; and Model 3 for fear sentiment and Bitcoin trading volume. Panel B reports test statistics of the Granger causality test for Model 1, Model 2, and Model 3. The sample period is from 11 February 2020 to 24 April 2020.
*** indicates 1% level significance, ** indicates 5% level significance, and * indicates 10% level significance.

find that Bitcoin trading volume is positively influenced by fear sentiment. Moreover, the results of Granger causality tests for all pairs of our variables are in favor of our findings, which is consistent with our full sample analysis.

6. Conclusion

In this paper, we explore how investors' fear sentiment influences Bitcoin price dynamics during the coronavirus pandemic. We construct a Google search-based fear sentiment measure to proxy investors' fear related to the coronavirus at a high frequency. Our results demonstrate that an increase in search interest in the pandemic is correlated with increased financial market uncertainty. We then examine the impact of fear of coronavirus on Bitcoin returns and investors' trading activity. We find that increasing fear of the coronavirus leads to negative Bitcoin returns and high trading volume, which indicates that Bitcoin behaves more like other financial assets rather than traditional safe-haven assets, such as gold, during times of market distress. Our research suggests that it may not be desirable for investors to allocate resources to Bitcoin to reduce their risk exposure, since it may not serve as a safe haven during the coronavirus pandemic.

Notes

1. See https://coinmarketcap.com/.
2. See https://www.cryptocompare.com.

3. See http://www.google.com/trends.
4. See https://trends.google.com/trends/explore?date=2020-01-15%202020-04-24.
5. See https://www.who.int/csr/don/archive/disease/novel_coronavirus/en.
6. The null hypothesis of causality tests is that fear sentiment does not Granger cause a change in VIX, Bitcoin returns and trading volume, respectively.
7. Another way to conduct a robustness test is to perform the out-of-sample predictions, as described by Sharma, Phan, and Narayan (2019) and Narayan et al. (2020).

Funding

Ningru Zhao would like to acknowledge financial support by the Applied Economics Department of Nanjing Audit University of the Priority Academic Program Development of Jiangsu Higher Education Institutions (Office of Jiangsu Provincial People's Government, [No. [2018] 87]

References

Adjei, F. 2019. Determinants of *Bitcoin* expected returns. *Journal of Finance and Economics* 7 (1):42–47. doi:10.12691/jfe-7-1-5.

Ali, M., N. Alam, and S. A. R. Rizvi. 2020. Coronavirus (COVID-19) — An epidemic or pandemic for financial markets. *Journal of Behavioral and Experimental Finance* 27:100341. doi:10.1016/j.jbef.2020.100341.

Apergis, E., and N. Apergis. 2020. Can the COVID-19 pandemic and oil prices drive the US partisan conflict index? *Energy Research Letters* 1 (1):13144. doi:10.46557/001c.13144.

Baig, A., H. A. Butt, O. Haroon, and S. R. Rizvi. 2020. Deaths, panic, lockdowns and US equity markets: The case of COVID-19 pandemic. Accessed 15 May 2020. Available at SSRN: https://ssrn.com/abstract=3584947.

Baker, M., and J. Wurgler. 2006. Investor sentiment and the cross-section of stock returns. *Journal of Finance* 61:1645–80. doi:10.1007/s11156-018-0756-z.

Bouri, E., R. Gupta, A. K. Tiwari, and D. Roubaud. 2017. Does Bitcoin hedge global uncertainty? Evidence from wavelet-based quantile-in-quantile regressions. *Finance Research Letters* 23:87–95. doi:10.1016/j.frl.2017.02.009.

Cheah, E. T., and J. Fry. 2015. Speculative bubbles in bitcoin markets? An empirical investigation into the fundamental value of bitcoin. *Economics Letters* 130:32–36. doi:10.1016/j.econlet.2015.02.029.

Ciaian, P., M. Rajcaniova, and D. A. Kancs. 2016. The economics of Bitcoin price formation. *Applied Economics* 48 (19):1799–815. doi:10.1080/00036846.2015.1109038.

Conlon, T., and R. Mcgee. 2020. Safe haven or risky hazard? Bitcoin during the covid-19 bear market. *Finance Research Letters* 101607. doi:10.1016/j.frl.2020.101607.

Corbet, S., A. Meegan, C. Larkin, B. Lucey, and L. Yarovaya. 2018. Exploring the dynamic relationships between cryptocurrencies and other financial assets. *Economics Letters* 165:28–34. doi:10.1016/j.econlet.2018.01.004.

Corbet, S., C. Larkin, and B. Lucey. 2020. The contagion effects of the covid-19 pandemic: Evidence from gold and cryptocurrencies. *Finance Research Letters* 101554. doi:10.1016/j.frl.2020.101554.

Da, Z., J. Engelberg, and P. Gao. 2015. The sum of all fears investor sentiment and asset prices. *Review of Financial Studies* 28 (1):1–32. doi:10.1093/rfs/hhu072.

Dyhrberg, A. 2016. Bitcoin, gold and the dollar – A GARCH volatility analysis. *Finance Research Letters* 16:85–92. doi:10.1016/j.frl.2015.10.008.

Gil-Alana, L. A., and M. Monge. 2020. Crude oil prices and COVID-19: Persistence of the shock. *Energy Research Letters* 1 (1):13200. doi:10.46557/001c.13200

Granger, C. W. J. 1969. Investigating causal relations by econometric models and cross-spectral models. *Econometrica* 37:424–38. doi:10.2307/1912791.

Guesmi, K., S. Saadi, I. Abid, and Z. Ftiti. 2019. Portfolio diversification with virtual currency: Evidence from bitcoin. *International Review of Financial Analysis* 63:431–37. doi:10.1016/j.irfa.2018.03.004.

Kristoufek, L. 2015. What are the main drivers of the Bitcoin price? Evidence from wavelet coherence analysis. *PLoS One* 10 (4):e0123923. doi:10.1371/journal.pone.0123923.

Mamaysky, H. 2020. Financial markets and news about the Coronavirus. Accessed 15 May 2020. Available at SSRN: https://ssrn.com/abstract=3565597.

Mele, A., Y. Obayashi, and C. Shalen. 2015. Rate fears gauges and the dynamics of fixed income and equity volatilities. *Journal of Banking & Finance* 52:256–65. doi:10.1016/j.jbankfin.2014.04.030.

Narayan, P. K., S. S. Sharma, D. H. B. Phan, and G. Liu. 2020. Predicting exchange rate returns. *Emerging Markets Review* 42:100668. doi:10.1016/j.ememar.2019.100668.

Panagiotidis, T., T. Stengos, and O. Vravosinos. 2019. The effects of markets, uncertainty and search intensity on bitcoin returns. *International Review of Financial Analysis* 63:220–42. doi:10.1016/j.irfa.2018.11.002.

Shahzad, J., E. Bouri, D. Roubaud, L. Kristoufek, and B. Lucey. 2019. Is bitcoin a better safe-haven investment than gold and commodities? *International Review of Financial Analysis* 63:322–30. doi:10.1016/j.irfa.2019.01.002.

Sharma, S. S., D. H. B. Phan, and P. K. Narayan. 2019. Exchange rate effects of US government shutdowns: Evidence from both developed and emerging markets. *Emerging Markets Review* 40:100626. doi:10.1016/j.ememar.2019.100626.

Tantaopas, P., C. Padungsaksawasdi, and S. Treepongkaruna. 2016. Attention effect via internet search intensity in Asia-Pacific stock markets. *Pacific-Basin Finance Journal* 38:107–24. doi:10.1016/j.pacfin.2016.03.008.

Tetlock, P. C. 2007. Giving content to investor sentiment: The role of media in the stock market. *Journal of Finance* 62:1139–68. doi:10.1111/j.1540-6261.2007.01232x.

Urquhart, A. 2018. What causes the attention of Bitcoin? *Economics Letters* 166:40–44. doi:10.1016/j.econlet.2018.02.017.

Whaley, R. E. 2000. The investor fear gauge: Explication of the CBOE VIX. *Journal of Portfolio Management* 26 (3):12–17. doi:10.3905/jpm.2000.319728.

Yermack, D. 2015. Is Bitcoin a real currency? An economic appraisal. *Handbook of Digital Currency* 31–43. doi:10.1016/B978-0-12-802117-0.00002-3.

Zaremba, A., A. Szyszka, H. Long, and D. Zawadka. 2020. Business sentiment and the cross-section of global equity returns. *Pacific-Basin Finance Journal* 61:101329. doi:10.1016/j.pacfin.2020.101329.

Appendix

Table A1. Stationarity tests for fear sentiment (Level) and Bitcoin prices.

	Panel A: Dickey-Fuller Test for Fear Sentiment (Level)			
	Test Statistic	1% Critical Value	5% Critical Value	10% Critical Value
Z(t)	−2.007	−3.430	−2.860	−2.570

MacKinnon approximate p-value for Z(t) = 0.2836

	Panel B: Dickey-Fuller Test for Bitcoin Prices (BTC/USD)			
	Test Statistic	1% Critical Value	5% Critical Value	10% Critical Value
Z(t)	−1.245	−3.430	−2.860	−2.570

MacKinnon approximate p-value for Z(t) = 0.6538

This table shows the results of stationarity tests for hourly data on fear sentiment and Bitcoin prices using the augmented Dickey-Fuller method. The sample period is from 15 January 2020 to 24 April 2020.
Critical values at the 10% level are smaller than corresponding T-statistics. Therefore, the null hypothesis that the two series are not stationary cannot be rejected at the 10% level.

Table A2. Stationarity tests for fear sentiment (difference), VIX, Bitcoin returns, and bitcoin trading volume.

	Panel A: Dickey-Fuller Test for Fear Sentiment			
	Test Statistic	1% Critical Value	5% Critical Value	10% Critical Value
Z(t)	−22.367***	−3.430	−2.860	−2.570

MacKinnon approximate p-value for Z(t) = 0.0000

	Panel B: Dickey-Fuller Test for VIX			
	Test Statistic	1% Critical Value	5% Critical Value	10% Critical Value
Z(t)	−2.913**	−3.430	−2.860	−2.570

MacKinnon approximate p-value for Z(t) = 0.0438

	Panel C: Dickey-Fuller Test for Bitcoin Returns			
	Test Statistic	1% Critical Value	5% Critical Value	10% Critical Value
Z(t)	−52.766***	−3.430	−2.860	−2.570

MacKinnon approximate p-value for Z(t) = 0.0000

	Panel D: Dickey-Fuller Test for Bitcoin Trading Volume			
	Test Statistic	1% Critical Value	5% Critical Value	10% Critical Value
Z(t)	−21.642***	−3.430	−2.860	−2.570

MacKinnon approximate p-value for Z(t) = 0.0000

This table shows the results of stationarity tests for hourly data on the first difference of fear sentiment, the VIX, Bitcoin returns, and Bitcoin dollar trading volume using the Dickey-Fuller method. The sample period is from 15 January 2020 to 24 April 2020.
All critical values at the 5% level are larger than corresponding T-statistics. Therefore, the null hypothesis that the four series are not stationary can be rejected at the 5% level.

Table A3. VAR estimations for fear sentiment and Bitcoin price dynamics (Subsample 1).

	Panel A: VAR Estimation				
	Model 1			Model 2	
	R_t	S_t	VOL_t		S_t
S_{t-1}	0.0007*	0.3872***	166.9879 **		0.3434***
S_{t-2}	0.0003	−0.1243***			
R_{t-1}	−0.0469	2.4606			
R_{t-2}	−0.0256	4.3220			
VOL_{t-1}			0.3795***		0.00001

Panel B: Granger Causality Test			
S_t does not Granger Cause R_t	5.230 *	R_t does not Granger Cause S_t	1.584
S_t does not Granger Cause VOL_t	4.249 **	VOL_t does not Granger Cause S_t	0.840

Panel A shows estimation results for two VAR models. Model 1 reports results for fear sentiment and Bitcoin returns and Model 2 for fear sentiment and Bitcoin trading volume. Panel B shows test statistics of the Granger causality test for Model 1 and Model 2. The sample period is from 15 January 2020 to 10 February 2020.
*** indicates 1% level of significance, ** indicates 5% of level significance, and * indicates 10% of level significance.

Constructing a Global Fear Index for the COVID-19 Pandemic

Afees A. Salisu and Lateef O. Akanni

ABSTRACT

This paper offers two main innovations. First, we construct a global fear index (GFI) for the COVID-19 pandemic to support economic, financial, and policy analyses in this area. Second, we demonstrate the application of the index to stock return predictability using OECD data. The panel data predictability results reveal the significance of the index as a good predictor of stock returns during the pandemic. Also, we find that accounting for "asymmetry" effect and macro (common) factors improves the forecast performance of the GFI-based predictive model for stock returns. With regular updates and improvements of the index, several empirical analyses can be extended to other macroeconomic fundamentals in future research.

1. Introduction

The interest to construct a global fear index for the novel coronavirus (COVID-19) is motivated by two factors. First, while viruses generally can infect people, the rate of infection of COVID-19 is unprecedented as it is found to be more infectious than other coronaviruses such as SARS [Severe Acute Respiratory Syndrome] and MERS-CoV [Middle East Respiratory Syndrome – Coronavirus] (WHO, 2020). Second, only COVID-19 outbreak among the class of coronaviruses was declared a global pandemic in less than 3 months of its emergence and therefore its impact on the global economy is more likely to be severe than other coronaviruses. The increasing number of reported cases and deaths associated with the COVID-19 pandemic has engendered palpable fear among investors due to its threat to the health and livelihood of the people as well as the global economic activity.[1] In fact, the action to lockdown the global economy was informed by the rising cases of infected persons and related deaths, therefore, using these numbers to construct the level of fear associated with the novel virus is justified. This is the main contribution of the study and there is none to the best of our knowledge that has utilized the same parameters to analyze the panic associated with the pandemic.

Information about the fear index is important for a number of reasons. First, policymakers are confronted with the choice between containing the virus and sustaining the economy. Information about the extent of the panic associated with COVID-19 and its impact on the economy (say financial market and real economic activity) will offer useful insights into how much sacrifice the economy will have to endure to contain the virus. The use of our index to predict macroeconomic indices is also demonstrated in this study with special focus on stock returns.[2] Thus, the fear index can also help in analyzing how much of distortions in the market can be attributed to the pandemic. Second, in addition to the impact assessment of the panic on the economy, we also demonstrate how the fear index can be used to project the future path of relevant macroeconomic series such as stock returns. This information is crucial for determining how long it will take the impact of this fear to fizzle e out over time. Investors seeking to maximize returns will find this information useful particularly in terms of portfolio diversification and hedging strategy.

Additionally, analyzing the effect of fear on stock market performance is not new in the literature and some of them have relied on the use of media generated panic (see Badshah et al. 2018; Economou, Panagopoulos, and Tsouma 2018; Gradinaru 2014; Haroon and Rizvi 2020; Narayan 2019; Westerhoff 2004). We also argue that the number of COVID-19 reported cases and deaths constitute an integral part of media report during the pandemic and therefore we hypothesize that the level of panic will increase as these numbers increase and by extension stock returns will decline. This is well demonstrated under the section for descriptive analyses of our proposed COVID-19 fear index. An alternative measure of fear is the one that relies on the implied volatility index (see Bouri et al. 2018; Shaikh and Padhi 2015) and prominent among them is the one introduced by the Chicago Board Options Exchange (CBOE) in 1993 and further modified in 2003 by Shaikh and Padhi (2015). Unlike the CBOE index which is limited to the US rather than global and only captures uncertainty due to the stock market (Bouri et al. 2018), one of the strengths of our proposed fear index lies in its coverage as all the countries and by extension regions and territories in the world are considered in the construction of the index. This makes it possible to link the panic to any relevant macroeconomic fundamental or market (financial market, real estate market, commodity market, or foreign exchange market, among others) and by extension its response to the panic can easily be evaluated using the newly proposed index. In other words, while the original fear index and its current extensions have played important role in explaining and predicting changes in stock market performance, their inability to capture the recent source of fear associated with COVID-19 suggests that their application may be inefficient. Thus, this study contributes to the literature by developing and applying an alternative fear index that incorporates the

COVID-19 parameters which have remained the barometer for actions/decisions taken at all levels, household, business, and government.

In order to promote wider acceptability of the newly constructed fear index, we assess its predictive power in the forecast of the OECD stock markets (as developed markets) and BRICS stock markets (as emerging markets).[3] Apparently, OECD countries have the most developed stock markets in the world and BRICS have the most advanced emerging stock markets (see Mensi et al. 1993). Relevant studies on the predictability of stocks with fear index include Bouri et al. (2018) and Zhu et al. (2019), with both finding that fear index is a good predictor of stock market performance. Our study however differs from Bouri et al. (2018) and Zhu et al. (2019) as it applies the newly developed index with COVID-19 effect. It also covers a group of developed and emerging markets as against Bouri et al. (2018) which only cover emerging markets of BRICS and Zhu et al. (2019), focusing on the US stock market.

Another contribution of this study is in the area of methodology drawn from panel data forecasting techniques. This is rather different from the GARCH-MIDAS method employed in Zhu et al. (2019) and the Bayesian Graphical Structural VAR model utilized in Bouri et al. (2018). Our choice model is considered suitable based on its ability to deal with short time period occasioned by the period between the outbreak of the COVID-19 pandemic and the period of writing this paper. In addition, the use of panel data forecast rather than pooling of individual forecasts of different markets with small T would tend to generate better results (see Baltagi 2013; Westerlund and Narayan 2016; Westerlund and Narayan (2016); for some discussions on panel data forecasting with short T).[4] For completeness and in the spirit of Westerlund and Narayan (2016), we allow for common factors such as global stock market volatility and commodity price volatility in the predictability of stock returns. The computational advantages of accounting for these factors are well documented in Westerlund and Narayan (2016). Notwithstanding the short T dimension of our panel data, we also offer some forecast evaluations to complement the predictability results. For robustness, we also compare the forecast performance of our proposed global fear index (GFI) for the COVID-19 pandemic with the existing fear index that is limited to the stock market. Overall, we find that the proposed index offers better predictability than the benchmark model (historical average or constant returns model). Similarly, an extended GFI-based model that accounts for "asymmetry" effect and macro factors further enhance the predictability of the index. Finally, the GFI is a better predictor of fear/panic in the stock market than the existing fear index. Our results offer meaningful generalizations about the behavior of the GFI given the coverage of the data scope (OECD and the BRICS emerging economies) which is a reasonable proxy for the global stock markets.

The remainder of the paper is structured as follows: Section 2 provides the procedures for the construction of fear index. Section 3 presents the trend and description of the fear index. Section 4 shows the empirical application of the global fear index in stock market predictability. It also presents and discusses the results. Section 5 concludes the paper.

2. Construction of the Global Fear Index

The World Health Organization (WHO) on March 11, 2020, noting the number of reported cases for preceding two weeks, declared COVID-19 as a global health pandemic.[5] The tragic health consequences of COVID-19 and the expectation of increase in number of cases pose some economic uncertainties and disruptions that came at a significant cost to the global economy. The global fear index (GFI) seeks to measure daily concerns and emotions on the spread and severity of COVID-19 since the pandemic declaration. Excessive fear could have significant implications on investment sentiments and decisions, and as such affecting prices such as stocks and oil prices. Relying on the official reports of COVID-19 cases and deaths globally,[6] the GFI is a composite index of two factors; Reported Cases and Reported Deaths, on a scale of zero to 100, respectively, indicating absence and presence of extreme fear/panic. We considered the incubation period expectation and daily reported cases and deaths in constructing the index. By incubation period expectation, we meant the time-expectations between catching the virus and emergence of symptoms of the disease (WHO 2020).

(i) Reported Cases Index (RCI)

It measures how far expectations from reported cases in a 14-day period ahead veered from the present reported case. Most estimates of the incubation period for COVID-19 range from 1-14 days (WHO 2020). Therefore, the choice of 14-day expectations represents the highest number of incubation days as defined by the WHO. The RCI is computed as:

$$RCI_t = \left(\frac{\sum_i^N c_{i,t}}{\sum_i^N \left(c_{i,t} + c_{i,t-14} \right)} \right) \times 100 \tag{1}$$

$$i = 1, 2, \ldots, N; t = 1, 2, \ldots, T.$$

where RCI_t denotes the Reported Cases Index computed for period t; $\sum_i^N c_{i,t}$ is the total number of COVID-19 reported cases at time t for all the countries in the world, $i = 1, 2, \ldots, N$ where N is the total number of cross-sections captured in the index; $c_{i,t-14}$ is the number of COVID-19 reported cases for each cross-section at the beginning of the incubation period, which is represented as the preceding 14th day. The multiplication by 100 provides the index on a scale of 0 to 100 with the highest value representing the highest level of fear during the pandemic and decreases as the index tends toward 0.

(ii) Reported Death Index (RDI)

Similar to the Reported Cases Index, the Reported Death Index mirrors the reported cases by relating the number of daily reported deaths to expectations from reported number of deaths in a 14-day period ahead in line with the assumption for RCI based on WHO declaration. The index is computed as:

$$RDI_t = \left(\frac{\sum_i^N d_{i,t}}{\sum_i^N (d_{i,t} + d_{i,t-14})} \right) \times 100 \tag{2}$$

where RDI_t denotes the Report Death Index; $\sum_i^N d_{i,t}$ is the total number of COVID-19 reported deaths at time t for all countries, denoted as N; $d_{i,t-14}$ is the number of COVID-19 reported deaths at the beginning of the incubation period, $t - 14$. The index is also given on a scale between 0 and 100 where the highest value signifies the highest level of fear due to the pandemic.

(iii) Global Fear (Composite) Index [GFI]

The construct of the GFI pulls the two indexes together with equal weights assigned to obtain the composite index. The composite index (GFI_t) is given as:

$$GFI_t = [0.5(RCI_t + RDI_t)] \tag{3}$$

As expressed in [3], the global fear index utilizes all the available data for both reported cases and deaths and therefore may be more representative in capturing the severity of fear due to the pandemic. Like the RCI and RDI, the global fear index is also given on a scale of 0 to100 where 50 signifies moderate level of fear and increases as the index tends toward 100.

2.1. Descriptive Statistics Using the Constructed GFI Data[7]

We render some descriptive statistics for the constructed GFI data obtained and thereafter evaluate its relationship with the stock returns of OECD and BRICS countries.[8] The start and end periods for data collection used in constructing the GFI is informed by the data availability and start period of COVID-19. However, to avoid the problem of zero weights, especially in the number of deaths[9] declared as well as to account for the incubation period, the start period is selected as 14 days after the recorded number of deaths exceeded10. This date which forms the start period of our analysis coincides with the 10th of February, 2020.

The summary of the mean, standard deviation, and relative standard deviation is presented in Table 1. Unlike the coefficient of variation that is commonly used, which divides the standard deviation by the mean, the relative standard deviation is the absolute value of the coefficient of variation. If the mean is negative, the coefficient of variation will be negative while the relative standard deviation used here will always be positive. Hence, the preference for the latter for evaluating the series variability. The average stock returns across most of the countries considered are negative over the period under consideration. This indicates an overall average decline in stock returns across the countries. On the stock return variability, the relative standard deviation statistics show that Latvia records the highest stock return variability over the period under consideration while Spain has the least variability. However, for the pool of countries, the average stock returns is given as −0.2639% with a relative standard deviation of 5.29%. Overall, the rate of change in GFI is more volatile compared to the variation in the stock returns across all the countries, as measured by the relative standard deviation given as 15.12%.

Following the descriptive analysis of the series, we conduct some scenario analyses of the relationship between the GFI and the stock returns across OECD and BRICS countries. We evaluate the behavior of stock returns to when the GFI increases or declines. Table 2 summarizes the average stock

Table 1. Summary statistics.

Country	Mean	Std. Deviation	R.Std (%)	Country	Mean	Std. Deviation	R.Std (%)
Stock Returns							
Australia	−0.4266	3.3653	7.89	Japan	−0.2848	2.6480	9.30
Austria	−0.6015	4.0952	6.81	Korea	−0.1980	2.9415	14.86
Belgium	−0.5005	3.5606	7.11	Latvia	−0.0817	3.1555	38.63
Brazil	2.5175	24.0264	9.54	Mexico	−0.3495	2.4087	6.89
Canada	−0.3259	4.1869	12.85	Netherland	−0.3302	3.0817	9.33
Chile	−0.2537	3.7907	14.94	New Zealand	−0.2081	2.8820	13.85
China	−0.0425	1.4419	33.89	Norway	−0.2706	2.9077	10.75
Czech	−0.4303	2.7726	6.44	Poland	−0.3932	3.1957	8.13
Denmark	−0.1459	2.1631	14.83	Portugal	−0.3739	2.8490	7.62
Finland	−0.3633	2.9905	8.23	Russia	−0.2579	2.9266	11.35
France	−0.4900	3.4540	7.05	Slovakia	−0.1227	0.9885	8.06
Germany	−0.3875	3.4557	8.92	Slovenia	−0.3516	2.4901	7.08
Greece	−0.6478	4.8145	7.43	South Africa	−0.2172	3.3776	15.55
Hungary	−0.4212	3.3666	7.99	Spain	−0.6323	3.4680	5.48
Iceland	−0.2043	2.2822	11.17	Sweden	−0.2918	2.9643	10.16
India	−0.3483	3.8551	11.07	Switzerland	−0.2441	2.6636	10.91
Ireland	−0.4142	3.3819	8.17	Turkey	−0.2810	2.5230	8.98
Israel	−0.3281	2.8955	8.82	UK	−0.4154	3.1669	7.62
Italy	−0.5821	3.9523	6.79	USA	−0.3294	4.3710	13.27
Australia	−0.4266	3.3653	7.89				
Panel	−0.2639	4.9892	5.29	GFI*	5.7626	38.1087	15.12

Note: Like the stock returns, the GFI* is computed as the rate of change in the index in order to allow for easy comparison between the two indices. The R.Std is the relative standard deviation statistic. It slightly differs from the commonly used coefficient of variation which is computed as the standard deviation divided by the mean. Here, we divide the standard deviation by the absolute value of the mean expressed in percentage (%). If the mean is negative, the coefficient of variation will be negative while the relative standard deviation used here will always be positive.

Table 2. Scenario analyses.

Country	Mean	Above	Below	Country	Mean	Above	Below
Column	**I**	**II**	**III**		**I**	**II**	**III**
Stock Prices							
Australia	−0.4266	−0.3575	−0.4542	Japan	−0.2848	0.0410	−0.4152
Austria	−0.6015	−0.7188	−0.5545	Korea	−0.1980	−0.0162	−0.2707
Belgium	−0.5005	−0.6387	−0.4453	Latvia	−0.0817	0.1746	−0.1842
Brazil	2.5175	10.1602	−0.5396	Mexico	−0.3495	−0.2398	−0.3933
Canada	−0.3259	−1.1296	−0.0045	Netherlands	−0.3302	−0.5486	−0.2428
Chile	−0.2537	−0.5240	−0.1456	New Zealand	−0.2081	0.3266	−0.4220
China	−0.0425	−0.0434	−0.0422	Norway	−0.2706	−0.6942	−0.1011
Czech	−0.4303	−0.4086	−0.4390	Poland	−0.3932	−0.9810	−0.1580
Denmark	−0.1459	−0.1848	−0.1303	Portugal	−0.3739	−0.5384	−0.3081
Finland	−0.3633	−0.5222	−0.2998	Russia	−0.2579	−0.5535	−0.1397
France	−0.4900	−0.4378	−0.5108	Slovakia	−0.1227	0.2734	−0.2811
Germany	−0.3875	−0.3943	−0.3848	Slovenia	−0.3516	−0.0268	−0.4815
Greece	−0.6478	−1.2160	−0.4205	South Africa	−0.2172	−0.3044	−0.1823
Hungary	−0.4212	−0.6983	−0.3103	Spain	−0.6323	−0.6523	−0.6243
Iceland	−0.2043	−0.2943	−0.1683	Sweden	−0.2918	−0.4162	−0.2420
India	−0.3483	0.1291	−0.5393	Switzerland	−0.2441	−0.4840	−0.1481
Ireland	−0.4142	−0.3903	−0.4237	Turkey	−0.2810	−0.0349	−0.3794
Israel	−0.3281	−0.6339	−0.2058	UK	−0.4154	−0.6906	−0.3054
Italy	−0.5821	−0.4276	−0.6439	USA	−0.3294	−0.5893	−0.2254

Note: the average values reported in each column indicate the average stock returns for each of the countries for three different scenarios over the period considered. The first scenario is the Mean which depicts the average stock returns at the overall average change in the global fear index (GFI). Above indicates the average returns when the changes in GFI is above its overall average, while Below connote the average stock returns when the GFI changes below its average value.

returns across the 38 countries, at the average change in GFI, as well as below and above its average. The reported average values in column II of the Table represent the average stock returns across all the countries at GFI values above the overall average change of 8.49 as earlier depicted in the lower pane of Table 1, while column III reports stock returns when the GFI is below the average change. It is evident from the analyses that as the change in GFI increases, stock returns decline across most of the countries considered. On the other hand, when the change in GFI declines, stock returns across the countries are above their averages.

In line with the standard practice in the literature, we also render some graphical illustrations of the GFI and stock prices across the countries considered (see Figure 1). We used the level series for both indices to be able to trace any potential or existing co-movement between the two of them. The graphical representations highlight the co-movements between our constructed GFI index and stock prices for the selected countries. The graphs show an inverse relationship between stock prices and the fear index, which is similar to findings from the scenario analyses.

2.2. Additional Descriptive Analysis

In addition to the global fear index computed and discussed above, we extend the analysis to evaluate the index across COVID-19 most affected countries across the

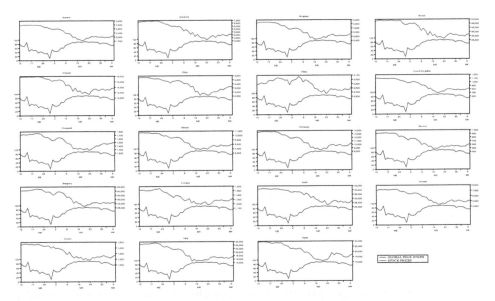

Figure 1. Trends in Stock prices and the Global Fear Index (GFI) for the COVID-19 pandemic. Note: Each graph plots stock prices against the fear index; the left axis depicts the global fear index while the right axis plots the stock prices for each country.

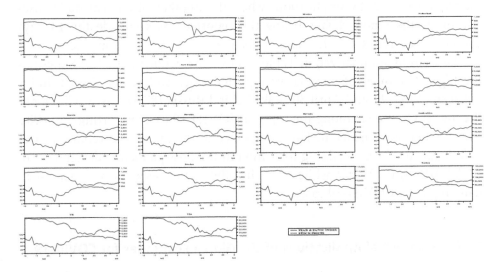

Figure 1. Continued.

globe. We concentrate mainly on countries with the highest reported cases. Table 3 summarizes the cumulative reported cases for the 10 countries with the highest reported cases as well as their average weekly GFI since the announcement of COVID-19 as a pandemic by the WHO. The last column labeled "Average" in Table 3 indicates the average GF index across the period considered between March 11, when COVID-19 was declared pandemic and April 30, 2020, selected based on most recent and latest available data on COVID-19.

Table 3. Fear index for top-ten cases reporting countries.

Country	COVID-19 Reported		Fear Index				
	Cases	Deaths	W1	W2	W3	W4	Average
United States	1,039,909	60,966	92.81	92.68	66.69	47.88	77.37
Spain	211,291	24,090	97.87	81.20	38.50	27.84	64.64
Italy	203,591	27,682	90.89	61.70	41.78	40.73	60.54
United Kingdom	165,221	22,473	96.48	91.67	66.77	45.30	77.22
Germany	159,119	6,288	96.56	82.97	52.81	40.18	70.87
France	128,442	24,087	95.38	83.02	50.94	31.64	68.54
Turkey	117,589	3,081	-	95.43	71.63	46.04	72.55
Russia	99,399	972	94.08	92.91	88.14	77.11	87.50
Iran	93,657	5,957	80.71	59.75	39.89	40.45	56.98
China	83,944	4,637	25.17	46.45	34.34	7.97	31.85

Note: Average indicates the average GF index across the eight-weeks period considered between March 11 and April 30, 2020. W1 indicates the first two weeks that follow the announcement by WHO that COVID-19 is a global pandemic; W2, W3 and W4 are respectively the successive two-weeks periods that followed W1; Cases indicate the cumulative number of reported cases for each of the country; while deaths is the total number of deaths recorded as at 30th April 2020.

A number of thought-provoking information emanates from the weekly distribution of the index and the analysis rendered. Recall that the construction GF index takes into consideration incubation expectations, which implies the reported cases and deaths 14 days earlier which marks the beginning of incubation period, by implication, when the number of current daily cases and/or deaths reported falls below the reported cases and deaths 14 days earlier, the current GF index tends to be lower than the previous index.

The analysis summarized in Table 3 shows that while the United States has the highest number of cumulative reported cases and deaths, its GF index between March 11 and April 30 ranks behind Russia (87.5). Lastly, China has the lowest GF index among the top-ten COVID-19 cases reporting countries over the period considered. This is expected as the number of reported cases and deaths has been declining for China in the post-pandemic declaration of COVID-19 by the WHO, while other the other countries witnessed increase in daily reported COVID-19 cases.

3. Some Empirical Applications of the Global Fear Index for COVID-19

The evident relationship between the constructed index and stock prices provides a strong motivation to probe further into the predictive power of the formulated index. Thus, we construct a predictive model for the stock returns of the OECD and BRICS stock markets where the GFI is used as a predictor and its predictive power is comparatively evaluated with other plausible forecast models for stock returns. The considered stock markets are good representations of the global stock market and by extension results obtained offer reasonable generalizations for other stock markets (Christou and Gupta 2019). In addition, pooling the stock markets helps to circumvent the problem of insufficient observations that may plague country-specific analyses.[10] Given the short time span of the available data for COVID-19, we employ homogenous panel data procedures.[11]

Consequently, the predictive models constructed in this paper for the return predictability are structured in panel form. We begin our analyses with the historical average (constant return) model which ignores any potential predictor of stock and is specified as[12]:

$$r_{it} = \alpha + e_{it}; \quad t = 1, 2, 3, \ldots, T; \quad i = 1, 2, 3, \ldots, N \tag{2}$$

where r_{it} denotes stock returns computed as log returns; α is a constant parameter; and e_{it} is the error term. Premised on the Investor Recognition hypothesis (see Merton 1987), we construct a single-predictor model using the Global Fear index as a regressor. The Investor Recognition hypothesis, by assuming incomplete market information, suggests that investors are not aware of all securities in a market and therefore they prefer to choose familiar stocks in constructing portfolios (for relevant literature see Adachi, Masuda, and Takeda 2017; Aouadi, Arouri, and Teulon 2013; Bank, Larch, and Peter 2011; Bodnaruk and Ostberg 2009; Da, Engelberg, and Gao 2011; Jacobs and Hillert 2016; Joseph, Wintoki, and Zhang 2011; Preis, Moat, and Stanley 2013; Zhu and Jiang 2018). The single-predictor model is given as:

$$r_{it} = \alpha + \sum_{k=1}^{5} \delta_k gfi_{i,t-k} + e_{it} \tag{3}$$

where gfi_{it} denotes the constructed Global Fear index expressed in natural logs, a measure of investors' emotion and attention. Note that we allow for up to five lags given the underlying frequency for our analysis which is daily and therefore the proximity of the data points can be exploited to account for more dynamics in the predictive model. Thus, in addition to the behavior of the individual parameters, testing for the overall sign and significance of these parameters jointly is crucial to arrive at a distinct conclusion on the predictability of GFI on stock returns. The testable null hypothesis of no predictability can therefore be expressed as $H_0 : \sum_{k=1}^{5} \hat{\delta} = 0$ against the alternative hypothesis of $H_0 : \sum_{k=1}^{5} \hat{\delta} \neq 0$. One important feature of daily stock returns is that they tend to exhibit day-of-the-week effect (see Zhang, Lai, and Lin 2017 for a review of the literature). To account for this feature and at the same time prevent parameter proliferation, we follow a three-step procedure. First, we regress the return series on dummy variables constructed for the five days of the week, that is, $r_{it} = \theta + \sum_{j=1}^{4} \gamma_j D_{jit} + v_{it}$ where $D_j = 1$ for each j and zero otherwise. Note that $j = 1, 2, 3, 4$ respectively denotes Monday, Tuesday, Wednesday, and Thursday while Friday is the reference day. The second step requires determining the day-of-the-week adjusted returns (r_{it}^d) which can be estimated as $r_{it}^d = r_{it} - \left(\hat{\theta} + \sum_{j=1}^{4} \hat{\gamma}_j D_{jit} \right)$ or simply $r_{it}^d = \hat{v}_{it}$. The third step involves regressing the latter on the GFI predictor series, that is,

$$r_{it}^d = \alpha + \sum_{k=1}^{5} \delta_k gfi_{i,t-k} + e_{it} \qquad (4)$$

We also test for possible asymmetry in the GFI series where positive and negative changes in the index are assumed to have distinct effects on stock returns. This idea is prominent when dealing with the predictability of stock returns (see, for example, Narayan 2019; Narayan and Gupta 2015; Salisu, Isah, and Akanni 2019d). Hypothetically, a decline in the GFI (negative asymmetry) is expected to impact positively on stock returns, while on the other hand, positive asymmetry, which implies increase in the COVID-19 GFI is expected to have a negative impact. The predictive model can be specified as $r_{it} = \alpha + \beta D_{1,it-1} + \rho \Delta gfi_{it-1} + \psi \Delta gfi_{it-1}^* + e_{it}$ where $D_{1,it} = 1$ if $\Delta gfi_{it} > 0$ and zero otherwise; $\Delta gfi_{it}^* = D_{1,it} * \Delta gfi_{it}$.[13] Therefore, the impact of positive changes in GFI on stock returns can be estimated as $(\rho + \psi)$ (i.e. evaluated at $D_{1,it} = 1$) while it is ρ for negative asymmetry (i.e. evaluated at $D_{1,it} = 0$). The differential slope coefficient between the two asymmetries is measured as ψ and its statistical significance implies the presence of asymmetry, otherwise, the positive and negative "asymmetry" effects are assumed identical.

For completeness, we also account for some other important factors that can influence stock returns (see also Bannigidadmath and Narayan 2015; Narayan et al. 2016; Devpura, Narayan, and Sharma 2018; Salisu, Swaray, and Oloko 2019a, 2019b, 2019c, 2019d and 2019e). The Arbitrage Pricing Theory offers the theoretical basis for incorporating systemic or macroeconomic risks in the predictability of stock returns. On this basis, we extend the single-predictor model as:

$$r_{it} = \alpha + \sum_{k=1}^{5} \delta_k \, gfi_{i,t-k} + Z_{it}'\phi + e_{it} \qquad (5)$$

where Z_{it}' is $(1 \times K)$ vector of additional (macroeconomic) variables, and ϕ is $(K \times 1)$ vector of parameters for the additional K regressors.[14] Again, to circumvent having so many parameters in the predictive model and in the spirit of Westerlund and Narayan (2016), we adopt the same procedure followed in the computation of the day-of-the-week-adjusted stock returns. In other words, we regress the return series on the selected macro variables, that is, $r_{it} = \vartheta + Z_{it}'\phi + u_{it}$ and thereafter, the macro-adjusted returns series is regressed on the GFI predictor. Ideally, the choice of the return series will be determined by the relative forecast performance of r_{it} and r_{it}^d from the single-predictor case.

Finally, the forecast evaluation of the predictor is rendered for both in-sample and out-of-sample periods. Since there is no formal procedure of splitting the data for this purpose,[15] we consider 75% and 25% split for the in-sample and out-of-sample periods, respectively. This choice is informed by the need to have sufficient observations that will allow for meaningful regression analyses from which the forecasts will be obtained. For robustness purpose, we also consider multiple out-of-sample forecast horizons – 5-day, 10-day and 15-day ahead forecasts. We adopt two pair-wise forecast measures, namely Campbell-Thompson (CT, 2008) and Clark and West (CW, 2007) tests for the forecast evaluation. These measures are particularly useful when dealing with nested predictive models. The (CT, 2008) test is specified as:

$$CT = 1 - (M\hat{S}E_u/M\hat{S}E_r) \tag{6}$$

where $M\hat{S}E_u$ is the mean squared error obtained from the unrestricted model, in this case the GFI-based model (Equation (3)) and $M\hat{S}E_r$ is the mean squared error obtained from the restricted model (for example, the historical average or constant return model, Equation (2)). In this case, Equation (3) outperforms Equation (2) if $CT > 0$ and vice versa. The CW (2007) test, on the other hand, is used to establish the statistical significance of the forecast evaluation procedure in the CT (2008). For a forecast horizon h, the CW (2007) test is specified as:

$$\hat{f}_{t+h} = M\hat{S}E_r - (M\hat{S}E_u - adj) \tag{7}$$

where $\hat{f}_{t+h}$ is the forecast horizon; $M\hat{S}E_r$ and $M\hat{S}E_u$ respectively are the squared errors of restricted and unrestricted predictive models and they are, respectively, computed as: $P^{-1} \sum \left(r_{i,t+h} - \hat{r}_{ri,t+h}\right)^2$ and $P^{-1} \sum \left(r_{i,t+h} - \hat{r}_{ui,t+h}\right)^2$. The term adj is included to adjust for noise in the unrestricted model and it is defined by $P^{-1} \sum \left(\hat{r}_{ri,t+h} - \hat{r}_{ui,t+h}\right)^2$; P is the amount of predictions that the averages are computed. Lastly, the statistical significance of regressing $\hat{f}_{t+h}$ on a constant confirms the CT test.

3.1. The Results of the Empirical Application of COVID-19 Global Fear Index

We demonstrate the empirical application of the global fear index (GFI) by evaluating its predictability of stock returns across OECD and BRICS countries. We estimate a single factor predictive model with the GFI as the predictor, and compared the forecast performance with the historical average model. We further extend the estimation to account for day-of-the-week effects by adjusting the stock returns series for possible day-of-the-week anomalies. The predictability results are summarized in Table 4 and the estimated coefficients show that the predictors are correctly signed and

Table 4. GFI predictability of stock return.

Coefficients	Model 1	Model 2
GFI_{t-j}	−1.3954*	−1.5378**
	(0.7636)	(0.7563)
	[−1.8275]	[−2.0332]

Note: Model 1 is the COVID-19 GFI predictability model of stock returns while in Model 2, the stock returns series is adjusted for the day-of-the-week effect; GFI_{t-j} is the sum of the lags of coefficients of global fear index where t period and j is the number of lags and it equals 1 to 5; The sign and significance of joint coefficient is evaluated using the Wald test for coefficient restriction; Standard errors are presented in parentheses while the t-statistics are in squared brackets. The asterisk ** & * indicate statistical significance at 5% and 10% levels respectively.

statistically significant. The joint coefficient of the GFI lags, after controlling for the day-of-the-week effects, is also negative and significant. By implication, the estimated predictabilities confirm that the COVID-19 GFI poses a negative impact on stock returns. More importantly, we find that accounting for other salient features of the stock return series such as the day-of-the-week effect improves the predictability results. This is in line with the extended predictive model previously specified in Equation (4) which assumes a role for these effects in the predictability of stock returns. This outcome also validates our findings from the descriptive statistics rendered in the immediate preceding section where an inverse relationship between the two series is also observed.

The forecast evaluation of the predictive models using both the in-sample and out-of-sample data periods is also carried out and the results are summarized in Table 5. The in-sample predictability evaluation, as described in the methodology section, is performed using 75% of the entire data sample for the in-sample forecasts and the balance for the out-of-sample forecasts. For robustness, we consider multiple out-of-sample forecast horizons using 5-day, 10-day, and 15-day ahead forecasts. For the predictability models evaluated, first we compare the performance of the single predictor with the GFI model (Model 1) with that of the historical average. Second, we compare the predictability performance between the model that accounts for day-of-the-week effects (i.e. Model 2) and the model that ignores the same (i.e. Model 1). The criteria for interpreting the forecast measures have been previously discussed. Based on the two forecast measures, the obtained results, both in-sample and out-of-sample forecast horizons, indicate that (i) the GFI predictability model for stock returns outperforms the historical average, and (ii) the stock return model that adjusts for day-of-the-week effects also outperforms the model that ignores the same. Thus, controlling for the day-of-the-week effects is imperative in stock return predictability (see also Boubaker et al. 2017; Zhang, Lai, and Lin 2017).

We further extend the analysis by accounting for the impact of asymmetries in the GFI predictability of stock returns. Hypothetically, it is expected that the decline in the COVID-19 GFI (negative asymmetry) would have a positive

Table 5. In-sample and out-of-sample forecast evaluation.

Forecast Evaluation	Model 1 Vs Historical Average	Model 2 Vs Model 1
In-sample		
CT statistic	0.1973	0.0484
CW test	0.8157***	1.5148***
	(0.2849)	(0.2977)
h = 1		
CT statistic	0.2063	0.0414
CW test	0.7917***	1.0436***
	(0.2037)	(0.2183)
h = 2		
CT statistic	0.2221	0.0369
CW test	1.0945***	0.8128***
	(0.1721)	(0.1664)
h = 3		
CT statistic	0.2244	0.0084
CW test	1.0796***	0.2185
	(0.1472)	(0.1501)

Note: Model 1 is the COVID-19 GFI predictability model of stock returns while in Model 2, the stock returns series is adjusted for the day-of-the-week effect. The C-T stat denotes the Campbell-Thompson (2008) test while the C-W test is the Clark and West (2007) test. ***, ** & * indicate statistical significance at 1%, 5% & 10% levels respectively.

impact on stock returns, while the reverse would be the case for positive asymmetry. The results are summarized in Table 6 as Model 3 and we find that positive asymmetry has a negative sign and statistically significant, while, on the other hand, the negative asymmetry has a positive coefficient as hypothesized. In other words, any increase in the COVID-19 GFI will impact stock returns negatively, while a decline in the index improves stock returns across the countries under consideration, on average. The statistical significance of the differential slope coefficient between the two asymmetries is reported in the lower pane of the Table and its statistical significance further

Table 6. Macroeconomic-adjusted and asymmetric stock returns predictability results.

Coefficients	Model 3	Model 4
GFI		−1.4992***
		(0.7738)
		[−1.9375]
GFI^P	−0.7999**	
	(0.4003)	
	[−1.9982]	
GFI^N	0.3096	
	(0.1327)	
	[4.7081]	
Asymmetry test	−1.1096**	

Note: Model 3 is the asymmetry GFI predictability model and Model 4 controls for macroeconomic volatility effects. GFI is the sum of the coefficients on the five-lag global fear index; GFI^P and GFI^N are respectively the positive and negative asymmetries of GFI. The asymmetry test reported is the coefficient of the differential slope coefficient and its statistical significance implies the presence of asymmetry. The reported standard error and t-stats, respectively in parentheses and squared brackets, are computed using the Wald test for coefficient restriction. The asterisks ***, ** and * respectively indicate statistical significance at 1%, 5% and 10% levels.

implies the presence of asymmetry. Consequently, positive and negative changes in the GFI will not have identical impact on stock returns.

Furthermore, the predictability estimates after controlling for macroeconomic variables show that the estimated Wald test for the joint coefficient of the five-period lagged GFI is negative and statistically significant conforming with the a priori expectation.

The evaluation of forecast performance for Models 3 and 4 is summarized in Table 7. The two models are, respectively, compared with the historical average and the baseline GFI predictability models. The results show positive CT statistics and statistically significant CW test statistics for both the in-sample and out-of-sample periods across the multiple forecast horizons [i.e. at 5-day, 10-day and 15-day ahead forecasts]. These results further imply that: (i) accounting for asymmetry in the forecast analyses is encourages as its forecasting power outperforms the model that ignores the same including the historical average, and (ii) controlling for macroeconomic variables such as stock and commodity markets volatilities, improves the forecasting performance of stock returns predictability.

3.2. Additional Results

The Chicago Board Options Exchange (CBOE) Volatility Index (VIX) has long been recognized in the empirical literature as a prominent index to measure fear sentiment in global stock markets.[16] Although similar measures are available and have also been applied in empirical studies, the VIX and its different components are adjudged as leading barometers of investor sentiment and market volatility relating to listed options.[17] One of such alternative

Table 7. Forecast evaluation for macroeconomic-adjusted and asymmetric stock returns models.

Forecast Evaluation	Model 3 Vs Historical Average	Model 3 Vs Model 1	Model 4 Vs Historical Average	Model 4 Vs Model 1
In-sample				
C-T stat	0.1629	0.0411	0.2481	0.0633
C-W test	1.9597***	1.4239***	2.5867***	1.9682***
	(0.3468)	(0.3489)	(0.4442)	(0.3668)
h = 1				
C-T stat	0.1634	0.0536	0.2456	0.0496
C-W test	1.6763***	1.0233***	1.8682***	1.2154***
	(0.2644)	(0.2535)	(0.3123)	(0.2643)
h = 2				
C-T stat	0.1643	0.0691	0.2562	0.0439
C-W test	1.5167***	0.7442***	1.8437***	0.9509***
	(0.2155)	(0.1952)	(0.2526)	(0.2026)
h = 3				
C-T stat	0.1413	0.0967	0.2147	−0.0125
C-W test	0.7906***	0.0808***	0.6798***	−1381
	(0.1977)	(0.1760)	(0.2536)	(0.2077)

Note: Model 3 is the asymmetry GFI predictability model and Model 4 controls for macroeconomic volatility effects. The C-T stat denotes the Campbell-Thompson (2008) test while the C-W test is the Clark and West (2007) test. ***, ** & * indicate statistical significance at 1%, 5% & 10% levels, respectively.

measures is the Equity Market Volatility (EMV) which was created based on the text-counts of newspaper articles including several keywords related to the economy and stock market volatility.[18] These alternative volatility indexes are mostly constructed using single or selected country information and are mostly available in monthly frequencies. However, the VIX has also been generally found to understate true volatility, and its estimation errors are found to be considerably enlarged during volatile markets and turbulence periods (Allechi and Niamkey 1994; Chow, Jiang, and Li 2018; Bongiovanni, De Vincentiis, and Isaia 2016). One of such periods could be the current global COVID-19 pandemic with impacts that cut across every facet of human and economic existence. Therefore, our additional analyses involved evaluating the stock return predictability of the constructed Global Fear Index versus the predictability performance of the VIX. Figure 2 depicts the graphical highlight of the co-movements between COVID-19 GFI and the VIX. For illustration purposes, we partitioned the graph into three phases; I, II, and III (see Figure 2). The graphs show a general positive co-movement between the two indexes in the first phase which is the period before the declaration of COVID-19 as a global pandemic by the WHO (correlation coefficient between the two for this period is about 94%). However, the VIX reflects a smooth decline in the second phase than the GFI. Overall the co-movement between GFI and VIX is positively indicated by the correlation coefficient of about 61%.

Next, the predictability performance of stock returns using the VIX is evaluated and compared with that of the historical average and the COVID-19 Global Fear index predictor models. The predictability and forecast evaluation results are summarized in Table 8. The estimated VIX predictability regression shows a negative and statistically significant relationship between

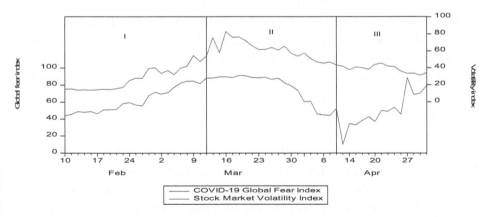

Figure 2. Co-movements between Global Fear Index (GFI) for COVID-19 and CBOE Volatility Index (VIX). Note: The left axis plots the COVID-19 global fear index and the CBOE volatility index is plotted on the right axis. The graph is portioned into three phases; I, II, and III, in order to depict the co-movements between the two indexes before and after the declaration of COVID-19 as a global pandemic by the WHO.

Table 8. VIX predictability of stock returns and forecast evaluation.

Coefficients	VIX-Predictor Model	
VIX_{t-1}	−0.6799*	
	(0.3860)	
	[−1.7616]	
Forecast Evaluation	VIX model Vs Historical Average	GFI Model Vs VIX Model
In-sample		
C-T stat	0.0253	0.2164
Clark & West	2.0418***	1.4040***
	(0.2947)	(0.3653)
Out-of-sample		
C-T stat	0.0307	0.2150
C-W test	1.5921***	1.0853***
	(0.2309)	(0.2514)

Note: VIX_{t-1} is the one-period lag volatility index. Standard errors and t-stats are respectively reported in parentheses and squared brackets. The C-T stat denotes the Campbell-Thompson (2008) test while the C-W test is the Clark and West (2007) test. ***, ** & * indicate statistical significance at 1%, 5% & 10% levels, respectively.

volatility index and stock returns. The forecast evaluation also reveals that it outperforms the historical average. However, when compared with the GFI-based predictive model, the latter tends to outperform the VIX-based model. This finding further attests to the underperformance of the VIX as a measure of fear during crisis/turbulent period.

4. Conclusion

This study motivates the literature to aid research on the COVID-19 pandemic. This becomes crucial given the need to analyze the potential negative impacts of the pandemic on the global economy whether developed, emerging, or developing economies. However, there is no standard measure of COVID-19 in a way that accommodates all the relevant parameters such as reported cases, deaths, and recoveries into a single index. This is the main contribution of the study. Thus, a composite index [Global Fear Index (GFI)] that accounts for the mentioned parameters and covers all the countries in the world is constructed. To validate the data, we demonstrate how it can be used to forecast economic and financial series using OECD and BRICS stock returns data. Expectedly, the model that incorporates the index during the pandemic period outperforms benchmark model. In addition, there may be need to account for "asymmetry" effect and macro-common factors in the GFI-based predictive model for stock returns to further improve its forecast performance. Finally, we show that the GFI is a better predictor of fear/panic in the stock market than the existing fear index (technically described as the Chicago Board Options Exchange (CBOE) Volatility Index (VIX)) at least during the pandemic period. We do hope to regularly update the database used for the index to encourage further extension of its application to other macroeconomic fundamentals.

Notes

1. Between February and March 2020 when the virus spread much rapidly and was declared a global pandemic (See World Health Organization [WHO] 2020), the US stock prices fell by 32%, the UK's by 27.9% and the Italy's by 39.3%. Emerging stock markets have also not been spared with the stock prices of Brazil declining by 40.5%, Russia's by 24.2% and China's by 10.1%. Some analysts have attributed the fall in stock prices to investors' panic, as many investors sold out of fear. See also World Economic Forum (https://www.weforum.org/agenda/2020/03/stock-market-volatility-coronavirus/).
2. A number studies have also investigated the connection between the COVID-19 pandemic and the energy sector (see Apergis and Apergis 2020; Fu and Shen 2020; Gil-Alana and Monge 2020; Liu, Wang, and Lee 2020; Narayan 2020;; Qin, Zhang, and Su 2020).
3. Notably, OECD denotes Organization for Economic Cooperation and Development while BRICS is the acronym for Brazil, Russia, India, China and South Africa.
4. A number of studies (see Narayan and Liu 2018 for a review) have suggested the use of GARCH models for forecasting stock returns, we however differ based on the time series dimension required for GARCH modeling and forecasting. The forecasts from GARCH models are found to be less optimal when confronted with small samples (see Ng and Lam 2006; Shumway and Stoffer 2000) and the same problem is evident even with panel GARCH models (see Pakel, Shephard, and Sheppard 2011).
5. See (WHO 2020): "WHO Director-General's opening remarks at the media briefing on COVID-19 – 11 March 2020" at: https://www.who.int/dg/speeches/detail/who-director-general-s-opening-remarks-at-the-media-briefing-on-covid-19—11-march-2020.
6. Daily data on official COVID-19 cases and deaths, based on reports from health authorities worldwide, is collected from the European Center for Disease Prevention and Control (ECDC) Epidemic Intelligence and it is available up-to-date at https://www.ecdc.europa.eu/en/geographical-distribution-2019-ncov-cases
7. We hope to publish the indices in the Data-in-Brief journal in order to make it publicly accessible. In the meantime, the data can be made available on request.
8. The Organization for Economic Co-operation and Development (OECD) countries comprise Austria, Australia, Belgium, Mexico, Canada, Chile, Czech Denmark, Finland, France, Germany, Greece, Hungary, Iceland, Ireland, Israel, Italy, Japan, South Korea, Latvia, Netherlands, New Zealand, Norway, Poland, Portugal, Slovakia, Slovenia, Spain, Sweden, Switzerland, Turkey, United Kingdom and United States. The BRICS are Brazil, Russia, India, China and South Africa. The daily data of stock price indices for each of the countries was collected from the Federal Reserve Bank of St. Louis database.
9. Although the first case of COVID-19 was reported on 31 December 2019. The first COVID-19 related death was reported on 11 January 2020. The preceding days are intermitted with both new cases and deaths reported as well as absence of occurrence. However, since 20 January 2020, there have been consistent reports on new cases and death globally. Hence and in order to account for the incubation period, 14-days after is selected as the start period for the index computation and this coincides with February 11, 2020.
10. Some of the advantages of using panel data over cross-section as well as time series data in estimation and testing has been well documented in Hsiao (2003), Baltagi (2008a, 2008b) and Baltagi (2013), among others.
11. See Baltagi (2013) and papers cited therein for computational advantages of using homogenous panel data approach when forecasting with short T.

12. This is not the first study to examine stock return predictability using historical average as the baseline model (see Bannigidadmath and Narayan 2015; Narayan and Gupta 2015; Phan, Sharma, and Narayan 2015; Narayan et al. 2016; Devpura, Narayan, and Sharma 2018; Salisu, Swaray, and Oloko 2019a,b,c,d,&e). What is however new is the use of panel data (i.e. pooling of countries) to achieve the same objective albeit with a different predictor.

13. This approach is similar in spirit to that of Shin, Yu, and Greenwood-Nimmo (2014), however, we favor the one used in this paper due to its simplicity and easy replication of results.

14. This idea is also technically motivated by the work of Westerlund and Narayan (2016) which provides some technical details and computational procedures on how to incorporate common factors in the predictability of stock returns. The approach followed in the estimation of this model is similar in spirit to that of Westerlund and Narayan (2016). One major attraction to this approach is that it does not require integration property of the common factors used in the predictive model.

15. Notwithstanding, researchers have adopted 50:50; 25:75 and 75:25 splits for the in-sample and out-of-sample periods where the first argument in each split is for the in-sample while the second argument is for the out-of-sample (see also Narayan and Gupta 2015). However, the first and second options (i.e. 50:50 and 25:75) may be used if the period is sufficiently large to accommodate regression analyses while the last option (i.e. 75:25) may be preferred for a small sample.

16. See Balcilar and Demirer (2015); Psaradellis and Sermpinis (2016); Taylor (2019); Wang (2019); Zhu et al. (2019) and Yun (2020).

17. See http://www.cboe.com/products/vix-index-volatility/volatility-indexes

18. Zhu et al. (2019) applied the GARCH-MIDAS method to quantify the in-sample explanatory and out-of-sample predictive powers of the EMV and VIX in the US stock markets. The empirical results show that VIX has larger in-sample impacts on US stock market volatility than EMV trackers. However, the out-of-sample volatility predictive performances of EMV trackers are generally superior to VIX across different US stock indices and prediction time horizons.

References

Adachi, Y., M. Masuda, and F. Takeda. 2017. Google search intensity and its relationship to the returns and liquidity of Japanese startup stocks. *Pacific-Basin Finance Journal* 46:243–57. doi:10.1016/j.pacfin.2017.09.009.

Allechi, M., and Niamkey, M. A. 1994. Evaluating the net gains from the CFA Franc Zone membership: A different perspective. *World Development* 22 (8):1147–1160. doi:10.1016/0305-750X(94)90082-5.

Aouadi, A., M. Arouri, and F. Teulon. 2013. Investor attention and stock market activity: Evidence from France. *Economic Modelling* 35:674–81. doi:10.1016/j.econmod.2013.08.034.

Apergis, E., and N. Apergis. 2020. Can the COVID-19 pandemic and oil prices drive the US partisan conflict index? *Energy Research Letters* 1 (1):13144. doi:10.46557/001c.13144.

Badshah, I., S. Bekiros, B. Lucey, and G. Salah Uddin. 2018. Asymmetric linkages among the fear index and emerging market volatility indices. *Emerging Markets Review* 37:17–31. doi:10.1016/j.ememar.2018.03.002.

Balcilar, M., and Demirer, R. 2015. Effect of global shocks and volatility on herd behavior in an emerging market: Evidence from borsa istanbul. *Emerging Markets Finance and Trade* 51 (1):140–59. doi:10.1080/1540496X.2015.1011520.

Baltagi, B. H. 2008a. *Econometric analysis of panel data*. Chichester: Wiley & Sons.

Baltagi, B. H. 2008b. Forecasting with panel data. *Journal of Forecasting* 27:155–73. doi:10.1002/for.1047.

Baltagi, B. H. 2013. Panel data forecasting. *Handbook of Economic Forecasting* 2 (B):995–1024.

Bank, M., M. Larch, and G. Peter. 2011. Google search volume and its influence on liquidity and returns of German stocks. *Financial Markets and Portfolio Management* 25 (3):239–64. doi:10.1007/s11408-011-0165-y.

Bannigidadmath, D., and P. Narayan. 2015. Stock return predictability and determinants of predictability and profits. *Emerging Markets Review* 26:153–73. doi:10.1016/j.ememar.2015.12.003.

Bodnaruk, A., and P. Ostberg. 2009. Does investor recognition predict returns? *Journal of Financial Economics* 91 (2):208–26.

Bongiovanni, A., De Vincentiis, P., and Isaia, E. 2016. The VIX Index: Forecasting power and perfomance in a risk management framework. *Journal of Financial Management, Markets and Institutions* 4 (2):129–144.

Boubaker, S., N. Essaddam, D. K. Nguyen, and S. Saadi. 2017. On the robustness of week-day effect to error distributional assumption: International evidence. *Journal of International Financial Markets, Institutions and Money* 47:114–30. doi:10.1016/j.intfin.2016.11.003.

Bouri, E., R. Gupta, S. Hosseini, and C. K. M. Lau. 2018. Does global fear predict fear in BRICS stock markets? Evidence from a Bayesian graphical structural VAR model. *Emerging Markets Review* 34:124–42. doi:10.1016/j.ememar.2017.11.004.

Campbell, J. Y., and S. B. Thompson. 2008. Predicting excess stock returns out of sample: Can anything beat the historical average? *Review of Financial Studies* 21:1509–31. doi:10.1093/rfs/hhm055.

Chow, V., Jiang, W., and Li, J. V. 2018. Does VIX truly measure return volatility? Available at SSRN 2489345.

Christou, C., and R. Gupta. 2019. Forecasting equity premium in a panel of OECD countries: The role of economic policy uncertainty. *The Quarterly Review of Economics and Finance* 76:243–248.

Clark, T. E., and K. D. West. 2007. Approximately normal tests for equal predictive accuracy in nested models. *Journal of Econometrics* 138:291–311. countries. Finance Research Letters, 20, 47-62. doi:10.1016/j.jeconom.2006.05.023.

Da, Z., J. Engelberg, and P. Gao. 2011. In search of attention. *The Journal of Finance* 66 (5):1461–99. doi:10.1111/j.1540-6261.2011.01679.x.

Devpura, N., P. K. Narayan, and S. S. Sharma. 2018. Is stock return predictability time varying? J. *Journal of International Financial Markets, Institutions and Money* 52:152–72. doi:10.1016/j.intfin.2017.06.001.

Economou, F., Y. Panagopoulos, and E. Tsouma. 2018. Uncovering asymmetries in the relationship between fear and the stock market using a hidden co-integration approach. *Research in International Business and Finance* 44:459–70. doi:10.1016/j.ribaf.2017.07.116.

Fu, M., and H. Shen. 2020. COVID-19 and corporate performance in the energy industry. *Energy Research Letters* 1 (1):12967. doi:10.46557/001c.12967.

Gil-Alana, L. A., and M. Monge. 2020. Crude oil prices and COVID-19: Persistence of the shock. *Energy Research Letters* 1 (1):13200. doi:10.46557/001c.13200.

Glosten, L., R. Jagannathan, and D. Runkle. 1993. On the relationship between the expected value and the volatility of the nominal excess return on stocks. *Journal of Finance* 48 (5):1779–801.

Gradinaru, A. 2014. The contribution of behavioral economics in explaining the decisional process. *Procedia Economics and Finance* 16:417–26. doi:10.1016/S2212-5671(14)00821-1.

Haroon, O., and S. A. R. Rizvi. 2020. COVID-19: Media coverage and financial markets behavior—A sectoral inquiry. *Journal of Behavioral and Experimental Finance* 100343. doi:10.1016/j.jbef.2020.100343.

Hsiao, C. 2003. *Analysis of panel data.* Cambridge, UK: Cambridge University Press.

Jacobs, H., and A. Hillert. 2016. Alphabetic bias, investor recognition, and trading behavior. *Review of Finance* 20 (2):693–723. doi:10.1093/rof/rfv060.

Joseph, K., M. B. Wintoki, and Z. Zhang. 2011. Forecasting abnormal stock returns and trading volume using investor sentiment: Evidence from online search. *International Journal of Forecasting* 27 (4):1116–27. doi:10.1016/j.ijforecast.2010.11.001.

Liu, L., E. Z. Wang, and C. C. Lee. 2020. Impact of the COVID-19 pandemic on the crude oil and stock markets in the US: A time-varying analysis. *Energy Research Letters* 1 (1):13154. doi:10.46557/001c.13154.

Mensi, W., S. Hammoudeh, L. Glosten, R. Jagannathan, and D. Runkle. 1993. On the relationship between the expected value and the volatility of the nominal excess return on stocks. *Journal of Finance* 48 (5):1779–801. doi:10.1111/j.1540-6261.1993.tb05128.x.

Merton, R. C. 1987. A simple model of capital market equilibrium with incomplete information. *The Journal of Finance* 42 (3):483–510. doi:10.1111/j.1540-6261.1987.tb04565.x.

Narayan, P. K. 2019. Can stale oil price news predict stock returns? *Energy Economics* 83:430–44. doi:10.1016/j.eneco.2019.07.022.

Narayan, P. K. 2020. Oil price news and COVID-19—Is there any connection? *Energy Research Letters* 1 (1):13176.

Narayan, P. K., D. H. B. Phan, S. S. Sharma, and J. Westerlund. 2016. Are Islamic stock returns predictable? A global perspective. *Pacific-Basin Finance Journal* 40 (A):210–23. doi:10.1016/j.pacfin.2016.08.008. doi:10.46557/001c.13176.

Narayan, P. K., and R. Gupta. 2015. Has oil price predicted stock returns for over a century? *Energy Economics* 48:18–23. doi:10.1016/j.eneco.2014.11.018.

Narayan, P. K., and R. Liu. 2018. A new GARCH model with higher moments for stock return predictability. *Journal of International Financial Markets Institutions and Money* 56:93–103. doi:10.1016/j.intfin.2018.02.016.

Ng, H. R., and K. P. Lam 2006. How does sample size affect GARCH models? 9th Joint International Conference on Information Sciences (JCIS-06), Kaohsiung, Taiwan: Atlantis Press.

Pakel, C., N. Shephard, and K. Sheppard. 2011. Nuisance parameters, composite likelihoods and a panel of GARCH models. *Statistica Sinica* 21 (1):307–29.

Phan, D. H. B., S. S. Sharma, and P. K. Narayan. 2015. Stock return forecasting: Some new evidence. *International Review of Financial Analysis* 40:38–51, 276. doi:10.1016/j.irfa.2015.05.002.

Preis, T., H. S. Moat, and H. E. Stanley. 2013. Quantifying trading behavior in financial markets using Google Trends. *Scientific Reports* 3 (1):1684. doi:10.1038/srep01684.

Psaradellis, I., and Sermpinis, G. 2016. Modelling and trading the US implied volatility indices. Evidence from the VIX, VXN and VXD indices. *International Journal of Forecasting* 32 (4):1268–1283. doi:10.1016/j.ijforecast.2016.05.004.

Qin, M., Y. C. Zhang, and C. W. Su. 2020. The essential role of pandemics: A fresh insight into the oil market. *Energy Research Letters* 1 (1):13166. doi:10.46557/001c.13166.

Salisu, A. A., I. D. Raheem, and U. B. Ndako. 2019b. A sectoral analysis of asymmetric nexus between oil price and stock returns. *International Review of Economics and Finance* 61:241–59. doi:10.1016/j.iref.2019.02.005.

Salisu, A. A., K. O. Isah, and I. D. Raheem. 2019e. Testing the predictability of commodity prices in stock returns of G7 countries: Evidence from a new approach. *Resources Policy* 64:101520. doi:10.1016/j.resourpol.2019.101520.

Salisu, A. A., K. O. Isah, and L. O. Akanni. 2019d. Improving the predictability of stock returns with Bitcoin prices. *The North American Journal of Economics and Finance* 48:857–67. doi:10.1016/j.najef.2018.08.010.

Salisu, A. A., R. Swaray, and T. F. Oloko. 2019a. Improving the predictability of the oil–US stock nexus: The role of macroeconomic variables. *Economic Modelling* 76:153–71. doi:10.1016/j.econmod.2018.07.029.

Salisu, A. A., W. Adekunle, W. A. Alimi, and Z. Emmanuel. 2019c. Predicting exchange rate with commodity prices: New evidence from Westerlund and Narayan (2015) estimator with structural breaks and asymmetries. *Resources Policy* 62:33–56. doi:10.1016/j. resourpol.2019.03.006.

Shaikh, I., and P. Padhi. 2015. The implied volatility index: Is "investor fear gauge" or "forward-looking"? *Borsa Istanbul Review* 15 (1):44–52. doi:10.1016/j.bir.2014.10.001.

Shin, Y., B. C. Yu, and M. Greenwood-Nimmo. 2014. Modelling asymmetric cointegration and dynamic multipliers in a Nonlinear ARDL framework. In *Festschrift in honor of peter schmidt: Econometric methods and applications*, ed. R. Sickels and W. Horrace, 281–314. New York: Springer.

Shumway, R. H., and D. S. Stoffer. 2000. Time series analysis and its applications. *Studies in Informatics and Control* 9 (4):375–76.

Taylor, N. 2019. Forecasting returns in the VIX futures market. *International Journal of Forecasting* 35 (4):1193–210. doi:10.1016/j.ijforecast.2019.01.009.

Wang, H. 2019. VIX and volatility forecasting: A new insight. *Physica A: Statistical Mechanics and Its Applications* 533. doi:10.1016/j.physa.2019.121951.

Westerhoff, F. H. 2004. Greed, fear and stock market dynamics. *Physica A* 343:635–42. doi:10.1016/j.physa.2004.06.059.

Westerlund, J., and P. Narayan. 2016. Testing for predictability in panels of any time series dimension. *International Journal of Forecasting* 32 (2016):1162–77. doi:10.1016/j. ijforecast.2016.02.009.

World Health Organization [WHO]. 2020. WHO director-general's opening remarks at the media briefing on COVID-19-3 March 2020. Retrieved from https://www.who.int/dg/ speeches/detail/who-director-general-s-opening-remarks-at-the-media-briefing-on-covid -19—3-march-2020

Yun, J. 2020. A re-examination of the predictability of stock returns and cash flows via the decomposition of VIX. *Economics Letters* 186 doi:10.1016/j.econlet.2019.108755.

Zhang, J., Y. Lai, and J. Lin. 2017. The day-of-the-Week effects of stock markets in different countries. *Finance Research Letters* 20:47–62. doi:10.1016/j.frl.2016.09.006.

Zhu, H., and L. Jiang. 2018. Investor recognition and stock returns: Evidence from China. *China Finance Review International* 8 (2):199–215. doi:10.1108/CFRI-11-2016-0127.

Zhu, S., Q. Liu, Y. Wang, Y. Wei, and G. Wei. 2019. Which fear index matters for predicting US stock market volatilities: Text-counts or option based measurement? *Physica A* 536:122567. doi:10.1016/j.physa.2019.122567.

Accounting Index of COVID-19 Impact on Chinese Industries: A Case Study Using Big Data Portrait Analysis

Pinglin He, Hanlu Niu, Zhe Sun ⓘD, and Tao Li

ABSTRACT

The novel coronavirus (COVID-19) outbreak has become a global pandemic and has greatly impacted the world economy. This article adopts the financial data of Listed companies in China and uses the synthetic index compilation method to compile an accounting index that captures the period before and after the COVID-19 outbreak. This index is based on big data portrait analysis and measures the impact of the COVID-19 on various Chinese industries. The study found that except for the basic industry, which was less affected by the epidemic, the rest of the industries were significantly affected by the epidemic. Besides, the costs of various industries have increased by varying degrees. The aviation, tourism and other service industries have been greatly impacted. New infrastructure, Chinese patent medicine and Internet industries have achieved great development.

1. Introduction and Literature Review

At the end of 2019, COVID-19 quickly spread, became a global pandemic, and greatly impacted the world economy. At present, COVID-19 is under control in China, and, as a result, most industries resumed production. How to assess the impact of COVID-19 on economic development remains an urgent problem. We draw on the compilation method of the economic prosperity cycle and combine accounting information of different industries to compile a set of industry accounting indicators to compare the impact of COVID-19 on various industries in China.

Accounting information is a comprehensive and detailed record of an enterprise's economic activities and can faithfully reflect the process of value movement at the micro level (2019). Aggregate corporate accounting information can reflect macroeconomic issues. Konchitchki and Patatoukas (2014) pointed out that accounting information is the main driver of macroeconomic growth. They show that accounting information does not only affect stock prices and monetary policy, it also predicts gross domestic product (GDP) growth. Luo, Zeng, and Fang et al. (2016) used a theoretical framework – from micro data to macro forecast – and tested whether the aggregated accounting surplus information has a predictive effect on GDP growth. They show that the aggregated accounting surplus information can predict GDP growth. From these studies, it is obvious that enterprise accounting information is of great significance for studying macroeconomic issues.

As an in-depth, refined, and highly integrated accounting information, the accounting index can intuitively and vividly reveal the economic operation situation and provide 'wind vane', 'monitor', and 'early warning device' for economic decision-making. Wang, Lu, and Zhang et al. (2012) believes that by understanding the microeconomic foundation from the perspective of the accounting index, we can grasp the macroeconomic trends. Existing literature focuses on different regions and industries from the perspective of economic accounting indexes. Erwin (2016) constructed a commercial real estate price index against the backdrop of the production accounting requirements of the National Accounting System (SNA), which measures the input, output and asset prices of the commercial real estate industry. Giri and Bansod (2019) constructed a Financial Condition Index (FCI) and used the autoregressive distribution lag model to explore the possible co-integration relationship between economic growth and FCI. Choi (2010) studied the correlation between accounting information and economic crisis, and analyzed the impact of different economic crises on the accounting and economic environment. Lee, Park, and lee (2013) studied various factors affecting the Korea Accounting Transparency Evaluation Index and found that increasing accounting transparency will reduce the cost of equity capital. Chen (2017) constructed an industry prosperity index for China's listed companies from the perspectives of production, sales, and investment. Ha et al. (2018) selected relevant indicators from manufacturing and agriculture, constructed the Korea Agricultural Accounting Index, classified the cultivation types of rice farms, and provided advice on farm consultations. In summary, the existing research applies economic accounting indexes to various fields, such as agriculture, industry and commerce, and manufacturing, and to scenarios, such as performance evaluation.

Assessing the impact of epidemics/pandemics on the economy is an important research topic in disaster economics. Existing research on major health events mainly focuses on SARS. For instance, Liu and Cai (2003) analyzed China's macroeconomy under SARS and found that SARS has a greater impact on the tourism, transportation and catering industries. Beutels et al. (2009) used the cross-correlation function to study the impact of SARS and found that the wholesale and retail industry and the daily necessities industry were less affected by the epidemic. With regards to COVID-19, there is a growing body of literature studying its impact on various aspects. Xu, Yang, and Liu (2020) conducted a comparative study of SARS in 2003 and COVID-19 in 2020, analyzed the functioning and evolution of China's insurance industry, and found that the insurance industry plays an active role in responding to public health events. Weersink, Massow, and Mcdougall (2020) believe that the

Canadian dairy products, poultry and egg industries suffered losses due to COVID-19 but are more resistant to COVID-19 than other industries. Iyke (2020a, 2020b)) demonstrated that COVID-19 can explain exchange rate and stock return and volatility. Apergis, and Apergis (2020) studied the impact of the COVID-19 pandemic and oil price volatility on the U.S. partisan conflict index. Ataguba (2020) analyzed the impact of COVID-19 and emphasized the importance of establishing a flexible health system. Zandifar, and and Badrfam (2020) discussed Iran's fight against COVID-19 and called on the government to maximize the use of existing resources to fight the pandemic. Lai et al. (2020) analyzed the pandemic situation and control measures in different countries and regions, and argued that the potential mechanism through which COVID-19 affected these economies needs to be further studied. Gil-Alana, and Monge (2020) discussed the impact of COVID-19 on crude oil prices. Liu et al., (2020) discussed the impact of COVID-19 on crude oil prices and stock prices in the US. Narayan (2020) analyzed the relationship between COVID-19 and oil price news. Qin et al., (2020) analysed the impact of the pandemic on oil markets. Wang (2019) analyzed the way that accounting information is used for macro decision making.

The outbreak of major health events has a serious impact on various industries, and the accounting index can better reflect the different trends of responses across industries. However, there are few existing studies on the combination of accounting indexes and major health events, and none studies the impact of COVID-19 on various industries from the perspective of accounting indexes. This study uses the synthetic index compilation method to compile an accounting index that captures the period before and after the COVID-19 outbreak. The purpose of this study is to discover the impact of COVID-19 on different industries, explore its impact mechanism, and provide guidance for the recovery of the industrial chain after the outbreak. The study found that the industry and commerce, life and technology, and culture and social industries are significantly affected by the pandemic, whereas the basic industries are less affected. The manufacturing, and sports and entertainment industries received development opportunities during the pandemic, while the hotels and catering, and residential service industries suffered heavy losses. At the same time, the pandemic also increased the cost of mining, manufacturing, information technology, sports and entertainment, and transportation industries by varying degrees. The study further found that the aviation, tourism, and other service industries are greatly impacted by the pandemic. New infrastructure, Chinese patent medicine, and other industries are steadily improving, similar to the medical equipment and internet industries.

The study's contribution is as follows. On the one hand, we develop the industry accounting index to discuss the impact of COVID-19 from the perspective of value creation, cost expenditure, inventory overstocking, and financial risk of the whole Chinese industry. On the other hand, we use big data portrait technology to provide a detailed map of the impact of COVID-19 on various industries, so that macroeconomic policymakers can intuitively understand the impact of COVID-19 on the industries, and how to promote the recovery of the industrial chain after the outbreak.

2. Industry Impact Index Design

The basic idea of compiling the industry accounting index is as follows. First, determine the calculation method for the industry accounting index and the required accounting subjects. Second, calculate the quarterly accounting index $a_i(t)$ of each company in the industry, and obtain the accounting index $A_i(t)$ for each industry i and quarter t by weighting the equity and weighted average. Finally, use the synthetic index compilation method to form an optimized industry accounting index $Y_i(t)$.

The industry accounting index has four dimensions, namely value creation, cost, leverage, and inventory indexes. The value creation index represents how stakeholders create value to the enterprise. The value creation index is the sum of net profit, financial expenses, taxes, and remuneration. The larger the index, the more value the stakeholders create and the better it is for the industry.

The cost index reflects the quarterly operating costs of the industry. The cost index is sum of operating costs, taxes and surcharges, sales expenses, and management expenses. The leverage index reflects the industry's quarterly debt pressure and is measured by financial expenses. The inventory index reflects the industry's quarterly inventory backlog. The cost, leverage, and inventory indexes are all negative indexes. Thus, a reduction in these indexes is conducive to the development of the industry.

The final industry accounting index is obtained after passing $A_i(t)$ through the synthetic index compilation method and standardization. The steps involved in the composite index compilation method are as follows.

Step 1: In order to reduce the influence of seasonal changes and irregular factors on the index calculation, we use the $A_i(t)$of the current period and the previous period as the base to find the symmetric change rate – so that whether the index rises or falls, the change is equal/symmetric. The calculation of the symmetric change rate is:

$$C_i(t)=\begin{cases} \frac{A_i(t)-A_i(t-1)}{A_i(t)+A_i(t-1)}*200, & A_i(t)>0 \\ \\ A_i(t)-A_i(t-1), & A_i(t)\leq 0 \end{cases} \tag{1}$$

where $C_i(t)$ is a symmetric change rate, $A_i(t)$ is an unoptimized industry accounting index, i represents industry, and t represents the quarter.

Step 2: In order to reduce the impact of excessive change in the index, we standardized the symmetric change rate. First, we obtained the standardization factor $U_i(t)$:

$$U_i(t) = \frac{\sum_{t=2}^{n} |C_i(t)|}{n-1} \tag{2}$$

In order to more clearly see the effect of COVID-19 on various industry indexes, the rate of change is amplified, while ensuring the stable change of the index (the leverage index changes are relatively obvious, so a relatively small amplification process is adopted relative to other indexes). The standardized rate of change $S_i(t)$ is obtained:

$$S_i(t) = \frac{U_i(t)}{A_i} * 10000 \tag{3}$$

Step 3: Taking January 1, 2011 as the base period, let $Y_i(1) = 100$, and calculate the composite index of each subsequent quarter, which is the final industry accounting index $Y_i(t)$:

$$Y_i(t) = Y_i(t-1) * \frac{200 + S_i(t)}{200 - S_i(t)} \tag{4}$$

3. Experimental Results and Analysis

We selected the A-share main board of Shanghai Stock Exchange and Shenzhen Stock Exchange, SME and GEM listed companies as the research sample, the research period is from January 1, 2019 to March 31, 2020. The financial data comes from the CSMAR database. We divided the industry according to the China Securities Regulatory Commission's 2012 industry classification guidelines. Due to the special accounting methods of the financial industry and the lack of data in the water conservancy environment and public facilities management industry, we removed it from the sample leaving us with 17 sub-sectors for our analysis. In order to facilitate analysis and comparison, we further classified these sub-sectors into four categories, namely basic industry, industry and commerce, life and technology, and culture and society, according to the nature of the industry. In what follows, we present an analysis of the accounting indexes for various industries.

3.1. Overall Analysis of the Industry

Table 1 lists the industry value creation indexes of 17 industries in China from January 1, 2019 to March 31, 2020. The value index of most industries during

Table 1. Industry-wide value creation index table.

Industry categories	Industry Code	Segment industry	20190101	20190331	20190630	20190930	20191231	20200331
Basic industry	A	Agriculture	100.000	109.369	110.628	110.931	111.033	111.614
	D	Electric & Heating	100.000	100.674	100.868	100.936	100.984	101.535
	E	Construction	100.000	100.004	100.013	100.019	100.073	100.153
	K	Real estate	100.000	100.005	100.009	100.011	100.013	100.167
		居民服务,修理和其他服务业					105.933	
Industry and Commerce	B	Mining	100.000	100.109	100.122	100.129	100.133	105.254
	C	Manufacturing	100.000	123.168	131.995	137.060	140.705	199.312
	G	Transportation	100.000	100.557	100.749	100.838	100.890	105.933
Life and Technology Industry	F	Wholesale & Retail	100.000	102.713	103.575	103.927	104.151	107.455
	L	Commercial service	100.000	100.108	100.168	100.210	100.280	107.133
	H	Hotels & Catering	100.000	100.156	100.221	100.257	100.283	−98.725
	O	Residential service	100.000	−99.934	98.230	−93.058	82.733	−81.342
	M	Scientific research	100.000	101.708	102.367	102.711	102.964	112.514
	I	IT	100.000	100.337	100.529	100.661	100.770	101.040
Culture and Social Industry	P	Education	100.000	100.769	101.034	101.174	101.277	105.804
	Q	Social & Health	100.000	100.747	100.922	100.995	101.061	102.385
	R	Sports&Entertainment	100.000	100.221	100.414	100.632	−98.056	100.693
	S	Public management	100.000	101.720	102.106	102.268	102.351	102.488

The value creation index = net profit + financial expenses + taxes + remuneration. In the table, the date on the abscissa represents the quarter of the industry, for example, 20190331 represents the first quarter of 2019. The industry code of this article comes from China's "SFC Industry Classification Guidelines 2012".

this period showed a steady upward trend. The COVID-19 outbreak impacted economic production, hotels, catering, and residential services – these industries are hard hit. Notwithstanding, most industries in China are still on the rise, and the manufacturing and sports & entertainment industry value creation index increased significantly. On the whole, the basic industries, and industry and commerce, which are related to national economy and people's livelihood, are more resistant to risks and have a higher stability in the face of the sudden COVID-19 outbreak.

Under the premise of ensuring the stability of the industry value creation index, the lower the industry's cost index is, the more favorable the industry's development will be. Table 2 shows the cost index of each industry, from which it can be seen that the cost of mining and manufacturing industries increased significantly under the influence of the pandemic, and the cost of scientific research and sports and entertainment increased slightly. This change shows that in the face of major public emergencies, the government should focus on supporting industries, such as industry, scientific research, and culture. In the process of resuming production after the pandemic, policymakers should accelerate the implementation of the "cost reduction" strategic concept and promote sustainable economic development.

To a certain extent, the leverage index reflects the production status and financial risks of enterprises. Table 3 shows that the leverage index of all industries increased by varying degrees under the pandemic situation. Among them, the manufacturing, information technology, and sports and entertainment industries are greatly affected by the pandemic (i.e. the leverage index significantly improved compared with other industries), and the financial risk is very high. However, the financial leverage of the basic industry remained stable. For companies with greater debt risk, they can use equity financing, debt-to-equity swaps, etc., to resolve the short-term liquidity pressure brought about by single debt financing, and further enhance their ability to resist risks. The government should also adopt policy assistance to reduce the financial risks of enterprises and give enterprises an active role in the process of epidemic prevention and control.

Table 4 shows the inventory index of various industries. The inventory index of various Chinese industries shows a certain upward trend under the influence of the pandemic. The sudden outbreak affected the original stable supply chain structure. The normal circulation of products is blocked, resulting in a backlog of inventory at the production end.

3.2. Analysis of Subdivided Industries

Figure 1 shows the value creation index of the sub-industries. The creativity of sports and entertainment declined before and a substantial increase after the

Table 2. Industry-wide cost index table.

Industry categories	Industry Code	Segment industry	20190101	20190331	20190630	20190930	20191231	20200331
Basic industry	A	Agriculture	100.000	100.208	100.266	100.294	100.309	100.427
	D	Electric & Heating	100.000	100.245	100.317	100.346	100.362	100.614
	E	Construction	100.000	100.014	100.017	100.019	100.020	100.219
	K	Real estate	100.000	100.371	100.438	100.469	100.482	100.656
		居民服务，修理和其他服务业						
Industry and Commerce	B	Mining	100.000	100.007	100.008	100.009	100.009	108.638
	C	Manufacturing	100.000	103.314	104.244	104.697	104.989	111.786
	G	Transportation	100.000	100.114	100.149	100.165	100.176	101.715
	F	Wholesale & Retail	100.000	100.135	100.172	100.190	100.201	100.447
	L	Commercial service	100.000	100.136	100.173	100.192	100.203	100.286
Life and Technology Industry	H	Hotels & Catering	100.000	100.099	100.128	100.142	100.151	101.150
	O	Residential service	100.000	100.390	100.505	100.540	100.557	100.775
	M	Scientific research	100.000	100.362	100.470	100.524	100.557	100.819
	I	IT	100.000	101.116	101.430	101.570	101.657	105.187
Culture and Social Industry	P	Education	100.000	100.306	100.392	100.434	100.462	101.144
	Q	Social & Health	100.000	100.075	100.097	100.108	100.116	100.229
	R	Sports&Entertainment	100.000	100.571	100.738	100.823	100.881	102.853
	S	Public management	100.000	100.232	100.297	100.327	100.346	100.481

Note: The cost index = operating costs + taxes and surcharges + sales expenses + management expenses. In the table, the date on the abscissa represents the quarter of the industry, for example, 20190331 represents the first quarter of 2019. The industry code of this article comes from China's "SFC Industry Classification Guidelines 2012".

Table 3. Industry-wide leverage index table.

Industry categories	Industry Code	Segment industry	20190101	20190331	20190630	20190930	20191231	20200331
Basic industry	A	Agriculture	100.000	100.063	100.084	100.098	100.107	100.237
	D	Electric & Heating	100.000	100.023	100.030	100.032	100.033	100.048
	E	Construction	100.000	100.018	100.023	100.025	100.027	100.123
	K	Real estate	100.000	100.072	100.087	100.094	100.098	100.125
		居民服务，修理和其他服务业						
Industry and Commerce	B	Mining	100.000	100.012	100.013	100.013	100.013	101.650
	C	Manufacturing	100.000	102.290	103.022	103.416	103.688	106.003
	G	Transportation	100.000	100.060	100.069	100.073	100.076	101.905
	F	Wholesale & Retail	100.000	100.104	100.133	100.147	100.156	100.313
	L	Commercial service	100.000	100.000	100.001	100.002	100.008	100.131
Life and Technology Industry	H	Hotels & Catering	100.000	100.041	100.054	100.060	100.063	100.221
	O	Residential service	100.000	126.317	147.254	148.663	149.342	151.172
	M	Scientific research	100.000	100.278	100.401	100.478	100.537	104.394
	I	IT	100.000	100.118	100.180	100.230	100.266	100.994
Culture and Social Industry	P	Education	100.000	100.063	100.084	100.096	100.102	100.406
	Q	Social & Health	100.000	100.001	100.003	100.005	100.014	100.120
	R	Sports&Entertainment	100.000	102.180	102.792	103.134	103.238	105.282
	S	Public management	100.000	100.050	100.065	100.073	100.076	100.084

The leverage index is measured by financial expenses. In the table, the date on the abscissa represents the quarter of the industry, for example, 20190331 represents the first quarter of 2019. The industry code of this article comes from China's "SFC Industry Classification Guidelines 2012".

Table 4. Industry-wide inventory index table.

Industry categories	Industry Code	Segment industry	20190101	20190331	20190630	20190930	20191231	20200331
Basic industry	A	Agriculture	100.000	100.015	100.023	100.029	100.035	100.042
	D	Electric & Heating	100.000	100.482	100.713	100.804	100.869	100.920
	E	Construction	100.000	100.001	100.002	100.002	100.003	100.093
	K	Real estate	100.000	100.003	100.005	100.006	100.007	100.008
		居民服务，修理和其他服务业	100.003	100.033				
Industry and Commerce	B	Mining	100.000	100.006	100.008	100.010	100.011	106.141
	C	Manufacturing	100.000	100.174	100.292	100.380	100.518	101.084
	G	Transportation	100.000	100.018	100.033	100.044	100.067	102.353
	F	Wholesale & Retail	100.000	100.003	100.007	100.012	100.017	100.059
	L	Commercial service	100.000	100.026	100.053	100.071	100.084	100.103
Life and Technology Industry	H	Hotels & Catering	100.000	100.051	100.079	100.099	100.121 100.145	100.145
	O	Residential service	100.000	100.118	100.177	100.216	100.491 100.687	100.687
	M	Scientific research	100.000	100.443	100.712	100.931	101.350	101.709
	I	IT	100.000	100.268	100.421	100.534	100.624	100.936
Culture and Social Industry	P	Education	100.000	100.017	100.028	100.037	100.050	101.715
	Q	Social & Health	100.000	100.034	100.075	100.109	100.135	100.156
	R	Sports&Entertainment	100.000	100.031	100.051	100.076	100.128	100.200
	S	Public management	100.000	100.004	100.007	100.010	100.014	100.019

The inventory index is measured by inventories. In the table, the date on the abscissa represents the quarter of the industry, for example, 20190331 represents the first quarter of 2019. The industry code of this article comes from China's "SFC Industry Classification Guidelines 2012".

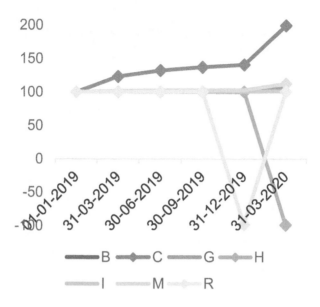

Figure 1. Value creation index by industry.

COVID-19 outbreak. The reason for this phenomenon is that, in order to control the spread of COVID-19, people are required to stay home, which caused an increase in the demand for internet, cultural, and sports entertainment services to meets people's spiritual needs. During the pandemic, people's demand for first aid materials increased significantly. Demand stimulated production, and coupled with the Chinese government's macro-policy control, the manufacturing industry expanded its production. As the outbreak approached the Chinese New Year, which is the peak season for hotels and catering sales, hotels and catering services suffered greatly from the pandemic via sharp decline in profits.

Figure 2 shows the cost index of the subdivided industries. It can be seen from the figure that, after the outbreak, the cost index of the mining and manufacturing industries increased significantly compared to other industries, and mining and manufacturing heavily depended on raw materials, labor, and various production equipment. The pandemic outbreak further expanded the scale of various costs and expenses, which, in turn, led to an increase in the cost index. COVID-19 caused an increase in costs across various industries, but information technology is least affected, indicating that information technology, as a high-tech industry, responded well to the impact of the pandemic.

Figures 3 and 4 show the leverage and inventory indexes, respectively, of the subdivided industries. Following the COVID-19 outbreak, the leverage index for the manufacturing, information technology, and sports and entertainment industries increased significantly. The increase in manufacturing costs caused companies to spend excessively. Due to their particularities and limited market demand, companies are unable to increase product prices by a large margin.

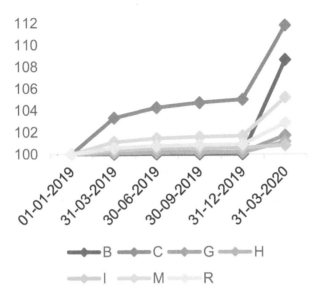

Figure 2. Cost index by industry. Note: B, C, G, H, I, M, R represent Mining, Manufacturing, Transportation, Hotels & Catering, IT, Scientific research, Sports & Entertainment.

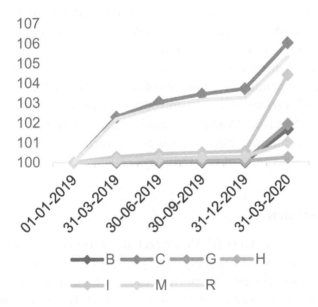

Figure 3. Leverage index by industry.

Therefore, the overall operation of the industry is under pressure and the ability to repay debts has been somewhat reduced – the financial risk has become more serious. For information technology, and sports and entertainment, because personnel are unable to carry out normal work on the job, various related activities stagnated leading to a decline in industry revenue,

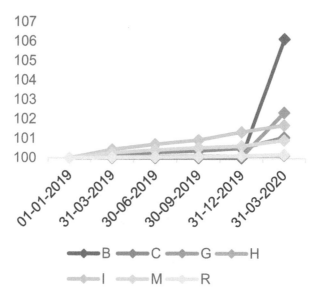

Figure 4. Stock index by industry. Note: B, C, G, H, I, M, R represent Mining, Manufacturing, Transportation, Hotels & Catering, IT, Scientific research, Sports & Entertainment.

which caused excessive pressure on corporate debts and increased the leverage index. Judging from the inventory situation, the outbreak and the road blocking measures adopted by various provinces was undoubtedly a direct blow to the transportation industry. The transportation of mining enterprises' products is highly dependent on the smoothness of the road. The COVID-19 outbreak forced various cities to introduce various restrictions on public transportation. The road blockade caused a large amount of inventory accumulation in the mining industry, which, in turn, was detrimental to the production and operation of this industry.

4. Further Research

To visually show the COVID-19 impact on various industries using the accounting indexes, we draw a big data portrait of the value creation index for all 17 industries. The big data portrait used in this article refers to obtaining the behavior index of various industries in China, using Internet technology to build efficient, accurate and rich big data samples, and then abstracting the characteristics of different industries under COVID-19. It can be clearly seen from Figure 5 that residential service and hotels are heavily impacted by the pandemic. In the face of the pandemic, manufacturing, and sports and entertainment showed the strongest response capacity, ranking first in the industry. The reason for this phenomenon can be attributed to the fact that the COVID-19 outbreak started around the Chinese New Year. With the promulgation of home segregation measures, the continuous extension of the Spring Festival

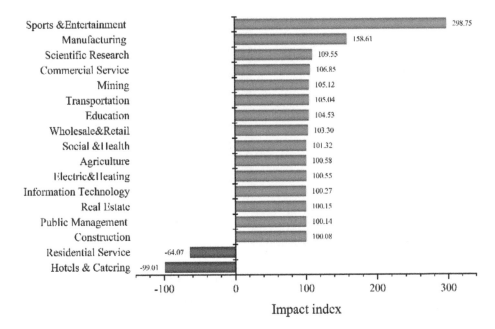

Figure 5. Big data portrait of changes in industry-wide value creation index. Note: The data in the figure is the change of the value creation index in the first quarter of 2020 relative to the end of 2019.

holiday, and the implementation stay-home policy, home activities, such as video games and entertainment videos increased, which has boosted the value creation index for the sports and entertainment industry.

In order to dig deeper into the industry heterogeneity of the impact of the COVID-19 pandemic on the Chinese economy, we re-divided the industry, selected representative enterprise samples, and further studied 25 industry sectors, such as China's new infrastructure, medicine, transportation, tourism, and the internet. As can be seen from Figure 6, the value creation index of the tourism, aviation, road transportation, pharmaceutical manufacturing, catering, radio and television, and hotel accommodation industries are obviously negative. COVID-19 has a strong negative impact on service industries, such as tourism, aviation, road transportation, catering, radio and television, and lodging.

The blocking of spatial position also changed people's work and lifestyle. Following the COVID-19 outbreak, government institutions at various levels and many enterprises in China actively promoted home office work. The number of home office workers surged, and the number of office communications, such as Dingding and Tencent conference users has increased vertically. In order to improve service capabilities, online office manufacturers successively increased server expansion. The increase in users and the improvement in service capabilities drastically improved the value creation capability of the internet industry. The internet value creation index was 287.10, the largest

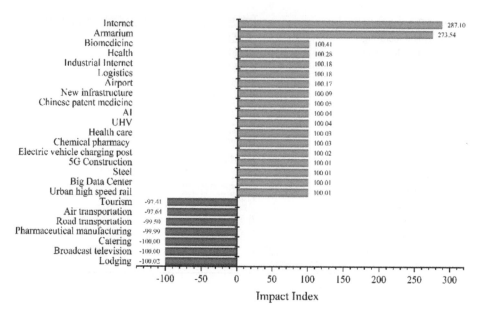

Figure 6. Big data portrait of the value creation index of 25 industries. Note: The data in the figure is the change of the value creation index in the first quarter of 2020 relative to the end of 2019.

increase among the 25 industries. Global COVID-19 outbreaks and people's awareness of preventive measures increased, and the demand for infrared temperature measurement equipment, ventilators, and other medical equipment in the world surged. And China's medical equipment has already been fully produced and dispatched to help countries fight the pandemic. This significantly enhanced the value creation ability of the medical equipment industry. The value creation capacity of the medical equipment industry was 273.54, ranking the second among the 25 industries.

Because Chinese patent medicine, biomedicine, health, and other medical and health fields actively fight against COVID-19, the value creation capability index increased to some extent. However, in the process of resisting the pandemic, the role played by traditional pharmaceutical manufacturing is negligible. In the short term, the value creation index shows a downward trend due to the impact of corporate rework time, employee arrival time, and sales. In addition, new infrastructure, such as UHV, 5 G construction, AI, industrial internet, urban highspeed rail, etc., which are China's key support projects, also showed a small increase during the outbreak. The State Grid of China specified that the annual investment in UHV construction for 2020 is 112.8 billion yuan, which is the historical peak, this injected vitality into China's new round of UHV construction, and promoted the development of new infrastructure industries such as UHV. This phenomenon shows that new infrastructure has better resisted the impact of COVID-19, and its industry value creativity needs a longer-term follow-up study.

5. Conclusions and Recommendations

This article uses the synthetic index compilation method to compile industry-wide accounting indexes that capture the period before and after the COVID-19 outbreak. These indexes are able to measure the impact of the pandemic on the Chinese economy at the industry level. The study found that the industrial and commercial, life and technology, and cultural and social industries were significantly affected by the pandemic. While the basic industries were relatively stable, the manufacturing, sports and entertainment, hotels, and catering and residential service industries (or sub-sectors) were greatly affected by the pandemic. The manufacturing, and sports and entry value creation index grew significantly, whereas the hotels, catering and residential services industries were hard hit by the pandemic. At the same time, the pandemic increased the cost of mining and manufacturing, the financial cost of information technology, cultural and entertainment industries, and the inventory cost of mining and transportation industries. Further digging into the industry heterogeneity of the value creation index reveals that the service industry has been significantly affected by the pandemic. New infrastructure, Chinese patent medicine, and other industries steadily improved, and the medical equipment and internet industries achieved great development.

The paper explored the impact of COVID-19 on the Chinese economy from four angles, namely value creation, cost, leverage, and inventory. It also explored the bigger picture of the impact of COVID-19 using a big data impact chart for various industries. This could help macroeconomic policymakers to better understand the impact of COVID-19 on different industries, better explore the impact mechanism, and would provide guidance for the recovery of the industrial chain after the pandemic.

Conflicts Of Interest

The authors declare no conflict of interest.

Funding

The National Social Science Fund of China [17BGL051], the Fundamental Research Funds for the Central Universities [2018QN068], the Fundamental Research Funds for the Central Universities [2019FR005] and the Beijing Social Science Fund [18GLB017], supported this work

ORCID

Zhe Sun ⓘ http://orcid.org/0000-0001-8890-0262

References

Apergis, E., and N. Apergis. 2020. Can the COVID-19 pandemic and oil prices drive the US partisan conflict index? *Energy Research Letters* 1 (1):13144. doi:10.46557/001c.13144.

Ataguba, J. E. 2020. COVID-19 pandemic, a war to be won: Understanding its economic implications for Africa. *Applied Health Economics and Health Policy* 10227. doi:10.1007/s40258-020-00580-x.

Beutels, P., N. Jia, Q.-Y. Zhou, R. Smith, W.-C. Cao, S. J. de Vlas, et al. 2009. The economic impact of SARS in Beijing, China. *Tropical Medicine & International Health* 14:85–91. doi:10.1111/j.1365-3156.2008.02210.x.

Chen, G. Z. 2017. Research on the construction of the prosperity index system of listed companies. *Shanghai Journal of Economics* 12:47–56. doi:10.19626/j.cnki.cn31-1163/f.2017.12.005.

Choi, K. 2010. The effect of economic crisis on the value relevance of accounting information. *Korean Accounting Journal* 19 (3):83–110.

Diewert, W. E., K. J. Fox, and C. Shimizu. 2016. Commercial property price indexes and the system of national accounts. *Journal of Economic Surveys* 30 (5) : 913–943. doi:10.1111/joes.12117.

Fu, M., and H. Shen. 2020. COVID-19 and corporate performance in the energy industry. *Energy Research Letters* 1 (1):12967. doi:10.46557/001c.12967.

Gil-Alana, L. A., and M. Monge. 2020. Crude oil prices and COVID-19: Persistence of the shock. *Energy Research Letters* 1 (1):13200. doi:10.46557/001c.13200.

Giri, A. K., and D. Bansod. 2019. Establishing finance-growth linkage for India: A financial conditions index (FCI) approach. *International Journal of Emerging Markets* 14 (5):1032–59. doi:10.1108/IJOEM-10-2017-0422.

Ha, J., S. Kim, T. Kim, and S. Seo. 2018. Farming types analysis of rice farms by financial index in agricultural accounting. *Korean Journal of Agricultural Management and Policy* 45 (3):522–44. doi:10.30805/KJAMP.2018.45.3.522.

Iyke, B. N. 2020a. *The disease outbreak channel of exchange rate return predictability: Evidence from COVID-19*. Emerging Markets Finance and Trade. 56 (10):2277–2297. doi:10.1080/1540496X.2020.1784718.

Iyke, B. N. 2020b. COVID-19: The reaction of US oil and gas producers to the pandemic. Working Paper.

Konchitchki, Y., and P. N. Patatoukas. 2014. Accounting earnings and gross domestic product. *Journal of Accounting and Economics* 57 (1):76–88. doi:10.1016/j.jacceco.2013.10.001.

Lai, C. C., C. Y. Wang, Y. H. Wang, S.-C. Hsueh, W.-C. Ko, P.-R. Hsueh. 2020. Global epidemiology of coronavirus disease 2019: Disease incidence, daily cumulative index, mortality, and their association with country healthcare resources and economic status. *International Journal of Antimicrobial Agents* 105946. doi:10.1016/j.ijantimicag.2020.105946.

Lee, H. Y., H. Y. Park, and Y. H. lee. 2013. Accounting transparency and cost of equity capital - evidence with the accounting transparency index of Korean accounting association. *Korean Accounting Journal* 22:219–52.

Liu, L., E.-Z. Wang, and -C.-C. Lee. 2020. Impact of the COVID-19 pandemic on the crude oil and stock markets in the US: A time-varying analysis. *Energy Research Letters* 1 (1):13154. doi:10.46557/001c.13154.

Liu, W., and Z. Z. Cai. 2003. The analysis and prospect of China's macroeconomic situation after SARS. *Red Flag Manuscript* 17:18–22. doi:CNKI:SUN:HQWG.0.2003-17-005.

Luo, H., Y. L. Zeng, J. X. Fang. 2016. The macro-predictive value of accounting information: A study based on China's institutional environment. *Accounting Research* 4:9–18. doi:10.3969/j..1003-2886.2016.04.002.

Narayan, P. K. 2020. Oil price news and COVID-19—Is there any connection? *Energy Research Letters* 1 (1):13176. doi:10.46557/001c.13176.

Qin, M., Y.-C. Zhang, and C.-W. Su. 2020. The essential role of pandemics: A fresh insight into the oil market. *Energy Research Letters* 1 (1):13166. doi:10.46557/001c.13166.

Wang, H. C., L. Lu, X. Zhang. 2012. Strengthen the study of accounting index to comprehensively enhance the influence of accounting in economic and social development. *Accounting Research* 11:7–11. doi:CNKI:SUN:KJYJ.0.2012-11-004.

Wang, Y. 2019. Analysis of the usefulness of accounting information in macroeconomic analysis. *Modern Marketing* 11:99.

Weersink, A., M. V. Massow, and B. Mcdougall. 2020. Economic thoughts on the potential implications of COVID-19 on the Canadian dairy and poultry sectors. *Canadian Journal of Agricultural Economics/Revue Canadienne D'agroeconomie* 1–6. doi:10.1111/cjag.12240.

Xu, X., H. Y. Yang, and B. L. Liu. 2020. The function and evolution of insurance in response to public health events– Based on a comparative perspective of the SARS epidemic in 2003 and the covid-19 epidemic in 2020. *The Theory and Practice of Finance and Economics* 41 (2):2–8. doi:10.16339/j.cnki.hdxbcjb.2020.02.022.

Zandifar, A., and R. Badrfam. 2020. Fighting COVID-19 in Iran; Economic Challenges Ahead. *Archives of Iranian Medicine* 23 (4):284–284. doi:10.34172/aim.2020.14.

How Does COVID-19 Affect China's Insurance Market?

Yating Wang, Donghao Zhang, Xiaoquan Wang (iD), and Qiuyao Fu

ABSTRACT

The insurance market has been greatly impacted by the out-break of the COVID-19 pandemic. We employ monthly provincial panel data and fixed-effects models to study how COVID-19 has impacted China's insurance market. The study finds that the commercial insurance premium income, the monthly year-on-year growth rate of premium, insurance density, and insurance depth have all decreased due to COVID-19. The negative impacts on property and personal insurances are both statistically significant. Raising the level of social security and digital insurance can alleviate the adverse impact of the pandemic on the insurance market.

1. Introduction

The novel Coronavirus (COVID-19) had spread across 215 countries and territories in all 5 continents by May 12, 2020. On January 30, 2020, the unrelenting spread of COVID-19 prompted the World Health Organization to declare it a public health emergency, and on March 12, 2020 COVID-19 was declared a pandemic. This pandemic has caused great social and economic disruptions, leading to a decline in consumption, investment, services, and industrial production activities around the world. In particular, the insurance market in mainland China has been severely affected. The year-on-year (YOY) growth rate of gross premium in the first quarter of 2019 was 15.8%, while the rate was 6.27% in the first quarter of 2020, indicating a decrease of 9.53 percentage points in growth rate. In addition, the monthly YOY growth rates of premium in the first three months of 2020 were −12.53%, −21.35%, and 1.93%, respectively, showing a sharp decline compared to the rates of 23.97%, 10.19%, and 6.76%, respectively, in the same periods of the previous year.[1]

While research on COVID-19 and equity markets globally is evolving (Ali, Alam, and Rizvi 2020; Haroon and Rizvi 2020), a literature has developed that examines the impact of pandemics on various energy issues (Apergis and Apergis 2020; Fu and Shen 2020; Gil-Alana and Monge 2020; Liu, Wang, and Lee 2020; Narayan 2020; Qin, Zhang, and Su 2020). In addition, there are also studies on socioeconomic factors (Fang, Long, and Yang 2020; Qiu, Xi, and Wei 2020), pandemic mitigation (Chudik, Pesaran, and Alessandro 2020), and households' spending and consumption (Baker et al. 2020; Eichenbaum, Sergio, and Mathias 2020). However, there is no empirical study on the impact of the pandemic on the insurance market. The fundamental function of insurance is to protect people from risks. Encountering the catastrophic hazard of COVID-19 has highlighted the importance of a well-functioning insurance market. Thus, it is of great practical and policy value to study how the pandemic affects the insurance market.

In this empirical study, we employ monthly provincial-level panel data and fixed-effects models to study the impact of COVID-19 on China's insurance market. We find that COVID-19 had a significant adverse impact on the insurance market in the short term due to the limitation of insurance marketing channels and the suppression of household insurance demand. The development of social security and digital insurance could help alleviate the negative impact of COVID-19 on the insurance market. This study provides insights into the impacts of COVID-19 on the Chinese insurance market.

The rest of the article is organized as follows: Section 2 introduces the data, defines the variables, along with the empirical models; Section 3 reports the empirical results, and the last section concludes the study.

2. Materials and Methods

2.1. Data Sources and the Definition of Variables

We use data for 29 provinces, municipalities, and autonomous regions of mainland China, excluding Tibet Autonomous Region and Qinghai Province. We select data of the first quarters of 2018, 2019, and 2020 to construct the balanced panel data for the benchmark analysis for two reasons. First, a popular saying among the insurers is that "a good start means the full success in the year," which is commonly known as "the auspicious start." To achieve the sales target, the insurance companies typically launch various marketing activities, such as increasing publicity, holding wine parties, discounting premiums, launching new insurance products, training agents, using distribution channels, subsidizing commission for the agents and brokers, and providing salary incentives for the employers in the last few months of the previous year. Thus, the premium income in the first few months tends to be significantly higher than that of other months, and it is incomparable between different quarters. Second, we can only collect the data on premium income up to the first quarter of 2020, so that the data of the first quarter of 2018 and 2019 can be directly compared with that of 2020. In addition, we will use the monthly balanced panel data from January 2018 to March 2020 for the robustness test.

2.2. Descriptive Statistics

Since all the provinces in mainland China started first-level response to major public health emergencies and implemented strict social isolation and traffic control measures in the last few days of January, and the premium data are provided on a monthly basis, we regard the February and March of 2020 as posterior to the pandemic and other months as prior to the pandemic. Table 2 shows the prior and posterior mean-variance test results, where the monthly YOY growth rates of the gross premiums before and after the outbreak are 4.97% and −2.07%, respectively. The average YOY growth rates of property, personal,[2] life, and accident insurances after the outbreak are significantly lower than before, whereas the monthly YOY growth rate of health insurance premium increases, although the result is insignificant. This more-or-less coincides with our expectations. Since the outbreak, the entire insurance industry has been impacted adversely, and the monthly YOY growth rates of all insurance products have declined by varying degrees. COVID-19 also instigated consumers' potential demand for health care; hence, the health insurance premium continued to grow steadily after the outbreak.

2.3. Empirical Models

The fixed-effects model to analyze the impact of COVID-19 on China's insurance market is expressed as follows:

$$Ins_{i,t} = \alpha_0 + \alpha_1 nCoV_{i,t} + \alpha_2 CPI_{i,t} + \alpha_3 PPI_{i,t} + \alpha_4 lnIncome_{i,t} + \alpha_5 lnGDP_{i,t} + \delta_i + \eta_t + \varepsilon_{it}$$

$$(1)$$

Table 1. Definition of variables. This table reports the definition of variables and data sources. The commercial insurance products include property, personal, life, accident, and health insurances.

Variables		Measurement	Data source
Explained variables	Ln (premium)	Ln (gross premium income (CNY))	Official website of the China Banking and Insurance Regulatory Commission and the provincial offices
	YOY growth rate	(Monthly gross premium YOY gross premium last year)/YOY gross premium last year ×100%	
	Insurance density	Monthly gross premium (CNY)/resident population last year	
	Insurance depth	Monthly gross premium/monthly GDP	
Explanatory variables	Confirmed cases	Cumulative number of confirmed cases at end of the month/100	Official website of National Health Commission of China
	Confirmed ratio	Cumulative number of confirmed/ population (10,000 per unit)	
Control variables	CPI	Monthly CPI (using the same month in 2018 as basis)	Official website of the National and Provincial Bureau of Statistics of China
	PPI	Monthly PPI (using the same month in 2018 as basis)	
	Ln (PDI)	Ln (monthly per capita disposable income (CNY))	
	Ln (GDP)	Ln (monthly GDP (CNY))	

Table 2. Mean-variance tests. This table reports the results of the mean-variance test of the insurance development prior and posterior to the pandemic. The symbols ***, **, and * represent significance levels of 1%, 5%, and 10%, respectively.

Monthly YOY growth rate	Prior to the pandemic			Posterior to the pandemic			t-test
	obs	mean	variance	obs	mean	variance	Mean (post.)-mean (prior)
Commercial insurance	203	4.97%	0.0120	58	−2.07%	0.0179	−7.04%***
Property insurance	203	9.73%	0.0086	58	−4.55%	0.0222	−14.27%***
Personal insurance	203	4.64%	0.0143	58	−1.38%	0.0212	−6.01%**
Life insurance	203	1.52%	0.0144	58	−9.55%	0.0208	−11.07%***
Health insurance	202	26.32%	0.0287	58	33.75%	0.0615	7.44%
Accident insurance	193	16.08%	0.0260	56	−12.23%	0.0385	−28.31%***

$Ins_{,it}$ indicates the insurance market development of province i at time t. We use gross premium income, YOY growth rate, insurance density, and insurance depth to measure the insurance market development. Subscript i stands for each of the 29 provinces, municipalities, and autonomous regions in mainland China, excluding Tibet and Qinghai. The t stands for months, from January 2018 to March 2020. The $nCoV_{i,t}$ are variables that represent the severity of the pandemic, including the number of confirmed cases and ratio to the local resident population. The $CPI_{i,t}$ and $PPI_{i,t}$ are consumer and producer price indexes, respectively, using the same month in 2018 as the basis. $lnIncome_{i,t}$ is the logarithm of per capita disposable income, the $lnGDP_{i,t}$ is the logarithm of GDP per capita, the δ_i and η_t are the provincial and time fixed effects, respectively, and ε_{it} is the error term.

We augment Equation (1) to study the impact of the pandemic on China's insurance market for the robustness test:

$$Ins_{it} = \alpha_0 + \alpha_1 COVID\_dummy_t + \alpha_2 CPI_{it} + \alpha_3 PPI_{it} + \alpha_4 LnIncome_{it} + \alpha_5 LnGDP_{it} + \delta_i + \varepsilon_{it} \qquad (2)$$

The variable representing the effect of the pandemic is a dummy variable, $COVID\_dummy_t$, which takes a value 1 if a province reports confirmed cases of COVID-19 on a monthly basis, and 0 otherwise. Since all provinces in the mainland had confirmed cases at the end of January 2020, the dummy variable is only valued in the time dimension. To eliminate complete collinearity, the monthly fixed effect will not be controlled in Equation (2).

3. Results

3.1. Using the Logarithm of Gross Premium as a Dependent Variable

To eliminate the effects of "an auspicious start" – a common feature of the Chinese insurance market – we use the data of various provinces from the first quarters of 2018, 2019, and 2020 to study the impact of COVID-19 on the insurance market based on the fixed-effects model. The confirmed ratio, which is the number of confirmed cases divided by the gross permanent resident population, is used to measure the severity of COVID-19. One unit of the confirmed ratio equals one confirmed case in every 10,000 people in a province. We use the logarithm of premium income, monthly YOY growth rate, monthly insurance density, and depth to proxy the development of the insurance market. First, COVID-19 may be detrimental to China's insurance market because it restricts insurance sales channels. Owing to the outbreak, individual agencies' businesses were largely suspended, banking channels restricted, and telemarketing businesses suspended because of their centralized office business-style, and direct sales business was greatly restricted.

As offline selling remains the main source of commercial insurance premium income in China, the proportion of online insurance premium income is very low. Therefore, the strict lockdown and social distancing measures are likely to have severe effects on the premium income and its growth. Second, COVID-19 may lead to rising unemployment rates and declining household incomes and may significantly restrict household demand for commercial insurance and intensify the negative impact of COVID-19 on the insurance market.

Table 3 reports the benchmark estimation results. First, Columns 1–2 show that COVID-19 has significantly reduced the gross premiums and monthly YOY growth rates of insurance premiums. For every unit increase in the confirmed ratio, the gross premiums and monthly YOY growth rate fall by 2.03% and 3.54%, respectively. Second, Columns 3–4 show that COVID-19 has significantly reduced the insurance density and depth. For every unit increase in the confirmed ratio, the monthly per capita premium income and proportion of premium to GDP fall by 13.21 yuan and 0.44%, respectively. The results further show that COVID-19 has significantly and negatively impacted the premium income, monthly premium YOY growth rate,

Table 3. Benchmark estimates of COVID-19's impact on the insurance market in China. This table reports the benchmark estimation results of COVID-19's impact on the insurance market in China based on Model (1). The symbols ***, **, and * represent significance levels of 1%, 5%, and 10%, respectively. The robust standard error of clustering at the provincial level is shown in parentheses.

	(1)	(2)	(3)	(4)
	Ln (premium)	YOY growth rate	Insurance density	Insurance depth
Confirmed ratio	−0.0203***	−0.0354**	−13.2077***	−0.0044***
	(0.0064)	(0.0145)	(2.9774)	(0.0012)
CPI	0.0208	−0.0375	−14.1398	−0.0015
	(0.0180)	(0.0233)	(16.6924)	(0.0024)
PPI	0.0004	0.0156	3.2223	−0.0002
	(0.0041)	(0.0102)	(2.5371)	(0.0005)
Ln(PDI)	0.6876***	1.9311***	463.1236**	−0.0022
	(0.2165)	(0.4950)	(219.9032)	(0.0336)
Ln(GDP)	−0.3735**	−1.2580***	−415.1421***	−0.1617***
	(0.1596)	(0.4004)	(98.2027)	(0.0311)
Prov FE	Y	Y	Y	Y
Month FE	Y	Y	Y	Y
N	261	261	261	261
Adj R-sq	0.9455	0.5319	0.7925	0.8727

insurance density, and depth in China's insurance market. Therefore, a quick and effective containment of COVID-19 would be helpful to the insurance market, while the laissez-faire approach to COVID-19 may have profound negative impacts on the development of the insurance market.

Additionally, Table 3 shows that per capita disposable income has a significant positive impact on the insurance market. The growth of disposable income increases the household demand for commercial insurance and promotes the growth of the insurance market. It also indicates that GDP influences the insurance market negatively. One possible reason is that households' income growth lags behind economic growth, and both the primary distribution and redistribution of national income show that the ratio of resident income decreases, and the ratio of corporate and government income rises in China (Zhang and Zhao 2014). Thus, it will directly inhibit household demand for commercial insurance. In addition, the duration for the data used in this study is too short to reflect the positive effect of GDP growth on the insurance market in the medium to long term.

3.2. Separate Regression Results for Property and Personal Insurances

In this sub-section, we analyze how COVID-19 has affected the property insurance and personal insurance markets separately. In China's insurance market, premium income mainly comes from personal insurance, and the proportion of property insurance is relatively low. The premium income of life insurance accounts for about 80% of personal insurance, while both health and accident insurances account for about 20%. The premium income of automobile insurance accounts for more than 60% of the property insurance premium income. The impact of COVID-19 on property and personal insurances may vary with the structures of insurance markets.

Table 4 displays the estimated results. First, Columns 1–2 show that COVID-19 affects the premium income of property insurance more severely than that of personal insurance. The increase in the confirmed ratio by one unit reduces the gross property insurance premium income by 3.86% and personal insurance premium income by 1.4%. Second, Columns 3–4 show that COVID-19 exerted almost the same negative impacts on property and personal insurances in terms of monthly YOY growth rate of the premiums. A unit increase in the confirmed ratio leads to a decrease of 3.08% and 3.33% in the monthly YOY growth rate of insurance premiums for property and personal insurances, respectively. Finally, Columns 5–8 indicate that COVID-19 has significantly reduced the insurance density and depth of property and personal insurances; however, the negative impact on personal insurance is greater than that on property insurance. For example, a unit increase in the confirmed ratio would result in a drop of 0.07% in the depth

Table 4. Regression results for property and personal insurances separately. This table reports the regression results of COVID-19's impact on the property and personal insurances based on Model (1). The symbols ***, **, and * represent significance levels of 1%, 5%, and 10%, respectively. The standard error of clustering at the provincial level is shown in parentheses.

	Insurance premium		YOY growth rate		Insurance density		Insurance depth	
	(1)property	(2)person	(3)property	(4)person	(5)property	(6)person	(7)property	(8)person
Confirmed ratio	-0.0386***	-0.0140*	-0.0308***	-0.0333**	-1.9347***	-11.3693***	-0.0007***	-0.0038***
	(0.0048)	(0.0079)	(0.0067)	(0.0153)	(0.2743)	(2.9997)	(0.0001)	(0.0011)
CPI	0.0012	0.0373*	-0.0084	-0.0309	-4.4289	-9.3266	-0.0002	-0.0012
	(0.0169)	(0.0214)	(0.0326)	(0.0286)	(4.1158)	(13.6512)	(0.0003)	(0.0024)
PPI	-0.0032	0.0012	-0.0023	0.0173	0.3524	2.8082	-0.0000	-0.0002
	(0.0054)	(0.0046)	(0.0086)	(0.0111)	(0.5911)	(2.1027)	(0.0001)	(0.0005)
Ln(PDI)	-0.0987	0.8315***	0.7498	2.0763***	-17.0055	484.7728**	-0.0046	0.0035
	(0.4128)	(0.2809)	(0.5791)	(0.5572)	(30.6251)	(225.4813)	(0.0080)	(0.0317)
Ln(GDP)	-0.3494**	-0.3020	-0.4584**	-1.3375***	-20.7263*	-397.1439***	-0.0209***	-0.1418***
	(0.1563)	(0.2173)	(0.2140)	(0.4443)	(11.5761)	(96.2648)	(0.0038)	(0.0290)
Prov FE	Y	Y	Y	Y	Y	Y	Y	Y
Month FE	Y	Y	Y	Y	Y	Y	Y	Y
N	261	261	261	261	261	261	261	261
Adj R-sq	0.9213	0.9348	0.4887	0.5097	0.7054	0.7883	0.8647	0.8496

of property insurance, compared to a significant drop of 0.38% in the depth of personal insurance.

The above-mentioned discrepancies between property and personal insurances may be attributed to the following factors. More than 60% of the property insurance premium income comes from auto insurance. During the outbreak, the sales of new cars dropped sharply or even to zero leading to the exact same decline in the premium income from new cars. Furthermore, many families do not renew their car insurances immediately upon expiry because they use them sparingly or not at all during the pandemic. Therefore, we can infer that COVID-19 has had the most severe impact on the auto insurance market, resulting in a larger decline in gross property insurance premiums than in personal insurance. At the same time, because property insurance accounts for a small share of China's insurance market, even though the premium income of property insurance itself has fallen greatly, changes in commercial insurance density and depth are still small.

3.3. Robustness Test

For the robustness test, we use the number of confirmed cases and the dummy variable of whether COVID-19 has broken out, to measure the severity of COVID-19. First, the more confirmed cases in a region, the more serious the pandemic and the more likely its negative impact on the insurance market. Second, the dummy variable can be used to directly compare the differences between the insurance markets before and after the COVID-19, to identify the impact of the pandemic on insurance market. As stated in Equation (2), we only control for the provincial fixed effect in the regression. Table 5 displays the estimated results; the alternative indicators of COVID-19 have the same results as that obtained in the benchmark regression, making the benchmark results robust.

We also employ monthly data for all 27 months in 29 provinces from January 2018 to March 2020 for the robustness test. Table 6 reports the estimated results; they show the robustness of our conclusion that the confirmed ratio has a significantly negative impact on the gross premium income, monthly premium YOY growth rate, insurance density, and insurance depth. However, considering that there are only first quarter data in 2020, it is impossible to compare the data with the full year data in 2018 and 2019. To exclude the effects of an auspicious start, we still use the estimated results of the 9 months' data in 29 provinces as the benchmark.

3.4. Heterogeneity Analysis

We further discuss whether COVID-19 had a heterogeneous impact on insurance market. First, considering that social security provides a means for

Table 5. Robust estimation results using other COVID-19 indicators. We use Model (1) to estimate Panel A, except using the confirmed cases to measure the $nCoV_{it}$. We control for the CPI, PPI, PDI, GDP, and provincial and monthly fixed effects in Panel A.; Meanwhile, we use Model (2) to estimate Panel B and do not control for the fixed effects of months. Owing to the limited space, not all the results of control variables are reported. The symbols ***, **, and * represent the significance levels of 1%, 5%, and 10%, respectively. The robust standard error of clustering at the provincial level is shown in parentheses.

	Ln (Premium)	YOY growth rate	Insurance density	Insurance depth
Panel A	(1)	(2)	(3)	(4)
Confirmed cases	−0.0003***	−0.0006**	−0.2175***	−0.0001***
	(0.0001)	(0.0003)	(0.0522)	(0.0000)
N	261	261	261	261
Adj R-sq	0.9455	0.5330	0.7924	0.8726
Panel B	(5)	(6)	(7)	(8)
COVID_dummy	−0.4931***	−0.1021***	−205.3983***	−0.0430***
	(0.0388)	(0.0256)	(26.7046)	(0.0041)
N	261	261	261	261
Adj R-sq	0.2920	0.1838	0.3101	0.3262

Table 6. Robust estimation results using the monthly data from January 2018 to March 2020. This table reports the robust estimation results using monthly data from January 2018 to March 2020 based on Model (1). The symbols ***, **, and * represent significance levels of 1%, 5%, and 10%, respectively. The standard error of clustering at the provincial level is shown in parentheses.

	(1)	(3)	(4)	(5)
	Ln (Premium)	YOY growth rate	Insurance density	Insurance depth
Confirmed ratio	−0.0101**	−0.0153***	−4.1961*	−0.0023***
	(0.0049)	(0.0040)	(2.2452)	(0.0008)
CPI	0.0062	−0.0150*	1.7837	0.0004
	(0.0101)	(0.0073)	(3.8504)	(0.0010)
PPI	0.0034	0.0028	0.7832	0.0002
	(0.0024)	(0.0027)	(0.7262)	(0.0002)
Ln(PDI)	−0.0896	−0.0386	40.0601	−0.0099*
	(0.0797)	(0.0250)	(58.0648)	(0.0049)
Ln(GDP)	−0.0912	−0.0181	−105.6219*	−0.1071***
	(0.1334)	(0.1074)	(56.0006)	(0.0227)
Prov FE	Y	Y	Y	Y
Month FE	Y	Y	Y	Y
N	783	783	783	783
Adj R-sq	0.9322	0.4420	0.8025	0.8927

households to cope with risks, and remarkable differences exist in the development of social security among provinces, we conduct a heterogeneous analysis based on social security. Second, with the rapid development of digital technology and financial technology in recent years in China, online sales have become an important channel for households to buy daily necessities, including commercial insurance. When the Chinese government enforced powerful lockdown measures to control the spread of the virus, the traditional offline insurance marketing channel was limited, whereas the online channel worked well. Therefore, we conduct heterogeneous analysis based on the degree of digital insurance development.

Specifically, we adopt the participation rate of unemployment insurance (UI), the participation rate of urban medical insurance (UMI), per capita spending of local finance on social security and employment, and local finance health-care expenditures to measure the development of social security. The larger the value of these indicators, the higher the degree of social security in the province. According to the results in Table 7, COVID-19 has a smaller negative impact on commercial insurance in regions with higher degree of social security; in contrast, it has significantly reduced the commercial insurance in regions with a low degree of social security. This is mainly because social security systems provide households with a risk management mechanism, helping them to manage the shocks such as unemployment and medical expenditures effectively during the pandemic, and to avoid the adverse effects on the demand for commercial insurance. The lack of social security coverage means poor ability to manage the pandemic-related risks, which has a significant negative impact on their demand for insurance.

We use the sub-index of insurance business in the digital inclusive financial index produced by the Digital Finance Research Center of Peking University to measure the development of digital insurance. A higher index value, the mean value of which is used to conduct group analysis, indicates a more digitalized insurance market. Table 7 shows that COVID-19 had a small negative impact on commercial insurance in regions with a high degree of digital insurance, while it significantly reduced the growth of commercial insurance in regions with a low degree of digital insurance. The offline channels, such as insurance agents and bank-insurance, were unable to carry out marketing activities effectively during the outbreak. In regions with a high degree of digital insurance, online marketing, to some extent, circumvented the inconvenience caused by the lockdown as experienced by the offline channels. However, in regions with a low level of digital insurance, online insurance marketing business was not effective enough to offset the significant negative impact of COVID-19 on the insurance market.

Heterogeneous analysis shows that improving the construction and coverage of social security system can reduce the adverse impacts of COVID-19 and other major public health emergencies on the insurance market by strengthening the risk management capacity of households. At the same time, with the rapid development of Fintech, digital insurance can be a beneficial supplement to traditional insurance marketing, and thus helps the insurance market cope with the adverse impact of major public health events such as COVID-19.

4. Conclusions

The outbreak of the COVID-19 pandemic has adversely affected global social and economic activities. This has attracted a growing literature on

Table 7. Heterogeneity estimation results of COVID-19's impact on insurance markets in different regions. This table reports the heterogeneity estimation results in different regions based on Model (1). The model controls for CPI, PPI, PDI, GDP, and the fixed effects of provinces and months. Owing to the limited space, all the control variable results are not reported. The symbols ***, **, and * represent the significance levels of 1%, 5%, and 10%, respectively. The standard error of clustering at the provincial level is shown in parentheses.

YOY growth rate	Higher participation rate of UI			Lower participation rate of UI		
	(1)gross prem.	(2)prop. prem.	(3)person. prem.	(4)gross prem.	(5)prop. Prem.	(6)person. prem.
Confirmed ratio	0.5565	−0.7430	1.0434	−0.0216**	−0.0264***	−0.0175*
	(0.5535)	(0.5117)	(0.6352)	(0.0088)	(0.0062)	(0.0085)
N	81	81	81	180	180	180
	Higher participation rate of UMI			Lower participation rate of UMI		
Confirmed ratio	0.5994	−0.0604	0.8367	−0.0279**	−0.0294***	−0.0250*
	(0.4499)	(0.4223)	(0.5324)	(0.0121)	(0.0064)	(0.0128)
N	126	126	126	135	135	135
	Higher per capita security spending			Lower per capita security spending		
Confirmed ratio	0.1937	−1.1798***	0.5120	−0.0144***	−0.0242***	−0.0108*
	(0.3148)	(0.3467)	(0.3084)	(0.0047)	(0.0031)	(0.0052)
N	99	99	99	162	162	162
	Higher per capita health-care spending			Lower per capita health-care spending		
Confirmed ratio	0.8012*	0.1106	0.9257*	−0.0246**	−0.0290***	−0.0206**
	(0.3700)	(0.4459)	(0.4505)	(0.0091)	(0.0065)	(0.0088)
N	108	108	108	153	153	153
	Higher development of digital insurance			Lower development of digital insurance		
Confirmed ratio	0.1207	−0.7350	0.3012	−0.0228**	−0.0275***	−0.0184**
	(0.4421)	(0.4248)	(0.3112)	(0.0086)	(0.0068)	(0.0081)
N	63	63	63	198	198	198

the effects of COVID-19. This empirical study examines the impact of COVID-19 on the insurance market in mainland China using the provincial level panel data and the fixed-effects model. The findings reveal that COVID-19 has had a significant negative impact on China's insurance market in the short term due to the limitation of insurance marketing channels and the suppression of household insurance demand. One new confirmed case per 10,000 people decreases the gross commercial insurance premium income, monthly YOY growth rate of premium, insurance density, and insurance depth by 2.03%, 3.54%, 13.21 yuan, and 0.44%, respectively. While COVID-19 has adversely impacted both the property and personal insurances, the negative impact on personal insurance is greater than that on property insurance from the perspective of insurance density and depth.

In addition, the study finds that the development of social security and digital insurance helps alleviate the negative impact of COVID-19 on the insurance market. This is because social security helps households cope with the impact of the pandemic on their work and income, and digital insurance helps to overcome the restrictions of offline insurance marketing against the backdrop of COVID-19.

This study makes the following policy recommendations to minimize the impact of severe health emergencies in general and on the insurance market in particular. First, resolute, effective, and quick measures should be taken to contain COVID-19 before it adversely affects the insurance market and other social and economic activities. Second, the social security system and income distribution should be optimized because they play an important role in enhancing the resilience of the regions against the outbreak of severe public health emergencies. Third, with the development of Fintech, the insurance market should be further digitalized to enhance its resilience against serious public health emergencies.

It should be cautioned that the study only sheds light on the short-term effect of COVID-19. Whether COVID-19 will have a long-term impact on the development of China's insurance market remains for future studies.

Notes

1. The insurance data come from the official website of China Banking and Insurance Regulatory Commission and the provincial offices.
2. In China's insurance market, life and personal insurances are statistically different from the concepts in the Western insurance markets. Life insurance includes universal life, unit-linked, participating life, and variable life, and endowment insurance, and excludes annuities, health insurance, and accident insurance, while personal insurance includes life insurance, annuities, health insurance, and accident insurance.

ORCID

Xiaoquan Wang ⓘ http://orcid.org/0000-0003-4915-410X

References

Ali, M., N. Alam, and S. A. R. Rizvi. 2020. Coronavirus (COVID-19)—an epidemic or pandemic for financial markets. *Journal of Behavioral and Experimental Finance* 27:100341. doi:10.1016/j.jbef.2020.100341.

Apergis, E., and N. Apergis. 2020. Can the COVID-19 pandemic and oil prices drive the US partisan conflict index? *Energy Research Letters* 1 (1):13144. doi:10.46557/001c.13144.

Baker, R. S., R. A. Farrokhnia, S. Meyer, M. Pagel, and C. Yannelis. 2020. Income, liquidity, and the consumption response to the 2020 economic stimulus payments. NBER Working paper No. 27097. May. DOI: 10.3386/w27097

Chudik, A., M. H. Pesaran, and R. Alessandro. 2020. Voluntary and mandatory social distancing: Evidence on COVID-19 exposure rates from Chinese provinces and selected countries. NBER Working paper No. 27039. April. DOI: 10.3386/w27039

Eichenbaum, M. S., R. Sergio, and T. Mathias. 2020. The macroeconomics of epidemics. NBER Working paper No. 26882. April. DOI: 10.3386/w26882

Fang, H., W. Long, and Y. Yang. 2020. Human mobility restrictions and the spread of the novel Coronavirus (2019-nCoV) in China. NBER Working paper No. 26906. March. DOI: 10.2139/ssrn.3559382

Fu, M., and H. Shen. 2020. COVID-19 and corporate performance in the energy industry. *Energy Research Letters* 1 (1):12967. doi:10.46557/001c.12967.

Gil-Alana, L. A., and M. Monge. 2020. Crude oil prices and COVID-19: Persistence of the shock. *Energy Research Letters* 1 (1):13200. doi:10.46557/001c.13200.

Haroon, O., and S. A. R. Rizvi. 2020. COVID-19: Media coverage and financial markets behavior—A sectoral inquiry. *Journal of Behavioral and Experimental Finance* 27:100343. doi:10.1016/j.jbef.2020.100343.

Liu, L., E. Z. Wang, and C. C. Lee. 2020. Impact of the COVID-19 pandemic on the crude oil and stock markets in the US: A time-varying analysis. *Energy Research Letters* 1 (1):13154. doi:10.46557/001c.13154.

Narayan, P. K. 2020. Oil price news and COVID-19—Is there any connection? *Energy Research Letters* 1 (1):13176. doi:10.46557/001c.13176.

Qin, M., Y. C. Zhang, and C. W. Su. 2020. The essential role of pandemics: A fresh insight into the oil market. *Energy Research Letters* 1 (1):13166. doi:10.46557/001c.13166.

Qiu, Y., C. Xi, and S. Wei. 2020. Impacts of social and economic factors on the transmission of coronavirus disease 2019 (COVID-19) in China. Global Labor Organization (GLO), Discussion paper. No. 494. DOI: 10.1101/2020.03.13.20035238

Zhang, J. W., and W. Zhao. March 2014. How to realize the growth of residents' income? *Studies in Labor Economics.* 2 (6). doi:10.12081/sle.2014.2.6.3.

Household Financial Decision Making Amidst the COVID-19 Pandemic

Pengpeng Yue(iD), Aslihan Gizem Korkmaz(iD), and Haigang Zhou(iD)

ABSTRACT

This paper investigates the impact of the COVID-19 pandemic on household investment decisions using a novel survey conducted by the Survey and Research Center for China Household Finance. We use linear probability and probit models to analyze the effects of COVID-19 at the household level. Our results show that households who know someone infected with COVID-19 lose confidence in the economy. They are more likely to change their risk behavior and become risk-averse. Further, COVID-19 increases the probability that a household will change its investment portfolio. More specifically, it causes a 9.15% decrease in the total investment amount.

1. Introduction

The year 2020 has brought unprecedented events since a new coronavirus outbreak (COVID-19) emerged in Wuhan, China, and spread to the rest of the world. Despite countries' efforts to slow the spread of the virus, the pandemic has infected 6,194,533 people and caused 376,320 deaths worldwide as of June 2, 2020.[1] The outbreak has also dramatically impacted global financial markets, creating an environment of uncertainty and volatility. At the time of writing this article, the pandemic is still evolving rapidly. Governments, medical practitioners, and academics are working hard to understand its effects, devise solutions to counteract them, and hopefully learn from this experience.

As the pandemic runs its course, academic literature in this area has also begun to flourish. For example, Corbet, Larkin, and Lucey (2020) document the impact COVID-19 has had on the volatility of both Shanghai and Shenzhen stock exchanges in China and discuss the potential of gold and cryptocurrencies as alternative asset categories to deal with the volatility and achieve diversification. Akhtaruzzaman, Boubaker, and Sensoy (2020) analyze the financial contagion that has occurred through listed firms between China and G7 countries. Ali, Alam, and Rizvi (2020) investigate the global financial market reaction to the pandemic as its epicenter moved from China to Europe, and the U.S. Zhang, Hu, and Ji (2020) map the general patterns of country-specific and systemic risks in the global financial markets.

While most of this early research has focused on financial markets, this is only one dimension of the pandemic's impact. Goodell (2020) posits that COVID-19 affects economies, financial markets, firm financing and cost of capital and industries such as banking and insurance, governments, and the public. Accordingly, Haroon and Rizvi (2020) and Corbet et al. (2020) focus on a different aspect of the pandemic by studying its psychological effects. In particular, the studies investigate sentiment generated by coronavirus-related news and reputational based contagion, that is the impact of the coronavirus outbreak on companies related to the term "corona", respectively. Additionally, Apergis and Apergis (2020), Fu and Shen (2020), Gil-Alana and Monge (2020), Liu, Wang, and Lee (2020), and Narayan (2020) examine the pandemic's impact on the energy industry to contribute to our understanding of this global phenomenon. Our paper contributes to this literature by analyzing COVID-19's effects at the household level and shows how households' investment portfolios changed in response to COVID-19 using a novel survey conducted by the Survey and Research Center for China Household Finance.

Studying the impact of a negative shock, such as a global pandemic at the micro level, is important because households are the key players in the economic system. Their perceptions and corresponding actions determine the extent of an outbreak's impact. Thus, we need more research in this area to attain a complete understanding of the household behavioral response to rare events.

Dietrich et al. (2020) and Knotek et al. (2020) present the results of a real-time survey conducted by Dietrich et al. (2020) of American households to inform policymakers and researchers about consumers' beliefs during the COVID-19 outbreak. Although they make significant contributions to the literature by presenting results from the U.S., our study contributes to the literature by presenting results from China, where the outbreak initiated.

According to the Centers for Disease Control and Prevention, the first confirmed case of COVID-19 in the U.S. came on January 21, 2020. According to the World Health Organization timeline, the novel coronavirus was identified on December 31, 2019.[2] But the South China Morning Post reported that the first confirmed case in China can be traced back to November 17, 2019.[3] The survey by Dietrich et al. (2020) started March 10, 2020.[4] The survey used in our paper started February 12, 2020. On one hand, both surveys have similarities that offer grounds for comparisons between the beliefs and expectations of American and Chinese households in an effort to offer a complete picture of the impact of a worldwide pandemic, but on the other hand, the survey used in our study differs in several ways that strengthen the contribution of this study. Namely, the survey used in this study has detailed information on Chinese households, and we are able to merge this data with the latest data from the China Household Finance Survey conducted in 2019 to perform a more in-depth analysis. Additionally, Dietrich et al. (2020) and Knotek et al. (2020) posit that the extent of the outbreak was not clear in the U.S. when the survey began because there were only about 1,000 confirmed cases. But according to the Johns Hopkins University & Medicine Coronavirus Resource Center, there were 44,759 confirmed cases in China when the survey began. So, our final dataset offers more detailed insight as to the impact of a pandemic on households to better enable policymakers to design policies that respond to negative shocks.

We use linear probability and probit models to examine how COVID-19 affects household behavior. Our results show that the COVID-19 pandemic causes households to lose confidence in the economy and change their risk preference. More specifically, they become risk averse. Accordingly, they change the composition of their financial portfolios. While households continue to hold financial assets, they decrease the total amount invested.

This paper contributes to the newly emerging branch of literature concerning the impact of a large-scale pandemic on finance by being the first to provide empirical evidence on household financial decision making during COVID-19.

2. Research Methods

2.1. Data and Variables

2.1.1. Data

This study uses a novel dataset based on the results of a recent survey conducted by the Survey and Research Center for China Household Finance. The survey was conducted in two consecutive periods with different households. The total number of responses from the two periods is equal to 3,553. 88% of this total sample consists of people who were surveyed during the last wave of the China Household Finance Survey (CHFS) in 2019.[5] After we merge these two datasets and drop missing values, the total sample includes 2,595 households. The U.S. survey discussed in Dietrich et al. (2020) and Knotek et al. (2020) included 3,954 responses.

Using the survey data for China, we employ figures similar to Knotek et al. (2020) and Dietrich et al. (2020) to compare American and Chinese households. Knotek et al. (2020) posit that the U.S. survey obtains 50 to 208 survey responses daily. Thus, for a daily average to be included in our figures, we require at least 50 survey responses. Accordingly, daily intervals on the horizontal axes vary. On the other hand, we use all responses in our regression analyses. Figure 1 depicts Chinese household expectations for the duration of the COVID-19 outbreak. Nearly 42% of households expected the outbreak to last one to two months. On February 12, 2020, 99.38% of the households expected a less than six-month duration. This number dropped to 95.34% on March 21, 2020.

Knotek et al. (2020) report that more than half of American households expected the outbreak to last less than six months, but this number dropped to about 33% in April 2020.

Figure 2 portrays Chinese household expectations for the economy. About 39% of households have a positive or very positive outlook on China's economy this year. This number increases to 74.91% of households for the three to five-year period. Knotek et al. (2020) and Dietrich et al. (2020) document that U.S. households expect higher inflation and a decline in GDP growth over the one year period starting from the day the survey is conducted.

Next, we investigate the income and consumption expectations of Chinese households for 2020 compared to 2019. Figure 3 shows that, on average, 68.28% expect a decrease in their income. The highest percentage of negative expectations occurred on February 13, 2020, with 80.39% of households expecting a decrease in their income. Yet, this number falls to 65% on March 21, 2020. Dietrich et al. (2020) also show a negative expectation, with U.S. households becoming less pessimistic toward April 1, 2020. About 51.40%

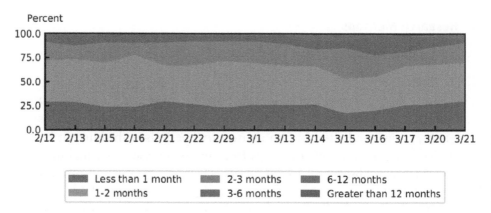

Figure 1. Expected duration of the coronavirus outbreak. This figure is created by using household responses to the survey question on the expected duration of the COVID-19 outbreak. The vertical axis shows the percentages of daily averages, and the horizontal axis shows the survey days with at least 50 responses.

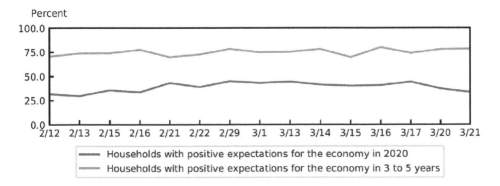

Figure 2. Household expectations for Chinese economy. This figure is created by using household responses to the survey question on household opinions about the Chinese economy in the short term, that is, the current year 2020, and in the long term, that is in 3 to 5 years. The vertical axis shows the percentages of daily averages, and the horizontal axis shows the survey days with at least 50 responses.

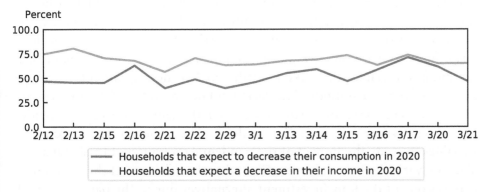

Figure 3. Household income and consumption expectations. This figure is created by using household responses to the survey question on income and consumption expectations of Chinese households for 2020 in comparison to the previous year 2019. The vertical axis shows the percentages of daily averages, and the horizontal axis shows the survey days with at least 50 responses.

of households expected to decrease their consumption. Dietrich et al. (2020) report that 70% of American households refrained from planning larger purchases.

Finally, we focus on household financial decision making in Figure 4. During our sample period, 19.97% of households changed their investment portfolio due to the COVID-19 outbreak and 8.47% of households decreased their total investment amount. Dietrich et al. (2020) report that 61% of American households changed their financial planning due to the outbreak.

2.1.2. Variables
Our first variable of interest is *COVID-19*, a dummy variable, which takes the value of 1 if the respondent has a family member, colleague, fellow

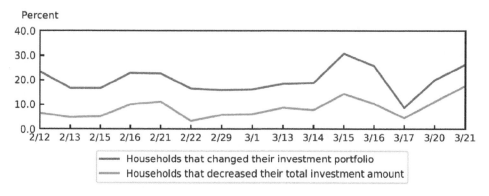

Figure 4. Household financial behavior. This figure is created by using household responses to the survey question on whether the household has or will change their investment portfolio due to the pandemic. The vertical axis shows the percentages of daily averages, and the horizontal axis shows the survey days with at least 50 responses.

student, friend, or acquaintance in the same community or village who has the virus. Next, we create two dummy variables to analyze household expectations of the economy in the short term, 2020, and in the long term, three to five-years. $ST\_Econ\_Confidence_i$ and $LT\_Econ\_Confidence_i$ are dummy variables that take the value of 1 if the respondent has a very positive or positive outlook. The variables take the value of 0 if the respondent expects the economic growth to remain the same as the current year or has a negative or very negative outlook. Then, we create two dummy variables to study the impact of the pandemic on household risk behavior. The first variable $Risk\_Behavior\_Chg_i$ takes the value of 1 if the respondent chooses one of the four investment alternatives due to the pandemic: high risk & high return, average risk & average return, low risk & low return, avoid risk altogether. The variable takes the value of 0 if the respondent's choice of investment alternative is not influenced by the pandemic. The second variable $Risk\_Seeking_i$ takes the value of 1 is the respondent chooses high risk & high return investment alternatives. Finally, we create two dummy variables to investigate the impact of COVID-19 on household financial decision making. The first variable $Inv\_Portfolio\_Chg_i$ takes the value of 1 if the respondent changes the portfolio composition or the total amount invested. The variable takes the value of 0 if the respondent keeps her portfolio the same. The second variable $Investment_i$ takes the value of 1 if the respondent maintains the same portfolio and 0 if she decreases the total investment amount. Figure 4 shows that 19.97% of households changed their investment portfolio due to COVID-19, and 8.47% of households decreased their total investment amount. Dietrich et al. (2020) report that 61% of U.S. households changed their financial planning due to the outbreak.

Following the household financial decision making and household welfare literature, we control for gender (e.g., Atella, Brunetti, and Maestas 2012; Gao, Liu, and Shi 2020; Heimer, Myrseth, and Schoenle 2019), age (e.g., Atella, Brunetti, and Maestas 2012; Berkowitz and Qiu 2006; Cardak and Wilkins 2009; Gao, Liu, and Shi 2020; Heimer, Myrseth, and Schoenle 2019; Rosen and Wu 2004), education (e.g., Atella, Brunetti, and Maestas 2012; Berkowitz and Qiu 2006; Cardak and Wilkins 2009; Gallagher and Hartley 2017; Gao, Liu, and Shi 2020; Heimer, Myrseth, and Schoenle 2019; Rosen and Wu 2004), marital status (e.g., Atella, Brunetti, and Maestas 2012), health status (e.g., Atella, Brunetti, and Maestas 2012; Berkowitz and Qiu 2006; Cardak and Wilkins 2009; Rosen and Wu 2004) government employment status (e.g., Gao, Liu, and Shi 2020), children (e.g., Cardak and Wilkins 2009; Rosen and Wu 2004), self-employment status (e.g. Cardak and Wilkins 2009; Gao, Liu, and Shi 2020), home ownership (e.g., Cardak and Wilkins 2009; Gao, Liu, and Shi 2020), family size (e.g., Atella, Brunetti, and Maestas 2012; Gao, Liu, and Shi 2020), whether the household has more than one working member (e.g. Cardak and Wilkins 2009; Gao, Liu, and Shi 2020), wealth (e.g., Atella, Brunetti, and Maestas 2012; Cardak and Wilkins 2009; Gao, Liu, and Shi 2020; Rosen and Wu 2004), income (e.g., Atella, Brunetti, and Maestas 2012; Berkowitz and Qiu 2006; Cardak and Wilkins 2009; Gallagher and Hartley 2017; Gao, Liu, and Shi 2020; Heimer, Myrseth, and Schoenle 2019; Rosen and Wu 2004), and rural residence (e.g., Karim 2018). Additionally, since the survey was conducted in two consecutive periods, we also include a dummy variable to control for the period.

Table 1. Summary statistics.

Variables	Obs	Mean/%	Std.	Min	Max
COVID-19	2,595	2.31%		0	1
ST_Econ_Confidence	2,171	40.21%		0	1
LT_Econ_Confidence	2,294	75.24%		0	1
Risk_Behavior_Chg	847	68.71%		0	1
Risk_Seeking	847	2.60%		0	1
Inv_Portfolio_Chg	1,249	18.73%		0	1
Investment	1,031	92.43%		0	1
Age	2,595	46.23	13.13	18	84
Education	2,595	12.51	3.67	0	22
Married	2,595	83.01%		0	1
Male	2,595	57.42%		0	1
Health	2,595	52.60%		0	1
Self_Employed	2,595	9.06%		0	1
Gov_Employee	2,595	7.36%		0	1
Multiple_Workers	2,595	62.50%		0	1
Children	2,595	38.54%		0	1
Family_Size	2,595	3.26	1.35	1	15
Homeowner	2,595	92.10%		0	1
ln(Netwealth)	2,595	1,458,524.10	1,998,225.72	1	9,548,500.00
ln(Income)	2,595	177,586.47	141,415.50	1	663,017.30
Rural	2,595	32.52%		0	1
Period	2,595	1.40	0.49	1	2

This table details the summary statistics. The table presents the percentages for categorical variables and means for continuous variables.

Table 1 presents summary statistics. A typical household consists of three members with 1,458,524 yuans of net wealth and 177,586 yuans of total household income.

2.2. Models

Caudill (1988) discusses the advantages of using the linear probability model (LPM), a special case of the ordinary least squares (OLS) regression method over logit and probit models. Similarly, Angrist (2001), and Angrist and Pischke (2008) give examples of research questions where the use of an LPM model is appropriate. Deke (2014) and Dovì (2019) use LPM models to estimate binary outcomes. Thus, we follow prior literature and use LPM models in our main analyses. In several tests, we also use probit models. In LPM models, X_i represents the vector of controls, and μ_i is the error term.

Using Equations (1a), (1b), (2a), and (2b), we investigate how the COVID-19 outbreak affects Chinese households' outlook on the economy.

$$ST\_Econ\_Confidence_i = \alpha + \beta COVID - 19_i + X_i\gamma + \mu_i \tag{1a}$$

$$Prob(ST\_Econ\_Confidence_i = 1|X_i) = Prob(\alpha + \beta COVID - 19_i + X_i\gamma > 0|X_i) \tag{1b}$$

$$LT\_Econ\_Confidence_i = \alpha + \beta COVID - 19_i + X_i\gamma + \mu_i \tag{2a}$$

$$Prob(LT\_Econ\_Confidence_i = 1|X_i) = Prob(\alpha + \beta COVID - 19_i + X_i\gamma > 0|X_i) \tag{2b}$$

We use Equations (3) and (4) to study the impact of the COVID-19 outbreak on households' risk behavior.

$$Risk\_Behavior\_Chg_i = \alpha + \beta COVID - 19_i + X_i\gamma + \mu_i \tag{3}$$

$$Risk\_Seeking_i = \alpha + \beta COVID - 19_i + X_i\gamma + \mu_i \tag{4}$$

Using Equations (5a), (5b), (6a), and (6b), we study the impact of the COVID-19 outbreak on households' financial decision making.

$$Inv\_Portfolio\_Chg_i = \alpha + \beta COVID - 19_i + X_i\gamma + \mu_i \tag{5a}$$

$$Prob(Inv\_Portfolio\_Chg_i = 1|X_i) = Prob(\alpha + \beta COVID - 19_i + X_i\gamma > 0|X_i) \tag{5b}$$

$$Investment_i = \alpha + \beta COVID - 19_i + X_i\gamma + \mu_i \tag{6a}$$

$$Prob(Investment_i = 1|X_i) = Prob(\alpha + \beta COVID - 19_i + X_i\gamma > 0|X_i) \quad (6b)$$

3. Results

3.1. Confidence in the Economy

Table 2 presents the results using Equations (1a), (1b), (2a), and (2b). In all columns, having a family member, colleague, fellow student, friend, or acquaintance in the same community or village who has COVID-19 has a negative impact on a household's outlook on the economy. However, these results are only significant for long-term expectations. In Columns (3) and (4), knowing someone with the virus decreases long-term confidence in the economy by 13.46% and 13.07%, respectively.

Table 2. Household confidence in the economy.

	Short-term Confidence		Long-term Confidence	
	(1) LPM	(2) Probit	(3) LPM	(4) Probit
COVID-19	−0.0507	−0.0545	−0.1346**	−0.1307**
	(0.0663)	(0.0716)	(0.0660)	(0.0572)
Age	−0.0055	−0.0053	−0.0096**	−0.0114**
	(0.0056)	(0.0057)	(0.0047)	(0.0051)
Age_sq/100	0.0119**	0.0116*	0.0146***	0.0170***
	(0.0059)	(0.0060)	(0.0048)	(0.0055)
Education	−0.0039	−0.0041	−0.0018	−0.0016
	(0.0035)	(0.0036)	(0.0029)	(0.0030)
Married	−0.0318	−0.0317	−0.0148	−0.0157
	(0.0352)	(0.0364)	(0.0309)	(0.0312)
Male	−0.0413*	−0.0422*	−0.0309*	−0.0312*
	(0.0217)	(0.0222)	(0.0186)	(0.0187)
Health	0.0231	0.0245	0.0071	0.0064
	(0.0218)	(0.0225)	(0.0191)	(0.0190)
Self_Employed	−0.0490	−0.0529	0.0119	0.0136
	(0.0364)	(0.0393)	(0.0332)	(0.0318)
Gov_Employee	0.0905**	0.0926**	0.1012***	0.1099***
	(0.0421)	(0.0422)	(0.0329)	(0.0374)
Multiple_Workers	−0.0075	−0.0082	0.0083	0.0095
	(0.0264)	(0.0269)	(0.0223)	(0.0220)
Children	−0.0184	−0.0204	0.0129	0.0173
	(0.0272)	(0.0281)	(0.0237)	(0.0234)
Family_Size	0.0176*	0.0184*	0.0036	0.0035
	(0.0104)	(0.0105)	(0.0085)	(0.0087)
Homeowner	−0.0498	−0.0509	0.0452	0.0471
	(0.0434)	(0.0439)	(0.0358)	(0.0358)
ln(Netwealth)	−0.0087	−0.0090*	−0.0115***	−0.0126***
	(0.0053)	(0.0053)	(0.0038)	(0.0048)
ln(Income)	−0.0025	−0.0026	0.0083	0.0079
	(0.0080)	(0.0081)	(0.0076)	(0.0068)
Rural	−0.0115	−0.0122	0.0074	0.0084
	(0.0231)	(0.0238)	(0.0199)	(0.0199)
Prov	Yes	Yes	Yes	Yes
Period	Yes	Yes	Yes	Yes
N	2,171	2,171	2,294	2,294
Adj. R-sq/Pseudo R-sq	0.0268	0.0355	0.0161	0.0334

This table shows how COVID-19 outbreak affects household confidence in the economy in the current year 2020, and in the next 3 to 5 year period. *** indicates significance at the 1% level, ** at the 5% level, and * at the 10% level.

3.2. Household Risk Behavior

In Table 3, we use Equations (3) and (4). Column (1) shows that knowing someone infected with COVID-19 changes a household's risk preference. The possibility that households will change their risk preference is 21.51%. In Column (2), the negative coefficient of the COVID-19 outbreak indicates that the possibility of becoming risk seeking will decrease by 3.19%.

3.3. Household Portfolio Decisions

In Table 4, we use Equations (5a), (5b), (6a), and (6b). Columns (1) and (2) show that knowing someone who has COVID-19 increases the probability of

Table 3. Household risk behavior.

	Risk Behavior Change	Risk-Seeking
	(1) LPM	(2) LPM
COVID-19	0.2151***	−0.0319*
	(0.0629)	(0.0168)
Age	0.0152*	0.0049
	(0.0086)	(0.0030)
Age_sq/100	−0.0200**	−0.0049
	(0.0091)	(0.0031)
Education	−0.0089*	0.0025
	(0.0054)	(0.0019)
Married	−0.0166	−0.0491**
	(0.0556)	(0.0249)
Male	0.0144	0.0043
	(0.0330)	(0.0110)
Health	−0.0165	0.0200*
	(0.0330)	(0.0104)
Self_Employed	0.0509	−0.0240
	(0.0549)	(0.0158)
Gov_Employee	−0.0863	−0.0292
	(0.0728)	(0.0187)
Multiple_Workers	−0.0484	0.0056
	(0.0410)	(0.0141)
Children	−0.0183	0.0100
	(0.0425)	(0.0163)
Family_Size	0.0173	0.0127
	(0.0152)	(0.0089)
Homeowner	−0.0671	0.0169*
	(0.0616)	(0.0093)
ln(Netwealth)	0.0173**	0.0029**
	(0.0075)	(0.0012)
ln(Income)	0.0044	−0.0072
	(0.0111)	(0.0060)
Rural	−0.0214	−0.0062
	(0.0344)	(0.0106)
Prov	Yes	Yes
Period	Yes	Yes
N	847	847
Adj. R-sq/Pseudo R-sq	0.0449	0.0065

This table shows the relationship between COVID-19 outbreak and household risk behavior. *** indicates significance at the 1% level, ** at the 5% level, and * at the 10% level.

Table 4. Household portfolio change.

	Investment Portfolio Change		Investment	
	(1) LPM	(2) Probit	(3) LPM	(4) Probit
COVID-19	0.1912**	0.1603**	−0.1565*	−0.0915**
	(0.0919)	(0.0641)	(0.0853)	(0.0356)
Age	−0.0011	0.0017	−0.0018	−0.0031
	(0.0057)	(0.0058)	(0.0041)	(0.0037)
Age_sq/100	−0.0012	−0.0043	0.0030	0.0045
	(0.0057)	(0.0061)	(0.0041)	(0.0041)
Education	0.0061	0.0066*	−0.0012	−0.0017
	(0.0038)	(0.0040)	(0.0030)	(0.0026)
Married	−0.0416	−0.0486	0.0351	0.0339
	(0.0429)	(0.0386)	(0.0348)	(0.0255)
Male	−0.0336	−0.0367*	0.0071	0.0072
	(0.0228)	(0.0220)	(0.0166)	(0.0132)
Health	−0.0377*	−0.0385*	0.0046	0.0057
	(0.0226)	(0.0224)	(0.0162)	(0.0130)
Self_Employed	0.1636***	0.1363***	−0.1703***	−0.0929***
	(0.0504)	(0.0375)	(0.0465)	(0.0204)
Gov_Employee	−0.0085	−0.0088	0.0359	0.0313
	(0.0424)	(0.0396)	(0.0270)	(0.0264)
Multiple_Workers	0.0165	0.0183	−0.0126	−0.0109
	(0.0281)	(0.0280)	(0.0207)	(0.0171)
Children	0.0372	0.0392	−0.0025	−0.0058
	(0.0301)	(0.0278)	(0.0227)	(0.0162)
Family_Size	−0.0073	−0.0063	−0.0015	−0.0012
	(0.0116)	(0.0111)	(0.0085)	(0.0062)
Homeowner	0.0028	0.0009	−0.0165	−0.0136
	(0.0475)	(0.0459)	(0.0296)	(0.0270)
In(Netwealth)	0.0005	0.0012	−0.0041	−0.0027
	(0.0074)	(0.0073)	(0.0063)	(0.0067)
In(Income)	0.0015	0.0004	−0.0028	−0.0024
	(0.0093)	(0.0096)	(0.0073)	(0.0072)
Rural	−0.0060	−0.0071	0.0043	0.0003
	(0.0255)	(0.0238)	(0.0197)	(0.0138)
Prov	Yes	Yes	Yes	Yes
Period	Yes	Yes	Yes	Yes
N	1,249	1,249	1,031	1,031
Adj. R-sq/Pseudo R-sq	0.0348	0.0732	0.0450	0.0877

This table shows the impact of the COVID-19 outbreak on household financial decision making. *** indicates significance at the 1% level, ** at the 5% level, and * at the 10% level.

changing portfolios by 19.12% and 16.03%, respectively. In Columns (3) and (4), the coefficient of COVID-19 shows that knowing someone with COVID-19 causes a 15.65% and 9.15% decrease in the total amount invested.

4. Robustness Tests

Tables 5 and 6 report the results of our robustness tests using Equations (5a), (5b), (6a) and (6b). In these tests, we exclude households older than 65, and households with already poor health from our sample and reinvestigate household portfolios. The results of these tests are similar to our main results.

Table 5. Robustness test: excluding households older than 65.

	Investment Portfolio Change		Investment	
	(1) LPM	(2) Probit	(3) LPM	(4) Probit
COVID-19	0.1987**	0.1708**	−0.1356	−0.0768*
	(0.0976)	(0.0707)	(0.0856)	(0.0403)
Age	−0.0016	0.0003	−0.0066	−0.0086
	(0.0078)	(0.0077)	(0.0056)	(0.0053)
Age_sq/100	−0.0009	−0.0032	0.0093	0.0120*
	(0.0086)	(0.0089)	(0.0062)	(0.0063)
Education	0.0073*	0.0075*	−0.0010	−0.0016
	(0.0042)	(0.0044)	(0.0033)	(0.0029)
Married	−0.0252	−0.0299	0.0275	0.0257
	(0.0455)	(0.0420)	(0.0371)	(0.0286)
Male	−0.0344	−0.0375	0.0040	0.0042
	(0.0243)	(0.0237)	(0.0177)	(0.0148)
Health	−0.0368	−0.0372	0.0033	0.0007
	(0.0242)	(0.0240)	(0.0176)	(0.0146)
Self_Employed	0.1746***	0.1484***	−0.1749***	−0.0998***
	(0.0520)	(0.0395)	(0.0482)	(0.0222)
Gov_Employee	−0.0027	−0.0030	0.0318	0.0282
	(0.0434)	(0.0415)	(0.0279)	(0.0288)
Multiple_Workers	0.0159	0.0206	−0.0067	−0.0076
	(0.0301)	(0.0300)	(0.0223)	(0.0193)
Children	0.0353	0.0378	0.0042	0.0047
	(0.0314)	(0.0298)	(0.0235)	(0.0182)
Family_Size	−0.0098	−0.0092	0.0010	0.0013
	(0.0123)	(0.0120)	(0.0090)	(0.0072)
Homeowner	−0.0088	−0.0114	−0.0154	−0.0146
	(0.0505)	(0.0488)	(0.0324)	(0.0310)
ln(Netwealth)	0.0001	0.0007	−0.0034	−0.0019
	(0.0078)	(0.0078)	(0.0066)	(0.0069)
ln(Income)	−0.0001	−0.0015	−0.0017	−0.0007
	(0.0106)	(0.0102)	(0.0085)	(0.0073)
Rural	−0.0039	−0.0060	−0.0013	−0.0056
	(0.0271)	(0.0254)	(0.0214)	(0.0154)
Prov	Yes	Yes	Yes	Yes
Period	Yes	Yes	Yes	Yes
N	1,133	1,133	926	896
Adj. R-sq/Pseudo R-sq	0.0337	0.0735	0.0473	0.139

This table shows the impact of the COVID-19 outbreak on household financial decision making after excluding households older than 65. *** indicates significance at the 1% level, ** at the 5% level, and * at the 10% level.

5. Conclusion

This paper uses a new survey conducted by the Survey and Research Center for China Household Finance between February 12, 2020, and March 22, 2020. Combining this survey with the 2019 wave of the China Household Finance Survey, we investigate the impact of COVID-19 on household financial decision making. COVID-19 changes households' outlook on the economy. The households who lose confidence in the economy are more likely to change their risk preference to risk averse. The probability that a household will change its investment portfolio is 16.03%. Namely, having a family member, colleague, fellow student, friend, or acquaintance in the same community or village with COVID-19 causes a 9.15% decrease in the total investment amount.

Table 6. Robustness test: excluding households with already poor health.

	Investment Portfolio Change		Investment	
	(1) LPM	(2) Probit	(3) LPM	(4) Probit
COVID-19	0.1725	0.1367*	−0.1418	−0.1009**
	(0.1169)	(0.0776)	(0.1060)	(0.0489)
Age	−0.0100	−0.0059	0.0095**	0.0082*
	(0.0074)	(0.0075)	(0.0046)	(0.0044)
Age_sq/100	0.0066	0.0021	−0.0077*	−0.0062
	(0.0075)	(0.0081)	(0.0046)	(0.0050)
Education	0.0106*	0.0111*	−0.0039	−0.0039
	(0.0054)	(0.0058)	(0.0041)	(0.0034)
Married	0.0567	0.0379	−0.0539	−0.0415
	(0.0604)	(0.0555)	(0.0466)	(0.0418)
Male	−0.0108	−0.0180	−0.0173	−0.0099
	(0.0316)	(0.0292)	(0.0230)	(0.0184)
Self_Employed	0.1617**	0.1374***	−0.2035***	−0.1206***
	(0.0662)	(0.0490)	(0.0602)	(0.0280)
Gov_Employee	0.0027	0.0108	0.0595*	0.0676*
	(0.0546)	(0.0490)	(0.0330)	(0.0381)
Multiple_Workers	−0.0016	−0.0031	−0.0439	−0.0411
	(0.0385)	(0.0376)	(0.0292)	(0.0262)
Children	0.0588	0.0544	−0.0217	−0.0205
	(0.0399)	(0.0362)	(0.0312)	(0.0237)
Family_Size	−0.0250	−0.0195	0.0203	0.0140
	(0.0157)	(0.0158)	(0.0125)	(0.0112)
Homeowner	−0.0071	−0.0287	−0.0218	−0.0312
	(0.0649)	(0.0648)	(0.0364)	(0.0543)
ln(Netwealth)	0.0075	0.0157	−0.0066	−0.0071
	(0.0077)	(0.0139)	(0.0062)	(0.0091)
ln(Income)	−0.0063	−0.0080	0.0054	0.0039
	(0.0140)	(0.0114)	(0.0114)	(0.0061)
Rural	−0.0074	−0.0100	−0.0087	−0.0132
	(0.0338)	(0.0314)	(0.0264)	(0.0191)
Prov	Yes	Yes	Yes	Yes
Period	Yes	Yes	Yes	Yes
N	696	696	584	523
Adj. R-sq/Pseudo R-sq	0.0285	0.0969	0.0587	0.192

This table shows the impact of the COVID-19 outbreak on household financial decision making after excluding households with already poor health. *** indicates significance at the 1% level, ** at the 5% level, and * at the 10% level.

Notes

1. Accessed on June 2, 2020. https://covid19.who.int
2. Accessed on May 6, 2020. https://www.who.int/news-room/detail/27-04-2020-who-timeline—covid-19
3. Accessed on May 6, 2020. https://www.scmp.com/news/china/society/article/3074991/coronaviru-chinas-first-confirmed-covid-19-case-traced-back
4. Accessed on May 6, 2020. https://www.cdc.gov/mmwr/volumes/69/wr/mm6918e2.htm
5. Survey and Research Center for China Household Finance. China Household Finance Survey. https://chfs.swufe.edu.cn/

Funding

This work was supported by the Beijing Technology and Business University [QNJJ2020-30].

ORCID

Pengpeng Yue (iD) http://orcid.org/0000-0002-5210-4309
Aslihan Gizem Korkmaz (iD) http://orcid.org/0000-0002-9151-0692
Haigang Zhou (iD) http://orcid.org/0000-0002-8201-5032

References

Akhtaruzzaman, M. D., S. Boubaker, and A. Sensoy. 2020. Financial contagion during COVID-19 crisis. *Finance Research Letters* 101604. doi:10.1016/j.frl.2020.101604.

Ali, M., N. Alam, and S. A. R. Rizvi. 2020. Coronavirus (COVID-19) – An epidemic or pandemic for financial markets. *Journal of Behavioral and Experimental Finance* 27:100341. doi:10.1016/j.jbef.2020.100341.

Angrist, J. D. 2001. Estimation of limited dependent variable models with dummy endogenous regressors: Simple strategies for empirical practice. *Journal of Business & Economic Statistics* 19 (1):2–28. doi:10.1198/07350010152472571.

Angrist, J. D., and J. S. Pischke. 2008. *Mostly harmless econometrics: An empiricist's companion.* Princeton, NJ: Princeton University Press.

Apergis, N., and E. Apergis. 2020. Can the COVID-19 pandemic and oil prices drive the US Partisan conflict index. *Energy Research Letters*, 1 (1), 13144. doi:10.46557/001c.13144.

Atella, V., M. Brunetti, and N. Maestas. 2012. Household portfolio choices, health status and health care systems: A cross-country analysis based on share. *Journal of Banking & Finance* 36 (5):1320–35. doi:10.1016/j.jbankfin.2011.11.025.

Berkowitz, M. K., and J. Qiu. 2006. A further look at household portfolio choice and health status. *Journal of Banking & Finance* 30 (4):1201–17. doi:10.1016/j.jbankfin.2005.05.006.

Cardak, B. A., and R. Wilkins. 2009. The determinants of household risky asset holdings: Australian evidence on background risk and other factors. *Journal of Banking & Finance* 33 (5):850–60. doi:10.1016/j.jbankfin.2008.09.021.

Caudill, S. B. 1988. Practitioners corner: An advantage of the linear probability model over probit or logit. *Oxford Bulletin of Economics and Statistics* 50 (4):425–27. doi:10.1111/j.1468-0084.1988.mp50004005.x.

Corbet, S., C. Larkin, and B. Lucey. 2020. The contagion effects of the COVID-19 pandemic: Evidence from gold and cryptocurrencies. *Finance Research Letters* 101554. doi:10.1016/j.frl.2020.101554.

Corbet, S., Y. Hou, Y. Hu, B. Lucey, and L. Oxley. 2020. Aye Corona! The contagion effects of being named Corona during the COVID-19 Pandemic. *Finance Research Letters* 101591. doi:10.1016/j.frl.2020.101591.

Deke, J. 2014. Using the linear probability model to estimate impacts on binary outcomes in randomized controlled trials. *Working paper.*

Dietrich, A., K. Keuster, G. J. Muller, and R. Schoenle. 2020. News and uncertainty about Covid-19: Survey evidence and short-run economic impact. *Working paper.*

Dovì, M. S. 2019. Does higher language proficiency decrease the probability of unemployment? Evidence from China. *China Economic Review* 54:1–11. doi:10.1016/j.chieco.2018.09.009.

Fu, M., and H. Shen. 2020. COVID-19 and corporate performance in the energy industry. *Energy Research Letters*, 1 (1), 12967. doi:10.46557/001c.12967.

Gallagher, J., and D. Hartley. 2017. Household finance after a natural disaster: The case of hurricane Katrina. *American Economic Journal: Economic Policy* 9:199–228.

Gao, M., Y. J. Liu, and Y. Shi. 2020. Do people feel less at risk? Evidence from disaster experience. *Journal of Financial Economics*, in press. doi:doi:10.1016/j.jfineco.2020.06.010.

Gil-Alana, L. A., and M. Monge. 2020. Crude oil prices and COVID-19: Persistence of the shock. *Energy Research Letters*, 1 (1), 13200. doi:10.46557/001c.13200.

Goodell, J. W. 2020. COVID-19 and finance: Agendas for future research. *Finance Research Letters* 101512. doi:10.1016/j.frl.2020.101512.

Haroon, O., and S. A. R. Rizvi. 2020. COVID-19: Media coverage and financial markets behavior – A sectoral inquiry. *Journal of Behavioral and Experimental Finance* 27:100343. doi:10.1016/j.jbef.2020.100343.

Heimer, R. Z., K. O. R. Myrseth, and R. S. Schoenle. 2019. Yolo: Mortality beliefs and household finance puzzles. *The Journal of Finance* 74 (6):2957–96. doi:10.1111/jofi.12828.

Karim, A. 2018. The household response to persistent natural disasters: Evidence from Bangladesh. *World Development* 103:40–59. doi:10.1016/j.worlddev.2017.10.026.

Knotek, E. S., II, R. Schoenle, A. M. Dietrich, K. Kuester, G. J. Muller, K. O. R. Myrseth, and M. Weber. 2020. Consumers and Covid-19: A real-time survey. *Economic Commentary* Federal Reserve Bank of Cleveland). doi:10.26509/frbc-ec-202008.

Liu, L., E.-Z. Wang, and C. C. Lee. 2020. Impact of the COVID-19 pandemic on the crude oil and stock markets in the US: A time-varying analysis. *Energy Research Letters*, 1 (1), 13154. doi:10.46557/001c.13154.

Narayan, P. K. 2020. Oil price news and COVID-19—is there any connection? *Energy Research Letters*, 1 (1), 13176. doi:10.46557/001c.13176.

Rosen, H. S., and S. Wu. 2004. Portfolio choice and health status. *Journal of Financial Economics* 72 (3):457–84. doi:10.1016/S0304-405X(03)00178-8.

Survey and Research Center for China Household Finance. *China household finance survey*. http://www.chfsdata.org/.

Zhang, D., M. Hu, and Q. Ji. 2020. Financial market under the global pandemic of COVID-19. *Finance Research Letters* 101528. doi:10.1016/j.frl.2020.101528.

Pandemic, Mobile Payment, and Household Consumption: Micro-Evidence from China

Taixing Liu ⓘ, Beixiao Pan, and Zhichao Yin

ABSTRACT

The novel coronavirus disease (COVID-19) outbreak has significantly affected many lives, as indicated by widespread lockdowns and restrictions. This study investigates the impact of COVID-19 on Chinese household consumption. It employs the China Household Finance Survey (CHFS) data and finds that there was a significant decline in household consumption during the outbreak period. Further heterogeneity analysis shows that the pandemic suppresses consumption in urban households; rural households are, however, less affected. Moreover, mobile payment promotes urban household consumption during the pandemic, while rural households remain unaffected.

1. Introduction

The coronavirus (COVID-19) outbreak in December 2019 attracted considerable media attention (Haroon and Rizvi 2020) and generated global panic (Ali, Alam, and Rizvi 2020), thereby causing much of the economy to halt (Narayan 2020). Moreover, the outbreak has significantly affected many lives, as indicated by the widespread lockdowns and restrictions to prevent further infections. This study employs Chinese survey data to investigate the impact of the COVID-19 pandemic on household consumption. As the initial outbreak took off in China and coincided with the Chinese Lunar New Year (which is a traditional festival characterized by high consumption levels),[1] the resultant rapid spread disrupted the consumption plans of many families. Moreover, it has deeply affected consumption behavior in the short- or even long-term.

Thus, the existing literature on the impact of the pandemic on consumption can be divided into short- and long-term impact research. Regarding short-term impact studies, irrespective of the focus on the overall changes in consumption (see Barro and Ursúa 2008; Barro, Ursúa, and Weng 2020; Chen, Qian, and Wen 2020; Correia, Luck, and Verner 2020), different category changes in consumption (see Jung et al. 2016), and dynamic changes in consumption (see Baker et al. 2020), most studies employ macro- or micro-level data. However, they either exist the small sample issue or lack sample representation. Moreover, such studies mainly focus on the degree of impact of the pandemic on consumption; few studies further discuss heterogeneity. Regarding long-term impact studies, scholars posit that isolation creates new consumption demands and patterns. Thus, the more the threat of the contagion prolongs, the further adaptive responses become ingrained and resistant to reversal (Cohen 2020). However, such studies do not discuss the consumption patterns that change during the pandemic.

Thus, unlike Jung et al. (2016), this study employs nationally representative household sampling survey data of China to address the shortcomings of having a small sample size in macro-level data and resolve the serious problem of sample representation in micro-level data. The study finds that COVID-19 suppresses Chinese household consumption significantly. Secondly, from the perspective of the urban-rural dual economy structure,[2] there is considerable heterogeneity in consumption changes between Chinese urban and rural households. Specifically, urban households suffer more declines; rural households are, however, less affected by the pandemic. Thirdly, since the long-term isolation results in significant changes in consumption patterns (Cohen 2020), as reflected in the transition from offline to online consumption, we further investigate the impact of mobile payment on household consumption during the pandemic period.[3] The results show that mobile payment promotes urban household consumption.

Hence, this study bridges the research gap in the literature by answering the following questions. How has household consumption responded to the pandemic? Is there heterogeneity among families? Can mobile payment change the impact of the pandemic on household consumption? By addressing these questions, we can obtain a more intuitive understanding of consumption adjustments during the pandemic and contribute to the literature on the evaluation of COVID-19. Moreover, we can provide empirical evidence for the formulation of consumption policies during (and even after) the pandemic.

We arrange the data of confirmed, recovered, and death COVID-19 cases of Chinese prefecture-level cities and match the data with the nationally representative sampling survey data to evaluate the impact of COVID-19 on household consumption during the Spring Festival. Our results show that household consumption is significantly affected by the pandemic; consumption continues to decline as the effect increases in severity.

Further, we explore the heterogeneity between urban and rural families regarding the differences in consumption patterns and human capital. Considering consumption patterns, China is a typical urban-rural dual economy. Moreover, there are significant differences in consumption patterns between urban and rural families. Considering commodity consumption, rural families mostly own the right to use village collective lands, which enables them to engage in agricultural production to provide surplus consumer goods for sale and satisfy their own consumption. Meanwhile, urban families always act as the demand side in the consumer goods market. Regarding human capital, given the low income in agricultural production, many rural labor transfers from agricultural production to non-agricultural sectors, such as the construction and service industries, comprise a large group of migrant workers. Generally, the human capital of migrant workers is relatively low. Thus, most workers engage in low-skilled jobs in the manufacturing, construction, and service industries. The pandemic has significantly affected many low-skilled jobs, which may lead to a sharp rise in the unemployment risk among migrant workers. Relatively urban families have higher human capital. Thus, they face lower unemployment risk and income uncertainty. However, our results show that the negative impact of the pandemic on household consumption is more obvious in urban families, while the self-sufficient rural families are less affected. The differences in consumption patterns dominate the impact of the pandemic on consumption.

Moreover, given that consumption patterns changed significantly during the pandemic, we evaluate the function of new payment tools. Notably, mobile payment tools can induce the transition from offline to online consumption, thus overcoming space-time limitations, reducing unnecessary personnel mobility, and meeting the needs of consumers and businesses during the pandemic. Mobile payment plays a significant role in promoting consumption during the pandemic; however, it is only evident in urban families.

This study contributes to the literature in three aspects. First, it is first to employ nationally representative sampling survey data to evaluate the impact of COVID-19 on household consumption. Insight from the findings addresses the overall situation in China regarding how household consumption responds to the pandemic on average. Second, this study employs the urban-rural dual economy structure as the division criteria to examine heterogeneity among urban and rural households. Nearly 600 million rural residents in China are not significantly affected by the pandemic. Thus, from the perspective of urban-rural economic activity differences,[4] consumption continues to decline as the dependence on the consumer goods market (urban households) increases. The study findings can supplement the literature on the heterogeneous impact of the pandemic on household consumption. Third, long-term isolation creates new consumption demands and patterns (Cohen 2020). Offline consumption may be significantly restricted, while online consumption may be less affected, given mobile payment. Thus, we further investigate whether mobile payment can alleviate household consumption during the pandemic. We find that mobile payment promotes urban household consumption during the pandemic, while rural households are unaffected. The findings can encourage the government to put more resources into developing the mobile payment market.

The rest of the paper is structured as follows. Section 2 provides an in-depth discussion of the data and describes the empirical specifications employed. Section 3 analyzes the estimation results. Section 4 concludes.

2. Data and Empirical Methodology

The data employed in the study can be grouped into two. The first group presents the confirmed, recovered, and death cases released by the health commission of various prefecture-level cities in China. The second group presents the data from the sampling survey on the impact of the COVID-19 pandemic on production and life. The survey was conducted by the Survey and Research Center for China Household Finance in the first quarter of 2020. The sample is partly (mostly) derived from a randomly selected individual sample (the 2019 CHFS individual sample, which is adjusted according to the sampling weight).[5] The samples are nationally representative, with which we match the data from the various prefecture-level cities to derived a sample size of 2,767. The online survey comprised two batches, and the questionnaire was launched from February 12 to March 22, 2020. The questionnaire includes subjects such as income and consumption, industrial and commercial operation, and financial market investment.

We use the ordinary least square (OLS) method to analyze the impact of the pandemic on household consumption. The econometric model was set as follows:

$$Consumption_{hc} = \alpha_0 + \beta' Confirmed_c + \gamma' X_{ihc} + \delta' Z_{hc} + \lambda_c + \varepsilon_{ihc} \quad (1)$$

From the pandemic survey questionnaire, *Consumption* refers to the changes in household consumption during the 2020 Spring Festival, as compared with 2019. *Confirmed* is the core explanatory variable that measures the pandemic intensity. X_{ihc} is the control variable at the individual interviewee level, Z_{hc} is the control variable at the household interviewee level, λ_c is the city-level fixed effect, and ε_{ihc} is the error term.

The two batches of questionnaires on the choice of consumption changes differ in the following ways. In the first batch, the consumption options include a sharp decrease, a slight decrease, basically unchanged, a slight increase, and a sharp increase. The second batch includes a decrease of more than 50%, decreases by 30% to 50% and 10% to 30%, and a decrease of less than 10%, as well as basically unchanged. It also includes an increase of less than 10%, increases by 10% to 30% and 30% to 50%, and an increase of more than 50%. We categorize the decrease of more than 30%, decrease of less than 30%, increase of less than 30%, and increase of more than 30% under sharp decrease, slight decrease, slight increase, and sharp increase, respectively, to integrate the two batches of consumption data.[6] We then set 1 to sharp decrease, 2 to slight decrease, in that order, until 5 is set to sharp increase.

Regarding the pandemic intensity variable, we first employ the number of newly confirmed cases during the Spring Festival to measure the pandemic intensity. Moreover, since the Spring Festival period coincided with the initial outbreak of COVID-19 in China, we also employ the number of cumulative and existing confirmed cases at the end of the Spring Festival to measure the pandemic intensity. We add 1 to the three indicators and take the logarithm to measure the pandemic intensity. Furthermore, the COVID-19 pandemic situation is exceptional in Wuhan. For instance, Wuhan observed the first confirmed cases more than one and a half months earlier than other cities. Thus, we exclude the Wuhan household samples in our estimation to avoid outliers that can interfere with the results.

We also control for several interviewee characteristics, following Campbell and Cocoo (2007) and Li and Chen (2014). There is strong evidence from the literature that households are heterogeneous in several dimensions. The age variable captures the consumption difference in the life cycle of different periods. Moreover, following Li and Chen (2014), we include the gender, marital status, educational background, and occupation of respondents to avoid missing variable problems since they might impact household consumption.

Several household characteristics that may affect household consumption are also included in our model. Moreover, it is intuitive and necessary to consider the family size variable in the consumption model (Campbell and Cocoo 2007) because the larger the population, the higher the consumption. We also control for the children and elderly ratios, following Li and Chen (2014), to capture the demography-induced consumption difference. Moreover, according to Dynan (2012) and Kukk (2016), household income and asset variables largely reflect the family's economic situation and determines its consumption ability. Thus, we include them in our model.

Moreover, to capture the impact of inherent differences or heterogeneity (such as cultural environment, regional consumption habits, and savings preferences) at the regional level on household consumption, we control for the city-level fixed effect following Chen, Qian, and Wen (2020). Table 1 presents the descriptive statistical results of variables.

3. Results and Discussion

Table 2 presents the estimation results of the OLS method. We find that pandemic intensity has a significantly negative impact on household consumption. From column 1, the pandemic coefficient is −0.095, which indicates that for every 10% increase in newly confirmed cases, household consumption decreases by nearly 0.01. Since the consumption variables are sequencing indicators, it is difficult to conduct a quantitative analysis. However, when viewed from the macro-level (such as city, province, and even national level),

Table 1. Descriptive Statistics.

	Obs.	Mean	Std. Dev.	Min	Max
Consumption	2575	2.201	1.085	1	5
Confirmed_Added	313	68.543	221.727	1	2410
Confirmed_Cumul	313	70.754	225.515	1	2436
Confirmed_Existing	313	64.559	212.554	0	2362
Age	2575	56.728	14.895	19	93
Age-sq	2575	34.398	16.364	3.61	86.49
Male = 1	2575	0.502	0.500	0	1
Married = 1	2575	0.824	0.381	0	1
Lower Secondary	2575	0.299	0.458	0	1
Higher Secondary	2575	0.173	0.379	0	1
College+	2575	0.182	0.386	0	1
Job-Employee	2575	0.248	0.432	0	1
Job-Business	2575	0.059	0.235	0	1
Job-Agriculture	2575	0.010	0.100	0	1
Family_Num	2575	3.017	1.443	1	11
Children _Pro	2575	0.091	0.157	0	0.667
Elderly_Pro	2575	0.422	0.433	0	1
Per Capita Asset	2575	511444.1	900771.1	−36300	9598000
Per Capita Income	2575	29476.08	36955.95	−10069.99	621076.9
Rural	2575	0.308	0.462	0	1

Job-Employee refers to employed individuals, Job-Business refers to individuals who engage in entrepreneurship activity, and Job-Agriculture refers to individuals who engage in agricultural production. The Children_Pro refers to the proportion of children under the age of 16 in the total number of households, and the Elderly_Pro refers to the proportion of the elderly aged 60 and above in the total number of households. Personal-level variables are adjusted according to personal-level weights, and household-level variables are adjusted according to household-level weights.

Table 2. The effect of the pandemic on the Spring Festival consumption in the full sample.

	Consumption		
Full Sample	(1)	(2)	(3)
Confirmed_Added	−0.095***		
	(0.016)		
Confirmed_Cumul		−0.083***	
		(0.015)	
Confirmed_Existing			−0.082***
			(0.015)
Controls	Yes	Yes	Yes
FE City	Yes	Yes	Yes
R^2	0.1496	0.1496	0.1495
No. of Observations	2575	2575	2575

Based on the OLS estimation under the full sample, the results are adjusted according to the household-level weight. Core explanatory variables vary by column, with columns (1) to (3) respectively showing newly confirmed cases, cumulative confirmed cases, and existing confirmed cases. Within the brackets are the robust standard errors clustered according to the city level. *** $p < .01$, ** $p < .05$, * $p < .1$.

the impact is significant. The explanation of the result can be approached from two perspectives. Areas with dire pandemic situations will not only adopt stricter countermeasures but also reduce the freedom of movement, given the high risk of infection. Columns 2 and 3 employ the number of cumulative and existing confirmed cases to measure the pandemic intensity, and the same results were obtained.

Furthermore, the pandemic may lead to a significant decrease in urban household consumption due to excessive dependence on the consumer goods market. It may, however, lead to higher unemployment risk for rural households due to lower human capital, thereby actively reducing household consumption to respond to the income decline that results from the potential unemployment risk.

To explore the heterogeneity between urban and rural households, we divide the sample into urban and rural categories. The first three columns of Table 3 show the rural sample estimation results. We find that the pandemic has no significant negative impact on rural household consumption. It indicates that, given a low dependence on the consumer goods market, rural household consumption is relatively stable during the pandemic.

The last three columns of Table 3 show the urban sample estimation results. The pandemic has a significant negative impact on urban household consumption. Column 4 shows that the pandemic coefficient is −0.083 and indicates that for every 10% increase in the newly confirmed cases, household consumption would decrease by 0.0083. From the perspective of the macrolevel, the impact is significant. It indicates that the dire pandemic situation has a greater impact on urban households that considerably depend on the consumer goods market.

The rapid spread of COVID-19 resulted in the closure of many restaurants, shopping malls, and supermarkets. Meanwhile, mobile payment can induce the transition from offline to online consumption, which may significantly alleviate the impact of the pandemic on business sales and resident consumption. However, as the pandemic situation worsens, even online consumption, given its reliance on logistics and transportation, has been considerably

Table 3. The effect of the rural-urban difference of the pandemic on Spring Festival consumption.

	Consumption					
	Rural Sample			Urban Sample		
	(1)	(2)	(3)	(4)	(5)	(6)
Confirmed_Added	−0.018			−0.083***		
	(0.062)			(0.020)		
Confirmed_Cumul		−0.017			−0.065***	
		(0.057)			(0.019)	
Confirmed_Existing			−0.016			−0.058***
			(0.058)			(0.020)
Controls	Yes	Yes	Yes	Yes	Yes	Yes
FE City	Yes	Yes	Yes	Yes	Yes	Yes
R^2	0.2844	0.2844	0.2844	0.1825	0.1824	0.1823
No. of Observations	873	873	873	1732	1732	1732

Columns (1) to (3) are based on the OLS estimation under the rural sample, and columns (4) to (6) are based on the OLS estimation under the urban sample. The results are adjusted according to the household-level weight. Core explanatory variables vary by column. Columns (1) and (4), (2) and (5), and (3) and (6) respectively present the newly confirmed cases, cumulative confirmed cases, and existing confirmed cases. Within brackets are the robust standard errors clustered according to the city level. *** $p < .01$, ** $p < .05$, * $p < .1$.

affected. Thus, to evaluate whether mobile payment is vital for promoting consumption during the pandemic, we set the following econometric model:

$$Consumption_{hc} = \alpha_0 + \beta' Confirmed_c + \gamma' MP_{hc} + \delta' Confirmed_c \times MP_{hc}$$
$$+ Controls + \lambda_c + \varepsilon_{ihc} \tag{2}$$

where MP is the mobile payment variable. If a household has access to a mobile payment tool, such as Alipay and WeChat, the mobile payment variable will be set to 1; otherwise, it is 0. δ is the interaction coefficient. If it is significantly positive, it indicates that the consumption of households with mobile payment tools is less affected during the pandemic. The other variables bare the same definition as those of equation (1).

Table 4 shows the estimation results after adding the interaction terms between mobile payment and pandemic intensity. We find that the total effect of the pandemic in column 1 is −7.79%, indicating the pandemic leads to a significant decline in household consumption. The coefficient of the interaction term is significantly positive, indicating that, as compared to households without mobile payment tools, mobile payment significantly increases consumption during the pandemic. The results of columns 2 and 3 are similar to that of column 1. The total effect of the pandemic on household consumption is −6.39% and −5.89%, respectively. The interaction coefficient is significantly positive at the 5% level, indicating that mobile payment has somewhat inhibited the negative impact of the pandemic on consumption. It shows that

Table 4. The interaction effect of mobile payment and the pandemic on Spring Festival consumption in the full sample.

Full Sample	Consumption		
	(1)	(2)	(3)
Confirmed_Added	−0.138***		
	(0.023)		
Confirmed_Added×MP	0.116**		
	(0.049)		
Confirmed_Cumul		−0.125***	
		(0.022)	
Confirmed_Cumul×MP		0.118**	
		(0.051)	
Confirmed_Existing			−0.120***
			(0.022)
Confirmed_Existing×MP			0.118**
			(0.049)
MP	−0.538**	−0.554**	−0.536**
	(0.238)	(0.247)	(0.236)
Controls	Yes	Yes	Yes
FE City	Yes	Yes	Yes
R^2	0.1542	0.1543	0.1543
No. of Observations	2575	2575	2575

Based on the OLS estimation under the full sample, the results are adjusted according to the household-level weight. Interaction terms vary by column. Columns (1) to (3) present the interaction terms between mobile payment and newly confirmed cases, cumulative confirmed cases, and existing confirmed cases, respectively. Within the brackets are the robust standard errors clustered according to the city level. *** $p < .01$, ** $p < .05$, * $p < .1$.

Table 5. The interaction effect of mobile payment and the pandemic on the Spring Festival consumption in the rural and urban sample.

	Consumption					
	Rural Sample			Urban Sample		
	(1)	(2)	(3)	(4)	(5)	(6)
Confirmed_Added	−0.022			−0.140***		
	(0.065)			(0.044)		
Confirmed_Added×MP	0.041			0.129*		
	(0.136)			(0.078)		
Confirmed_Cumul		−0.021			−0.123***	
		(0.061)			(0.044)	
Confirmed_Cumul×MP		0.031			0.136*	
		(0.139)			(0.080)	
Confirmed_Existing			−0.020			−0.114***
			(0.062)			(0.044)
Confirmed_Existing×MP			0.035			0.138*
			(0.134)			(0.079)
MP	−0.158	−0.126	−0.136	−0.629*	−0.669*	−0.656*
	(0.444)	(0.464)	(0.430)	(0.356)	(0.371)	(0.356)
Controls	Yes	Yes	Yes	Yes	Yes	Yes
FE City	Yes	Yes	Yes	Yes	Yes	Yes
R^2	0.2847	0.2846	0.2847	0.1877	0.1880	0.1881
No. of Observations	873	873	873	1732	1732	1732

Columns (1) to (3) are based on the OLS estimation under the rural sample, and columns (4) to (6) are based on the OLS estimation under the urban sample. The results are adjusted according to the household-level weight. The interaction terms vary by column. Columns (1) and (4), (2) and (5), and (3) and (6) respectively present the interaction terms between mobile payment and newly confirmed cases, cumulative confirmed cases, and existing confirmed cases. Within brackets are the robust standard errors clustered according to the city level. *** $p < .01$, ** $p < .05$, * $p < .1$.

mobile payment remains essential in promoting consumption during the pandemic.

Given that the pandemic has no significant impact on rural households during the Spring Festival, it means that they are less dependent on the consumer goods market and can satisfy their consumption demand through self-sufficiency. Thus, can mobile payment tools improve rural household consumption during the pandemic? The first three columns of Table 5 show the estimation results. We find that mobile payment does not have a significant effect on rural household consumption during the pandemic.

The last three columns of Table 5 show the urban sample estimation results. The main effect of the pandemic intensity in column 4 is estimated as −6.26%; thus, the pandemic reduced urban household consumption significantly. The interaction coefficient between pandemic intensity and mobile payment is significantly positive; hence, mobile payment still promotes urban household consumption, despite the strict countermeasures. The total effects of the pandemic in columns 5 and 6 are −4.14% and −3.12%, respectively. Moreover, the coefficients of the interaction term are significantly positive at the 10% significance level, which shows that mobile payment tools reduce the negative effect of the pandemic on urban household consumption.

4. Conclusion

We employ nationally representative sampling survey data to analyze the impact of the COVID-19 pandemic on Chinese household consumption. We find that the pandemic has a significant negative impact on household consumption. Heterogeneity analysis shows that the negative impact is mainly reflected in urban households that depend considerably on the consumer goods market. However, rural households are less affected.

Mobile payment can improve transaction efficiency and facilitate consumption while overcoming the traditional space-time limitations. Thus, mobile payment can induce the transition from offline to online consumption. Our study finds that although the pandemic has somewhat constrained consumption ability, mobile payment can still promote household consumption. However, we find that it only applies to urban households. For rural households, mobile payment cannot significantly improve consumption. Thus, the empirical evidence gives scope for the formulation of consumption policies during (and even after) the pandemic. The findings, for instance, provide empirical grounds for the government to treat the development of the mobile payment market with urgency.

Notes

1. Data from the National Bureau of Statistics of China show that during the seven days of the Spring Festival in 2019, tourism by Chinese residents generated 513.9 billion yuan, accounting for 7.75% of the tourism consumption for the year. The number of tourists reached 415 million, accounting for 6.91% of the total number of tourists for the year. The film industry generated 5.84 billion yuan, accounting for 9.09% of the total film industry revenue for the year.
2. The urban-rural dual economy structure of developing countries refers to the segmentation phenomenon between urban and rural areas. Generally, the biggest difference is that industrial production is prevalent in urban areas, while agricultural production is prevalent in rural areas. Typical dual economy countries include India, China, Vietnam, Brazil, and Mexico.
3. Mobile payment can directly replace cash payment (Yin, Gong, and Pan 2019b) and change people's consumption habits (Yin et al. 2019a). Thus, it played an important role during the pandemic period when isolation measures were encouraged.
4. As mentioned above, the biggest difference is that industrial production dominates urban areas, while agricultural production dominates rural areas. It indicates that urban households have higher dependence on the consumer goods market, while rural households have a relatively low dependence.
5. CHFS is a nationwide sampling survey conducted by the Survey and Research Center for China Household Finance (Li, Wu, and Xiao 2020; Yin, Wu, and Gan 2015). It is mainly used to collect household finance information at the micro level. The CHFS project conducted its first survey in 2011 and conducts a tracking survey every two years. In 2019, the survey collected over 30,000 household micro-data.
6. Although the survey includes two batches, consumption during the Spring Festival occurred before the surveys. Thus, the combination of the two batches of consumption data is appropriate.

Funding

This work was supported by the Chinese National Funding of Social Sciences [grant number: 16AZD014].

ORCID

Taixing Liu ⓘ http://orcid.org/0000-0003-2363-4316

References

Ali, M., N. Alam, and S. A. R. Rizvi. 2020. Coronavirus (COVID-19)—An epidemic or pandemic for financial markets. *Journal of Behavioral and Experimental Finance* 27:100341. doi:10.1016/j.jbef.2020.100341.

Baker, S. R., R. A. Farrokhnia, S. Meyer, M. Pagel, and C. Yannelis. 2020. How does household spending respond to an epidemic? Consumption during the 2020 COVID-19 pandemic. *NBER Working Paper Series.* doi:10.3386/w26949.

Barro, R. J., and J. F. Ursúa. 2008. Macroeconomic crises since 1870. *Brookings Papers on Economic Activity* 39 (1):255–350. doi:10.3386/w13940.

Barro, R. J., J. F. Ursúa, and J. Weng. 2020. The coronavirus and the great Influenza epidemic: Lessons from the "Spanish Flu" for the coronavirus's potential effects on mortality and economic activity. *NBER Working Paper Series.* doi:10.3386/w26866.

Campbell, J. Y., and J. F. Cocco. 2007. How do house prices affect consumption? Evidence from micro data. *Journal of Monetary Economics* 54 (3):591–621. doi:10.3386/w11534.

Chen, H., W. Qian, and Q. Wen. 2020. The impact of the COVID-19 pandemic on consumption: Learning from high frequency transaction data. *SSRN Electronic Journal.* doi:10.2139/ssrn.3568574.

Cohen, M. J. 2020. Does the COVID-19 outbreak mark the onset of a sustainable consumption transition? *Sustainability: Science, Practice and Policy* 16 (1):1–3. doi:10.1080/15487733.2020.1740472.

Correia, S., S. Luck, and E. Verner. 2020. Pandemics depress the economy, public health interventions do not: Evidence from the 1918 Flu. *SSRN Electronic Journal.* doi:10.2139/ssrn.3561560.

Dynan, K. 2012. Is a household debt overhang holding back consumption? *Brookings Papers on Economic Activity* 43 (1):299–362. doi:10.1353/eca.2012.0001.

Haroon, O., and S. A. R. Rizvi. 2020. COVID-19: Media coverage and financial markets behavior—A sectoral inquiry. *Journal of Behavioral and Experimental Finance* 27:100343. doi:10.1016/j.jbef.2020.100343.

Jung, H., M. Park, K. Hong, and E. Hyun. 2016. The impact of an epidemic outbreak on consumer expenditures: An empirical assessment for MERS Korea. *Sustainability* 8 (5):454–69. doi:10.3390/su8050454.

Kukk, M. 2016. How did household indebtedness hamper consumption during the recession? Evidence from micro data. *Journal of Comparative Economics* 44 (3):764–86. doi:10.1016/j.jce.2015.07.004.

Li, J., Y. Wu, and J. Xiao. 2020. The impact of digital finance on household consumption: Evidence from China. *Economic Modelling* 86:317–26. doi:10.1016/j.econmod.2019.09.027.

Li, T., and B. Chen. 2014. Real assets, wealth effect and household consumption: Analysis based on China Household survey data. *Economic Research Journal* 3:62–75. doi:CNKI:SUN:JJYJ.0.2014-03-006.

Narayan, P. K. 2020. Oil price news and COVID-19—Is there any connection? *Energy Research Letters* 1 (1):1–5. https://erl.scholasticahq.com/article/13176-oil-price-news-and-covid-19-is -there-any-connection.

Yin, Z., X. Gong, and B. Pan. 2019a. The effect of mobile payments on household money demand: Micro evidence from the China Household Finance Survey. *Journal of Financial Research* 10:40–58. doi:CNKI:SUN:JRYJ.0.2019-10-003.

Yin, Z., X. Gong, P. Guo, and B. Pan. 2019b. What drives entrepreneurship in digital economy? Evidence from China. *Economic Modelling* 82:66–73. doi:10.1016/j.econmod.2019.09.026.

Yin, Z., Y. Wu, and L. Gan. 2015. Financial availability, financial market participation and household portfolio choice. *Economic Research Journal* 3:87–99. doi:CNKI:SUN:JJYJ.0.2015-03-008.

The Response of the Labor Force Participation Rate to an Epidemic: Evidence from a Cross-Country Analysis

Zhen Yu, Yao Xiao ⓘ, and Yuankun Li

ABSTRACT

Coupled with data on the occurrence of historical epidemics, this study examines the impact of an epidemic on the labor force participation rate of the affected country. We find robust evidence that the outbreak of an epidemic alters human behavior and negatively affects the labor force participation rate. The negative impact could be attributed to cultural attitudes toward uncertainty avoidance. A country with a higher uncertainty avoidance index will suffer from a more significant decline in the labor force participation rate. The negative impact is more pronounced among males and younger workers in low- and middle-income countries.

1. Introduction

The advent of an epidemic can have a major impact on human morbidity and mortality. According to the World Health Organization, an epidemic is defined as the occurrence of health-related events in a particular region which are clearly in excess of the normal expectancy. Epidemics will lead to both direct and indirect losses in affected countries. These losses include deterioration of physical and mental health among the affected population as well as the destruction of business activities. In this article, we aim to examine the impact of epidemic shocks on labor market outcomes. Specifically, we assess the economic impact of historical epidemics on the overall labor force participation rate of the affected country. From a historical perspective, humans remain vulnerable in their encounters with diseases and continue to persist under the burden of epidemics. During the fourteenth century, the spread of the Black Death and smallpox swept across Europe, leading to tens of millions of deaths (Oxley 2003). In the twentieth century, the deadly wave of the 1918 Spanish flu killed up to 50 million people worldwide (Brainerd and Siegler 2003). Today, infectious diseases, both old and new, continue to haunt human beings. Long-established diseases such as cholera often return by surprise, while newly discovered diseases such as COVID-19 pose a vital threat to human life and demand urgent attention from public agencies. Given the frequent reemergence of diseases in human society, it is of vital importance to examine the impact of epidemics.

With regard to the destructiveness of epidemics, previous studies have been limited to the channel of health deterioration among affected populations (Almond 2006; Bleakley 2007; Levinsohn et al. 2013; Thirumurthy, Zivin, and Goldstein 2008). Subsequently, affected countries may experience reduced economic activities and business shutdowns (Béland, Brodeur, and Wright 2020; Coibion, Gorodnichenko, and Weber 2020; Karlsson, Nilsson, and Pichler 2014; Lee and Cho 2017). However, epidemics will also induce changes in human behavior, which is an aspect that has seldom been investigated in the research on labor market outcomes. In this article, we expand the scope of this research by assessing the impact of epidemics through behavioral economics with novel and interesting results. Based on a cross-country panel of historical epidemics, we found that the changing attitudes toward labor force participation could be explained by varied cultural dimensions across countries. Fear of infection and risk aversion cause workers to drift away from engaging in daily production activities with person-to-person contact. We found that a country with a higher uncertainty avoidance index will suffer from a more significant decline in the labor force participation rate. In addition, we conducted a heterogeneity analysis to investigate whether the consequences of epidemics were larger for specific demographic groups. The findings showed that males and young workers were more strongly affected by the epidemic. Relative to high-income countries, the negative impact mainly occurred in low- and middle-income countries.

This article builds on previous research in two ways. First, we investigate the impact of an epidemic on the labor force participation rate. We relate to the literature that documents the economic impact of epidemics and diseases (Acemoglu and Johnson 2007; Ambrus, Field, and Gonzalez 2020; Bleakley 2007; Karlsson, Nilsson, and Pichler 2014; Voigtländer and Voth 2013). Second, we identify a novel channel related to human behavior that drives this impact. We elaborate on the negative impact of epidemics from the standpoint of cultural economics, along with consideration of national characteristics. We complement existing literature on the interpretation of human behavior with regard to the uncertainty avoidance induced by epidemics (Kozak, Crotts, and Law 2007; Pennings, Wansink, and Meulenberg 2002). A country with a higher uncertainty avoidance index will suffer a more significant decline in the labor force participation rate. Our study provides a reference for decision-makers. In order to reduce uncertainty during health emergencies, practices such as maintaining hygiene in public areas and committing to transparency should be taken into consideration.

The remainder of the article is organized as follows: Section 2 reviews the literature and develops the research hypotheses, Section 3 introduces the estimation methodology, Section 4 reports the empirical results, and Section 5 provides a conclusion.

2. Literature Review and Hypotheses Development

2.1. Influence of Epidemics on Labor Force Participation Rate

Researchers have studied the correlation between epidemics and labor force participation in terms of health status (Nwosu and Woolard 2017). Better health is likely to foster an increased probability of labor force participation. On the contrary, health deterioration may negatively affect labor supply, both temporarily and permanently, by deterring individuals from participating in market-related activities.

Moreover, an epidemic is likely to alter human psychology and behavior (Ali, Alam, and Rizvi 2020; Haroon and Rizvi 2020). Given the contagion effect of an epidemic, it is more likely for workers to become infected if their occupations require human interaction. Thus, the labor supply, influenced by risk aversion behaviors, is almost certain to be reduced to a great extent (Evans et al. 2015). Two events demonstrating risk aversion behavior are the Middle East Respiratory Syndrome (MERS) in Korea and the COVID-19 in the United States. When MERS first emerged in Korea, tragic stories of MERS cases spread quickly in newspapers and public media. The unemployment rate in urban areas of Korea worsened, and this was especially significant for workers aged 50 years and above (Lee and Cho 2017). Accordingly, the arrival of COVID-19 has had a drastic impact on the labor market worldwide. The virus has generally caused a decline in the labor force participation rate and a decrease in hours of work in both the United States and Canada (Béland, Brodeur, and Wright 2020). Notably, given the relatively high risk of working, those affected may choose to leave the labor market voluntarily and permanently. Therefore, we hypothesize that the outbreak of an epidemic will have a negative impact on the overall labor force participation rate.

2.2. Uncertainty Avoidance, Epidemics, and Labor Force Participation Rate

From the perspective of cultural economics, collective mental programming and patterns of thinking vary across countries. According to the theory of cultural dimensions, public behavior under certain events can be attributed to cultural dimensions at the country level (Hofstede 1983; Hofstede and McCrae 2004). The uncertainty avoidance index expresses the degree to which members of a society feel uncomfortable with uncertainty. Countries exhibiting strong uncertainty avoidance show anxiety and distrust in the face of the unknown, while societies with weak uncertainty avoidance maintain more relaxed attitudes toward ambiguity.

The outbreak of an epidemic emerges as an important source of uncertainty. Two examples demonstrating uncertainty avoidance triggered by epidemics are the mad cow disease scare in Europe and the 2003 Hong Kong visitor survey. The spread of bovine spongiform encephalopathy (commonly referred to as mad cow disease) across Europe in 2000 led to a change in consumption patterns. As consumers became fearful of contracting the disease through contaminated beef, the consumption of beef fell on a large scale. According to a survey conducted with consumers of different nationalities, Germans, reported by Hofstede to be a culture featuring strong uncertainty avoidance, exhibited the lowest consumption intentions among European countries (Pennings, Wansink, and Meulenberg 2002). In addition, an international visitor survey conducted in Hong Kong in 2003 revealed that the threat of perceived risk would alter travelers' destination choices (Kozak, Crotts, and Law 2007). In other words, it was found that travelers from high uncertainty avoidance index groups were more inclined to change their travel plans due to infectious disease spread or terrorist attacks at the destination. Therefore, we hypothesize that the negative impact of epidemics on the labor force participation rate is more pronounced in countries with higher uncertainty avoidance indices.

3. Estimation Methodology

3.1. Model Setting

This study aimed to examine the causal effect of an epidemic on labor force participation from a cross-country perspective. The purpose of the analysis was to illuminate the complexities of a general phenomenon. We employed an ordinary least squares approach, and the regression model was set as follows:

$$LFPR_{it} = \beta_0 + \beta_1 Shock_{it} + \beta_2 X_{it} + \delta_i + \delta_t + \varepsilon_{it} \tag{1}$$

where $LFPR_{it}$ represents the labor force participation rate in country i in year t, and $Shock_{it}$ is a dummy variable representing the occurrence of an epidemic in country i in year t. δ_i and δ_t refer to country fixed effect and year fixed effect. By employing fixed effect models, the bias from unobserved time-invariant confounders is reduced. Moreover, the panel data set may suffer from a problem of serial correlation. Clustered standard errors can capture the unspecified correlation between observations in the same country in different years (Petersen 2008). Thus, in the rest of the article, we apply standard errors clustered at the country level to account for serial correlation.

In order to test whether uncertainty avoidance exerts a moderating effect on the relationship between the outbreak of an epidemic and labor force participation, the regression model was set as follows:

$$LFPR_{it} = \beta_0 + \beta_1 Shock_{it} + \beta_2*UAI_i + \beta_3 Shock_{it}*UAI_i + \beta_4 X_{it} + \delta_i + \delta_t + \varepsilon_{it}$$

$$(2)$$

where UAI_i represents the uncertainty avoidance index in country i.

3.2. Research Variables

We retrieved data on outbreaks of epidemics from EM-DAT, the International Disaster Database. This database is a widely acknowledged resource for research on disaster-related topics (Boudreaux, Escaleras, and Skidmore 2019; Caruso 2017). To double-check the accuracy of the data, we manually verified the records in the database with information from the World Health Organization, Wikipedia, and official reporting. Data on dynamic labor market outcomes and economic indicators were obtained from the World Development Indicators. Data on cultural dimensions are gathered from Hofstede (Hofstede 1983; Hofstede and McCrae 2004).

The dependent variable in this study is the indicator of the labor force participation rate. The labor force participation rate is calculated as the proportion of the working-age population that is economically active. Specifically, people who supply labor for the production of goods and services are regarded as economically active. Labor force participation generally includes all workers who are employed or actively seeking employment. Thus, in this case, it measures the willingness of workers to actively participate in the labor market.

We focus on the overall labor force participation rate, which is calculated for those aged 15 and above. We also collected data on gender and age groups for comparative analysis. The youth labor force participation rate is calculated for workers aged 15 to 24, while the labor force participation rate for the prime working-age group is calculated for workers aged 25 and above.

The independent variable is denoted as the evaluation of the epidemic. An epidemic is recorded in the database if more than 10 people died or more than 100 people were affected during the course of the disease. In this article, three variables are presented as indicators of an epidemic. First, we construct a dummy variable that is equal to 1 if an epidemic occurs during the period, and 0 otherwise. Second, we use the ratio of total deaths to the total population as a proxy for the severity of the epidemic. For a robustness check, we also apply the ratio of infected cases to the total population as a proxy variable for the extent of the epidemic.

In order to eliminate potential confounding factors that may have affected both the outbreak of an epidemic and the labor force participation rate, we added a set of economic indicators as control variables. Consistent with previous studies on external shocks, we include economic indicators such as GDP per capita, trade openness, and FDI inflow in the regression (Berlemann and Wenzel 2018; Berrebi and Ostwald 2016; Boudreaux, Escaleras, and Skidmore 2019). Wars and disasters other than epidemics may also interfere with labor market outcomes, so we add them as control variables as well. Since the outbreak of an epidemic is closely related to the medical and hygienic conditions of the impacted country, we incorporate hospital beds per capita and physicians per capita as control variables in the regression.

In this article, we are interested in the determinants behind the variation in the labor market. It is assumed that varying attitudes toward an epidemic could be attributed to cultural dimensions at the country level. Therefore, we set the uncertainty avoidance index as the moderating variable. Lower index values represent tolerance for uncertainty, while higher index values represent uncertainty avoidance.

3.3. Descriptive Statistics

From the International Disaster Database, we gathered country-level data on the outbreak of epidemics from 1970 to 2015. Next, we merge the data with economic indicators from the World Bank. After excluding data with missing values, we obtained 2999 records for 134 countries. Figure 1 presents the

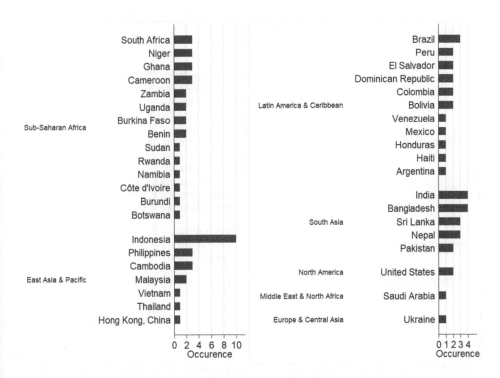

Figure 1. Epidemic shocks by region and country. This graph provides detailed information on the geographical distribution of epidemic shocks across continents and countries. During the sample period, a total of 85 epidemics occurred in 40 countries throughout the seven continents.

geographical distribution of epidemic shocks across continents and countries. During the sample period, a total of 85 epidemics occurred in 40 countries throughout the seven continents. It can be observed from Figure 1 that countries in Sub-Saharan Africa, East Asia Pacific, and Latin America Caribbean suffer suffered the highest epidemic burden.

Figure 2 provides detailed information on the type and name of the epidemic shocks in the sample. Epidemics are classified into four types in the database: bacterial diseases, viral diseases, parasitic diseases, and other diseases. During the sample period, bacterial and viral diseases showed the most frequent outbreaks, accounting for over 90% of the total amount. Moreover, the database also provides specific names for each disease. It can be observed from Figure 2 that cholera is the most common bacterial disease. Among viral diseases, dengue fever and respiratory infectious diseases occur frequently during this period. The records on respiratory infectious disease reflect the outbreak of severe acute respiratory syndrome in 2003 and H1N1 swine flu in 2009, respectively.

Table 1 provides detailed definitions of the major variables, and Table 2 presents the descriptive statistics of these variables. All continuous variables

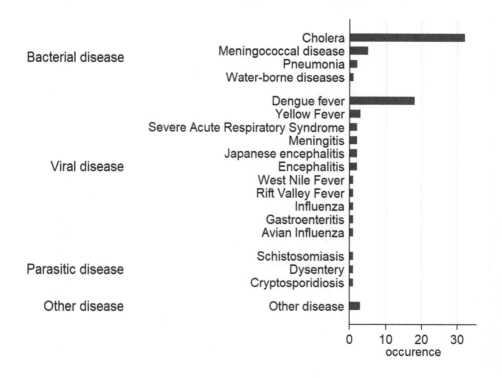

Figure 2. Epidemic shocks by type and name. This graph provides detailed information on the type and name of epidemic shocks in the sample. According to the type of the disease, epidemics are classified into four categories in the database: bacterial diseases, viral diseases, parasitic diseases, and other diseases. The database also provides the specific names of each disease.

Table 1. Definitions of major variables.

Variables	Definition
LFPR	Labor force participation rate
MLFPR	Labor force participation rate, male
FLFPR	Labor force participation rate, female
LFPR1524	Labor force participation rate for aged 15–24
LFPR25	Labor force participation rate for aged 25 and above
Shock	Dummy variable equals 1 if an epidemic occurs during the period and equals 0 otherwise
Ln Mortality ratio	Logarized ratio of total death caused by epidemic to total population
Ln Infection ratio	Logarized ratio of infected cases caused by epidemic to total population
UAI	Uncertainty avoidance index
Ln capita	Logarized GDP per capita (constant PPP)
Trade to GDP	Foreign trade to GDP
FDI to GDP	Net inflow of foreign direct investment to GDP
Per bed	Hospital beds per 1000 population
Per phy	Physicians per 1000 population
War	Dummy variable regarding the occurrence of war during the period
Other	Dummy variable regarding the occurrence of natural disasters during the period

This table reports the definitions of the major variables.

Table 2. Summary statistics of major variables.

Variables	N	Mean	p25	p50	p75	Std. Dev.	Min	Max
LFPR	2999	59.70	53.57	60.30	65.23	9.493	17.99	93
MLFPR	2999	72.88	67.75	73.75	79.29	9.137	32.52	96.10
FLFPR	2999	46.88	38.67	48.24	55.95	14.62	2.440	94
LFPR1524	2620	48.42	38.83	47.69	57.92	13.00	13.04	91.47
LFPR25	2620	63.79	58.02	63.50	68.75	8.991	34.38	94.95
Shock	2999	0.0280	0	0	0	0.166	0	1
Mortality ratio	2999	0	0	0	0	0	0	0.00100
Infection ratio	2999	0	0	0	0	0.00100	0	0.0520
UAI	1947	66.54	49	70	86	23.48	8	100
Ln capita	2999	9.077	8.142	9.132	10.25	1.339	5.439	11.63
Trade to GDP	2999	65.79	38.28	53.47	80.49	49.54	6.622	940.2
FDI to GDP	2999	4.266	0.658	2.011	4.666	7.699	−3.496	55.08
Per bed	2999	4.528	2	3.700	6.200	3.412	0.100	19.90
Per phy	2999	1.875	0.824	1.800	2.857	1.249	0.00700	6.108
War	2999	0.00600	0	0	0	0.0790	0	1
Other	2999	0.201	0	0	0	0.401	0	1

This table reports the summary statistics of the major variables.

are winsorized at the 1% level. The labor force participation rate varies between countries, with a maximum value of 93% and a minimum value of 17.99%. In general, males exhibit a higher labor force participation rate than females. The average value of the labor force participation rate for males is 72.88%, which is almost one-and-a-half times the average value of the labor force participation rate for females. Compared with the prime working-age group, the labor force participation rate is lower among youth. The uncertainty avoidance index ranges from eight to 100. The variances of GDP per capita, trade openness, FDI inflow, and health capacity imply that the included countries have a wide range of income levels. We also consider the occurrence of wars and other natural disasters. It can be inferred that natural disasters occurred frequently during this period.

4. Empirical Results and Analysis

The structure of the empirical analysis is organized as follows. First, we describe how we conduct the baseline regression regarding the impact of epidemics on the labor force participation rate. To validate the baseline results, several robustness checks are subsequently performed. Then, we discuss the mechanism behind the phenomenon and provide an interpretation of our results. Finally, we explore the significance of the heterogeneity analysis with respect to gender, age group, and income level.

4.1. Baseline Results

Columns (1) to (3) of Table 3 present the results for the baseline regression. It is estimated from Column (1) that a one-percentage-point increase in the probability of an epidemic outbreak is associated with a 1.98% lower labor force participation rate. In Columns (2) to (3), $MortalityRatio_{it}$ and $InfectionRatio_{it}$ represent the proportion of total death and infected cases caused by the epidemic with respect to the total population of country i in year t. As evidenced by Column (2), a one-percentage-point increase in the total number of deaths caused by the epidemic, as a proportion of the total population, brings about a 0.46% reduction in the labor force participation rate. It is inferred from Column (3) that a one-percentage-point increase in infected cases caused by an epidemic, as a proportion of the total population, results in a 0.22% lower labor force participation rate. From the baseline results, it is found that the advent of an epidemic is associated with a decline in the willingness to work.

4.2. Robustness Check

To test whether the above results are biased by confounding factors, we conduct several robustness checks to validate our results.

Table 3. Results for labor force participation rate.

Variables	Dependent Variable: Labor Force Participation Rate		
	(1)	(2)	(3)
Shock	−1.98**		
	(0.81)		
Ln Mortality ratio		−0.46***	
		(0.15)	
Ln Infection ratio			−0.22**
			(0.09)
Country FE	Y	Y	Y
Year FE	Y	Y	Y
Control	N	N	N
R^2	0.710	0.711	0.710
N	2999	2999	2999

This table reports the baseline results for the labor force participation rate. All regressions control for country fixed effects and year fixed effects. Robust standard errors are clustered at the country level. *p < 0.10, **p < 0.05, ***p < 0.01.

One concern is that the outbreak of epidemics is related to geographical characteristics. In fact, it is widely acknowledged that certain diseases are region-specific. For instance, malaria is endemic to countries in the tropical zone and not to countries in the temperate zone. Because we control for the country fixed effect and year fixed effect in the baseline regression, the problem of time-invariant factors is mitigated to some extent. Moreover, we add a fixed effect at both the region-year level and income-year level to control for potential time-invariant factors across region and income group levels. The classifications of region and income group levels for countries are derived from the World Bank. The results after the addition of the fixed effects are shown in Table 4. Given the addition of the fixed effects, the coefficients of interest in Columns (1) to (3) remain significant. It can be inferred from Table 4 that time-invariant factors on the region level and income group level will not affect the robustness of our results.

Another concern is that the outbreak of epidemics is associated with the hygiene and health conditions of the specific country. Therefore, we incorporate additional control variables to cover the strength of the overall health system in each country. Specifically, variables such as hospital beds per capita and physicians per capita are added to the baseline regression as indicators of health capacity and healthcare access. Columns (4) to (6) of Table 4 report the estimation results. After adding control variables such as GDP per capita, occurrence of war, occurrence of natural disasters, and health capacity, the results hardly change when compared to the baseline results. All the coefficients of the independent variable are significant, confirming that our results are not driven by potential variations in health system strength across countries.

Table 4. Robustness test with more control variables.

Variables	Dependent Variable: Labor Force Participation Rate					
	(1)	(2)	(3)	(4)	(5)	(6)
Shock	−2.21***			−2.06**		
	(0.84)			(0.81)		
Ln Mortality ratio		−0.51***			−0.46***	
		(0.16)			(0.15)	
Ln Infection ratio			−0.21**			−0.22**
			(0.09)			(0.09)
Country FE	Y	Y	Y	Y	Y	Y
Year FE	Y	Y	Y	Y	Y	Y
Region*Year FE	Y	Y	Y	N	N	N
Income level*Year FE	Y	Y	Y	N	N	N
Control	N	N	N	Y	Y	Y
R^2	0.772	0.772	0.771	0.716	0.716	0.716
N	2963	2963	2963	2999	2999	2999

This table reports results with more control variables. Columns (1) to (3) control for the fixed effect at the region-year level and income-year level. All regressions control for country fixed effects and year fixed effects. Robust standard errors are clustered at the country level.
*$p < 0.10$, **$p < 0.05$, ***$p < 0.01$.

An epidemic may be induced by an outbreak of a natural disaster. Natural disasters such as hurricanes and earthquakes can destroy residents' dwellings. Thus, the affected population may be forced to leave the disaster site and relocate to temporary shelters. Although the displacement process is a common adaptation to natural disasters, it will increase the risk of injury, infection, or death from adverse health consequences. Owing to the worsening hygienic conditions under such circumstances, communicable disease transmission is likely to increase among the affected population as a secondary disaster. Exposure to natural disasters has been found to increase the risk of additional vulnerability to secondary disasters (Loebach and Korinek 2019). In Table 5, we exclude the occurrence of secondary disasters in the regression. The coefficients of the independent variable remain negative and significant at the 5% level in Columns (1) to (3). The baseline effect remains unchanged after excluding secondary disasters from the sample. Therefore, it can be interpreted that our results are not driven by the occurrence of secondary disasters.

4.3. Impulse-Response Analysis

In this section, we apply the panel vector autoregression method to analyze the response of the labor force participation rate to an epidemic. The impulse-response function traces the impact of an external shock from a variable on another variable. In this case, it depicts how the labor market adjusts to the outbreak of an epidemic. Figure 3 presents graphs of the impulse-response functions. The variables are demeaned to eliminate unobservable heterogeneity among different countries. In line with previous literature, the results are generated by Monte Carlo simulation with 1000 repetitions at the 5% confidence level (Kang and Min 2016; Sierra and Vidal Alejandro 2019). Across each of the graphs in Figure 3, the labor market responds immediately and significantly to the advent of an epidemic. The labor force participation rate

Table 5. Robustness test with exclusion of secondary disaster.

Variables	Dependent Variable: Labor Force Participation Rate		
	(1)	(2)	(3)
Shock	−2.11**		
	(0.83)		
Ln Mortality ratio		−0.47***	
		(0.16)	
Ln Infection ratio			−0.23**
			(0.09)
Country FE	Y	Y	Y
Year FE	Y	Y	Y
Control	Y	Y	Y
R^2	0.715	0.715	0.715
N	2997	2997	2997

This table reports the results excluding the occurrence of secondary disasters. All regressions control for country fixed effects and year fixed effects. Robust standard errors are clustered at the country level. *p < 0.10, **p < 0.05, ***p < 0.01.

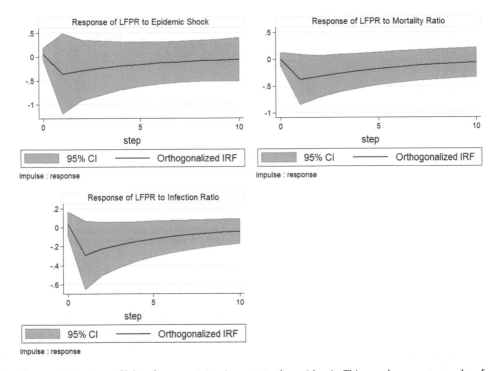

Figure 3. Response of labor force participation rate to the epidemic. This graph presents graphs of the impulse-response functions. The variables are demeaned to eliminate unobservable heterogeneity among different countries. The results were generated by Monte Carlo simulation with 1000 repetitions at the 5% confidence level.

displays a declining trend in the face of an epidemic. However, the negative impact is only temporary and gradually fades away. The labor market of the affected country will recover from the external shock and return to normal five years after the epidemic. These findings are consistent with the results from the ordinary least squares approach.

4.4. Mechanism Analysis

It is concluded that an epidemic exerts a negative impact on the labor force participation rate of the affected country. Next, we explore the mechanism behind this phenomenon in detail.

Table 6 presents the moderating effect of cultural dimensions on the labor force participation rate. As shown in Column (2), the coefficients on the interaction term are found to be negatively significant at the 5% level. It is revealed that countries with higher uncertainty avoidance indices suffer more significant declines in the labor force participation rate. Nonetheless, the coefficients of the epidemic shock and the infection ratio were found to be insignificant. It is therefore implied that when compared with the infection ratio, the mortality ratio better reflects the severity of an

Table 6. Moderating effect of cultural dimensions.

Variables	Dependent Variable: Labor Force Participation Rate		
	(1)	(2)	(3)
Shock	3.02		
	(2.80)		
Ln Mortality ratio		1.09*	
		(0.59)	
Ln Infection ratio			0.47
			(0.32)
Interaction with UAI	−0.06	−0.02**	−0.01
	(0.05)	(0.01)	(0.01)
Country FE	Y	Y	Y
Year FE	Y	Y	Y
Control	Y	Y	Y
R^2	0.732	0.734	0.733
N	1947	1947	1947

This table reports the moderating effect of cultural dimensions on the labor force participation rate. All regressions control for country fixed effects and year fixed effects. Robust standard errors are clustered at the country level.
*$p < 0.10$, **$p < 0.05$, ***$p < 0.01$.

epidemic. Fear of death is more pronounced in fatal diseases. Thus, the perception of risk matters only if the epidemic has serious adverse consequences.

4.5. Heterogeneity Analysis

In this section, we explore the variations across gender, age group, and income level regarding the causal relationship between an epidemic and the labor force participation rate.

Generally, each gender is assigned different roles and functions in the construction of social identity. Males are perceived as breadwinners, while females are more likely to play the role of housekeepers. Accordingly, men tend to have a higher labor force participation rate than women (Cho et al. 2012; Hyde, George, and Kumar 2019). Given the lower labor force participation rate for females relative to males, the slumping effect is more significant for males than for females. Unit record data from the Australian National Health Surveys show that chronic illnesses negatively affect the probability of labor force participation among males (Zhang, Zhao, and Harris 2009). Additionally, evidence from the outbreak of COVID-19 in the United States has revealed that the negative impact on labor market outcomes is larger for men (Béland, Brodeur, and Wright 2020).

Table 7 displays the estimation results for the labor force participation rate for both males and females. Columns (1) to (3) show the results for the labor force participation rate for males, and Columns (4) to (6) show the results for females. Compared with the baseline results in Table 3, the advent of an epidemic appears to lead to a larger decline in the labor force participation rate among males. It can be observed that the coefficients in Columns (1) to (3)

Table 7. Results for heterogeneity analysis on gender.

Variables	Panel A: Labor Force Participation Rate, Male			Panel B: Labor Force Participation Rate, Female		
	(1)	(2)	(3)	(4)	(5)	(6)
Shock	−2.33**			−1.66*		
	(1.04)			(0.95)		
Ln Mortality ratio		−0.46**			−0.44**	
		(0.19)			(0.18)	
Ln Infection ratio			−0.28**			−0.17*
			(0.11)			(0.09)
Country FE	Y	Y	Y	Y	Y	Y
Year FE	Y	Y	Y	Y	Y	Y
Control	Y	Y	Y	Y	Y	Y
R^2	0.629	0.629	0.629	0.837	0.837	0.837
N	2999	2999	2999	2999	2999	2999

This table reports results on labor force participation rate for both males and females. Panel A reports results on labor force participation rate for males, while Panel B reports results on labor force participation rate for females. All regressions control for country fixed effects and year fixed effects. Robust standard errors are clustered at the country level.
*$p < 0.10$, **$p < 0.05$, ***$p < 0.01$.

are greater than those in Columns (4) to (6). The significance levels are also higher for the coefficients in Columns (1) to (3). These findings are consistent with those of previous studies showing that ill health affects the probability of labor force participation more significantly for males. Since men generally have a higher workforce participation rate than women, the declining trend is, therefore, likely to be more pronounced among men.

Given their lack of work experience, young people are often perceived as unskilled rather than professional or skilled labor (Smith 2012). Young workers are more likely to take on jobs with fewer educational requirements. On the contrary, owing to increased completion rates in terms of education and the attainment of relevant work experience, mature-age workers exhibit higher confidence in gaining employment. As evidenced by the Global Financial Crisis in 2008, the labor force participation rate and unemployment rate among the young workers went through a slower recovery compared with the corresponding rates for the prime working-age group (Denny and Churchill 2016). Since young people possess a lower level of human capital and productivity, the impact of an economic crisis is greater for them (Cho et al. 2012). In addition, it is estimated that the COVID-19 pandemic in the United States has engendered greater effects on younger workers' labor force participation (Béland, Brodeur, and Wright 2020).

Table 8 shows the estimation results for the labor force participation rate by age group. In Columns (1) to (3), the dependent variable is set as the labor force participation rate for the young workers, while in Columns (4) to (6), the dependent variable is the labor force participation rate for the mature-age group. The outbreak of an epidemic is associated with a 1.76% decrease in the labor force participation rate among young people. A one-percentage-point increase in the total deaths caused by an epidemic, as a proportion of the total population, brings about a 0.57% reduction in the labor force participation rate for the young. It can be

Table 8. Results for heterogeneity analysis on age group.

Variables	Panel A: Population Aged 15–24			Panel B: Population Aged 25 and Above		
	(1)	(2)	(3)	(4)	(5)	(6)
Shock	−1.76*			−1.06		
	(1.06)			(0.65)		
Ln Mortality ratio		−0.57**			−0.32**	
		(0.22)			(0.13)	
Ln Infection ratio			−0.16			−0.11
			(0.11)			(0.07)
Country FE	Y	Y	Y	Y	Y	Y
Year FE	Y	Y	Y	Y	Y	Y
Control	Y	Y	Y	Y	Y	Y
R^2	0.798	0.799	0.798	0.819	0.820	0.819
N	2620	2620	2620	2620	2620	2620

This table reports results on labor force participation rate by age group. Panel A reports results on labor force participation rate for the youth, while Panel B reports results on labor force participation rate for mature-age group. All regressions control for country fixed effects and year fixed effects. Robust standard errors are clustered at the country level.
*p < 0.10, **p < 0.05, ***p < 0.01.

noticed that the coefficients of interest in Columns (4) to (6) are lower than the coefficients in Columns (1) to (3), indicating that the young are more susceptible to external shocks such as epidemics.

In less developed countries, the overall labor force participation rate is higher due to lower educational participation (O'Higgins 2003). Table 9 reports the estimation results on the labor force participation rate by income group level. Columns (1) to (3) show the results for low- and lower-middle-income countries, Columns (4) to (6) show the results for upper middle-income economies, and Columns (7) to (9) report the results for high-income economies. The coefficients of interest in Columns (1) to (3) are all significant. For low- and lower-middle-income countries, the outbreak of an epidemic is associated with a 2.38% decrease in the labor force participation rate. A one-percentage-point increase in the total deaths, as a proportion of the total population, leads to a 0.45% reduction in the

Table 9. Results for heterogeneity analysis on income level.

Variables	Panel A: Low & Lower Middle Income Countries			Panel B: Upper Middle Income Countries			Panel C: High Income Countries		
	(1)	(2)	(3)	(4)	(5)	(6)	(7)	(8)	(9)
Shock	−2.38**			−1.02			−0.42		
	(0.99)			(2.04)			(0.64)		
Ln Mortality ratio		−0.45**			−0.55			−0.82	
		(0.18)			(0.56)			(0.57)	
Ln Infection ratio			−0.23**			−0.12			−0.27
			(0.11)			(0.20)			(0.24)
Country FE	Y	Y	Y	Y	Y	Y	Y	Y	Y
Year FE	Y	Y	Y	Y	Y	Y	Y	Y	Y
Control	Y	Y	Y	Y	Y	Y	Y	Y	Y
R^2	0.679	0.679	0.678	0.812	0.813	0.812	0.787	0.788	0.787
N	1340	1340	1340	658	658	658	998	998	998

This table reports results on labor force participation rate by income level. Panel A reports results on labor force participation rate for low- and lower middle-income countries, Panel B reports results on labor force participation rate for upper middle-income economies, while Panel C reports results for high-income economies. All regressions control for country fixed effects and year fixed effects. Robust standard errors are clustered at the country level.
*p < 0.10, **p < 0.05, ***p < 0.01.

labor force participation rate. Accordingly, a one-percentage-point increase in the infected cases, as a proportion of the total population, results in a 0.23% lower labor force participation rate. In contrast, the coefficients in Columns (4) to (9) are all insignificant, indicating that the negative impact is only valid for countries with low- and lower-middle-income levels.

5. Conclusion

The outbreak of an epidemic exerts a considerable influence on economic activities and human behavior. Coupled with cross-country data recording the occurrence of epidemics from the 1970s onwards, we examined the response of the labor market to historical epidemic shocks. Based on the results, we arrived at the following conclusions. First, an epidemic has a significant negative impact on the overall labor force participation rate for the affected country. The results were robust to specification checks. Second, cultural and behavioral economics could account for this phenomenon. The negative impact was found to be more pronounced in countries with higher uncertainty avoidance indices. Moreover, the negative impact varies across gender, age group, and income level. Compared with females, males were found to exhibit more extensive declines with respect to their labor force participation rate. Relative to the mature-age group, young workers were found to be more strongly affected. The negative impact was more apparent in low- and middle-income countries than in high-income ones.

Our study underscores that the outbreak of an epidemic is likely to affect human behavior, and these results have illuminating policy implications. First, a comprehensive understanding of the epidemic shock can facilitate policy-making to properly cope with this issue. The solution to mitigate the negative impact lies in concerted efforts to reduce exposure to potential risks. Measures such as maintaining hygiene in public areas and committing to transparency during health emergencies could alleviate potential panic. Second, the scale of the impact varies across groups. Thus, the group that suffers the most from the burden of an epidemic ought to receive the most support. Services such as training courses will assist discouraged workers in gaining hands-on knowledge so that they can return to the labor market. Financial aid programs specifically targeting the vulnerable will help them overcome the hardships of the post-epidemic period. Third, the recurrence of an epidemic would trigger an evolu-tion in the work style of an entire generation. In order to curb the spread of contamination, workers should temporarily work from home. In the short term, work-from-home should be adopted as a self-quarantine measure to combat the epidemic, while in the long run, workers may need to adjust to working in the home office on a permanent basis. Such practices are likely to eliminate the negative impact of a potential epidemic in the future.

Funding

This work was supported by the Ministry of Education of the People's Republic of China [Grant Number: 18JZD034 and 18YJA790099]; Fundamental Research Funds for the Central Universities.

ORCID

Yao Xiao ⓘ http://orcid.org/0000-0002-2258-9421

References

Acemoglu, D., and S. Johnson. 2007. Disease and development: The effect of life expectancy on economic growth. *Journal of Political Economy* 115 (6):925–85. doi:10.1086/529000.

Ali, M., N. Alam, and S. A. R. Rizvi. 2020. Coronavirus (COVID-19) – An epidemic or pandemic for financial markets. *Journal of Behavioral and Experimental Finance* 27:100341. doi:10.1016/j.jbef.2020.100341.

Almond, D. 2006. Is the 1918 influenza pandemic over? Long-term effects of in utero influenza exposure in the post-1940 U.S. population. *Journal of Political Economy* 114 (4):672–712. doi:10.1086/507154.

Ambrus, A., E. Field, and R. Gonzalez. 2020. Loss in the time of cholera: Long-run impact of a disease epidemic on the urban landscape. *American Economic Review* 110:475–525. doi:10.1257/aer.20190759.

Béland, L., A. Brodeur, and T. Wright. 2020. The short-term economic consequences of COVID-19: Exposure to disease, remote work and government response. *Working paper.*

Berlemann, M., and D. Wenzel. 2018. Hurricanes, economic growth and transmission channels: Empirical evidence for countries on differing levels of development. *World Development* 105:231–47. doi:10.1016/j.worlddev.2017.12.020.

Berrebi, C., and J. Ostwald. 2016. Terrorism and the labor force: Evidence of an effect on female labor force participation and the labor gender gap. *Journal of Conflict Resolution* 60:32–60. doi:10.1177/0022002714535251.

Bleakley, H. 2007. Disease and development: Evidence from hookworm eradication in the American South. *The Quarterly Journal of Economics* 122:73–117. doi:10.1162/qjec.121.1.73.

Boudreaux, C. J., M. P. Escaleras, and M. Skidmore. 2019. Natural disasters and entrepreneurship activity. *Economics Letters* 182:82–85. doi:10.1016/j.econlet.2019.06.010.

Brainerd, E., and M. V. Siegler. 2003. The economic effects of the 1918 influenza epidemic. CEPR Discussion Paper, No. 3791. London, UK.

Caruso, G. D. 2017. The legacy of natural disasters: The intergenerational impact of 100 years of disasters in Latin America. *Journal of Development Economics* 127:209–33. doi:10.1016/j.jdeveco.2017.03.007.

Cho, Y., D. Margolis, D. Newhouse, and D. Robalino. 2012. Labor markets in low and middle income countries: Trends and implications for social protection and labor policies. *World Bank Social Protection Discussion Paper*, 67613.

Coibion, O., Y. Gorodnichenko, and M. Weber. 2020. Labor markets during the Covid-19 crisis: A preliminary view. *University of Chicago, Becker Friedman Institute for Economics Working Paper*, 6–20.

Denny, L., and B. Churchill. 2016. Youth employment in Australia: A comparative analysis of labour force participation by age group. *Journal of Applied Youth Studies* 1:5.

Evans, D., F. Ferreira, H. Lofgren, M. Maliszewska, M. Over, and M. Cruz. 2015. Estimating the economic impact of the 2014-2015 Ebola epidemic: CGE based analysis. *Conference paper.* Melbourne, Australia.

Haroon, O., and S. A. R. Rizvi. 2020. COVID-19: Media coverage and financial markets behavior—A sectoral inquiry. *Journal of Behavioral and Experimental Finance* 27:100343. doi:10.1016/j.jbef.2020.100343.

Hofstede, G. 1983. National cultures in four dimensions: A research-based theory of cultural differences among nations. *International Studies of Management and Organization* 13 (1--2):46–74. doi:10.1080/00208825.1983.11656358.

Hofstede, G., and R. R. McCrae. 2004. Personality and culture revisited: Linking traits and dimensions of culture. *Cross-Cultural Research* 38:52–88. doi:10.1177/1069397103259443.

Hyde, M., S. George, and V. Kumar. 2019. Trends in work and employment in rapidly developing countries. In *Handbook of disability, work and health*, 1–20. Cham Springer International Publishing.

Kang, S., and S. Min. 2016. Effect of the sovereign credit ratings in East Asia Countries: Evidence from panel vector autoregression. *Emerging Markets Finance and Trade* 52:1121–44. doi:10.1080/1540496X.2015.1103122.

Karlsson, M., T. Nilsson, and S. Pichler. 2014. The impact of the 1918 Spanish flu epidemic on economic performance in Sweden: An investigation into the consequences of an extraordinary mortality shock. *Journal of Health Economics* 36:1–19. doi:10.1016/j.jhealeco.2014.03.005.

Kozak, M., J. C. Crotts, and R. Law. 2007. The impact of the perception of risk on international travellers. *International Journal of Tourism Research* 9:233–42. doi:10.1002/jtr.607.

Lee, A., and J. Cho. 2017. The impact of city epidemics on rural labor market: The Korean Middle East respiratory syndrome case. *Japan and the World Economy* 43:30–40. doi:10.1016/j.japwor.2017.10.002.

Levinsohn, J., Z. M. McLaren, O. Shisana, and K. Zuma. 2013. HIV status and labor market participation in South Africa. *Review of Economics and Statistics* 95:98–108. doi:10.1162/REST_a_00237.

Loebach, P., and K. Korinek. 2019. Disaster vulnerability, displacement, and infectious disease: Nicaragua and Hurricane Mitch. *Population and Environment* 40:434–55. doi:10.1007/s11111-019-00319-4.

Nwosu, C. O., and I. Woolard. 2017. The impact of health on labour force participation in South Africa. *South African Journal of Economics* 85:481–90. doi:10.1111/saje.12163.

O'Higgins, N. 2003. Trends in the youth labour market in developing and transition countries. *World Bank Social Protection Discussion Paper Series*. Washington, DC: World Bank Group.

Oxley, D. 2003. 'The seat of death and terror': Urbanization, stunting, and smallpox. *The Economic History Review* 56:623–56. doi:10.1111/j.1468-0289.2003.00264.x.

Pennings, J. M. E., B. Wansink, and M. T. G. Meulenberg. 2002. A note on modeling consumer reactions to a Crisis: The case of the mad cow disease. *International Journal of Research in Marketing* 19:91–100. doi:10.1016/S0167-8116(02)00050-2.

Petersen, M. A. 2008. Estimating standard errors in finance panel data sets: Comparing approaches. *The Review of Financial Studies* 22:435–80. doi:10.1093/rfs/hhn053.

Sierra, L. P., and P. Vidal Alejandro. 2019. The impact of emerging Asia's demand on the Pacific Alliance Countries. *Emerging Markets Finance and Trade* 1–19. doi:10.1080/1540496X.2019.1693362.

Smith, C. L. 2012. The impact of low-skilled immigration on the youth labor market. *Journal of Labor Economics* 30:55–89. doi:10.1086/662073.

Thirumurthy, H., J. G. Zivin, and M. Goldstein. 2008. The economic impact of aids treatment labor supply in Western Kenya. *Journal of Human Resources* 43:511–52. doi:10.1353/jhr.2008.0009.

Voigtländer, N., and H.-J. Voth. 2013. The three horsemen of riches: Plague, war, and urbanization in early modern Europe. *Review of Economic Studies* 80:774–811. doi:10.1093/restud/rds034.

Zhang, X., X. Zhao, and A. Harris. 2009. Chronic diseases and labour force participation in Australia. *Journal of Health Economics* 28:91–108. doi:10.1016/j.jhealeco.2008.08.001.

Implications of COVID-19 Pandemic on the Global Trade Networks

C. T. Vidya and K. P. Prabheesh

ABSTRACT

This article measures the trade interconnectedness among countries before and after the COVID-19 outbreak, and forecasts the future direction of trade. Using Trade Network Analysis and Artificial Neural Networks, our findings show that: (1) There is a drastic reduction in trade interconnectedness, connectivity, and density among countries after the COVID-19 outbreak. (2) There is a visible change in the structure of trade-network (3) China's 'center' position in the trade network is not affected by the pandemic. (4) There will be a drastic decline in trade of most of the economies until December 2020.

1. Introduction

The COVID-19 pandemic is going to be the most serious global economic crisis after the economic depression of the 1930s. The scope for complacency is somewhat limited for most of the countries across the globe facing falling economic growth, decelerating trade, burgeoning global imbalances, and debilitating financial markets leading to freezing of the monetary system. If the crisis which happened a decade ago in 2008 was a massive blow to both global trade and financial markets, then the current pandemic crisis may result in disruptions both in demand and supply. As per the World Bank (2020) projection, the world Gross Domestic Product (GDP) is expected to decline considerably in 2020 due to the COVID-19 pandemic (Figure 1). Advanced economies are projected to shrink by 7% in 2020, whereas the emerging and developing economies by 2.5%. Similarly, global trade is also expected to decline by more 13% in 2020, which is more than that of World War II (Figure 2). These figures indicate a significant decline in global trade owing to the COVID-19 pandemic. Countries such as China, Korea, Italy, Japan, the US, and Germany witnessed a significant increase in the COVID-19 cases in March 2020. A lockdown was implemented in order to contain the spread of the infection. As a result of the lockdown, the manufacturing sector came to a complete standstill in these economies. As manufacturing production in

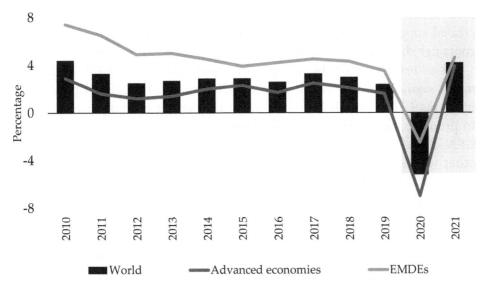

Figure 1. Trends in Global GDP growth. The figure presents the trends in real GDP growth of world, advanced, and emerging and developing economies. The data come from Global Economic Prospects, World Bank June, (2020). Where the shaded area indicates forecasts. Similarly, EMDEs denotes emerging markets and developing economies. Data for 2019 are estimates. Aggregate growth rates calculated using GDP weights at 2010 prices and market exchange rates.

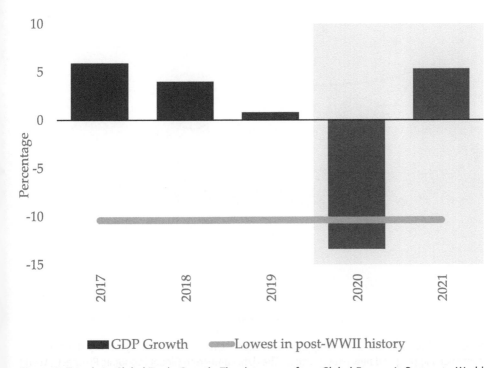

Figure 2. Trends in Global Trade Growth. The data come from Global Economic Prospects, World Bank June, (2020). Where the shaded area indicates forecasts. Trade is the average of import and export volumes and represented in percentage terms.

these countries is interlinked with the global trade network, the pandemic has created supply chain disruptions. There has been a reduction in volume of container shipping, as a result of shrinking global trade (Figure 3).

Let us briefly revisit the scenario of world trade before COVID-19. The major segment of the world trade was characterized by global production networks (GPN) which benefited many developing economies and helped to promote industrialization and thereby increase productivity. Because of GPN, the gap between the center and periphery regions was narrowed. In other words, trade diversification and fragmentation of production led to higher trade in intermediaries, and thus countries like India, China, and Korea emerged as the leaders and export hubs of goods in the global market (Vidya, Prabheesh., and Sirowa 2020). In particular, China, Japan, and Korea turned out to be the 'centre' of the global supply chains in most manufactured goods due to their comparative advantage in production and distribution. China turned out to be the supplier of industrial parts and components and emerged as a 'workshop of the world'. Similarly, Japan, Korea, and India became hubs of 'factory Asia' for Information and communication technology (ICT) services (Baldwin and Tomiura 2020).

We hypothesize that the COVID-19 pandemic has distorted the trade network due to the suspension of production in many countries and the

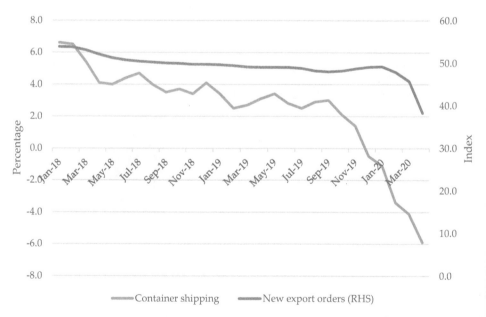

Figure 3. Trends in Container Shipping and Export Orders. The figure presents the trends in container shipping and new export orders. The data come from Global Economic Prospects, World Bank June, (2020). Where container shipping measured in percentage terms, new export orders are for manufacturing and measured by Purchasing Managers' Index (PMI). PMI readings above (below) 50 indicate expansion (contraction) in economic activity.

unavailability of intermediate products. In the GPN, the intermediate inputs cross the border several times before the final product is shipped to the last customer (Eichengreen and O'rourke 2009; Escaith, Lindenberg., and Miroudot 2010). Hence, a negative supply shock would disrupt the trade networks through the cessation of production processes and hindered transportation and logistics. Baldwin and Freedman (2020) argue that trade and supply chain disruptions in the global supply chains due to the present pandemic may lead to high contraction of demand. Theoretically, the production network and locations can be distorted due to random shocks[1] which may lead to shifts in economic fundamentals (Krugman 1997). The existing studies in this context mostly focussed on the impact of natural disasters and financial crisis on trade (Ando and Kimura 2012; Escaith et al. 2011; Korniyenko, Pinat, and Dew 2017; Martin, Alexander, and Robert 2006). The global financial crisis 2008–09 distorted the production network through a reduction in demand from the crisis originated in developed countries. In contrast, the COVID-19 pandemic disrupted GPN through a reduction in the supply of intermediate products, through suspension of production owing to lockdown. However, recent studies on the impact of the COVID-19 pandemic have mostly focussed on financial markets (Ali, Alam, and Rizvi 2020; Apergis and Apergis 2020; Fu and Shen 2020; Gil-Alana and Monge 2020; Haroon and Rizvi 2020; Liu et al., 2020; Narayan 2020; Phan and Narayan 2020; Qin, Zhang., and Su 2020). Hence, the present study tries to analyze the impact of COVID-19 pandemic on the world trade network. More specifically, the study addresses the following questions: (i) Has there been any considerable change in the trade network due to the pandemic? (ii) Has there been any decline in trade interconnectedness among countries? (iii) Does the pandemic lead to a reduction in trade density? (iv) How long will the trade shrinkage be prolonged?

Our approach toward testing the above issues is as follows. To examine the trade network, we apply Trade Network Analysis on the top 15 global trading countries for the pre- and post- COVID-19 outbreak period. These include Canada, the US, UK, Germany, France, Italy, Japan, South Korea, China, Hong Kong, India, Indonesia, Russia, Netherlands, and Singapore. We use network centrality parameters such as degree, closeness, eigenvector, and density to examine the trade structure. Finally, we applied the Artificial Neural Network (ANN) to forecast the duration of the trade shrinkage due to COVID-19. Our empirical findings reveal that: (1) There has been drastic reduction in trade interconnectedness, connectivity, and density among countries in 2020Q1 as compared to 2008. (2) There is a noticeable change in the structure of the trade-network. (3) China's 'center' position in the trade network is not affected by the pandemic. (4) It is predicted that the trade shrinkage will continue until the end of 2020.

This study is one of the first attempts to analyze the impact of COVID-19 on the global trade network, and hence, the findings of the study provide a valuable guide to frame policies to promote international trade at present and in the post-pandemic scenario. The rest of the article is organized as follows. Section 2 and 3 present data methodology; Sections 4 presents the empirical results and Section 5 presents the conclusions.

2. Data

We addressed the research issue from the top 15 global trading countries, based on their contribution to global trade. These countries include Canada, US, UK, Germany, France, Italy, Japan, South Korea, China, Hong Kong, India, Indonesia, Russia, Netherlands, and Singapore. Data has been drawn from the CEIC database and WTO database. To represent the trade network, we compared the structure of the trade network for two periods. One is based on annual data for the year 2018, and the second is based on quarterly data, for 2020Q1, to examine the changes in network due to the COVID-19 pandemic. For a network analysis of raw bilateral trade data, we calculated an export matrix, and the value of every cell in the matrix is the mean of exports of country A to country B and imports of B from A. Finally, to forecast the exports and imports, we use quarterly data from 2016Q4-2020Q1 of the eight economies due to the unavailability of data and its inconsistencies.

3. Methodology

In this section, we first discuss the key methodologies we have applied in the article. First, we discuss Artificial Neural Networks that is applied to forecast the exports and imports during the pandemic. Second, trade network analysis is used to understand the center–periphery interface.

3.1. Trade Network Analysis

The network is a mathematical representation of the state of a system at a given point in time in terms of nodes and links (Fagiolo, Reyes., and Schiavo 2010). In this article, we examine the trade interconnectedness and density using this methodology.[2] Network analysis sees the relationship between different elements in terms of nodes and edges. Nodes act as individual actors and edges are relationships between nodes, where out-degree is the number of outgoing edges, and the in-degree is the number of incoming edges. Every node has in-degree and out-degree. At the outset, we construct the trade structure from a network perspective which involves building centrality parameters, such as degree, closeness, eigenvector, and overall density. Where degree and closeness indicate the interconnectedness and geodesic distance, respectively. Whereas eigenvector measures network connectivity (See Appendix A for details). We construct the network by preparing an undirected network matrix with N = 15 countries for the years 2018 and 2020Q1.

3.2. Artificial Neural Networks (ANN)

In the present article, we use ANN to forecast exports and imports. The major strength of ANN as compared to time series models is as follows. First, it deals with problems of seasonality, non-stationarity, and varying patterns of non-linearity present in economic and financial time series (Tseng, Yu, and Tzeng 2002). Second, the functional form for the model is not necessary as the model is adaptively formed based on the features present in the data, making it appropriate for situations where a priori theoretical expectations are unknown, not accounted for, or even outright violated (Chuku, Impasa, and Duor 2019).[3] We applied what is called Long Short-Term Memory (LSTM) variant of Recurrent Neural Networks (RNN) in this context. LSTM has the capability to store a long-running memory about the sequence along with short-run memory of the most recent network outputs. Therefore, it allows the network to draw upon broad contextual features in the data (long-run memory) as well as information provided by only the most recent elements in a sequence (short-run memory) (Cook and Hall 2017). LSTM is more appropriate for modeling economic data where there is a long-term dependence in time series due to the lagged effect (Hao et al. 2020). A simple description of the LSTM is given in Appendix B. In order to forecast the exports, we took standard variables such as domestic income, proxied by industrial production index and exchange rate as inputs. Similarly, to forecast the imports, global income proxied by industrial production index of the US and exchange rate, was taken as inputs. We use monthly data and split 60% of the data for training and 40% for forecasting and validation. An LSTM model with the following specifications is built: Input Layers = 1, Hidden layers = 1 (50 units) and Output layers = 1. This model is trained on our training set data for 5000 epochs. The model is optimized such that the MSE (mean-square error) is minimized. After training and evaluating the forecast, we predict the future values of exports and imports up to the end of the year 2020.

4. Empirical Findings

The impact of COVID-19 on world trade has been severe. We took two periods for comparison 2018 and 2020Q1 to analyze the network and corresponding network centrality parameters which are reported in Table 1. It can be seen that all parameters such as degree, closeness, and eigenvectors have declined in 2020Q1 as compared to 2018 in all selected countries. This indicates there is less interconnectedness and fall in trade connectivity

Table 1. Network Centrality Parameters, 2018 and 2020 Q1.

	Degree		Closeness		Eigenvector	
	2018	2020Q1	2018	2020Q1	2018	2020Q1
Canada	1.07	NA	0.78	NA	0.23	NA
China	2.00	1.21	1.00	0.67	0.30	0.24
France	1.64	0.53	0.78	0.74	0.23	0.27
Germany	1.78	0.53	0.93	0.69	0.28	0.27
Hong Kong	1.35	0.48	0.78	0.74	0.22	0.28
India	1.85	0.96	0.88	0.80	0.26	0.26
Indonesia	1.21	0.54	0.64	0.74	0.15	0.29
Italy	1.57	0.50	0.78	0.74	0.22	0.31
Japan	1.92	1.03	1.00	0.74	0.30	0.27
Netherlands	1.71	0.50	0.93	0.74	0.28	0.31
Russia	1.42	0.45	0.74	0.75	0.21	0.27
Singapore	1.64	0.45	0.88	0.77	0.26	0.29
South Korea	1.92	0.58	1.00	0.74	0.30	0.29
UK	1.92	0.81	1.00	0.72	0.30	0.28
US	1.92	0.75	1.00	0.74	0.30	0.28
Overall Trade Density	0.833 (2018)				0.429 (2020Q1)	

This table shows the result from trade network analysis. Degree, closeness, eigenvector and density are centrality parameters derived from network analysis. Where degree and closeness indicate the interconnectedness and geodesic distance, respectively. Whereas eigenvector measures network connectivity. The network is constructed by preparing an undirected network matrix with N = 15 countries for the years 2018 and 2020Q1.

among the trading countries. The COVID-19 pandemic has severely hit trade interconnectedness of countries such as Germany, Italy, France, USA, UK as these countries show a steep reduction in degree centrality. It is important to note that the overall trade density has declined from 0.833 to 0.429 during the same period. This indicates that there has been more than 50% reduction in the trade density among the countries in the network in 2020 Q1 compared to the 2018.

The network graphs (Figures 4 and 5) present an interesting picture. In 2018, the countries that are in the 'center' of the trade network are China, South Korea, India, USA, and UK, and China is exactly in the middle. As China is considered as the 'factory of the world', many countries in the world are dependent on Chinese exports for their production. But the network of 2020Q1 shows there is a slight deviation of China from the 'centre' to a repositioning but still within the 'circle of centre' countries. This clearly indicates that even though the COVID-19 pandemic originated in China in December 2019 and impacted its trade, the country's relative position in the trade network has not changed drastically. The other countries in the center of the network in 2020 were Japan and India. Another important observation is that the position of South Korea has drastically changed in 2020 and it has become a peripheral economy from having been a center economy. Finally, the overall trade density has declined in 2020 as compared to 2018 implying reduction in the volume of trade.

Finally, we make a forecast for exports and imports in the leading trading countries in the world as the world is faced with the prospect that the catastrophe of COVID-19 will penetrate the world, using ANN. Figures 6 and 7 show the

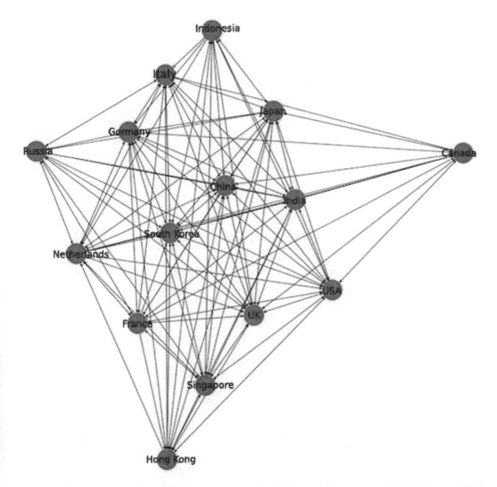

Figure 4. Trade-Network in 2008. This figure shows the network graph derived from Network Analysis for the period 2008. The number of countries included are Canada, US, UK, Germany, France, Italy, Japan, South Korea, China, Hong Kong, India, Indonesia, Russia, Netherlands, and Singapore.

result of the forecast of exports and imports in the leading trading countries. The forecasted exports and imports show a decline in all countries till December 2020. The overall findings show that there will be a significant decline in trade in these economies due to the adverse impact of COVID-19 pandemic.

5. Conclusions

The COVID-19 pandemic has had a stressful impact on the world economy. World GDP and world trade experienced a massive contraction in recent years. The pandemic originated in China, but the spread effect was huge by spreading through the whole world. In this study, we selected leading trading economies in the world to address the issue of (i) measuring the

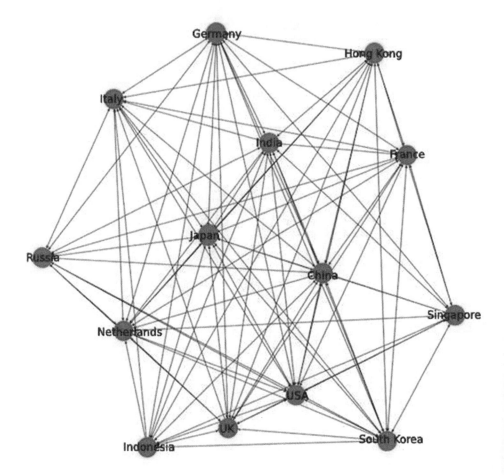

Figure 5. Trade-Network in 2020Q1. This figure shows the network graph derived from Network Analysis for the period 2020Q1. The number of countries included are USA, UK, Germany, France, Italy, Japan, South Korea, China, Hong Kong, India, Indonesia, Russia, Netherlands, and Singapore.

trade interconnectedness and density before and after the COVID-19 out-break period (ii) how long the impact will last and forecast for next six months.

We analyzed the trade interconnectedness and density among the leading trading economies in the world are: Canada, US, UK, Germany, France, Italy, Japan, South Korea, China, Hong Kong, India, Indonesia, Russia, Netherlands, and Singapore. We applied trade network analysis for two specific points of time, 2018 and 2020 Q1. Trade density has decreased considerably from 0.833 to 0.429. The COVID-19 pandemic has severely hit countries such as Germany, Italy, France, USA, UK. These countries show a steep reduction in degree centrality. Evidently, there is noticeable change in the trade network structure in 2020Q1 compared to 2018.

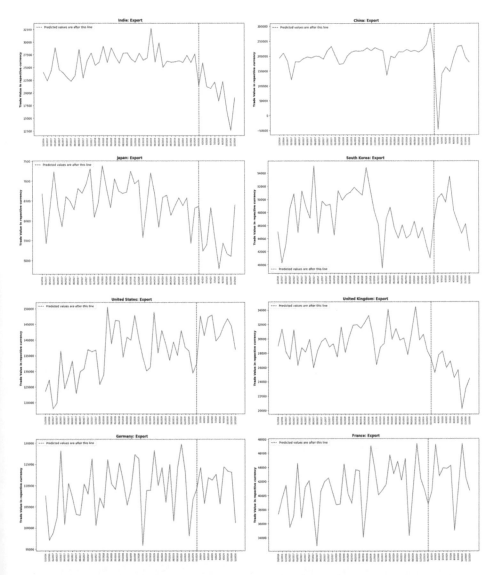

Figure 6. Export forecast based on Artificial Neural Network. This figure shows forecast of exports using Artificial Neural Network for eight countries, including India, China, Japan, South Korea, United States, United Kingdom, Germany, and France.

However, we could find that China was the key center of the trade during 2018 and is slightly repositioned toward 'circle of centre' by 2020Q1. It clearly indicates that even though the COVID-19 pandemic originated in China in December 2019 and impacted its trade, the country's relative position in the trade network has not changed drastically. Finally, we made a forecast for exports and imports using Artificial Neural Networks (ANN). The forecasted exports and imports show a decline in all countries till December 2020. The overall findings show that there will be a significant decline in trade in these economies due to the adverse impact of COVID-19 pandemic.

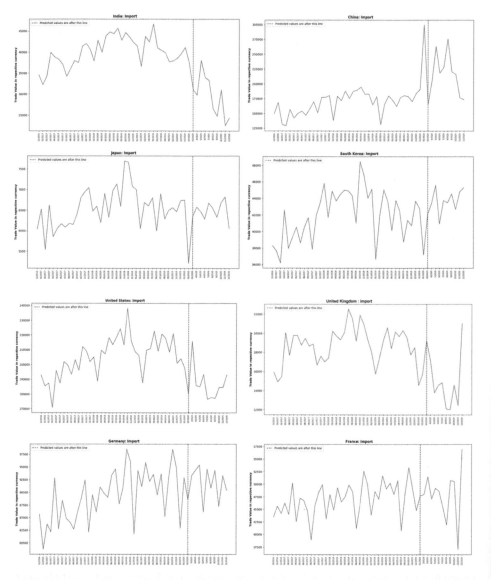

Figure 7. Import forecast based on Artificial Neural Network. This figure shows forecast of imports using Artificial Neural Network for eight countries, include India, China, Japan, South Korea, United States, United Kingdom, Germany, and France.

Notes

1. The theory of locational fundamentals developed by Krugman (1997) asserts that location is based on economic fundamentals that in turn contain random elements. This approach predicts that as fundamentals are unchanged, agglomeration patterns are maintained after temporary shocks. Long term changes in regional local patterns are explained by random and sustainable shifts in economic fundamentals (Rivera-Batiz and Oliva 2003, 129).

2. Network analysis is applied to examine the center-periphery relationship among countries in trade (Benedictis and Tajoli 2011; Kali and Reyes 2007).

3. Some of the commonly applied forecasting techniques include; autoregressive time series models etc. Many studies showed that ANN outperforms as compared to times series models in the forecast of economic variable (Giusto and Piger 2017; Heravi, Osborn., and Birchenhall 2004; Tkacz 2001).

References

Ali, M., N. Alam, and S. A. R. Rizvi. 2020. Coronavirus (COVID-19) – An epidemic or pandemic for financial markets. *Journal of Behavioral and Experimental Finance* 27:100341. doi:10.1016/j.jbef.2020.100341.

Ando, M., and F. Kimura. 2012. How did the Japanese exports respond to two crises in the international production networks? The global financial crisis and the great east Japan earthquake. *Asian Economic Journal* 26:261–87. doi:10.1111/j.1467-8381.2012.02085.x.

Apergis, N., and E. Apergis. 2020. Can the COVID-19 pandemic and oil prices drive the US Partisan conflict index. *Energy Research Letters* in press. doi:10.46557/001c.13144.

Baldwin, R., and E. Tomiura. 2020. Thinking ahead about the trade impact of COVID-19. In *Economics in the Time of COVID-19* 59, ed. Baldwin and di Mauro, 257–58. VoxEU..

Baldwin, R., and R. Freedman. 2020. Supply chain contagion waves: Thinking ahead on manufacturing 'contagion and reinfection' from the COVID concussion. https://voxeu.org/article/covid-concussion-and-supply-chain-contagion-waves.

Benedictis, D. L., and L. Tajoli. 2011. The world trade network. *The World Economy* 34 (8):1417–54. doi:10.1111/j.1467-9701.2011.01360.x.

Chuku, C., A. S. Impasa, and J. O. Duor. 2019. Intelligent forecasting of economic growth for developing economies. *International Economics* 159:74–93. doi:10.1016/j.inteco.2019.06.001.

Cook, R. T., and A. S. Hall. 2017. Macroeconomic indicator forecasting with deep neural networks. kc Fed Research Working Paper, Federal Reserve Bank of Kansas City.

Eichengreen, B., and K. H. O'rourke. 2009. A tale of two depressions. *VoxEU. Org* 1.

Escaith, H., A. Keck, C. Nee and R. Teh (2011). Japan's earthquake and tsunami: International trade and global supply chain impacts. VoxEU, 28 April.

Escaith, H., N. Lindenberg., and S. Miroudot. 2010. Global value chains and the crisis: Reshaping international trade elasticity. Global Value Chains in A Postcrisis World: A Development Perspective. Washington: The World Bank, 73–124.

Fagiolo, G., J. Reyes., and S. Schiavo. 2010. The evolution of the world trade web: A weighted-network analysis. *Journal of Evolutionary Economics* 20 (4):479–514. doi:10.1007/s00191-009-0160-x.

Fu, M., and H. Shen. 2020. COVID-19 and corporate performance in the energy industry. *Energy Research Letters* 1 (1):12967. doi:10.46557/001c.13154.

Gil-Alana, L. A., and M. Monge. 2020. Crude oil prices and COVID-19: Persistence of the shock. *Energy Research Letters* in press. doi:10.46557/001c.13200.

Giusto, A., and J. Piger. 2017. Identifying business cycle turning points in real time with vector quantization. *International Journal of Forecasting* 33 (1):174–84. doi:10.1016/j.ijforecast.2016.04.006.

Hao, M., J. Fu., D. Jiang, F. Ding, and S. Chen. 2020. Simulating the linkages between economy and armed conflict in India with a long short-term memory algorithm. *Risk Analysis* 40:1139–50. doi:10.1111/risa.13470.

Haroon, O., and S. A. R. Rizvi. 2020. COVID-19: Media coverage and financial markets behavior—A sectoral inquiry. *Journal of Behavioral and Experimental Finance* 27:100343. doi:10.1016/j.jbef.2020.100343.

Heravi, S., D. R. Osborn., and C. Birchenhall. 2004. Linear versus neural network forecasts for European industrial production series. *International Journal of Forecasting* 20 (3):435–46. doi:10.1016/S0169-2070(03)00062-1.

Kali, R., and J. Reyes. 2007. The architecture of globalization: A network approach to international economic integration. *Journal of International Business Studies* 38 (4):595–620. doi:10.1057/palgrave.jibs.8400286.

Korniyenko, Y., M. Pinat, and B. Dew. 2017. Assessing the fragility of global trade: The impact of localized supply shocks using network analysis. IMF Working paper 17/30, International Monetary Fund.

Krugman, P. 1997. *Development, geography, and economic theory.* Cambridge: MIT Press.

Liu, L., E. Z. Wang, and C. C. Lee. 2020. Impact of the COVID-19 pandemic on the crude oil and stock markets in the US: A time-varying analysis. *Energy Research Letters* 1 (1):13154. doi:10.46557/001c.13154

Martin, G., K. Alexander, and T. Robert. 2006. The impact of disasters on international trade. WTO Staff Working Paper, No. ERSD-2006-04, World Trade Organization (WTO), Geneva. doi:10.30875/64e59051-en.

Narayan, P. K. 2020. Oil price news and COVID-19—Is there any connection? *Energy Research Letters* 1 (1):13176. doi:10.46557/001c.13176

Phan, D. H. B., and P. K. Narayan. 2020. Country responses and the reaction of the stock market to COVID-19—A preliminary exposition. *Emerging Markets Finance and Trade* 56 (10):2138–2150. doi: 10.1080/1540496X.2020.1784719

Qin, M., Y. C. Zhang., and C. W. Su. 2020. The essential role of pandemics: A fresh insight into the oil market. *Energy Research Letters* 1 (1):13166. doi:10.46557/001c.13166

Rivera-Batiz, L. A., and M. A. Oliva. 2003. *International trade: Theory, strategies, and evidence.* New York, NY: Oxford University Press.

Smadi, M. A., B. Talafha., M. Al-Ayyoub, and Y. Jararweh. 2018. Using long short-term memory deep neural networks for aspect-based sentiment analysis of Arabic reviews. *International Journal of Machine Learning and Cybernetics.* doi:10.1007/s13042-018-0799-4.

Tkacz, G. 2001. Neural network forecasting of Canadian GDP growth. *International Journal of Forecasting* 17 (1):57–69. doi:10.1016/S0169-2070(00)00063-7.

Tseng, F. M., H. C. Yu, and G. H. Tzeng. 2002. Combining neural network model with seasonal time series ARIMA model. *Technological Forecasting and Social Change* 69:71–87. doi:10.1016/S0040-1625(00)00113-X.

Vidya, C. T., K. P. Prabheesh., and S. Sirowa. 2020. Is trade integration leading to regionalization? Evidence from cross-country network analysis. *Journal of Economic Integration* 35 (1):10–38. doi:10.11130/jei.2020.35.1.10.

Appendices

Appendix A. Construction of Networks

We constructed the trade patterns from a network perspective. First, we constructed the network variables by preparing an undirected network matrix with N = 15 countries for two periods 2018 and 2020Q1. In order to obtain the network, the following steps were applied. An export matrix (A) was calculated. The value of A_{ij} denotes the average of exports from i to j and imports to j from i. It is referred to as trade matrix henceforth. An edge exists between two nodes i and j if the value is greater than 0. A threshold of 0 is considered here. Network analysis sees the relationship between different elements in terms of nodes and edges (connections). Nodes act as individual actors and edges are relationships between nodes. Where out-degree is

Table 2. Terms and Descriptions used in Network Analysis.

Term	Description
Centrality	A variable that tells us about how a node is positioned in a network and how important it is.
Degree	Defined as the number of total edges connected with that vertex; it includes both arrows pointing toward it as well as arrows going outward from it.
In-degree	Defined as the total number of arrows pointing toward the node; it represents import trade, that is, trade flowing toward the country (vertex).
Out-degree	Defined as the total number of arrows pointing away from the node; it represents export trade, theat is, trade flowing away from the country (vertex).
Closeness centrality	A variable that tells how close one node (in terms of topological distance) is with respect to all other nodes. The smallest path connecting country i and country j is denoted by the geodesic distance between i and j.
Eigenvector Centrality	Indicates how important a node is to the nodes around it; countries that carry a high value of eigenvector centrality are the ones that are connected to many other countries which are, in turn, connected to many others.
Betweenness Centrality	The betweenness centrality for each vertex is the number of shortest paths that pass through the vertex.

the number of outgoing edges and the in-degree is the number of incoming edges. Every node has an in-degree and an out-degree. The out-degree is the number of outgoing edges and the in-degree is the number of incoming edges. Some of the important terms and descriptions of the employed unweighted network analysis are provided in Table 2.

Appendix B. Artificial neural networks

In the present article, we use ANN to forecast exports and imports. We applied what is called Long Short-Term Memory (LSTM) variant of Recurrent Neural Networks (RNN) in this context. The RNN draws information from the temporal structure of the input data and draw upon the sequence in which the input data is presented to the model. That is, the RNN accept input not only from the current input in a sequence but also from the state of the network that arose when considering previous inputs in that sequence (Cook and Hall 2017). However, RNNs suffer from the vanishing gradient problem when handling long sequence of data. LSTM neural networks is a solution for this problem and have proven to be efficient in many natural languages related problems. At each learning step, LSTM use a weighted sum of input values with a nonlinear activation unit. More specifically, LSTM process a sequence of input as pairs $(x_i, y_i) \ldots (x_z, y_z)$. For each pair of (x_i, y_i) at each time step t, an LSTM maintains a hidden vector h_t and a memory of m_t, and which is responsible for controlling state updates and outputs to produce the target output y_i based on the past state of x_i (i.e. $x_i \ldots x_{i-1}$) (Smadi et al. 2018).

COVID-19 and Air Quality: Evidence from China

Wen Ming, Zhengqing Zhou, Hongshan Ai, Huimin Bi, and Yuan Zhong

ABSTRACT

To test the impact of the COVID-19 pandemic on air quality, this article matches the city-level real-time air quality monitoring data with the big data on population migration provided by Baidu. The article uses urban samples from the same data sample of the Chinese lunar calendar in 2019 to construct the counterfactual status of the COVID-19 pandemic. Then, the difference-in-differences (DID) model is employed to estimate the impact of the COVID-19 pandemic on air quality. It is found that the COVID-19 pandemic caused PM2.5 and AQI to decrease by about 7 $\mu g/m^3$ and 5-points, respectively.

1. Introduction

During the COVID-19 pandemic, China imposed strict restrictions on the movement of people to reduce the spread of the COVID-19 virus, which led to a significant reduction in the intensity of population travel and also forced companies to stop production activities which has affected economy (Guan et al. 2020). We investigate the impact of COVID-19 on the air quality.

To address this issue, this article employs a quasi-experiment to estimate the effect of COVID-19 on air quality in China.

There are two main types of literature involved in this article. The first type of literature is the impact of government policies, measures, and other exogenous events on air quality. These studies focus on finding the causes of air pollution. The effectiveness of policy measures varies. Some studies discussed the impact of short-term policies on air quality which are usually aimed at optimizing air quality over important dates by prohibiting industrial production and controlling short-term emissions around important areas (Chen et al. 2013b). Generally speaking, the impact of short-term policies on air quality is often transient. Short-term government policies can significantly improve short-term air quality, such as a series of political blue skies in Beijing (He, Fan, and Zhou 2016; Li et al. 2017), as well as changes in government officials and gasoline prices (Guo and Shi 2017; Xi and Liang 2015b). Although such a temporary blue sky is beautiful, it is not sustainable. If the haze control relies on such temporary regulations, it may worsen the environment in the long run (Shi, Guo, and Chen 2016). Some scholars also study the factors, such as the impact of straw burning, that cause air pollution in the short term (Balwinder-Singh et al. 2019; He, Liu, and Zhou 2020) and the deterioration of air quality caused by winter heating in northern China (Chen et al. 2013a; 2017; Fan, He, and Zhou 2020).

Short-term government policy research will help governments design targeted air pollution measures to achieve immediate results, but controlling air pollution also requires long-term institutional arrangements and the application of breakthrough technologies (Alvarez-Herranz et al. 2017). In terms of medium and long-term policy measures, a series of environmental policies and targeted measures of the Chinese government have also achieved certain results (Chen and Li 2018). Macro environmental policies, such as the revision of Law of the People's Republic of China on the Prevention and Control of Atmospheric Pollution (APPCL2000), have improved air quality and total factor productivity in pollution-intensive industries (Li and Chen 2013). Pilot policies, such as the construction of "low-carbon cities", have significantly improved air quality (Song, Sun, and Chen 2019). The targeted centralized regulation of scattered coal has effectively reduced the concentration of PM2.5 (Xie, Ai, and Deng 2020). Meanwhile, transportation is also an important measure to control air pollution. The construction of high-speed rail and other public transportation infrastructure will significantly improve air quality (Fu and Gu 2017; Lalive, Luechinger, and Schmutzler 2018; Liang and Xi 2016; Mérel et al. 2014; Sun, Luo, and Yao 2019). In general, government policy measures, technological innovation, and transportation can optimize air quality. However, the heavy haze in Beijing-Tianjin-Hebei and surrounding areas during the COVID-19 pandemic is inconsistent with previous studies. Therefore, it is necessary to conduct a more in-depth study on the air quality conditions in China during the COVID-19 pandemic.

Another type of literature mainly focused on the complex relationship between air pollution and macroeconomic. On the one hand, high-speed development of the macroeconomic is often accompanied by high levels of air pollution (Grossman and Krueger 1995). On the other hand, air pollution may in turn limit macroeconomic by causing environmental degradation and affecting economic activity (Azam 2016). Specifically, haze slows down urbanization, restricted the incremental benefits of urban scale and the effective performance of agglomeration effects, thereby inhibiting the macroeconomic (Hanlon 2016). Air pollution can also suppress macroeconomic by slowing the accumulation of human capital (Chang et al. 2016; Greenstone and Hanna 2014). Air pollution increases the hours that workers are absent from work due to illness, which in turn affects macroeconomic (Neidell 2017). Air pollution can lead to a range of psychological problems, such as insomnia and cognitive decline, leading to decreased productivity (Chen, Oliva, and Zhang 2018; Heyes and Zhu 2019; Schlenker and Walker 2016; Zhang, Chen, and Zhang 2018). In addition, some scholars have worked on the health costs of smog production as a way to estimate the economic costs of air pollution (Zhang and Mu 2018; Zhi et al. 2013). In conclusion, air pollution will impose a reverse inhibitory effect on macroeconomic. Therefore, we can further estimate the economic impact of the COVID-19 pandemic through the impact of COVID-19 on air pollution.

The marginal contributions of this article are as follows: First, this article estimates the macroeconomic response to the COVID-19 pandemic through air quality improvement. Second, in previous studies, real-time population monitoring is difficult to measure. To cope with this problem, this article combines the population travel big data with air quality data and uses the high-dimensional and high-quality advantages of this data to conduct a detailed study and evaluation of the impact of COVID-19 on the air quality. Third, the source of air pollution has been further identified. In the case of extremely restricted population movement, the mechanism of temporary blue-sky formation can help us to realize the main direction of air pollution control in the future.

2. Research Background

On January 23, 2020, following an outbreak of COVID-19, a lockdown was declared in Wuhan, China. The Chinese government then began urging people to quarantine in their homes to prevent the spread of the virus. Two days after the Wuhan lockdown, came the annual Chinese New Year holiday. Chinese New Year is the equivalent of Christmas, which means it is one of the most important holidays in China. Every year, people return to their home-towns to celebrate the Spring Festival with their families. Therefore, during the Spring Festival, the whole country goes on a holiday for seven days. During this period, factories stop production. The outbreak of the COVID-19 pandemic led to the isolation of the Chinese people, which greatly extended the date of resumption of business and production of enterprises (CCTV 2020a). This phenomenon provides an identification strategy for our research in this article. Workers should have returned to their jobs on the seventh day after the Spring Festival, but due to the COVID-19 pandemic, they were unable to return to work. It was not until two weeks after the Spring Festival holiday that companies gradually resumed production (CCTV 2020b).

Therefore, by comparing the counterfactual results of the same period a year before the outbreak of the COVID-19 pandemic with the certain period in the year of the outbreak, the average treatment effect of corporate shut-downs on macroeconomic during the COVID-19 pandemic can be estimated. This article divides the basis of whether the enterprise should resume production at the end of the Spring Festival, and uses the sample year as a grouping basis to construct a DID model to study the impact of the COVID-19 pandemic outbreak on air quality and macroeconomic.

3. Data and Methodology

3.1. Data

There are two main categories of research data covered in this article, the first being air quality data and the second being population travel data.

In this article, PM2.5 concentrations, AQI, and PM10 concentrations are selected to measure air quality. These data come from the Chinese Air Quality Real-time Publishing Platform published by the China Environmental Monitoring General Station. Air quality data are collected from more than 1,000 monitoring stations across the country in real-time, and we aggregated this data by day and city to form a daily-city panel consisting of 367 cities.

Population travel data comes from Baidu's Population Migration Platform. Baidu is a search engine company in China, and its social status in China is similar to that of Google in the US. "Baidu Location System" provides geographic location services (LBS) for hundreds of thousands of APPs, processing third-party user location requests for more than 3.5 billion times a day in 2013, and is the most extensive data and technical service platform for LBS data sources in China. "Baidu Migration" big data is a public product that Baidu Corporation provides to the public for free after collecting the migration data of third-party users. We used the daily travel intensity per city published on the Baidu migration platform to measure the travel status of China's population during the COVID-19 pandemic. The specific algorithm of the travel intensity index is the result of indexing the ratio of the number of people who travel in the city to the number of people living in the city.

The sample in this article matches the above two sets of data to finally obtain a sample of 344 cities. This sample consists of daily data around the Chinese New Year in 2020 and 2019. Spring Festival is a traditional Chinese festival that uses the lunar calendar for counting. We convert the date counting method of the sample to the lunar calendar and select the data of 2020 and the same period of 2019 for comparison. The reasons are as follows: firstly, the date of the Spring Festival would be different in each year if counted according to the lunar calendar; secondly, the COVID-19 pandemic outbreak occurred two days before the Chinese Spring Festival. Therefore, the switching of the sample counting method to the lunar calendar can effectively eliminate the confounding of the study results by the production shutdown during the Spring Festival holiday.

The sampling period is from 30 days before the Chinese New Year holiday to 45 days after. The sample time interval was chosen for the following reasons:

First, after the outbreak of the COVID-19 pandemic in Wuhan, the city of Wuhan was locked down, the incubation period of the COVID-19 virus is generally 14 days. Therefore, if the residents are not sick, it is very likely to rule out the possibility of infection with COVID-19 after 14 days of family isolation. However, due to the presence of asymptomatic carriers of the virus, it will take another 14 days to rule out asymptomatic infections. As a result, the total quarantine period is 28 days. Second, when the company resumes production, the air pollution situation still requires an additional observation period.

3.2. Summary Statistics

Table 1 shows the descriptive statistics for the sample, where Panel A contains descriptive statistics for the whole sample; Panel B has descriptive statistics for the control group; and Panel C contains descriptive statistics for the treatment group. It can be seen that from the overall average of one month before and after the Spring Festival, China's air quality is in good condition, but there are cities with air pollutant outbreaks in both the control and treatment groups during the sample period. Air quality is better and travel intensity is lower in 2020 than in 2019, both in terms of overall average and extreme values, within the sample interval.

Table 2 shows the mean differences between treatment and control groups. Panel A provides a comparison of the control group before and after the

Table 1. Summary statistics.

Variable	N	Mean	Std. Dev.	Min	Max
Panel A. Full sample					
Day	52,136	38.5000	21.9376	1	76
City	52,136	172	99.0161	1	343
AQI	51,958	75.4927	51.8946	6.2000	500
PM 2.5	51958	51.0536	43.0185	1.2917	1349.0870
PM 10	51958	78.5365	75.2194	3.2609	5700.6310
dd	52,136	0.2961	0.4565	0	1
Trip-intensity	52,136	4.1056	1.2076	0.3003	8.8778
Panel B. 2019 sample					
Day	26,068	38.5000	21.9378	1	76
City	26,068	172	99.01705	1	343
AQI	25,979	79.1993	52.2290	6.2000	500.0000
PM 2.5	25,979	53.1987	44.7209	2.1429	1349.0870
PM 10	25,979	86.8700	83.6234	4.3333	5700.6310
dd	26,068	0	0	0	0
Trip-intensity	26,068	4.4954	0.7710	0.8953	8.8106
Panel C. 2020 sample					
Day	26,068	38.5000	21.9378	1	76
City	26,068	172	99.01705	1	343
AQI	25,979	71.7861	51.2918	9.0833	500.0000
PM 2.5	25,979	48.9108	41.1372	1.2917	553.9167
PM 10	25,979	70.2222	64.7142	3.2609	2606.0830
dd	26,068	0.5921	0.4915	0	1
Trip-intensity	26,068	3.7158	1.4206	0.3003	8.8778

Note: This table reports the summary statistics of major variables. *Panel A.* reports the full samples summary statistics. *Panel B.* keep the samples in 2019. *Panel C.* keep the samples in 2020.

Table 2. Mean differences.

Panel A.	2019			2020		
	Mean (Before)	Mean (After)	Mean-diff	Mean (Before)	Mean (After)	Mean-diff
AQI	87.655	73.440	−14.216***	87.591	60.882	−26.709***
PM 2.5	60.384	48.191	−12.193***	64.090	38.438	−25.652***
PM 10	95.387	81.021	−14.366***	82.759	61.582	−21.177***
Trip intensity	4.517	4.483	−0.035***	4.604	3.105	−1.499***

Panel B.	Before			After		
	Mean (2019)	Mean (2020)	Mean-diff	Mean (2019)	Mean (2020)	Mean-diff
AQI	87.655	87.591	−0.065	73.357	61.342	−12.015***
PM 2.5	60.384	64.090	3.706***	48.179	38.905	−9.273***
PM 10	95.387	82.759	−12.628***	80.766	61.806	−18.960***
Trip intensity	4.517	4.604	0.087***	4.486	3.092	−1.394***

Note: This table reports the mean differences of the samples. *Panel A.* compares the mean values before and after the shock in the control group and treatment group. *Panel B.* report mean differences between the control group and treatment before the shock, and the mean differences between the control group and treatment after the shock.

Spring Festival holiday and the comparison of the treatment group before and after the Spring Festival holiday. It shows that the air quality improved in 2019 and 2020 after the Spring Festival holiday, especially in 2020, the national average PM2.5 concentration changed from "good" before the Spring Festival to "excellent" after the Spring Festival (from 53.2 μg/m³ in 2019 to 48.91 μg/m³). However, this value is still some distance away from the World Health Organization's first-stage standard (35 micrograms/cubic meter), which still requires more long-term efforts. Panel B contains the mean difference between the treatment group before and after the Spring Festival holiday and the control group before and after the Spring Festival holiday. The difference between the mean difference in air quality between the control group and the treatment group before the Spring Festival holiday is not significant, but the air quality of the treatment group after the Spring Festival holiday improved. Combining the results from Tables 1 and 2, it can be seen that the air quality is significantly better after the Spring Festival holiday in 2020 compared to 2019.

In this article, a DID model is used to study the impact of the COVID-19 pandemic on the air quality status of firms with the delayed resumption of production. One of the most important assumptions used in the DID model is the satisfaction of the parallel trend assumption, i.e., a consistent trend between the treated and control groups in the absence of the COVID-19 pandemic outbreak. Therefore, the air quality in 2020 should be close to the same period of 2019 in the lunar calendar, after the resumption of production and before the adoption of forced measures to restrict the traffic of people in all regions. In order to compare the dynamic trends of the treatment group and the control group, this article illustrates the daily averages of AQI, PM2.5, and PM10 in each city as a line graph (see Figures 1-3). The black-dotted line

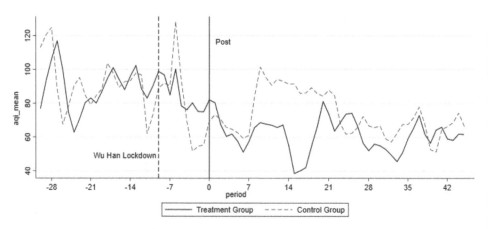

Figure 1. The trend of AQI in the treatment group and control group. Figure 1 shows the trend of AQI in 2020 and 2019. The vertical axis is the daily mean of the AQI for the sample cities. "Post" represents the end day of the Chinese New Year holiday.

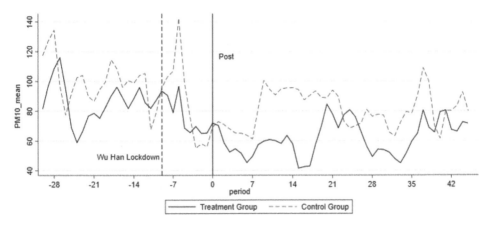

Figure 2. The trend of PM2.5 in the treatment group and control group. Figure 2 shows the trend of PM2.5 concentrations in 2020 and 2019. The vertical axis is the daily mean of the PM2.5 concentrations for the sample cities. "Post" represents the end day of the Chinese New Year holiday.

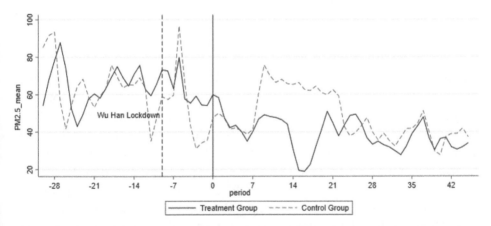

Figure 3. The trend of PM10 in the treatment group and control group. Figure 3 shows the trend of PM10 concentrations in 2020 and 2019. The vertical axis is the daily mean of the PM10 concentrations for the sample cities. "Post" represents the end day of the Chinese New Year holiday.

shows the date of Wuhan lockdown, while the black solid line represents the end of the Chinese New Year holiday on the seventh day of the first lunar month. After the seventh day of the first lunar month, the three air quality indicators were remarkably better in the treatment group. This gap did not shrink until a large number of firms resumed production around the 20th day after the end of the Spring Festival holiday.

To study the air quality distribution in Chinese cities before and after the Spring Festival, this article visualizes the air quality situation. Figure 4a–e show the PM2.5 concentration distribution of Chinese cities for 2 weeks before the start of the Spring Festival and 2 weeks after the end of the Spring Festival. Based on evidence in these Figures, the following results can be found: First, the areas with the most

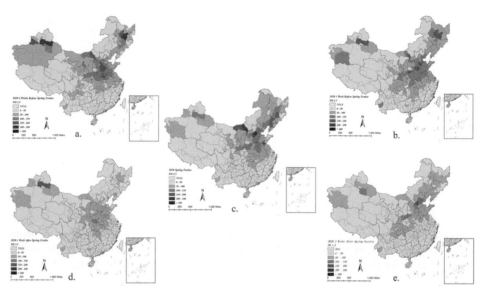

Figure 4. Air quality during the COVID-19 pandemic period in China. Figure 4 Graphs the PM2.5 concentration distribution during the COVID-19 pandemic period in China. a. to e. shows the PM2.5 concentration distribution of Chinese cities for 5 weeks from 2 weeks before the start of the Spring Festival to 2 weeks after the end of the Spring Festival.

serious air pollution in China are concentrated in the northern part of the country, represented by Beijing-Tianjin-Hebei. Second, the AQI value in the southern region is better than that in the northern region. Again, Beijing-Tianjin-Hebei experience serious air pollution during the Spring Festival but there was a significant drop in AQI in various cites of China one week after the Spring Festival. Finally, when companies began to resume production two weeks after the end of Chinese New Year, AQI in north China began to rise. Our assumption that the delayed return to work by companies does optimize air quality seems to be true. Therefore, based on a descriptive statistical analysis of air quality data, the following hypothesis can be formulated.

Hypothesis: The COVID-19 pandemic extended the Chinese New Year holiday and delayed the resumption of work by companies in various cities, leading to a reduction in production intensity and improved air quality.

To confirm our assumption, a DID model is implemented to verify the improving effect of delayed work resumption by firms on air quality.

3.3. Empirical Research

In this article, a quasi-experiment is employed to construct a DID model to estimate the impact of reduced production intensity on air quality. The model is as follows:

$$Air_{i,c,j} = \alpha_i + \delta_c + \gamma_j + \lambda_{i,c} + \beta_{i,c,j} * dd_{i,c,j} + \varpi_{i,c,j}X_{i,c,j} + \varepsilon_{i,c,j} \qquad (1)$$

where $Air_{i,c,j}$ represents the air quality level of city i on day j before the end of Chinese New Year holiday in year c, $dd_{i,c,j}$ is the core estimation variable constructed in this article, which equal to 1 if the sample is the city i after the Chinese New Year holiday in 2020, and equal to 0 if city i before the Chinese New Year holiday. $X_{i,c,j}$ is a vector of relevant control variables. α_i is the city fixed effect, δ_c is the year fixed effect, γ_j is the daily fixed effect, $\lambda_{i,c}$ is the individual fixed effect, and $\varepsilon_{i,c,j}$ is the residual. $\beta_{i,c,j}$ for the air quality impact coefficient of delayed rework by firms. If $\beta_{i,c,j}$ is negative then the hypothesis of this article is confirmed, and if $\beta_{i,c,j}$ is positive then the hypothesis of this article cannot be confirmed.

The application of the DID model requires the satisfaction of some assumptions. First, the event shock must be sufficiently exogenous. In this article, the outbreak of the COVID-19 pandemic in China is used as a quasi-experiment, and the COVID-19 outbreak in Wuhan, China can be described as a "black swan" that no one could have predicted in late 2019. Therefore, the event shock of the COVID-19 outbreak as a DID model meets the exogenous assumption. Second, the intervention of the exogenous shocks on the treatment group should not affect the control group. In other words, the exogenous event shocks only affected the treatment group. In this article, the cities before and after the Chinese New Year holiday in 2020 were selected as the treatment group and the cities during the same period of the lunar calendar in 2019 were selected as the control group. Obviously, the COVID-19 pandemic in 2020 cannot affect the air quality level before and after the Chinese New Year in 2019. Again, the treatment and control groups should be trending the same before being shocked by an exogenous event, that is, the treatment and control groups need to meet the parallel trend assumption.

To test the parallel trend assumption, a dynamic model is built to capture the impact of delayed resumption on air quality at each lunar date. The model is as follows:

$$Air_{i,c,j} = \alpha_i + \delta_c + \gamma_j + \lambda_{i,c} + \sum_{j=-30}^{45} \beta_{i,c,j} * dd_{i,c,j} + \varpi_{i,c,j}X_{i,c,j} + \varepsilon_{i,c,j} \qquad (2)$$

The trend between the treatment group and the control group can be found by observing the variation on the coefficient of the core estimation variable. The parallel trend assumption is satisfied when the following two situations occur simultaneously. The first is that $\beta_{i,c,j}$ is statistically insignificant before the event shock. The other is that a remarkable difference can be easily observed in post-intervention coefficients compared to pre-intervention.

4. Primary Empirical Results

4.1. Main Result

Table 3 shows the main results of the DID model, where Panels A, B, and C are the estimate using PM2.5, AQI, and PM10 as a proxy variable for air quality, and the standard errors of all estimates are clustered to each individual of the groups. Column (1) mixes all the sample and uses the pooled OLS estimator. Panel data can help to capture the unobservable fixed factors. Column (2) sets up the panel data by day j and individual i, c. In Column (3), the daily fixed effect is controlled to exclude the time-varying factor of air quality such as whether, and the individual fixed effect is also controlled to eliminate the influence of the time-invariant factor at the individual level.

Table 3. Main results.

	(1) pool	(2) model 1	(3) model 2	(4) model 3	(5) model 4	(6) log
Panel A. PM2.5						
dd	−17.907***	−25.278***	−13.423***	−13.423***	−6.931***	−0.107***
	(−53.48)	(−17.91)	(−7.82)	(−7.79)	(−3.94)	(−4.13)
Trip intensity					4.431***	
					(10.75)	
Trip intensity_l						0.232***
						(10.26)
_cons	56.357***	58.539***	69.530***	55.029***	34.910***	3.370***
	(229.82)	(47.55)	(38.69)	(107.84)	(18.12)	(95.92)
r^2	0.036		0.148	0.419	0.423	0.536
r^2-adj	0.04		0.15	0.41	0.41	0.53
Panel B. AQI						
dd	−20.736***	−26.444***	−12.552***	−12.552***	−5.034**	−0.050**
	(−47.56)	(−14.50)	(−5.89)	(−5.87)	(−2.35)	(−2.39)
Trip intensity					5.132***	
					(10.69)	
Trip intensity_l						0.187***
						(9.77)
_cons	81.631***	83.326***	94.776***	79.208***	55.905***	3.898***
	(285.07)	(55.66)	(47.19)	(125.05)	(25.14)	(134.44)
r^2	0.033		0.129	0.449	0.454	0.528
r^2-adj	0.03		0.13	0.44	0.44	0.52
Panel C. PM10						
dd	−24.095***	−21.276***	−6.762**	−6.762**	1.294	0.011
	(−35.93)	(−9.33)	(−2.39)	(−2.38)	(0.43)	(0.49)
Trip intensity					5.501***	
					(10.43)	
Trip intensity_l						0.237***
						(10.85)
_cons	85.677***	84.861***	99.204***	80.540***	55.565***	3.790***
	(210.95)	(49.38)	(47.05)	(95.54)	(21.21)	(116.36)
r^2	0.021		0.057	0.352	0.354	0.568
r^2-adj	0.02		0.06	0.34	0.34	0.56
City FE	NO	NO	NO	YES	YES	YES
Year FE	NO	NO	NO	YES	YES	YES
Day FE	NO	NO	YES	YES	YES	YES
Individual FE	NO	NO	YES	YES	YES	YES
Cluster (id)	YES	YES	YES	YES	YES	YES
N	51958	51958	51958	51958	51958	51958

Note: ***, ** and *, indicate the 1%, 5% and 10% significance levels, respectively. Number of Clusters (id) = 684.

Due to the Spring Festival holiday, some enterprises will also reduce the intensity of production before the Spring Festival. So, will changes in air quality be affected by the Spring Festival holiday? To exclude the impact of the Chinese New Year holiday on the estimation results, the same period of the 2019 lunar calendar is selected as the control group. Considering that the economic, international, and institutional environment may be different between 2020 and 2019, and each city has its unique characteristics, column (4) of Table 3 further controls year fixed effects and city fixed effects to exclude other factors. In column (4), results show that the variation of core estimated coefficient is relatively small but still significant.

It has been shown that air quality is also affected by car exhaust emissions (Mérel et al. 2014), and the Chinese government's strict travel restrictions during the COVID-19 pandemic led to a significant reduction in the intensity of population travel during the Spring Festival. Could air quality improvement, therefore, be a result of the reduced intensity of population travel following the COVID-19 outbreak? In order to exclude the interference of reduced travel intensity on our results, this article further uses the daily travel intensity of each city provided by the Baidu Migration data as a control variable. This allows to exclude the effect of reduced vehicle exhaust generated by reduced travel intensity. Column (5) further controls for population travel intensity and finds that the estimated coefficients have become remarkably smaller. Specifically, the delayed resumption of work due to the COVID-19 pandemic reduces PM2.5 by about 7 $\mu g/m^3$ and AQI by at least 5 points. And the estimated coefficients for PM2.5 and AQI remain significant but those for PM10 become insignificant. Therefore, the vehicle exhaust might be the source of PM10. Column (6) makes a log transformation to estimate percentage changes based on column (5), and the estimates are similar to column (5). The results from columns (1) to (6) show that the COVID-19 pandemic does improve air quality, but it has more than one pathway. Both reductions in production intensity and population travel intensity are pathways to improve air quality.

Thus, the delay in the resumption of production caused by the COVID-19 pandemic will at least reduce the PM2.5 concentration by 6.93 $\mu g/m^3$. China's per capita GDP in 2019 as about 10,127 USD. By sorting the existing literature on haze pollution and economic growth coefficients, it is concluded that the air quality improvement caused by the pandemic will increase GDP per capita by 109 USD to 115 USD. According to our estimation, it is found that an increase of 1% in PM2.5 concentration will decrease the per capita GDP by 0.072%. Therefore, the air quality improvement caused by the COVID-19 pandemic is equivalent to an increase in per capita GDP by 103 USD. It is closer to the estimated value obtained from previous literatures (Chen, Oliva, and Zhang 2018; Hao et al. 2018). To sum up, the potential benefit of China's COVID-19 pandemic on air quality improvement will at least increase per capita GDP by 103 USD. This is the main economic importance of our result.

4.2. Parallel Trend Test

The DID models need to satisfy the assumption that there is a common trend between the treatment and control groups before the event shock, and this article uses an event study approach to construct the dynamic effects models (Jacobson, LaLonde, and Sullivan 1993). Figure 5a,b shows the dynamic effects of AQI as a proxy variable for air quality within or without trip intensity, respectively. From Figure 5a, it can be seen that the estimated coefficients before the Wuhan lockdown fluctuated around 0 and were insignificant. During the Spring Festival, the estimated coefficient experiences a significant increase, which probably is due to the shortage of pandemic prevention materials at the beginning of the COVID-19 pandemic. The estimated coefficients gradually decreased after the end of the Spring Festival holiday and were significantly negative one week after the end of the Spring Festival. In

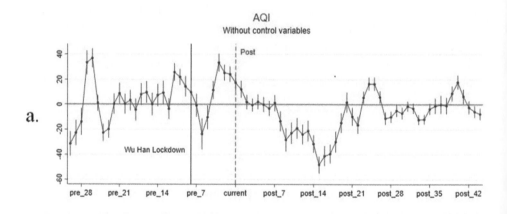

a.

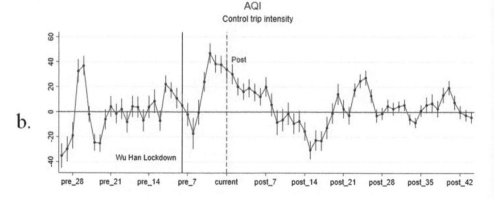

b.

Figure 5. Dynamic effect on AQI. Figure 5a,b shows the dynamic effects of AQI as a proxy variable for air quality within or without trip intensity, respectively.

summary, the control and treatment groups of the sample in this article passed the parallel trend test.

Furthermore, this article analyzes the dynamic effects of the COVID-19 pandemic on air quality. It can be seen that in the second week after the Chinese New Year holiday, population movements were gradually eased and the estimated coefficients of the core variables increased. One month after the end of the Spring Festival holiday, the core variables estimation coefficients returned to the state before the Wuhan lockdown, indicating that the dynamic impact of the COVID-19 pandemic on air quality largely disappeared. The results in Figure 5b are largely consistent with those shown in Figure 5a, except for the small absolute value of the estimated coefficient after the end of the pandemic. Figure 6a,b shows the results of not controlling the travel intensity and controlling the travel intensity, respectively, by using PM2.5 as an air quality proxy variable.

Figure 7a,b replace the dependent variable with PM10, and the results are similar to those estimated for AQI, PM2.5. Only after controlling for travel intensity, the absolute value of the PM10 coefficient becomes smaller after the Chinese New Year holiday compared to the time when the travel intensity was not controlled, which is consistent with the estimates of PM10 in the main regression.

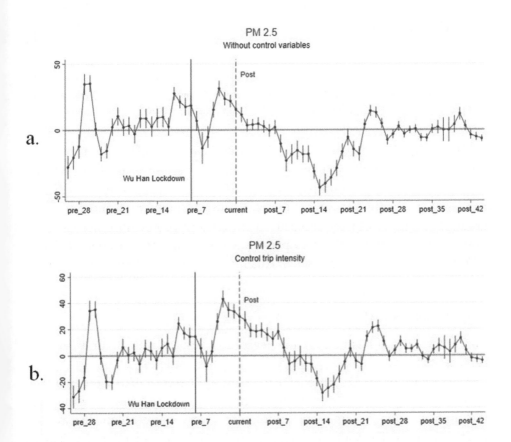

Figure 6. Dynamic effect on PM2.5. Figure 6a,b shows the dynamic effects of PM2.5 concentration as a proxy variable for air quality within or without trip intensity, respectively.

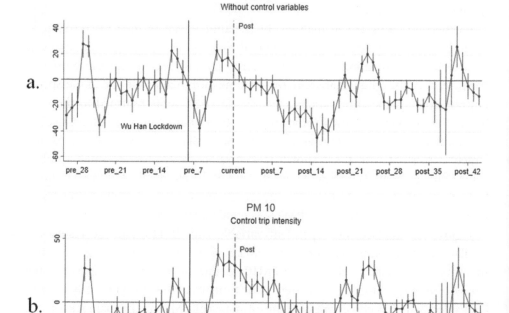

Figure 7. Dynamic effect on PM10. Figure 7a,b shows the dynamic effects of PM10 concentration as a proxy variable for air quality within or without trip intensity, respectively.

Taken together, these estimates suggest that air quality in China has improved significantly and the macroeconomic response has been positive during the COVID-19 outbreak. However, as the impact of the COVID-19 pandemic gradually decreases, the restrictions on population movement are gradually relaxed, and the intensity of travel and production increases, the optimal effect of the COVID-19 pandemic on air quality (and potentially on GDP) will slowly disappear and air quality will return to its original level.

4.3. Robustness Test

To confirm the robustness of the regression results, we set up a series of robustness tests.

The essence of the DID model is to create a difference before the intervention and the difference after the intervention between the treatment group and the control group to eliminate confounding factors and obtain the average treatment effect. Therefore, the selection of the sample time interval will affect the robustness of the estimation results. In our model, many companies have resumed production in the third week after the Spring Festival. The model includes samples after the third week, which could make the average value of the sample after the intervention of the treatment group larger. This can partially offset the impact of delayed reproduction of companies. Therefore, the results estimated in this article will be more stringent. To further verify the robustness of the estimation results, the article changes the window width of the sample time and uses the placebo test to achieve our goal.

4.3.1. Transform Sample Range

Table 4 shows the results of changing sample width. Columns (1) to (4) are estimates of different sample time interval set from the interval between 1 week before the seventh day to 1 week after the seventh day of the Chinese

Table 4. Robust test results.

	(1)	(2)	(3)	(4)
	1 week	2 weeks	3 weeks	4 weeks
Panel A. AQI				
dd	−7.503***	−12.687***	−14.337***	−8.627***
	(−3.34)	(−7.02)	(−6.86)	(−4.34)
Trip intensity	2.777**	4.382***	5.118***	5.536***
	(2.06)	(7.15)	(8.55)	(9.27)
_cons	63.481***	63.791***	62.174***	58.132***
	(12.83)	(25.22)	(25.19)	(23.09)
r^2	0.600	0.573	0.503	0.485
r^2-adj	0.55	0.55	0.48	0.47
Panel B. PM2.5				
dd	−6.549***	−12.393***	−15.446***	−10.832***
	(−3.48)	(−8.10)	(−8.81)	(−6.52)
Trip intensity	2.942**	4.403***	4.654***	4.932***
	(2.41)	(8.50)	(9.79)	(10.46)
_cons	41.066***	40.450***	40.552***	37.149***
	(9.23)	(18.93)	(20.58)	(18.58)
r^2	0.570	0.552	0.500	0.477
r^2-adj	0.51	0.52	0.48	0.46
Panel C. PM10				
dd	−2.801	−6.486***	−5.724**	0.510
	(−1.30)	(−3.80)	(−2.58)	(0.25)
Trip intensity	3.014**	4.847***	5.267***	5.667***
	(1.99)	(7.37)	(8.03)	(8.44)
_cons	58.946***	58.879***	59.243***	56.170***
	(10.73)	(22.10)	(22.05)	(20.06)
r^2	0.590	0.578	0.485	0.478
r^2-adj	0.54	0.55	0.46	0.46
City FE	YES	YES	YES	YES
Year FE	YES	YES	YES	YES
Day FE	YES	YES	YES	YES
Individual FE	YES	YES	YES	YES
Cluster (id)	YES	YES	YES	YES
N	8880	18456	28031	37604

Note: Column (1) set the time interval as from 1 week before the seventh day to 1 week after the seventh day of the Chinese New Year. Column (2) set the time interval as from 2 weeks before the seventh day to 2 weeks after the seventh day of the Chinese New Year. Column (3) set the time interval as from 3 weeks before the seventh day to 3 weeks after the seventh day of the Chinese New Year. Column (4) set the time interval as from 4 weeks before the seventh day to 4 weeks after the seventh day of the Chinese New Year. ***, ** and *, indicate 1%, 5%, and 10% significance levels, respectively. Number of Clusters (id) = 684.

New Year and the interval between 4 weeks before the seventh day to 4 weeks after the seventh day of the Chinese New Year. The results show that regardless of whether the time window width is adjusted to 1 week, 2 weeks, 3 weeks, or 4 weeks, the coefficient of core variables is still significantly negative. So, the conclusion that delayed reproduction of enterprises during the COVID-19 pandemic can reduce air pollution is robust. Besides, the absolute value of the core explanatory variable estimation coefficient reaches its maximum when the sample time window width is controlled within 3 weeks before and after the seventh day of the first lunar month. When the pandemic was controlled around the fourth week after the Spring Festival, the restrictions on population movement weakened and enterprises began to resume production. In this time interval, the coefficient of the core explanatory variable shrinks, which further verifies the conclusion of this article.

4.3.2. Placebo Test

In order to exclude the influence of other interfering factors on our estimation results, this article further verifies the robustness of the estimation results by randomly setting treatment groups and control groups repeatedly (Chetty, Looney, and Kroft 2009; Murphy, Shleifer, and Vishny 1989). The specific operation is to randomly assign a certain city in a certain year to the treatment group and construct a virtual $dd_{i,c,j}$ variable. Then, the next step is to regress the virtual control group and the treatment group, and repeat this random process to obtain the estimated results of multiple random processing. Sorting these results from small to large, we can get an empirical distribution of the estimated results of random processing. If the average value of the empirical distribution is 0, and the true estimation results fall outside of the confidence interval of random process results, then the true estimation results can be proved robust.

All of the three proxy variables of air quality are repeatedly conducted randomly 1,000 times. The true estimation results of PM2.5, AQI, and PM10 are −6.931, −5.034, and 1.294, respectively, which are obviously outside the empirical distribution of the random processing results; therefore, the estimation results of this article are robust. Al results are available upon request.

4.4. Heterogeneity Test

Different kinds of cities will differ in the intensity of policy implementation. Given city heterogeneity, we set municipalities, cities specifically designated in the state plan and capital cities as virtual variable Metropolis. Municipalities, cities specifically designated in the state plan, and capital cities are defined as 1, and ordinary cities are defined as 0. Then, we can estimate the heterogeneity of delayed reproduction of enterprises on air quality improvement between large cities and ordinary cities during the COVID-19 pandemic. Results are available upon request. A brief discussion of main finding follows. The results suggest that the estimated coefficients of PM2.5 and AQI are significantly negative. That is the air quality improvement degree of large cities is higher than that of ordinary cities after the Spring Festival. There may be two reasons: First, the governance capability of large cities in China is stronger. Second, the economic development level of large cities is much higher than that of ordinary cities, that is to say, the production and operation intensity of large cities in China will be higher than that of ordinary ones, which also proves our conclusion that production and operation of enterprises are the sources of air pollution, particularly PM2.5.

The living habits of southerners and northerners in China are also very different, especially in winter, northern cities will central heating systems, and heating is one of the main factors accelerating air pollution. According to the Qinling Mountain–Huaihe River boundary line, this article separates the samples from southern cities and northern cities to construct virtual variables. Northern cities are be defined as 1, and southern cities are defined as 0. Detailed results are available upon request. The estimated coefficients of the three proxy variables of air pollution are significantly negative, and the air quality improvement in northern cities will be better than that in southern cities after the Spring Festival. Combining Figure 4a-e and the results of heterogeneity of the southern cities and northern cities, the reason why the air quality in southern cities is not as optimized as in northern cities might be that the pollution in northern cities is more serious than that in southern cities. Northern cities hold a larger air pollution foundation, and the potential for deterioration is also greater.

5. Conclusion

This article uses a quasi-experiment to estimate the impact of the delayed reproduction by enterprises during the Spring Festival on air quality. The conclusions are as follows:

First, the air quality during the COVID-19 pandemic has improved. Second, the delayed reproduction of enterprises has indeed improved air quality. We construct the counterfactual state that China has not encountered the COVID-19 pandemic before and after the Spring Festival in 2020 based on the air quality status of the same period as in the 2019 lunar calendar. Using the DID model to estimate the effect of delayed reproduction of enterprises during the COVID-19 pandemic in 2020, we found that the delayed reproduction by enterprises temporarily optimized air quality. It is conservatively estimated that the delayed reproduction of enterprises will reduce PM2.5 by 6.93 $\mu g/m^3$ and AQI by 5 points.

Third, by improving air quality, we estimate an improvement in GDP. On average, we estimated, that GDP per capita increased by approximately US\$103.

Fourth, the effect of the COVID-19 pandemic on improving air quality is temporary. Through the estimation of the dynamic effect of delayed reproduction by enterprises during the COVID-19 pandemic, we found that with the increased control over the spread of the COVID-19 pandemic in China, companies gradually began to resume production in two weeks after the Spring Festival, and the improvement effect of delayed reproduction on air quality has gradually weakened.

Acknowledgments

We acknowledge the financial support from the National Natural Science Foundation of China (Nos. 71974054,71773028, 71703120, 71603079, 71804044), and National Social Science Foundation of China (No.18BJL041), the Hunan Natural Science Foundation (No. 2019JJ40039). Science-Technology innovation Platform and Talents Program of Hunan Province, China (2019TP1053).

Declaration Of Interests

The authors declare that they have no known competing financial interests or personal relationships that could have appeared to influence the work reported in this article.

Disclosure Of Financial Interest

There has been no significant financial support for this work that could have influenced its outcome.

Funding

This work was supported by the Science-Technology innovation Platform and Talents Program of Hunan Province [2019TP1053]; National Social Science Fund of China [18BJL041]; Hunan Natural Science Foundation [2019JJ40039]; National Natural Science Foundation of China [71974054,71773028, 71703120, 71603079, 71804044].

References

Alvarez-Herranz, A., D. Balsalobre-Lorente, M. Shahbaz, and J. M. Cantos. 2017. Energy innovation and renewable energy consumption in the correction of air pollution levels. *Energy Policy* 105:386–97. doi:10.1016/j.enpol.2017.03.009.

Azam, M. 2016. Does environmental degradation shackle economic growth? A panel data investigation on 11 Asian countries. *Renewable and Sustainable Energy Reviews* 65:175–82. doi:10.1016/j.rser.2016.06.087.

Balwinder-Singh, A. J. McDonald, A. K. Srivastava, and B. Gerard. 2019. Tradeoffs between groundwater conservation and air pollution from agricultural fires in northwest India. *Nature Sustainability* 2 (7):580–83. doi:10.1038/s41893-019-0304-4.

CCTV. 2020a. Latest! Beijing holiday extended to Feb. 10. http://news.cctv.com/2020/01/31/ARTIufpX4Dxnw4jG0WVm0jKz200131.shtml.

CCTV. 2020b. Scientific and orderly resumption of work and production to ensure smooth economic development. http://news.cctv.com/2020/02/25/ARTIDwGZ0aLAFcSTFSrUDU96200225.shtml.

Chang, T., J. Graff Zivin, T. Gross, and M. Neidell. 2016. Particulate pollution and the productivity of pear packers. *American Economic Journal: Economic Policy* 8 (3):141–69. doi:10.1257/pol.20150085.

Chen, K., and Y. Li. 2018. A review of air pollution control policy development and effectiveness in China. *Energy Management for Sustainable Development*. doi:10.5772/intechopen.74928.

Chen, S., and D. Chen. 2018. Air pollution, government regulations and high-quality economic development. *Economic Research Journal* 53 (2):20–34. (In Chinese).

Chen, S., P. Oliva, and P. Zhang. 2018. Air pollution and mental health: Evidence from China. Working Paper No. 24686; Working Paper Series, National Bureau of Economic Research. doi:10.3386/w24686.

Chen, Y., A. Ebenstein, M. Greenstone, and H. Li. 2013a. Evidence on the impact of sustained exposure to air pollution on life expectancy from China's Huai River policy. *Proceedings of the National Academy of Sciences* 110 (32):12936–41. doi:10.1073/pnas.1300018110.

Chen, Y., G. Z. Jin, N. Kumar, and G. Shi. 2013b. The promise of Beijing: Evaluating the impact of the 2008 Olympic Games on air quality. *Journal of Environmental Economics and Management* 66 (3):424–43. doi:10.1016/j.jeem.2013.06.005.

Chetty, R., A. Looney, and K. Kroft. 2009. Salience and taxation: Theory and evidence. *American Economic Review* 99 (4):1145–77. doi:10.1257/aer.99.4.1145.

Ebenstein, A., M. Fan, M. Greenstone, G. He, and M. Zhou. 2017. New evidence on the impact of sustained exposure to air pollution on life expectancy from China's Huai River Policy. *Proceedings of the National Academy of Sciences* 114 (39):10384–89. doi:10.1073/pnas.1616784114.

Fan, M., G. He, and M. Zhou. 2020. The winter choke: Coal-Fired heating, air pollution, and mortality in China. *Journal of Health Economics* 71:102316. doi:10.1016/j.jhealeco.2020.102316.

Fu, S., and Y. Gu. 2017. Highway toll and air pollution: Evidence from Chinese cities. *Journal of Environmental Economics and Management* 83:32–49. doi:10.1016/j.jeem.2016.11.007.

Greenstone, M., and R. Hanna. 2014. Environmental regulations, air and water pollution, and infant mortality in India. *American Economic Review* 104 (10):3038–72. doi:10.1257/aer.104.10.3038.

Grossman, G. M., and A. B. Krueger. 1995. Economic growth and the environment. *The Quarterly Journal of Economics* 110 (2):353–77. doi:10.2307/2118443.

Guan, D., D. Wang, S. Hallegatte, S. J. Davis, J. Huo, S. Li, Y. Bai, T. Lei, Q. Xue, D. Coffman, et al. 2020. Global supply-chain effects of COVID-19 control measures. *Nature Human Behaviour* 1–11. doi:10.1038/s41562-020-0896-8.

Guo, F., and Q. Shi. 2017. Official turnover, collusion deterrent and temporary improvement of air quality. *Economic Research Journal* 52 (7):155–68. (In Chinese).

Hanlon, W. W. 2016. *Coal smoke and the costs of the industrial revolution*. National Bureau of Economic Research Working Paper No. 22921. Cambridge, MA: NBER. https://www.nber.org/papers/w22921

Hao, Y., H. Peng, T. Temulun, L. Liu, J. Mao, Z. Lu, and H. Chen. 2018. How harmful is air pollution to economic development? New evidence from PM2.5 concentrations of Chinese cities. *Journal of Cleaner Production* 172:743–57. doi:10.1016/j.jclepro.2017.10.195.

He, G., M. Fan, and M. Zhou. 2016. The effect of air pollution on mortality in China: Evidence from the 2008 Beijing Olympic Games. *Journal of Environmental Economics and Management* 79:18–39. doi:10.1016/j.jeem.2016.04.004.

He, G., T. Liu, and M. Zhou. 2020. Straw burning, PM2.5, and death: Evidence from China. *Journal of Development Economics* 145:102468. doi:10.1016/j.jdeveco.2020.102468.

Heyes, A., and M. Zhu. 2019. Air pollution as a cause of sleeplessness: Social media evidence from a panel of Chinese cities. *Journal of Environmental Economics and Management* 98:102247. doi:10.1016/j.jeem.2019.07.002.

Jacobson, L. S., R. J. LaLonde, and D. G. Sullivan. 1993. Earnings losses of displaced workers. *The American Economic Review* 83 (4):685–709. JSTOR.

Lalive, R., S. Luechinger, and A. Schmutzler. 2018. Does expanding regional train service reduce air pollution? *Journal of Environmental Economics and Management* 92:744–64. doi:10.1016/j.jeem.2017.09.003.

Li, S., and G. Chen. 2013. Environmental regulation and the growth of productivity in China — Evidence from the revision of air pollution prevention and control law in 2000. *Economic Research Journal* 48 (1):17–31. (In Chinese).

Li, X., Y. Qiao, J. Zhu, L. Shi, and Y. Wang. 2017. The "APEC blue" endeavor: Causal effects of air pollution regulation on air quality in China. *Journal of Cleaner Production* 168:1381–88. doi:10.1016/j.jclepro.2017.08.164.

Liang, R., and P. Xi. 2016. Heterogeneous effects of rail transit on air pollution—An empirical study with RDID. *China Industrial Economics* 3:83–98. (In Chinese).

Mérel, P., A. Smith, J. Williams, and E. Wimberger. 2014. Cars on crutches: How much abatement do smog check repairs actually provide? *Journal of Environmental Economics and Management* 67 (3):371–95. doi:10.1016/j.jeem.2013.12.006.

Murphy, K. M., A. Shleifer, and R. Vishny. 1989. Income distribution, market size, and industrialization. *The Quarterly Journal of Economics* 104 (3):537–64. doi:10.2307/2937810.

Neidell, M. 2017. Air pollution and worker productivity. *IZA World of Labor* 363–363. doi:10.15185/izawol.363.

Schlenker, W., and W. R. Walker. 2016. Airports, air pollution, and contemporary health. *The Review of Economic Studies* 83 (2):768–809. doi:10.1093/restud/rdv043.

Shi, Q., F. Guo, and S. Chen. 2016. Political blue sky' in Fog and Haze governance—Evidence from the local annual 'Two Sessions' in China. *China Industrial Economics* 5:40–56. (In Chinese).

Song, H., Y. Sun, and D. Chen. 2019. Assessment for the effect of government air pollution control policy: Empirical evidence from 'Low-carbon City' construction in China. *Management World* 35 (6):95–108. +195. (In Chinese).

Sun, C., Y. Luo, and X. Yao. 2019. The effects of transportation infrastructure on air quality: Evidence from empirical analysis in China. *Economic Research Journal* 54 (8):136–51. (In Chinese).

Xi, P., and R. Liang. 2015b. The impact of gasline price fluctuations on the air pollution: Through the channel of motor vehicle use. *China Industrial Economics* 10:100–14. (In Chinese).

Xie, X., H. Ai, and Z. Deng. 2020. Impacts of the scattered coal consumption on PM2.5 pollution in China. *Journal of Cleaner Production* 245:118922. doi:10.1016/j.jclepro.2019.118922.

Zhang, J., and Q. Mu. 2018. Air pollution and defensive expenditures: Evidence from particulate-filtering facemasks. *Journal of Environmental Economics and Management* 92:517–36. doi:10.1016/j.jeem.2017.07.006.

Zhang, X., X. Chen, and X. Zhang. 2018. The impact of exposure to air pollution on cognitive performance. *Proceedings of the National Academy of Sciences* 115 (37):9193–97. doi:10.1073/pnas.1809474115.

Zhi, C., W. Jn, M. Gx, and Z. Ys. 2013. China tackles the health effects of air pollution. *Lancet (London, England)* 382 (9909):1959–60. doi:10.1016/s0140-6736(13)62064-4.

Index

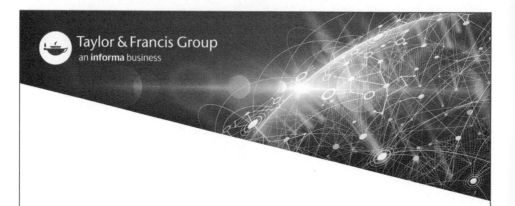